Second edition November 2011
First published July 2009

City T

thecityt

The City Trail travel guides provide independent advice. We do not accept
any payment in return for endorsing any place or business. We also do
not accept discounts in exchange for positive coverage.

A small number of advertisements have been included within the book.
Such inclusion in no way implies endorsement by City Trail Publishing
Ltd., and we accept no responsibility whatsoever for services offered by
other companies.

Text copyright © 2011 Blake Evans-Pritchard and Violetta Polese
Maps © 2011 City Trail Publishing Ltd.
Photographs © individual photographers

British Library Cataloguing in Publication Data
A catalogue record for this book is available from the British Library

ISBN 978-0-9559274-2-3

Cover photographs by Violetta Polese and Blake Evans-Pritchard
(The Khatmiyah Mosque just outside Kassala and a traditional village in
South Sudan)

Typesetting by City Trail Publishing Ltd.
Printing by AGE, Urbino, Italy

Audio files for this guidebook can be downloaded from www.thecitytrail.com
Audio Download Code: UKY73291LN

"The Sudan sounds a note unlike any we have met in Africa so far – of animation, confidence and spontaneity. It is crowded with zest to get ahead: it boils and sparkles with euphoria."

John Gunthar, US historian, 1955

Contents

Part 2: Khartoum

Part 3: Around the country

Part 4: Appendices

Maps

Khartoum bus maps

The Trail Guide to

North Sudan

&

South Sudan

Second edition
2012

The guidebook for travellers and expats

BLAKE EVANS-PRITCHARD
VIOLETTA POLESE

www.thecitytrail.com
City Trail Publishing Ltd.

Our Guides

Violetta Polese has been independently exploring the world for the past 15 years. Her travels have taken her all across Europe and the United States of America — and as far afield as Vietnam, India, Japan and Peru. She has spent some years living in Belgium, France, Spain, Portugal, Vietnam and Sudan. She is now based in The Netherlands.

Violetta was born in Italy. She studied Translation at university before deciding to pursue a life of travel, writing and photography.

Violetta is passionate about other cultures and strongly believes in living as the locals do. Her honed language skills come in useful when blending in with local customs and practices. She has found living in Sudan a great experience, and it has given her some excellent exposure to the Arabic language.

Violetta continues to write articles for publication all around the world — in French, Italian and English. She is currently codirector of City Trail Publishing.

Blake Evans-Pritchard is a professional journalist. He has been writing for a number of years about Africa, particularly Sudan. He also likes to think he knows something about economics, and regularly writes on this subject for a variety of British publications.

Like Violetta, Blake is passionate about travel and has spent many years roaming the world. Although his travels have taken him all over the place, the lure of Africa has been too strong — and he has always found himself drifting back to the continent.

Blake studied computer science at university. Then one day, whilst he was travelling between Byron Bay and Cairns in Australia, it suddenly dawned on him that he wanted to be a journalist and writer instead. He has never looked back.

He cofounded City Trail Publishing in 2008, which he still has a hand in running. He now lives in the Netherlands.

THE CITY TRAIL TEAM

Additional researchers

Mohammed Abdelwahab Ali, Ahmed Abouelnour, Luke Addis, Taha Sharif, Jenn Warren

Proof-readers

William Baldwin, Sheila Evans-Pritchard, John Evans-Pritchard, Rebecca McCoy, David Wilkinson

Photographers

Luke Addis, Blake Evans-Pritchard, Antoine Luc, Audrey Olivetti, Lara Palmisano, Isabelle Sauser, Taha Sharif, Violetta Polese, Jenn Warren (🖥 www.jennwarren.net)

Sales representatives

Stuart Coster (United Kingdom), Carmine Rossi (Italy), Taha Sharif (Sudan)

Archaeological consultation

Derek Welsby

Arabic language consultation

Laura Mann, Taha Sharif

Additional support

John Akec, Ahmed Badawi, Aymen Ahmed El-Mustafa, Arnaud Poussier, Isabelle Sauser, Dave Wilkins

HOW WE WORK

Our guidebooks are unique in that they are researched by people who have spent time actually living in, and not just visiting, the places that they are writing about.

Unlike the guidebooks of our competitors, all updates to our titles are made through extremely detailed on-the-ground research. We do not cut corners. We make sure that we re-visit every place that we have written about, to make sure that nothing has changed. We do not simply rely on phone calls or the internet. We actually go to the places. Even those places that are a really, really long way away.

We have excellent teams of researchers permanently based in the countries that we write about, and these people provide invaluable input during the update process. They will be among the first to know when things change in the places about which they are researching.

HOW TO SUPPORT INDEPENDENT PUBLISHING

We do our best to make our guidebooks the most accurate, up-to-date and useful of any destination that we write about.

We spend innumerable hours researching, investigating and writing our guides. Every single member of our team has the dedication, passion and determination to bring you the very best in travel guidebooks.

However, the publishing industry is tough and things are not always easy for the smaller player. Giant retailers and distributors take a significant share of profits for selling our book. They can sometimes demand as much as a 60% cut, which makes it very difficult for us to earn any money when we sell through third-parties.

We want to continue to offer quality books — but we need your help!

Buying directly from us (⌨ www.thecitytrail.com) not only helps us maintain our commitment to quality. It could also save you a bit of money, since buying the book from our website is usually cheaper than from any-where else. Suggest to your friends to buy directly from us, too!

We make every effort to provide you with the best and most up-to-date guidebook possible. But, of course, things will always change. We'd be really grateful if you could let us know of anything that has changed, so we can include this in the regular updates that we provide to our readers.

You can send us an email at @ thecitytrail@thecitytrail.com. We will give credit to every correction or amendment that we include.

TRANSLITERATION

There is a great deal of inconsistency throughout the world in the way in which Arabic writing is rendered in English, and no satisfactory system of transliteration has yet been developed. The same name in Sudan can be spelt in half a dozen different ways — or more! — depending on where you read it.

In our guidebook, we have generally tried to render names and words in Arabic using the Roman alphabet according to how a native English speak-er might pronounce them. This means that, whilst you will find a consist-ent application of transliteration throughout this book, the words will not always match the exact spelling that you encounter elsewhere. Also, note that it is simply not possible to accurately reflect all Arabic sounds using the Roman script.

Occasionally, we have chosen to use the English spelling of a particular place name according to common usage, even though it might not follow best convention as far as pronunciation goes. For example, most of the time we write the Arabic word for 'the' as 'al' or 'ah', but occasionally you will find that 'el' is a more common rendition. This is often the case in well-known place names, such as El-Obeid. Writing this name using 'al' instead of 'el' would cause unnecessary confusion.

On this theme, we have also decided to render common Arabic words — such as *sharia* (street), *kubri* (bridge) and *masjid* (mosque) — in English when they form part of a name. Therefore, we write 'Sharia al-Nil' as 'Nil Street' and 'Masjid al-Kabier' as 'Kabier Mosque'. We have decided to make *souq* (market) an exception to this rule, since many people from the expat community in Sudan identify the names of markets with this Arabic word. For example, most will find 'Souq as-Shabi' clearer than writing 'Shabi Market'.

The Arabic word for 'the' is used sparingly. When we render Arabic names in English, we tend to drop the article at the start of the name. So, for example, 'Sharia al-Mashtal' becomes 'Mashtal Street'. The exception to this is when article appears in the middle of an Arabic name. In this case, we keep it, since taking it out would change the meaning of the name. Thus, we write 'the tomb of Hamed al-Nil'.

THE SUDANESE CURRENCY

As we discuss in the book, the North Sudanese currency is the pound or the *jenayh*. The official abbreviation for this currency is 'SDG', although you may find other abbreviations in text elsewhere, such as 'SDD' or 'SP'. In this guidebook we have decided to stick to the official abbreviation. In South Sudan, the official currency is the South Sudanese Pound, which is abbreviated as 'SSP'.

SYMBOLS USED IN THIS BOOK

In the text

☎	Telephone number	☒	Opening times
💻	Website address	💰	Price
@	Email address	╪	How to get there
🔊	GPS co-ordinates	🍽	Type of restaurant

On maps

🚌	Bus station	☕	Where to drink
📖	Bookshop	▼	What to do
⛪	Church or Christian Centre	◎	What to see
💡	Education and learning	🏛	Embassy or government building
🛏	Accommodation	✉	Post office
❶	Information	🍽	Where to eat
@	Internet point	🛒	Where to shop
⟲	Market	🚆	Train station
☪	Mosque		

Foreword

The first edition of the City Trail Guide to Sudan was published more than three years ago. Since then, an astonishing amount has changed in the country.

Of course, the biggest change has been that now when we talk about Sudan, we actually speak of two countries.

On 9 July 2011, South Sudan finally got what it had been calling for ever since British colonialists pulled out of the country: independence from the North.

On the evening before independence, we were sitting with some good Sudanese friends on the roof of a fourth-floor apartment block in the Manshea district of Khartoum.

We were watching the sky turn crimson, as the sun dipped behind the horizon, when we suddenly noticed some frantic activity in the streets below.

Horns were being sounded, flags were being waved, people were cheering. We tottered to the edge of the roof and peered over at the cavalcade below to see exactly who was making such a ferocious racket and disturbing our idle reverie.

The procession of merrymakers stretched far into the distance. Men standing on the back of Toyota pick-up trucks were shouting incomprehensibly and waving the South Sudan flag with almighty gusto. Some were even banging drums.

But these were not men from South Sudan. There were Arabs from North Sudan, who had turned out in force to express solidarity with the South and wish them well in their newfound independence.

The scene was quite touching and made one reflect that, if the North and the South can move forwards in a spirit of co-operation and mutual respect for one another, then the future of the two autonomous nation states is a bright one.

There are challenges ahead. Not only for the newly-independent South, but also for the North, which has itself become a brand new country.

There is a whiff of optimism in the air, though. Both the South and the North buzz with a fresh sense of ambition and opportunity, and a realisation that anything has suddenly become possible.

We would like to dedicate this edition of the book to the memories of those that have struggled so hard for the future that now lies ahead of both countries, and express our sincere hope that the countries' leaders make the most of it.

Blake Evans-Pritchard

Violetta Polese

November 3, 2011

Travel Itineraries

The following travel itineraries are suggestions for trips that you might like to make whilst in Sudan, depending on the time that you have available. Remember: when choosing a travel itinerary, you should set aside at least three days for sorting out relevant paperwork and permissions: **photography permit**, **travel permit** and **registration**. See p28 for information about obtaining the various permits that you might need.

KHARTOUM (ONE WEEK)

You can travel round Khartoum fairly easily without your own vehicle, simply by relying on taxis, *amjads*, rickshaws and the city's expansive bus network.

A week is probably enough to see all the major sites. Allocate three days to see **Omdurman** (p102) and a further three for **Central Khartoum** (p101). You'll probably need no more than a day for visiting **Bahri** (p103). Make sure that you spend at least one Friday evening in the city, which will give you the opportunity to see either the **Whirling Dervishes** (p132) in Omdurman or **Nuba Wrestling** (p129) in Bahri, which frustratingly take place at the same time.

Start with Omdurman. Spend the morning of the first day visiting the **Khalifa's House** (p130) and the **Mahdi's Tomb** (p130), before moving on to the treasures of **Souq Omdurman** (p184) in the afternoon. On day two, take a walk along the banks of the Nile, starting at **Nilein Mosque** (p136) and the **Moreda fish market** (p183). This route will take you past the **fortifications of Omdurman** (p130), the **traditional boatbuilder** (p131) and **Souq as-Shigiara** (p185), a local handicraft market. In the evening, you can return to the Moreda area to eat fresh fish. The third day can be spent browsing through the trinkets in **Omdurman's sprawling markets** (p184). If it is a Friday, it is worth heading over to the tomb of Hamed al-Nil in the late afternoon to watch the ceremony of the **Whirling Dervishes** (p132).

Moving on to central Khartoum, spend at least a few hours strolling through the farmland of **Tuti Island** (p133). You could even have a picnic lunch there. Back on the mainland, stop off at the **National Museum** (p138) to delve into Sudan's ancient past. Spend the second day walking along the banks of the Nile, past the **Palace Museum** (p138), the **Ethnographic Museum** (p139) and **Kabier Mosque** (p136). On the third day visit some of Khartoum's vibrant markets, such as **Souq as-Shabi** (p183) and **Souq al-Merkhazi** (p184). In the evening, check out Khartoum's limited but growing **live entertainment** scene (p141).

Bahri has less to offer than the other two areas of the city. Start in the morning at **Souq Bahri** (p185). When you have grown tired of looking at the trinkets on display, head over to the ruins of the **Al-Shifa pharmaceutical factory** (p128), bombed by the United States in 1998 as they were hunting for Osama bin Laden.. If you are exploring on a Friday, don't forget to check out **Nuba Wrestling** (p129).

THE NORTH (10 DAYS)

For this itinerary, you ideally need your own vehicle, although parts of the route are served by public transport.

Spend a day travelling from Khartoum up to **Dongola** (p217), stopping for a few hours at the medieval ruins of **Old Dongola** (p216) on the way. If you have time, you can also visit one of the picturesque farming communities in the area. Spend the following day relaxing in Dongola and wandering around the local *souqs*. The next morning, drive up to the **Third Cataract** (p210), before continuing further northwards to explore the temple ruins of **Soleb**, **Sesibi** and **Sedeinga** (p211). Spend the night in Abri. The following morning, visit the ancient settlements on **Sai Island** (p221). Return south to Dongola, stopping at **Kerma** (219) on the way. Spend another night in Dongola before driving on to **Karima** (p210), passing through **Kawa** (p219) if you have time. Spending about three days in Karima, using the town as a base to visit the beautiful **Jebel Barkal** (p213), the pyramids of **Nuri** (p214), and the tombs of **El-Kurru** (p215). Spend a day travelling east to **Merowe** (p210) and then on to the railway town of **Atbara** (p208). The final leg of this itinerary is to drive southwards back to Khartoum — visiting **Meroe** (p207), **Naqa** (p221), **Mussawarat** (p210) and the **Sixth Cataract** (p210). This will be quite a long day, so you might want to break it up by stopping overnight at the **Tented Camp in Meroe** (p208).

KOSTI AND THE NUBA MOUNTAINS (10 DAYS)

You can follow this itinerary either with your own vehicle or by using the regular buses that run along the route.

The drive from Khartoum to **Kosti** (p246) takes around five hours. On the way, stop off at **Aba Island** (p250), the spiritual home of the Mahdi movement, for a few hours. Spend two nights in Kosti. This will give you enough time to soak up the relaxed charm of the town. Upon leaving, make your way westwards to **El-Obeid** (p253). You will probably not want to stay much longer than a day in the town, before starting on your journey into the Nuba Mountains. You will find travel slow here, due to poorly-maintained roads. You can spend up to three days in **Dilling** (p257), which is a lovely African market town. If the security situation allows it — and lately things have been very tense in the Nuba Mountains — you can make your way further south to **Kadugli** (p258). From here, you have a choice. You can either take a bus directly from the town all the way back to Khartoum — if you get up early enough in the morning — or you can head back to El-Obeid and then take a bus from there. If the thought of all this bus travel puts you off this itinerary, consider flying directly to El-Obeid and starting your trip from there.

KASSALA AND THE RED SEA (THREE WEEKS)

Drive (or take a bus) from Khartoum to **Kassala** (p239). On the way, you will pass through the university towns of **Wad Medani** (p246) and **Gedaref**, where you might want to spend a day or two. Spend around four days in Kassala, before making your way northwards to **Port Sudan** (p230). A week is probably a good period of time to spend here. This includes time for some activities (such as diving or snorkelling in the Red Sea), a day trip to **Suakin** (p235) and another day trip to **Arkowit** (p236). On the way back, rather than return to Khartoum the same way, consider visiting the railway town of **Atbara** (p208). Spend a day or two in this town before making the short hop south, back to Khartoum. If all this road travel is not for you, you could also fly direct to Port Sudan and explore the region from there.

DINDER PARK (ONE WEEK)

You really need your own transportation to do this itinerary, as public buses do not run all the way to Dinder Park (p243). Three days are probably enough to explore all parts of the park that are accessible to tourists, but, if you are not pressed for time, the park is a relaxing place to stay longer. On the way to Dinder Park, you will pass through **Wad Medani** (p246), **Sennar** (p247) and **Sinja**. Each town is worth exploring in its own right. If you have a little more time, you might like to think about driving south to **Ed-Damazin** to admire the picturesque villages and the dam there.

JUBA (ONE DAY)

One day is probably enough to see all the main sites of Juba. It helps to have your own car for sight-seeing in the city, but it is isn't essential — you can easily see everything on this itinerary by relying on *boda-bodas* or, if you're feeling particularly adventurous, the local bus network.

Start in central Juba by taking a leisurely stroll around the **Konyo-Konyo** (p276) and **Old Customs markets** (p275). Both markets are close together and, although the authorities have tried to move them elsewhere, the areas have retained much of their mercantile charm. When you're done with the markets, drop in on the **John Garang memorial** (p279) before making your way several kilometres eastwards to **Jebel Kujur** (p279), where you will see men, women and children crushing rocks to make gravel for roads. If the blistering Juba sun becomes too much for you, you can swing by the **Jebel Lodge** (p282) for some cool refreshment and a dip in their pool. To round off the day, choose one of the camps along the banks of the Nile, where you can have a drink whilst watching the sun slide behind the horizon.

THE BEST OF SUDAN (ONE MONTH)

If your time in Sudan is limited, you may have to plan carefully which are the most important sights to see.

In Khartoum, make sure to see traditional **Nuba Wrestling** (p129) or the religious ceremony of the **Whirling Dervishes** (p132). Since they both take place at the same time — Friday evening — you may have to be selective about which one to see. You should also sample the fresh fish in **Moreda fish market** (p183) and visit the **traditional boatbuilder** (p131). The **Khalifa's house** (p130) and the **Mahdi's tomb** (p130) are also must-see destinations. **Tuti Island** (p133) is something special, too.

Heading north, the top archaeological sites to visit are **Meroe** (p207), **Karima** (p210), **Jebel Barkal** (p213), **El-Kurru** (p215), **Old Dongola** (p216), **Kerma** (p219) and **Soleb** (p211).

South of Khartoum, try and visit **Aba Island** (p250), where the Mahdi once preached. Stop for a night in **Kosti** (p246) before heading westwards to **El-Obeid** (p253). The delightful town of **Dilling** (p257), on the fringes of the Nuba Mountains, is worth visiting if you have time.

Dinder Park (p243), in the east, is a great place to spend a few days on safari. The best way to get there is to drive from Khartoum.

From Dinder, you can head northwards to the beautiful town of **Kassala** (p239), surrounded by sugarloaf mountains.

Further north will take you to **Port Sudan** (p230), where you can do some diving. You should also make an effort to visit the old port of **Suakin** (p235), noted for its ruined buildings and oversized cats.

Given the difficulties in travelling around South Sudan, your principal destination in this region should be **Juba** (p269), which you can easily fly to from Khartoum. Spend a few days relaxing in the bars and restaurants of the city: a well-earned break from all the frantic sight-seeing.

North and South Sudan
The Essentials

It is one of Sudan's great tragedies that so many people who have not visited the country have a negative impression of it.

The media must take a large share of the blame for this. Over the years, news reports have tended to focus on the grimmer parts of the country, such as the fighting in South Sudan and in Darfur.

It is true that some parts of Sudan are less safe than others. Carjackings, armed robberies and kidnappings are still a big problem in Darfur (in the west of the country) and travel by road is not advisable. There is also banditry in the South.

However, it is important to remember that Sudan is vast. Taken together, the North and the South span a territory that is one-fifth the size of Europe. So whilst some areas may be unsafe, many others are open for independent travel. This includes the northern deserts, the Red Sea region, the east of the country and the central sweep that leads down to the Nuba Mountains. South Sudan is also starting to open up and roads west of Juba, all the way to Wau, are safer than they use to be.

Check with your embassy for the latest travel advice before you set off.

For those who look, Sudan has many hidden charms. This guidebook provides a good way of uncovering them.

WHEN TO GO

The weather can have a big effect on any travel plans.

Travelling during the rainy months is particularly difficult, especially in the South where most of the roads are little more than dirt tracks. The timing and duration of the rainy season varies from region to region. In the South, the rains usually start around April, whilst in Khartoum they don't tend to start until at least July. Some places, such as the northern deserts and parts of Darfur, see very little if any rainfall throughout the year.

Travelling around the country is most pleasant between January and March, when the temperature becomes a little cooler and the rains have not yet arrived.

During the summer months (April to June), Sudan can become exceedingly hot, regularly hitting 50°C (122°F) in parts of the country. The North tends to be more arid than the South, which can become unpleasantly humid and sticky during the summer.

Many expats living in Sudan take their main holiday in July and August, leaving the country at the height of summer and coming back when the temperature has cooled. Accordingly, travel agencies and tour operators often close their offices during this time, making it harder to book trips.

Visiting North Sudan during the holy Muslim month of Ramadan is an interesting experience and, if you are lucky enough, you might end up sharing a Ramadan breakfast with the hospitable Sudanese. However, things are more likely to be shut during this period.

When it is Ramadan, most restaurants in the north remain closed during the day. However, in Khartoum some of the places popular with expats have now been given permission to open.

Shops also have more restricted opening hours during Ramadan and may refuse to sell certain food items that are for immediate consumption.

Another inconvenience of Ramadan is that it can be difficult to find taxis in the early hours of the evening, when the Sudanese are eating.

The same restrictions do not apply in the non-Muslim South.

TIME ZONE

Sudan operates according to East Africa Time. In winter-time, it is three hours ahead of Greenwich Mean Time (GMT) and two hours ahead of Central European Time (CET). The country does not have daylight saving time and so, in the summer-time, the difference is plus two hours and plus one hour respectively.

LANGUAGE

Sudan has two official languages: Arabic and English.

Arabic is the working language of the north, and you will find that many people have only a fairly basic knowledge of English.

Prior to 1989, most university courses in Sudan were taught in English. However, when Omar al Bashir came to power, he quickly saw that Arabic became the de-facto teaching language and discouraged the teaching of English in schools. As a result, you will find that many of the older generation speak excellent English whilst younger people often do not.

Sudanese Arabic is distinct from the Arabic dialects spoken in other countries. Many people in the South speak a version of the language known as Juba Arabic, which is heavily influenced by tribal dialects.

English is the official language of the South, although not everyone speaks the language, especially in the more remote regions.

In total, there are more than 100 different languages currently in use in Sudan.

See p298 for help learning Arabic.

TOURIST INFORMATION

If you are already in Khartoum, then you could pop along to the Ministry of Tourism and Wildlife in Riyad (🏠 Mashtal Street, near Street 117; ☎ 0183 482 626; @ admin@sudan-tourism.gov.sd; 🖵 www.sudan-tourism.gov.sd). The Ministry staff are very helpful and can provide a few leaflets, mostly about the Red Sea and the northern deserts. They sometimes have booklets of postcards too.

It is here that you should come if you want to get a travel and photography permit (p28).

Their website now has a section in English.

In other cities outside of Khartoum, your best bet for tourist information is to try the desks of the larger hotels, which are used to dealing with foreigners, or to speak to others that have been to the region.

Consider whether you want to explore the country on your own or as part of an organised tour.

If you prefer to join a tour, there are several options available, with more and more cropping up all the time. You can contact most local tour agencies from abroad, and they will be happy to arrange your

TOUR OPERATORS AND BOOKING AGENCIES

North Sudan

Raidan Travel and Tours (☎ 0120 820 009 or 0912 301 928; @ raidantravel@gmail.com; ⌨ www.raidantravel.com) offers a good range of tailor-made packages to suit most budgets.

Air Booking Centre (☎ 0183 776 731 or 0912 305 188; @ nilein@gmail.com or info@abctravelplus.com; ⌨ www.abctravelplus.com) can arrange domestic and international flights at reasonable prices. Hotel booking, car hire and travel insurance are also available.

Sudan Travel and Tourism Club Agency (New Abu Alela Building, Barlaman Street; ☎ 0183 743 118/20/21; @ info@sudantravelclub.com; ⌨ www.sudantravelclub.com) can arrange tours in and around Khartoum and help with car hire.

Ace's Travel and Tourism Agency (Malik Street in the Industrial Development Bank building, Amarat; ☎ 0183 472 350/32; @ aces_tourism@yahoo.com) is useful for booking flights around Sudan, but the staff speak only a very little English.

The Italian Tourism Company (🏠 Street 31, Amarat; ☎ 0183 487 961 or +39 02 349 345 28; ⌨ info@italtoursudan.com or info@deserti-viaggilevi.it; ⌨ www.italtoursudan.com) specialises in package tours of the northern deserts.

Undiscovered Destinations (⌨ www.undiscovered-destinations.com; ☎ +44 191 296 2674; @ info@undiscovered-destinations.com) is a tour company specialising in travel to out-of-the-way destinations, such as Sudan. It offers a range of overland excursions, from one to three weeks.

Bestway Tours and Safaris (⌨ www.bestway.com; ☎ +1 604 264 7378; @ bestway@bestway.com) offers tours of the northern deserts, which can be combined with a more expansive package that also includes trips to neighbouring countries.

Wild Frontiers (☎ +44 20 7736 3968; ☎ info@wildfrontiers.co.uk; ⌨ www.wildfrontiers.co.uk) offers package adventure holidays to countries throughout the world, including Sudan.

South Sudan

Bahr El Jebel Safaris (☎ +52 647 428 1493 or +256 701 998 444 or +256 702 757 000; @ bahreljebel@yahoo.com; ⌨ www.bahr-el-jebel-safaris.com) can help to arrange safaris by plane and riverboat in Nimule National Park on Sudan's border with Uganda.

Red Sea

Red Sea Dives (☎ 0912 341 282 or 00882 1631 111 139; @ arnesen@bodmiscombe.demon.co.uk; ⌨ www.redseadives.com) operates live-aboard dive excursions for one week or more. They do not have offices in Port Sudan, so you usually have to book before you get there.

Diving World (☎ +44 20 7407 0019; @ info@diving-world.com; ⌨ www.divingworld.co.uk), a British company, also offers Red Sea diving in Sudan.

trip ahead of your arrival in the country.

One advantage of using tour operators is that they can help cut through any red tape, sorting out all visas and permits that you might need and generally saving a lot of hassle.

Unlike some destinations, it is not necessarily cheaper to go through a local tour operator based in Sudan than arranging things from abroad.

See p8 for a list of suggested travel itineraries.

See p92 for travelling around the country.

GETTING THERE AND AWAY

By air

There are two main international airports in Sudan — one in Khartoum and the other in Juba.

To Khartoum

The only air carrier that now flies between the **UK** and North Sudan is British Midland Airways (BMI). Flights will usually go via Lebanon.

Egypt Air offers good deals to North Sudan from **France** and **Italy**, flying via Cairo.

Lufthansa flies direct to Khartoum from Frankfurt in **Germany**, whilst KLM flies direct to the city from Amsterdam in **The Netherlands**.

Due to sanctions, it is not currently possible to fly direct from the **United States** to North Sudan. Travellers who wish to make this trip should fly via an intermediary country such as Amman, Dubai or Cairo.

There are no direct flights to Khartoum from **New Zealand**, **Australia** or **Canada**, so you will probably have to come via the Middle East.

To Juba

The easiest way of getting to South Sudan is to fly via Khartoum or one of its southern neighbours, such as Kenya or Uganda.

Several airlines fly between **Khartoum** and Juba, including Sudan Airways, Marsland Aviation and Air West. However, now that South Sudan has gained independence, prices could start creeping upwards.

From **Kenya**, Kenya Airways, Marsland Aviation and Sudan Airways all offer regular flights.

From **Uganda**, Uganda Air is your best choice.

By water

A ferry runs between **Aswan in Egypt** and Wadi Halfa at the top of North Sudan. The ferry leaves Aswan on Monday and Wadi Halfa on Wednesday. The overnight crossing takes around 16 hours.

A train formerly ran between Wadi Halfa and Khartoum, but this has been discontinued. Fast buses now cover the distance in ten hours — although, if you choose to do the journey in a single hop, you will be missing out on some of the wonders that the northern deserts have to offer (p203). It is also possible, and relatively safe, to hitchhike (p87).

Ferry tickets can be purchased at the ferry terminal or from travel agencies in Khartoum or Cairo. In Khartoum, try **Nivin Travel Agency** (☎ 0185 333 807 or 0122 233 165), located within the train station in Bahri. Nivin can also arrange overnight bus transportation to Wadi Halfa for 85 SDG. The price for the ferry is identical whether you buy a ticket in Khartoum or at the port.

Although the ferry generally leaves in the late afternoon, try to get there a few hours in advance

DIRECT FLIGHTS TO KHARTOUM'S INTERNATIONAL AIRPORT

Bahrain: Manama
Gulf Air — www.gulfair.com
Bahrain Air — www.bahrainair.net

Chad: N'Djamena
Sudan Airways — www.sudanair.com

Egypt: Cairo
Egypt Air — www.egyptair.com
Ethiopian Airlines — www.ethiopianairlines.com
Kenya Airways — www.kenya-airways.com
Sudan Airways — www.sudanair.com
Nasair — www.flynas.com

Eritrea: Asmara

Ethiopia: Addis Ababa
Ethiopian Airlines — www.ethiopianairlines.com
Sudan Airways — www.sudanair.com

Germany: Frankfurt
Lufthansa — www.lufthansa.com

Jordan: Amman
Royal Jordanian — www.rj.com
Sudan Airways — www.sudanair.com

Kenya: Nairobi
Kenya Airways — www.kenya-airways.com
Marsland Aviation — www.marsland-avi.com
Sudan Airways — www.sudanair.com
Nasair — www.flynas.com

Kuwait: Kuwait City
Jazeera Airways — www.jazeeraairways.com
British Midlands — www.flybmi.com

Lebanon: Beirut
Flying Carpet — www.flyingcarpet.com.lb

Libya: Tripoli
Afriqiyah Airways — www.afriqiyah.aero
Sudan Airways — www.sudanair.com

Netherlands: Amsterdam
KLM Royal Dutch Airlines — www.klm.com

Qatar: Doha
Qatar Airways — www.qatarairways.com
Sudan Airways — www.sudanair.com

Saudi Arabia: Jeddah
Saudi Arabian Airlines — www.saudiairlines.com
Sudan Airways — www.sudanair.com

Saudi Arabia: Riyadh
Saudi Arabian Airlines — www.saudiairlines.com
Sudan Airways — www.sudanair.com

United Arab Emirates: Sharjah   Air Arabia   www.airarabia.com
Syria: Damascus   Syrian Arab Airlines   www.syriaair.com
  Sudan Airways   www.sudanair.com
Turkey: Istanbul   Turkish Airlines   www.turkishairlines.com
Uganda: Entebbe   Sudan Airways   www.sudanair.com
United Arab Emirates: Abu Dhabi   Etihad Airways   www.etihadairways.com
  Sudan Airways   www.sudanair.com
United Arab Emirates: Dubai   Emirates   www.emirates.com
  Sudan Airways   www.sudanair.com
United Kingdom London   British Midlands   www.flybmi.com
Yemen: Sana'a   Yemenia   www.yemenia.com

DIRECT FLIGHTS TO JUBA'S AIRPORT

Kenya: Nairobi   African Express Airways   www.africanexpress.co.ke
  East African Safari Air   www.bookeastafrican.com
  JetLink Express   www.jetlink.co.ke
  Marsland Aviation   www.marsland-avi.com
  Sudan Airways   www.sudanair.com
Uganda: Entebbe   Air Uganda   www.air-uganda.com
  Eagle Air   www.flyeagleuganda.com
  Royal Daisy Airlines   www.royaldaisy.com
Ethiopia: Addis Ababa   Ethiopian Airlines   www.ethiopianairlines.com

The Essentials

AIRPORTS

Khartoum's International Airport is conveniently located close to the city centre (a short ten-minute taxi or bus ride). A new international airport is being built one hour's drive from the city, in Omdurman, to replace the current one as the main international airport. The official opening date of the airport is spring 2012, but will probably be delayed. The German contractors say that the opening of the airport is unlikely to take place before 2013. Others say that it could be even later, since fundamental problems have been found with the ground of the designated site and a new area may have to be chosen for the airport.

A taxi from the airport should cost you a maximum of 15 SDG for most destinations in the city.

If you are travelling to Amarat or Khartoum 2 and 3, you shouldn't pay more than 7 SDG. For Riyad or the centre of town, you might pay slightly more, but you should set a maximum limit of 10 SDG.

You should only pay more if you want to travel to Omdurman or Bahri.

You may need to haggle quite hard to get a good deal, though. Remember that taxis leaving from the airport are used to being tough on foreigners.

Drivers now have to pay a small charge when they leave the airport, which pushes up the price for taxis. Consider leaving the airport compound before hailing a taxi.

A cheaper option is to take one of the buses that run up and down Afriqia Street, often called Matar (Airport) Street by the locals. To get to this street, simply walk for a few minutes away from the airport.

If you catch a bus heading to your right, you will eventually end up in the centre of Khartoum. Buses heading left will take you to the Amarat and Riyad districts.

A bus ride anywhere in the city will cost between 50 *piastras* and 1 SDG, depending on the type of bus that you take (p*88*). To get to Omdurman or Bahri, you will need to change in the centre of town.

For airport information, you can call ☎ 0183 774 405 or 0183 788 194 or 0183 780 129. There are a few shops within the airport where you can buy a phone SIM card for your mobile phone. There is also an exchange bureau and car rental services. Free wi-fi is available at the airport, although it is not always working. There are also a few terminals where you can use the internet for free.

Juba's Airport is situated to the north of the city. A little frustratingly, security concerns mean that minibuses do not go to the airport. You either have to rely on motorcycles (*boda-bodas*), which can take you to most places in town for around 5 SSP, or the more expensive taxis (expect a ride to cost between 10-15 SSP). Most of the time, you will need to haggle in order to get the fair prices quoted in this book.

Facilities at Juba's airport are limited. The grocery chain JIT has just opened a duty-free store there and there is a small restaurant area. Across the parking lot there is a more modern cafeteria. It is here that you will also find the main airline offices.

PRICE OF THE FERRY BETWEEN WADI HALFA AND ASWAN		
class	return	single
1st	274 SDG	155 SDG
2nd	168 SDG	95 SDG

in order to make sure all necessary checks and controls are completed on time — and to fight for your seat, if you are travelling second-class.

The ship itself is pretty basic. The first-class cabins are simple and not overly spacious, although they do have air-conditioning. In second-class, you will have to make do with sleeping on padded benches. It is wonderful to watch the passing landscape from the upper deck, although the ship can get extremely busy, making it difficult to take in the views.

Try to be out on deck when passing the temples of Abu Simbel. Travelling from Wadi Halfa, you will pass these in the evening. If you come from Aswan, you will pass them in the morning.

A series of shallow stretches of water along the Nile — known as the Nile Cataracts (p210) — make river travel between Khartoum and Egypt unfeasible.

However, you can now travel between **Kosti**, south of Khartoum, and **Juba** by boat. Such a trip, though, is not for those who like to travel in comfort. The journey, which is usually on-board a cargo boat, takes ten days and will see you travelling through mosquito-infested swampland under often unbearable heat. Expect to pay between 100 and 150 SDG for the experience. To arrange this, simply turn up at the docks in Kosti and speak to the people there (p246).

From the **Red Sea port of Suakin**, it is possible to take a boat to Jeddah in Saudi Arabia (this costs around 200 SDG and takes 13 hours — see p229), although passenger traffic is not what it once was. There are no regular ferry services to other destinations on the Red Sea.

By land

The easiest way to enter and leave North Sudan by land is via **Ethiopia**. In South Sudan, the best land crossing is through **Uganda**.

At present, the border between Sudan and the **Central African Republic** is closed, as is the overland border to **Egypt**. The overland crossing to the **Democratic Republic of Congo** remains dangerous. You should also proceed with caution when crossing into Kenya — public buses do not yet serve the route due to the threat of banditry.

The situation on the border between Sudan and **Eritrea** remains tense. Although the border to **Chad** is now officially open, travel in Darfur and between the two countries is risky. The border with **Libya** was closed in July 2010.

There are no direct bus or train routes from Khartoum to other countries. Regular buses run from Juba to destinations in Uganda.

There are no train services into and out of the country.

TRAVELLING AROUND

Within cities

Buses are the cheapest way of travelling around cities. Most journeys will cost you between 50 *piastras* and 1 SDG. They also allow you to really appreciate a side of the local culture that is simply not possible if you use taxis or private vehicles all the time. However, without a good knowledge of the city, you are almost certain to get lost and frustrated when the bus veers off in a quite unexpected direction.

More modern air-conditioned buses have now arrived in Khartoum, although many Sudanese still prefer to take the old rickety African-style buses. The newer buses cost slightly more: within the city, prices are usually 1 SDG, irrespective of where you can on and off.

Taxis are another possibility, although remember that there is no guarantee that taxi drivers know where they are going any better than you do. Most city trips by taxi should cost no more than 15 SDG.

An alternative to the taxi, available mainly in northern cities, is the **amjad**. These are usually nondescript blue vans, although they can in fact be any colour. As a general rule of thumb, they tend to have lower prices and more honest drivers than taxis.

The **motor rickshaw** is popular in many cities in North Sudan. You will usually be charged a few SDG pounds for most journeys. Whilst rickshaws may be cheaper, there are more and more rickshaw-free zones being introduced, meaning that taxis are often the better option.

In the South, the easiest and cheapest way to get round cities is to hop on the back of a **bicycle** or **motorbike**. These are known as *boda-bodas*, a corruption of the English word "border" because, until quite recently, this mode of transport was the only way of crossing the borders between Kenya and Uganda. A ride on a motorbike should cost you no more than 5 SDG to most destinations within a city, whilst bicycles are usually a couple of SDG cheaper. Bicycles tend to be more popular in rural towns and may not be easily available in urban settings.

If you want more freedom, you could consider **hiring a car**, although driving in Sudanese cities can be a pretty hair-raising experience. Alternatively, if you are going to be here for a while, it might make sense to purchase a car — but note that a high import tax can make this prohibitively expensive.

See p86 for more information about available transportation.

Around the country

If you are planning on travelling a long distance, the quickest way is to fly.

Most major cities are connected to Khartoum by air, and you can usually **fly** anywhere within the country in just a few hours. Juba is slightly less well-connected, though there are still a good range of local flights leaving from the city.

Domestic flights are cheap, but remember that safety standards are lower than for international trips.

If you do not fancy flying, long-distance **buses** are also very convenient in the North, and are starting to become more popular in the South.

Overland travel in some areas of South Sudan and in Darfur can be risky due to occasional outbreaks of fighting and banditry on some of the roads. Road travel in North Sudan is generally safer, but you are strongly advised to contact your country's embassy for the latest travel advice.

When travelling long distances, make sure you that you take precautions against the heat, which can make you very ill.

Safety standards for buses are below those found in Europe or America and it is not unknown for bus drivers to be behind the wheel for 15 hours or longer with barely a break.

Travel permits — which foreigners need to obtain to most destinations — are more likely to be checked if you are travelling by bus than if you are in a private vehicle.

If you plan to drive yourself, remember that roads outside the main cities are not always in the best condition (especially in the South), and when it rains quickly turn to rivers of mud that can become perilous.

Sudan's **rail** network is not what it once was. Trains run along it very infrequently and usually take far longer than the equivalent bus journey, inexplicably stopping for lengthy periods of time at points along the way.

p92 for more information about travelling around Sudan.

WHAT TO TAKE

In the larger cities, it is possible to find many of the items that you might be missing from back home, but prices are often much higher.

In the North, this is largely because of the high level of taxation that the government levies on imported goods, in order to promote self-sufficiency within the country.

In the South, high prices can be blamed on poor infrastructure and high transportation costs.

Sudan is hot throughout the year so make sure that you pack accordingly. Loose comfortable **clothes**, preferably cotton, are best. It can get cold during winter nights, though, so a few extra clothes might not be a bad idea. It is better to take more light clothes than a few heavy items, so that you can peel them off as the day gets hotter.

Women who plan to visit the North should bring modest clothes that don't show too much flesh. A headscarf is an optional extra.

Sandals or light shoes are good for short walks around town, although it is also sensible to pack some comfortable shoes for more heavy-duty walking. Many city streets can be difficult to negotiate without proper footwear, since they are often poorly paved and pitted with gaping holes. If you are thinking of exploring the countryside outside of the major cities, consider bringing proper trekking shoes.

If you want to **camp** whilst in the country, it is a good idea to bring your own tent and sleeping bag. Some sites have permanently-erected tents, but these can be very expensive to stay in. For many locals, camping means sleeping on a mat under the stars. Thus camping equipment tends to be in short supply.

The Sudanese sun can be pretty fierce, and so sunglasses and high-factor sun-cream are a good idea. You might also think about wearing a hat, although this will inevitably mark you out as a tourist.

A flashlight is useful in case of power failures. This will also help to avoid potholes and other hazards when walking in the street at night. Street lighting in towns and cities, including Khartoum, remains poor.

You should make photocopies of all travel documents (passport, flight ticket, visa and insurance policy) in case you lose them. One handy trick is to email them to yourself — that way you will be able to print them out whenever you need.

Include several passport-sized photographs in your document wallet, because you'll certainly need to attach them to some form or other.

General medications (including antibiotics) can be bought in the pharmacies of main towns. Some supermarkets have also started selling basic **medicine** such as painkillers.

However, if you are dependent on special medication, make sure that you take an ample supply as it may not be so easy to when you are here.

You can get malaria tablets in the main cities, but they can be pricey. If possible, take enough to last the duration of your stay here.

Many pharmacies are well-equipped to test for malaria, so don't hesitate to use them if you think that you have contracted the disease.

Mosquitoes are a real nuisance throughout Sudan. To counter them, bring a good insect repellent that contains at least 50% DEET. This is a chemical compound that is particularly effective against mosquitoes but can be harmful if used for a prolonged period of time. You might want to bring a mosquito net, too, although this is an item that can be found quite cheaply in most cities.

If you are planning to do any **sport** in the country, it is best to bring the necessary equipment from back home. Tennis and squash racquets, for example, are extremely hard to find in the country.

Women may find that the one-piece swimming costumes sold in the North are not to their liking. These are designed to be as modest as possible, covering the entire body and the top part of the legs. If you do not want to bring your own costume from back home, remember not to choose one that is too revealing. If you do, many public swimming pools will not let you in.

There is not a great variety of internationally-recognised **perfumes** in Sudan so you might want to pack some of your favourite brands. The local brands of perfume, with their distinctively exotic aroma, are worth trying for a change.

Clothes and electronic equipment can be expensive and of poor quality.

CONNECTING WITH LOCALS AND EXPATS

There are a number of social networks that it is worth getting involved with, especially if you are going to be in Khartoum for any length of time. Even if you are just passing through, these groups may be able to give you some very useful information.

There is a group on **Facebook** (⌨ www.facebook.com) called 'Khartoum Klub', which can provide valuable information on many subjects to do with the city. You must be invited to join, though.

On **InterNations** (⌨ www.internations.org) you can find locals and foreigners working in Sudan. You need to be invited by an existing member in order to register.

CouchSurfing (⌨ www.couchsurfing.org) and Hospitality Club (⌨ www.hospitalityclub.org) are two groups that bring local and expats together all around the world. You can use the services to find people to host you for a few nights, but the main point of them is as a cultural exchange. If you are not interested in using the service to understand other cultures and make new friends, don't sign up!

In Khartoum, the **Hash House Harriers** (p145) hosts running events and also provides a forum for socialising with other expats. Unfortunately, the group has recently decided to bar local Sudanese from participating.

MONEY

The local currency

Following independence of the South, both Khartoum and Juba have issued new currencies.

The currency change-over was prompted by South Sudan's unexpectedly early introduction of the South Sudanese Pound, officially abbreviated as SSP.

This caused panic among central bankers in Khartoum, who feared that a sudden influx of old-currency notes from the South could have a destabilising effect on the North's economy.

Taken a little by surprise, the North Sudan's central bank immediately put in place currency controls that limit the amount of money that can enter and leave the country (as we were going to press, such controls were still in place) and prepared for the introduction of its own brand new currency.

The new currency of North Sudan, which was introduced at the end of July 2011, is still known as the *jenayh* and officially abbreviated as SDG.

It is actually the third time that the currency has been changed since 1992, which has created widespread confusion among ordinary people about how much things are worth.

The *dinar* was brought into circulation in 1992, in order to combat

BLACK MARKET

A small but thriving black market is to be found in most of the larger cities in Sudan. In Khartoum, black-market touts usually gather around Souq al-Arabi. In Juba, they are mostly found around near Old Customs Market, just across from the Nyakuron Cultural.

The poor rate for converting money into the local currency has further encouraged the development of the black market, and many shops and other businesses have started offering exceedingly attractive conversion rates (4.6 SDG for €1, for example).

Although you can save a lot of money if you go through the black market, such transactions can be risky.

For one thing, there are strict penalties for using the black market, which can include up to three months in prison and a fine.

Moreover, there have been several reported cases of foreigners being mugged whilst trying to exchange money in this way. The usual ploy is to lure the foreigner away from the crowded streets, under the pretext of needing to avoid the police. Once in this quieter spot, the unwitting foreigner is often surrounded by a larger group of men and forced to hand over his or her money.

A safer way of beating the official exchange rate is to swap money with someone that you know in the country. Many people who are planning to return home shortly are looking to get rid of their Sudanese pounds in return for dollars or euros.

the excessively high inflation that the country had suffered during the 1980s. However, most of the population never really adapted to the new currency, and so the decision was taken, as part of the 2005 Comprehensive Peace Agreement, (p66) to switch back to the *jenayh*.

When the *dinar* was introduced in 1992, 1000 of the old *jenayh* was equivalent to one of the new currency. With the changeover in 2007, one *jenayh* was worth 100 *dinar*. The latest currency has been introduced at parity with the previous *jenayh*, but even so widespread confusion remains.

Since many Sudanese never really got used to the *dinar* in the first place, prices are arbitrarily quoted in old *jenayh*, *dinar* and new *jenayh*. This can result in a bewildering number of zeros being added to the cost of everyday items. Therefore, don't be alarmed if you are asked to pay 200 or even 2000 for a rickshaw ride that should cost only two — just check carefully which currency is being used.

In both the North and the South, the old currency will cease to be legal tender three months after the introduction of the new one. This will be at the beginning of November.

A pound in both North and South Sudan can be divided into 100 *piastras*.

CURRENCY VALUE

£1	4.30 SDG
€1	3.89 SDG
$1	2.68 SDG
CA$1	2.78 SDG
AU$1	2.87 SDG
NZ$1	2.21 SDG

PRICES IN THIS BOOK

You will notice that a number of different currencies are quoted in this book — including the US dollar ($), the euro (€), the North Sudanese Pound (SDG) and the South Sudanese Pound (SSP). This may at first appear confusing, but there is a logic to it.

In North and South Sudan, we use the respective currencies — SDG or SSP. Sometimes, though, hotels and travel agencies, especially the more international ones, prefer to give their prices in a currency that is less likely to fluctuate — normally the US dollar or sometimes the euro. It made sense to follow their lead in this book, otherwise, if the SDG or SSP fell suddenly, the prices that are quoted here would quickly become out of date.

Paying for things

The North is currently subjected to US sanctions, which limits the way in which you can access money from abroad. Although sanctions on the South have been officially lifted, it will take some time before international payment systems are fully integrated into the banking environment.

US dollar travellers' cheques are not accepted by any bank in North Sudan, since banks cannot be reimbursed for them. The Central Bank of Sudan says that there are no such restrictions on travellers' cheques in other denominations, but many banks in the country still do not offer such exchange services. A few exchange bureaux in the city may offer to cash euro or sterling travellers' cheques, but expect to pay well over the odds for this. For a list of exchange bureaux, p326. Travellers' cheques have yet to take hold in the South, but expect them to become more popular in the future.

International payment cards are not widely accepted in Sudan. In the North, this is because of the US sanctions. In the South, this is because the electronic payment system is still under-developed.

In the North, some small exchange bureaux are starting to accept these cards, but expect the cost to be high, since such services have to be directed through a third country.

ATMs exist throughout Sudan, but they do not accept cards from Europe or America. However, you can find ATMs that will accept many cards from Middle Eastern and East African countries.

It is not possible to use PayPal in the country. Paying for some services over the internet can also be difficult — not just because of the US sanctions in the north, but also because companies in the West often suspect online transactions from Sudan of being fraudulent.

Taking money with you

Because of all the problems listed above, it is not surprising that many Sudanese spurn the banking system in favour of the old keeping-your-savings-under-your-mattress trick.

In Khartoum and other cities in the north, crime remains low, although it is rising (p34). In most of Darfur and South Sudan, crime is far more prevalent.

Taking ample cash is the best option for the short-term visitor to Sudan. The US dollar remains the most useful currency, in both the North and the South. Some shops and restaurants will accept this in lieu of the local currency. Euro or

sterling are less readily accepted, although they can easily be changed at an exchange bureau. Be careful not to change more money than you need, though, as changing the money back can be difficult. In North Sudan, you can only do this at the airport and you must produce proof of your departure. Even then, you will not be able to change more than €500.

If you do bring dollars, you should only carry notes that were printed after 2003. Many shops will not take older notes because of fears that they can be easily forged.

For those intending to stay longer, bringing hard currency is likely to be impractical and a local bank account might be a better option (p200).

THE COST OF LIVING

Sudan, perhaps a little surprisingly, is not a cheap country — at least not in the way that some of its neighbours are.

In general, prices are fixed in supermarkets and shops, whilst some haggling is expected in the market. Prices are also negotiable with rickshaw, taxi, *amjad* and *boda-boda* drivers.

In shops, prices of goods are not always marked. However, the Sudanese are usually fairly honest and so you are unlikely to be swindled just because you are foreign (although, of course, there are always exceptions). Prices tend to be fairly standard and do not vary significantly between shops.

Many of the international supermarkets, which sell goods specifically aimed at foreigners, display the prices on what they sell. Such shops are generally more expensive than those catering for the locals, but are handy for finding anything that you might be missing from back home.

See p174 for some useful tips about shopping.

MAIL AND COMMUNICATION

The postal service

Mail sent overseas from Sudan can take a long time to arrive at its destination, and so it is best not to rely on the national postal system for anything urgent. The Chinese-owned Express Mail Service (🖵 www.ems.com.cn) has become particularly popular for sending goods to North Sudan, and is generally reliable. Other international shipping companies, which offer services to both North and South Sudan, include DHL (🖵 www.dhl.com) and TNT (🖵 www.tnt.com).

There is no door-to-door postal service in Sudan, but many of the bigger cities and towns operate a *poste restante* system. This allows you to pick up your mail at the town's central post office. Mail sent in this way should be clearly marked 'poste restante' and addressed to the main post office in the town. There is no charge for collecting letters.

Alternatively, if you are going to be staying in the country for some time, you might like to think about opening a private PO Box (p191). Using the regular postal service to send to a PO Box can be significantly cheaper than relying on an international shipping company.

Certain restrictions apply to the types of goods you can ship to Sudan. Food and drink is not allowed, nor is anything that might be considered pornographic or contrary to the Islamic faith. These restrictions also exist in South Sudan, although

some of them might be eased in the coming months.

In North Sudan, custom officials often confiscate DVDs and other items for censorship reasons. As long as items are deemed permissible, you can usually get them back for a small administrative fee.

Internet

There are a growing number of wireless internet hotspots in both Khartoum and Juba. Many of the fancier hotels and restaurants now have wi-fi.

Wi-fi is less common elsewhere in the country, although internet cafés are relatively easy to find. In the North, internet cafés usually charge a few SDG an hour, but in the South things are much more expensive, with the typical cost of an hour's surfing being around 10 SSP.

If you are staying for a long time in North Sudan, you might want to consider subscribing to an internet service. ADSL broadband has been available in North Sudan since 2004. Sudani and Canar are the main providers. It is not yet available in the South.

Telecommunications companies Sudani, MTN and Zain now offer an internet service through a dongle that plugs into your computer's USB port. You can either take out a monthly subscription for this or pay on a daily basis.

This service works extremely well in Khartoum and other large cities in the North. Coverage is also rapidly improving in South Sudan.

Canar offers a dial-up package that allows you to make calls and connect to the internet throughout Sudan, providing that there is network coverage. Again, this works well in cities like Khartoum and coverage is slowly being extended to other parts of the country.

See p*189* for further information.

Phone

The country code for North Sudan is +249 and +211 for the South. Many people in the South still use Ugandan-registered phones (country code +256), although this is changing.

In North Sudan, mobile numbers in the country start with 091 (for Zain), 092 (for MTN) or 0121 (for Sudani). Numbers for Canar begin with 0155. Zain and MTN are also popular in the South. Vivacell (network code 095) only works in the south, as does the Ugandan operator Gemtel. A Sudanese number that begins with any other digit is likely to be a landline.

Sudan is served by a dual-band system, which means that any unblocked mobile phone should work there. Most international SIM cards work, as long as you have credit. Local pay-as-you-go SIM cards cost between 5 and 20 SDG/SSP, depending on the network, and can easily be purchased from street vendors or in shopping malls. They are also sold at Khartoum's airport, although not the one in Juba. Top-up cards are widely sold by street vendors or in local shops.

Note that once you have purchased a SIM card, you will usually have to take it to an office of the relevant network provider, within 24 hours, so that it can be registered.

Mobile phones do not work in remoter regions of Sudan, which is why many people also use satellite phones. The main satellite phone company is Thuraya. A Thuraya phone number is prefixed with 00882. You will occasionally see Thuraya phone numbers in this book. Remember, though, that the cost of calling such phones can be very high.

Fixed landlines are generally not popular in Sudan, but Sudani can provide more information about installing one if you want.

The 'Living and Working' sections of this book contains more information about postal, internet and phone services in the country. See p189 for North Sudan and p266 for South Sudan.

PRESS

In the North, the margins of press freedom have improved significantly since the signing of the Comprehensive Peace Agreement (p66), although some say that the improvements in freedom of speech have been exaggerated. It is true that there continue to be cases of newspapers, perceived to be anti-government, being temporarily shut down and members of staff arrested. But this is nothing compared to what things were like before 2005.

In general, the Arabic press is targeted more often than the English media, which has a smaller reading population and can therefore get away with much more. The most popular English newspaper (*The Khartoum Monitor*) has a daily readership of 3000-4000, whilst the largest Arabic newspapers (*Al-Ray al-Aam* and *Al-Sudani*) have a circulation of 60,000 each.

The media in South Sudan is much less developed than the media in the North, and there is a concerted effort at the moment to help it develop.

Recently, *The Khartoum Monitor*, established in 2000 to give southerners a voice in the north-south conflict, relocated from Khartoum to Juba.

The Sudan Tribune, published in English, also gives a good insight into southern politics. Note that it is totally unrelated to the online version (💻 www.sudantribune.com), which is an independent website based in France.

The Citizen is also known to be sympathetic to southern causes, but it has just divided into two. One edition is published from Juba and the other from Khartoum. They are editorially independent.

The Juba Post is a weekly newspaper, which also represents southern views.

The Sudan Vision is widely regarded as a pro-northern newspaper, supportive of the Khartoum regime. It continues to enjoy considerable influence.

English-language newspapers are usually sold by street vendors. Not all Sudanese newspapers are available in the South; *The Citizen* and *The Sudan Tribune* are the most readily available, along with a smattering of Ugandan titles.

There are 14 Arabic-language dailies. The main ones are *Al-Ray al-Aam, Al-Sudani, Ak-Khair Lahza, Al-Sahafa, As-Skhbar* and *Al-Youm*.

In terms of foreign news outlets, the *BBC* has a full-time correspondent in Sudan and *Reuters* has reporters in both Khartoum and Juba. *The Voice of America* periodically has journalists stationed in Khartoum. Journalists from other international newspapers occasionally flit in and out of Sudan. Most daily English and American papers cover the country from Nairobi or Cairo.

International newspapers and magazines are available in Sudan's major cities. You can buy them from street vendors, at small kiosks along the side of the road or in the markets.

In Khartoum, you can browse foreign newspapers and magazines at a number of locations usually frequented by expats. Hotels like the Acropole stock a good selection,

as does the library of the British Council. Solitaire and Ozone cafés also have a selection of foreign newspapers.

ELECTRICITY

Power shortages in the main cities of North Sudan are rarer than they used to be, although they still happen occasionally. In remoter towns and villages, and in the South, they are more common.

Power cuts don't tend to last more than a few hours, but it is a good idea to keep a flashlight, or some candles and matches, close at hand.

The standard voltage in Sudan is 220. Sockets are either the British three-pin or the round two-pin plug — there is no fixed rule. It is not uncommon to find both of them in the same building. You should bring an adaptor for both kinds of plug.

In general, the quality of plugs and extensions is very poor. Moreover, the spacing between the pins is not always consistent. This means that, when you plug something in, it is often either too loose or doesn't fit at all.

VISAS AND PERMITS

Entry visas are required by most nationalities, and are usually for one or two months.

Different embassy representations will handle your visa inquiry depending on whether you plan to visit North or South Sudan. A visa to the North does not guarantee you access to the South and vice-versa. However, the requirements and process for obtaining the different visas remain broadly the same.

North Sudan

Egyptian nationals are exempt from visa requirements when visiting North Sudan. You will not be allowed to enter the North if your passport shows evidence of a previous visit to Israel.

A **tourist visa** to North Sudan usually takes between one and two months to arrive, depending on the efficiency of the embassy through which you are applying. You can speed up the process by getting a Sudanese national to invite you — the approval process can then take as little as one or two weeks. However, embassies abroad and ministries in Sudan do not always agree on the procedure, with the result that personal invitations are not always accepted. Check with your nearest Sudanese embassy.

Prices for all tourist visas vary according to your nationality. Europeans pay around €60 for a tourist visa, whilst US citizens pay around €110.

Transit visas are available and allow a maximum two week stay in the country. You can sometimes pick transit visas up at the border, depending on where you are crossing (although don't bank on this). Again prices vary. A two-week transit visa purchased on the Ethiopian border costs around 50 SDG.

If you are working for an NGO in Sudan, your employer may be able to expedite the visa application process. Some NGOs claim that they can get their staff visas within a period of between 24 and 48 hours.

North Sudan requires **registration** within three days of arriving in the country — Fridays and Saturdays are included within this time-window. If you fail to register, you

THE TRIBULATIONS OF BEING A FOREIGNER

One of the truly great things of being a foreigner — or *khawadja* — in Sudan is just how welcoming the locals are. In general, the ordinary Sudanese don't care what country you are from. As long as you treat them and their culture with respect, they will do the same for you. It is one of the reasons that so many Europeans and Americans, as well as other nationalities, have chosen to pack up and move to Sudan.

Unfortunately, though, this blind acceptance of other cultures and faiths does not always extend to the security forces.

As a foreigner in Sudan, it is not unusual to be stopped and questioned by the police about what you are doing in a particular area. You are likely to arouse suspicion if you loiter too close to governmental buildings, military installations, banks or police headquarters. Taking photographs also increases the risk of drawing attention to yourself — just make sure you have your photography permit with you. You may also be stopped just because it is unusual to see foreigners in the particular place that you have visited.

Often the policemen who stop you may be wearing civilian clothes and refuse to show any ID. They will usually ask you to accompany them to a police station. Remember to remain calm and cheerful. Being detained by the police can be frustrating, but it is rarely intimidating.

However, there have been cases of ordinary people pretending to be policemen in order to extort money. Be alert to such behaviour. Do not agree to part with any money and report any unacceptable behaviour to your embassy.

will incur a fine of 10 SDG per day until you do. If you have been given a residence permit — which might be the case if, for example, you work for an international organisation — then you are exempt from registering.

Most hotels in Khartoum will register for you in return for a fee. If you want to do the registration yourself, simply turn up at one of the **Aliens Registration Offices** ('*Maktab Tasgil al-Agganib*') around the city. The easiest one to find is located on Afriqia Street, just opposite the Al-Salam Rotana Hotel. There is also one in the Mogran area of downtown Khartoum, near the Botanical Gardens, and one at the end of Street 61.

Registration costs around 117 SDG, but prices can fluctuate quite arbitrarily by about 5 or 10 SDG.

Visas on arrival are also possible, but usually only for those that have been invited by a company for a specific purpose. This is considerably more expensive, requiring a payment of 150 SDG for issuing the invitation and a further $110 (300 SDG) when you arrive at the airport in Khartoum.

To travel around North Sudan, you must first obtain a **travel permit** from either the Ministry of Tourism or the Ministry of Humanitarian Affairs.

The Ministry of Tourism is by far the easiest option and can issue travel permits for many popular destinations in a matter of minutes. The travel permit is usually combined with a **photography permit** (see box).

The procedure at the Ministry of Humanitarian Affairs is usually much more protracted, and it takes at least 24 hours for one to be issued. You will need to provide five copies of your passport information

---

THE PHOTOGRAPHY PERMIT

This is what the tourist office in Khartoum has to say about photography in the country: "Military areas, bridges, train stations, broadcasting and public utilities such as water, gas, petrol and electricity works are not to be filmed. Slum areas, beggars and other defaming subject [sic] are not to be photographed."

---

page, five copies of your visa and two passport-sized photos. You will also need to provide a photocopy of the ID of the person that invited you, unless you are on a tourist visa.

The main reason for going to the Ministry of Humanitarian Affairs, rather than the Ministry of Tourism, is if you want to travel to areas that have more restricted access, or if you are travelling on official or company business.

The **Ministry of Tourism** is located in Riyad, along Mashtal Street, not far from Street 117. Buses heading to and from Jeref as-Gara travel down this street.

The **Ministry of Humanitarian Affairs** is just south of Qurashi Park in Khartoum 2. Buses running between Jackson Station in central Khartoum and Sahafa Zalat can drop you off nearby.

Both ministries are closed on Fridays and Saturdays.

Travel permits issued by the Ministry of Tourism are free. If you apply through the Ministry of Humanitarian Affairs, you will have to pay a nominal tax (around 5 SDG).

Of course, some destinations are still off-limits to the casual traveller (such as large swathes of Darfur and parts of the Nuba Mountains) and permission to travel to these areas is much harder to come by.

If you book a trip through an established tour operator, they will usually sort out the necessary permits, although some try to shift responsibility for this onto their customers. Check who has the responsibility for the permits before booking.

Officially, you are not allowed to take photos in Sudan without a photography permit. Expect to be harassed if you do. Even with permission, there is still a list of places in North Sudan, such as slum areas and bridges, which you are not allowed to take photographs of (see box). The Ministry of Tourism is responsible for such permits.

You no longer have to pay a 35 SDG tax for leaving the country.

If you are planning on a longer stay in North Sudan, see p186 for full details about visa requirements.

South Sudan

Visa requirements for the South are somewhat fluid at the moment, but expect to pay the equivalent of around $50 for a month's stay. South Sudan representations in Europe and America will tell you that you need an invitation letter from someone in South Sudan before you can get a visa, but many embassies in Africa will be happy to issue you a visa without one.

You do not need additional permits to travel around the South — your entry visa will be sufficient.

Even in the South, though, you should obtain a photography permit in order to avoid being hassled by the police. The Ministry of Information, on Ministries Road in Juba, can help with the process.

HEALTH AND VACCINATIONS

This section outlines what health precautions you should take if travelling to Sudan. However, since health and vaccination requirements can change all the time, you are strongly advised to consult your local health clinic for the latest information. All visitors should take out a good health insurance policy before travelling.

Whatever length of time you are staying in Sudan, you should be vaccinated against **typhoid**, **tetanus** and **polio**. Vaccination against **hepatitis A** is also recommended if you are staying in the country for more than four months. For a longer stay, vaccination against **meningococcal meningitis** is a good idea. **Hepatitis B** is present in the country, but it is usually only contracted through intimate contact with a carrier. **Rabies** is also common and a rabies vaccine is recommended for those at high risk of animal bites. Should you get bitten by an animal during your stay, seek immediate medical attention; rabies can be fatal.

If you are travelling from a country where **yellow fever** is prevalent, you will need to have with you a yellow-fever vaccination certificate. You will also need to have a yellow-fever certificate if you plan to travel to Egypt during your stay in Sudan.

Malaria (see box on following page) is widespread in Sudan, so preventative medication should be taken before, during and after your trip. Malaria favours wetter conditions over drier climes, and therefore it is more common in the South. However, despite what you might hear, malaria is present in the North — and you must decide whether it is a big enough risk to warrant taking medication during your stay there.

Larium (otherwise known as mefloquine) is often recommended as the best medication to take as a

MALARIA TRAVEL ADVICE

Malaria can prove fatal if left untreated, and so you should seek medical advice if you start exhibiting any symptoms of the illness. Telltale signs of malaria are similar to severe flu: fever, sweating and shivering, headache, nausea and vomiting, diarrhoea, aching muscles and joints, and backache.

Malaria can spread rapidly, especially cerebral malaria, which is the most deadly form of the disease. Always seek medical advice if you have any suspicion that you may have contracted the disease. You must get customised advice about how to protect yourself against malaria. What precautions you take will depend on your medical history, what medications you are currently taking, where you are going, what you will be doing, what time of year you will be travelling and for how long you will be staying.

Some key things that you should do to deal with malaria effectively:

- Avoid getting bitten in the first place. This means using effective insect repellents (ideally containing at least 50% DEET) and wearing appropriate clothes to cover arms and legs.
- Take malaria prevention tablets, according to what your travel clinic advises — and take them consistently, as per instructions.
- Treat any symptoms without delay, ideally within eight hours and certainly within 12 hours of them starting.
- Consider taking an emergency treatment kit, especially if you are likely to be in a region where immediate treatment will be hard to obtain.

Malaria can strike several weeks, and sometimes more than a year, after that fateful mosquito bite. Continue taking your tablets for the full length of time recommended and immediately report any suspicious symptoms to your nearest emergency department, even if it is in the middle of the night.

guard against the strain of malaria found in Sudan. Follow your medical professional's advice regarding dosage: it is usually taken as a weekly tablet for the duration of your stay in the country. Some people experience side-effects with larium — including dizziness and paranoia. The best thing to do is to try larium a few weeks before your departure and, if you are one of those unfortunate people who do experience bad side-effects, consider switching to another drug. Your local health centre can give you more information on the drugs available.

Water quality varies in Sudan. The government in North Sudan insists that there is no serious problem with the water supply in Khartoum, and locals drink it all the time without any worries. However, water safety standards are still below the level of those in America and Europe and so, to avoid any problems, you might prefer to stick to the bottled drinking water that is available (2 SDG for one-and-a-half litres). Water purification filters are also available from household stores, costing around 60 SDG.

Outside of the capital, you should be more wary of the water.

Throughout Sudan, you will notice large urns of communal drinking water by the side of the road. Whilst this is an excellent way of making sure that no one ever goes thirsty, it is also a good way of passing germs around.

AIDS is present in Sudan, but is less common than in many other African countries. Figures from the United Nations put the number of those living with HIV, the virus that causes AIDS, at 1.4% of the total adult population. Nonetheless, if you have any sexual relations whilst in the country, it is always a good idea to use protection.

In North Sudan, you must have an AIDS test if you plan to work in Sudan for longer than a month. This requirement does not apply in the South.

The AIDS test must be carried out by the Department of Aliens. A certificate from outside the country, or even from a hospital within Sudan, is not considered valid.

Advice from the British Embassy in Sudan warns that **hospitals in the country** are not suitable for elective problems and are only suitable for stabilisation of serious medical conditions prior to evacuation.

Food poisoning is common in Sudan. Symptoms include stomach cramps, vomiting and being unable to eat and drink. To minimise the risk of getting food poisoning, be careful where you buy your food and be particularly careful when it comes to meat products. Look for food that has just been cooked. In general, frying food gets rid of more bacteria because it is cooked at a higher temperature.

For further information about the health requirements of Sudan, visit:

- 🖥 www.nathnac.org
- 🖥 www.fitfortravel.nhs.uk

ISLAMIC HOLIDAYS

Eid al-Fitr ('the feast of breaking the fast') marks the end of Ramadan, the holiest month in the Muslim calendar. The holiday, which lasts between three and four days, begins on the first day following the night in which the new moon has been sighted. It is an occasion of great feasting and an opportunity to visit friends and neighbours.

Eid al-Adhah ('the feast of the sacrifice'), often known as *Eid al-Kabier* ('the big feast'), commemorates Ibrahim's willingness to sacrifice his son to Allah. The festival takes place on the tenth day of Dhul Hijja, marking the day when Muslim pilgrims who undertake the Hajj (p73) descend from Mount Arafat. Most Muslim families will celebrate this festival by slaughtering a ram, to mark the sacrifice that Ibrahim was prepared to make. Celebrations usually last between four and five days

Moulid al-Nabi ('the Prophet's birthday') is celebrated 90 days after Eid al-Adhah. Thousands of people assemble at the public square closest to their homes to enjoy entertainment, greet friends and partake of sweets and refreshments.

Sham al-Nassim ('spring holiday') is celebrated on the first Monday following the Easter weekend. This celebration traces its origins back to ancient times and is still honoured in many Arabic countries. In Sudan, the festival is otherwise known as Coptic Easter and is an important date in the calendar of the Coptic Church.

PUBLIC HOLIDAYS AND WEEK-ENDS

Until fairly recently, the official weekend in North Sudan consisted of just a single day: Friday. A two-day weekend (Friday and Saturday) was introduced in January 2009. However, not all companies respect the two-day weekend.

All government ministries and offices have both days off, but for the private sector it is up to the discretion of the individual company and many of them still work on the Saturday. In particular, businesses with European origins tend to favour the one-day weekend.

Many offices — including embassies and government ministries — close early on Thursday.

In the South, the official weekend is two days: Saturday and Sunday.

Sudan has a number of official holidays, when most companies and public offices are closed. In the North, the dates for many holidays follow the Islamic calendar and therefore fall on different dates each year compared to the Gregorian calendar (see box below).

Islamic holidays are not so important in South Sudan. Instead, the country observes most major Christian holidays such as Easter and Christmas.

South Sudan also observes Comprehensive Peace Agreement Signing Day (January 9) SPLM/A Day (May 16), when the rebellion was launched, Martyr's Day (July 30), to commemorate those that have fallen during the struggle, and Constitution Day (5 December).

North and South Sudan celebrate their **independence** on different days. For the North, Independence Day is celebrated on January 1 and represents the day when the country got its independence from Britain. In the South, Independence Day is celebrated on July 9, when the country officially seceded from the North.

CRIME AND SAFETY

Most cities in North Sudan are surprisingly safe — especially when compared to other urban centres in Africa.

The **security** situation in southern towns, and in Darfur, is slightly more precarious and you should exercise greater caution.

Even in the North, it always pays to be on your guard, particularly after dark and around the market areas. The local Sudanese say that incidences of petty theft have been on the rise in recent years.

House break-ins are also becoming more prevalent in the North. Due to the obstacles with banking

ISLAMIC CALENDAR

Hijra Year	Moulid al-Nabi	Ramadan Begins	Eid al-Fitr	Eid al-Adhah
1433	04.02.12	20.07.12	19.08.12	26.10.12
1434	24.01.13	09.07.13	08.08.13	15.10.13
1435	13.01.14	28.06.14	28.07.14	04.10.14
1436	03.01.15	18.06.15	17.07.15	23.09.15

DEALING WITH BEGGARS

In the North, if you don't want to give money to beggars, a polite Arabic phrase to use is: *'Allah karima'*. Literally, this can be translated as 'God is generous', the implication being that God will provide for the beggar's needs.

However, since a growing number of beggars in the north are refugees that do not speak Arabic or are not Muslim, the phrase is not always understood.

in the country, many people stow their money under mattresses or between cushions — providing ripe pickings for the burglar.

As in urban environments the world over, begging is a common sight in Sudanese towns and cities, especially around marketplaces and bus stations, and it is increasing. Many of these beggars come from countries outside of Sudan such as Chad. The beggars are persistent but rarely threatening.

Sharia law was introduced into Sudan in 1983 and still applies to the North (although not to the South).

This means that certain crimes, which may seem trivial by Western standards, carry with them harsh penalties.

The 2005 Comprehensive Peace Agreement (CPA) sought to prevent *sharia* law from being applied to non-Muslims. However, since July 2011, the CPA is no longer enforce and it remains to be seen whether *sharia* law will now also apply to those not of the Muslim faith. President Omar al-Bashir has said that it will, but others in his government are taking a softer line.

The best advice is to always be on your guard and to avoid doing anything that might bring you into conflict with the authorities. If you are imprisoned, there is only a limited amount that your national government can do to secure your release.

Sudan has both capital and corporal punishment. Crimes that carry the death penalty include murder, armed robbery, prostitution and drug trafficking. Under the *sharia* legal system, the penalty for consuming alcohol is 40 lashes. Possession and distribution of pornography is also prohibited.

There have been reports in Khartoum of Westerners being arrested and accused of spying. It is always best to be on your guard and to be careful about where you are pointing your camera, especially near government and military areas.

There remains a slight threat of terrorism in Sudan. Al-Qaeda terrorist cells are believed to exist in the country, and there have been recent threats made towards Western embassies.

Always keep in mind the political situation in the country, and pay close attention to the news to see if things are likely to change. In 2005, following the death of the charismatic rebel leader John Garang (p64), there was widespread rioting throughout Sudan. In September 2007, rumours that Salva Kiir, then the vice-president of Sudan, had been killed sparked fears of fresh rioting.

You should register with your national embassy when you arrive in Sudan, and keep in touch throughout your stay.

About Sudan

Taken together, the Republic of North Sudan and the newly-created Republic of South Sudan make up the largest landmass in Africa.

Prior to July 9, 2011, the two countries were run by a unity government that consisted of the Sudan People's Liberation Movement (SPLM), the political arm of the former southern rebels, and the northern National People's Party (NCP).

This was only an interim measure, established under the 2005 Comprehensive Peace Agreement (CPA) that brought years of bloodshed and civil war to an end.

One of the provisions under the CPA was to give the South the chance to vote for secession from the North — which they did, overwhelmingly, on January 9, 2011.

Governing North and South Sudan as a single country was always going to be problematic, given the religious and cultural distinctions between the two regions.

North Sudan is typified by a predominantly Muslim population, unified by a common belief in Islam, whilst the South brings together a multifaceted Christian and animist society.

The British, when they governed Sudan, made certain that the two regions were kept separate. But, when negotiations started on granting the colonies independence, it was generally agreed that the poorer South would not be able to survive without being bound to the North. This decision had tragic consequences.

Now that the chord binding the North and South has at last been severed, it remains very uncertain what the future will hold for the two sovereign states. One thing is clear — in both Khartoum, the capital of the North, and Juba, the capital of the South, people are optimistic about the future.

For all the differences between the North and the South, many similarities remain. This is unsurprising since the two countries share such a close history with one another.

This is why the decision has been made to cover both countries in a single guidebook. Where differences occur, they will be pointed out in the relevant sections.

The two countries may diverge over time as they go their separate ways. The two governments say that they want to retain close ties with one another, but it is inevitable that more and more differences will start to emerge as the 193rd member of the United Nations forges its own way in the world.

GEOGRAPHY AND CLIMATE

The Republic of South Sudan shares borders with Ethiopia (to the east), Kenya and Uganda (to the south-east), the Democratic Republic of the Congo and the Central African Republic (to the southwest) and of course North Sudan.

Besides bordering South Sudan, North Sudan shares borders with Egypt (to the north), Eritrea and Ethiopia (to the east), Chad (to the west), the Central African Republic (to the south-west) and Libya (to the north-west). Sudan also borders the Red Sea, to the east, which is important for international trade.

SUDAN AT A GLANCE
(SEPARATE STATISTICS FOR NORTH AND SOUTH DO NOT YET EXIST)

Land area:	2,505,810 km^2
Land boundaries:	7687 km
Coastline:	853 km
Population:	45,047,502 (July 2011)
Population growth rate:	2.484% (2011)
Birth rate:	38.12 births/1,000 population (2011)
Death rate:	11 deaths/1,000 population (2011)
Total fertility rate:	4.84 children born per woman (2011)
Life expectancy at birth:	55.42 years (2011)
Ethnic groups:	black 52%, Arab 39%, Beja 6%, foreigners 2%, other 1%
Religions:	Sunni Muslim 70%, Christian 5%, indigenous beliefs 25%
Timezone:	GMT+3, no Daylight Saving Time
GDP:	$100 billion (2010)
GDP real growth rate:	5.1% (2010)
GDP per capita:	$2300 (2010)
Main exports:	Oil, cotton, sesame, livestock and hides, gum arabic

NORTH SUDAN

Capital:	Khartoum
Official language:	Arabic
President:	Omar al-Bashir
Vice-president	Ali Osman Taha
Independence:	January 1, 1956
Dialing code:	+249
Currency:	Sudanese Pound (SDG)
Internet suffix:	.sd

SOUTH SUDAN

Capital:	Juba
Official language:	English
President:	Salva Kiir
Vice-president	Riek Machar
Independence:	July 9, 2011
Dialing code:	+211
Currency:	South Sudanese Pound (SSP)
Internet suffix:	.ss

The northern part of North Sudan is fairly flat and mostly covered by desert, although there are a few rocky outcrops — such as Jebel Barkal (p213) — in the midst of all the sand. There are some mountains to be found near the border with the South and in Darfur in the west. North Sudan's highest point is Jebel Marra in Darfur, rising to 3042 metres above sea level. There are also some hills in the east, around Port Sudan and Kassala.

South Sudan is more hilly, with the highest point — Mount Kinyeti near the Ugandan border — rising to 3187 meters above sea level. Swamps and rainforests permeate the South, including the notorious mosquito-infested Sudd. British explorer Samuel Baker, for whom the Sudd proved particularly frustrating, described the swampish stretch of the Nile as heaven for mosquitoes and a "damp hell for man".

The **River Nile** flows through both South and North Sudan. It enters the South as two separate rivers — the White Nile coming in from Uganda and the Blue Nile from Ethiopia. The rivers then converge in Khartoum to form a single body of water that flows northwards through Egypt to the Mediterranean Sea.

Spanning 6695 km, the Nile is widely thought to be the longest river in the world, although researchers in Brazil have claimed that the Amazon is actually longer.

The White Nile is the river's longest tributary, although its exact source is as-yet undetermined. The Blue Nile brings in most of the water.

Sudan's **climate** varies significantly between the northern and southern regions.

In the northern desert regions, the weather is dry and arid. Moving south, however, the conditions quickly become more tropical, with very heavy rainfall for parts of the year, making travel during this period exceedingly tricky.

The time and duration of the rainy season varies from region to region, and can also depend upon air flows from elsewhere in the world.

From January to March, dry north-easterly winds blow in from the Arabian Peninsula. During this time, there is practically no rainfall in either the North or the South, apart from a small area in northwestern Sudan, which occasionally experiences light showers coming in from the Mediterranean.

By early April, moist southwesterly winds start sweeping into the country from the Congo River's

	Jan	Feb	Mar	Apr	May	Jun	Jul	Aug	Sep	Oct	Nov	Dec
Khartoum												
Min °C	16°	17°	20°	24°	27°	28°	26°	26°	26°	26°	21°	17°
Max °C	31°	33°	37°	40°	42°	41°	39°	38°	39°	39°	35°	32°
Rain (mm)	0.0	0.0	0.1	0.0	3.9	4.2	29.6	48.3	26.7	7.8	0.7	0.0
Juba												
Min °C	20	22	24	23	23	22	21	21	21	21	21	20
Max °C	37	38	38	35	34	32	31	32	33	34	35	36
Rain (mm)	5.1	11	36.7	111.5	129.9	117.8	144.7	127.5	103.7	114.5	43.1	8.2

basin, causing heavy rainfall in the South.

By July, the moist air has reached Khartoum and, in August, it has extended to its northern limits around Abu Hamed.

In some years, the humid air can even reach the Egyptian border. In September, the dry north-easterly winds begin to strengthen and to push south and, by the end of December, they cover both countries.

THE PEOPLE

To appreciate something of the richness of Sudanese heritage, you have only to look at the diverse range of people who are spread across its vast land surface.

Ethnographers have identified 19 core ethnic groups in Sudan, which can be sub-divided into 597 distinct tribes. There are over 100 different languages currently in use in Sudan.

Sudanese tribes are often pigeon-holed into one of two groups: Arab or non-Arab. Whilst such a distinction can be helpful in understanding the cultural heritage, one must be careful in being too cut-and-dry. In a country such as Sudan, with its long history of internal migration and foreign conquest, uncovering accurate data about its ethnic mix is notoriously difficult.

Arabs have frequently married non-Arab Africans, leading to an ethnic group that lies somewhere between the two, though is still labelled, for convenience, with the all-encompassing Arab or non-Arab tag.

Arab tribes

The Arabs are by far the largest ethnic group in North Sudan, estimated to number some 16 million. There are very few Arabs in the South, however.

The label 'Arab' refers to cultural, rather than religious, heritage, although Islam is practiced by almost all Arabs in the country. However, the interpretation of the faith is often influenced by ancestral customs and therefore differs widely between tribal groups.

The origin of most Sudanese Arabs can be traced back to the Bedouin nomads who, centuries ago, wandered the deserts of what is now modern-day Saudi Arabia.

With the passage of time, many Arabic groups have intermarried with African tribes, which has given them darker skin tones and Negroid features.

Beja

Nicknamed 'the Fuzzy Wuzzies' by the British, because of their unique crop of short curly hair, the Beja tribe was crucial in supporting the campaign of the Mahdi against British colonial forces at the end of the 19th century (p56).

The Beja are a nomadic tribe, living mainly in the east of North Sudan, although some are to be found in Ethiopia and Eritrea as well. Their origin is not known for certain, but many believe that they came from Egypt because of their resemblance to people depicted on ancient Egyptian monuments.

Their nomadic lifestyle, and their aloofness to foreigners, has given the Beja something of a reputation for being a sullen and hostile people.

The Beja worshipped the Egyptian goddess Isis until the 5th or 6th century, when they started to adopt Christianity. However, their association with this religion was short-lived. In the 13th century, the spread of Bedouin tribes into Sudan brought the Beja into direct contact

About Sudan

FUZZY WUZZY BY RUDYARD KIPLING

One of those that immortalised the prowess of the Beja as warriors was the British writer Rudyard Kipling, who laments the defeat of the British forces at the hands of the 'Fuzzy Wuzzy' in one of his poems. In the poem, he refers to the breaking of the British square, which was a four-sided defensive infantry formation considered to be impenetrable — until one fateful day in 1885 at Abu Klea when the Beja managed to break through.

We've fought with many men acrost the seas,
    An' some of 'em was brave an' some was not:
The Paythan an' the Zulu an' Burmese;
    But the Fuzzy was the finest o' the lot.
We never got a ha'porth's change of 'im:
    'E squatted in the scrub an' 'ocked our 'orses,
'E cut our sentries up at Suakim,
    An' 'e played the cat an' banjo with our forces.
    So 'ere's to you, Fuzzy-Wuzzy, at your 'ome in the Soudan;
    You're a pore benighted 'eathen but a first-class fightin' man;
    We gives you your certificate, an' if you want it signed
    We'll come an' 'ave a romp with you whenever you're inclined.

We took our chanst among the Khyber 'ills,
    The Boers knocked us silly at a mile,
The Burman give us Irriwaddy chills,
    An' a Zulu impi dished us up in style:
But all we ever got from such as they
    Was pop to what the Fuzzy made us swaller;
We 'eld our bloomin' own, the papers say,
    But man for man the Fuzzy knocked us 'oller.
    Then 'ere's to you, Fuzzy-Wuzzy, an' the missis and the kid;
    Our orders was to break you, an' of course we went an' did.
    We sloshed you with Martinis, an' it wasn't 'ardly fair;
    But for all the odds agin' you, Fuzzy-Wuz, you broke the square.

'E 'asn't got no papers of 'is own,
    'E 'asn't got no medals nor rewards,
So we must certify the skill 'e's shown
    In usin' of 'is long two-'anded swords:
When 'e's 'oppin' in an' out among the bush
    With 'is coffin-'eaded shield an' shovel-spear,
An 'appy day with Fuzzy on the rush
    Will last an 'ealthy Tommy for a year.
    So 'ere's to you, Fuzzy-Wuzzy, an' your friends which are no more,
    If we 'adn't lost some messmates we would 'elp you to deplore;
    But give an' take's the gospel, an' we'll call the bargain fair,
    For if you 'ave lost more than us, you crumpled up the square!

FUZZY WUZZY BY RUDYARD KIPLING (CONT.)

'E rushes at the smoke when we let drive,
    An', before we know, 'e's 'ackin' at our 'ead;
'E's all 'ot sand an' ginger when alive,
    An' 'e's generally shammin' when 'e's dead.
'E's a daisy, 'e's a ducky, 'e's a lamb!
    'E's a injia-rubber idiot on the spree,
'E's the on'y thing that doesn't give a damn
    For a Regiment o' British Infantree!
    So 'ere's to you, Fuzzy-Wuzzy, at your 'ome in the Soudan;
    You're a pore benighted 'eathen but a first-class fightin' man;
    An' 'ere's to you, Fuzzy-Wuzzy, with your 'ayrick 'ead of 'air —
    You big black boundin' beggar — for you broke a British square!

---

with Islam, which they have been practising ever since.

The Beja are not strict adherents to many of the popular Muslim decrees, though. For example, they often forego the saying of regular prayers and do not consider it necessary to make the required pilgrimage to Mecca. Although they subscribe to *sharia* law, they have developed their own interpretation of it, which they call 'salif law'. *Salif* law is an unwritten penal code, generally administrated by tribal leaders.

The Beja continue to be fearful of the *jinn* (evil spirits that can inflict illness or injury on individuals).

Beja life is centred around social gatherings, when they celebrate love and war in songs and poetry. Many tribal members play the traditional *rababa*, which is similar to the guitar. Spiced Sudanese coffee (*jabana*) plays a very important part in such gatherings.

The Beja are currently aligned with the Rashaida tribe in a bid for greater autonomy in Sudan's eastern region (p42).

RASHAIDA

The Rashaida are closely related to the Saudi-Arabian Bedouin, who migrated to Sudan from the Arabian Peninsula about 150 years ago. Most Sudanese Rashaida live in the east of North Sudan, on the outskirts of Kassala, although a large number inhabit neighbouring Eritrea. The Rashaida are practising Muslims.

Many members of the tribe still live a nomadic lifestyle, dwelling in rudimentary tents and earning a living from herding and breeding goats and sheep. Rashaida women also make jewellery and clothes, which are sold in local markets. Camel racing has become a big part of the tribe's culture and large bets are waged on races, even though gambling is widely regarded as contrary to Islam.

A distinctive feature of the Rashaida tribe is the full veil that the women wear. To protect their modesty, a young Rashaida girl will begin to cover her mouth and the lower part of her nose at about eight years old — and this veil remains in place whenever she is out in public, even when eating.

It is considered impolite to ask a male member of the Rashaida tribe for the name of his mother or for the names of other female family members. Expect a cold response from traditional tribal members if you do.

THE EASTERN FRONT

In 2005, the Beja and Rashaida tribes joined forces to fight against what they saw as the increased marginalisation of eastern Sudan, particularly the failure of the government to adequately distribute oil profits to the region.

This united force brought together two independent movements that were already in existence — the Beja Congress, which launched an armed struggle against the government in 1994, and the Rashaida-led Free Lions, established in 1999.

This eastern rebel movement has provoked the government into strengthening its military presence in the region. The consequence is that any foreigners in the region are likely to be subjected to rigorous security checks — so make sure that you have your permit handy!

The Rashaida are known for being fiercely independent and tend to be very wary of strangers, which means that taking photos of them can be extremely difficult or even impossible, unless you have a personal introduction to some tribal members.

KABABISH

The Kababish are a group of nomadic people considered to be midway between Arab and African. They dwell in harsh desert conditions in northern Kordofan, on the edge of the Libyan desert, and traditionally have wandered across the desert with their camels in search of food and water. Although most Kababish consider themselves Muslim, they do not adhere to the strict Islamic rules due to their harsh desert lifestyle. Many Kababish also have a fairly limited education, which makes it difficult to read Qur'anic texts.

A number of Kababish have moved away from their nomadic roots, to settle in villages to the west of Khartoum, although they are still known to wander frequently from place to place.

The Kababish originated in Arabia, but intermarried with various north African tribes. Because of this, it is difficult to define the Kababish identity.

Affiliations are loose and administrative control is hard to enforce because their territory is so broad.

The Kababish have darker skin than traditional Arabs do, but are not quite as dark as their southern neighbours.

Because life in the desert can be very dangerous, most Kababish men wear sheathed daggers on their left arms. A number of them also carry swords and sometimes even shotguns or rifles.

While the Kababish men move across the desert with their camel herds, the women and children tend to stay at home. The women often go to the camel markets in order to sell tea and coffee to the traders. Kababish children are sent to herd animals out in the desert sands almost as soon as they can walk.

BAGGARA

The Baggara are nomadic cattle herders ('baggara' is an Arabic word meaning 'those who look after cattle'). They live mainly on the western edge of North Sudan and in eastern Chad. Their origins can be traced back to the Bedouin Arabs of Saudi Arabia. Their dark skin comes from their intermarriage with the native Africans of Sudan.

The Baggara are known for being hardened fighters, although many other tribes often perceive them as uncouth barbarians. Very much on the frontline of Sudan's civil war, the Baggara have often been condemned for their part in raiding southern civilian villages. However, because of a lack of education, few Baggara are involved in the political arena in the same way that, for example, the Dinka are.

Tribal members typically follow Islam, though their faith is tinged with traditional beliefs. For example, they believe strongly in the 'evil eye', and are anxious to protect their cattle from jealous onlookers. They also place a large amount of faith in witch doctors.

A good example of how Islam has been combined with traditional beliefs is the way children who are ill often carry a small pouch containing Qur'anic verses around their necks or wrists.

Circumcision for both men and women is a big part of Baggara culture. Women who have not been circumcised are often deemed unfit for marriage.

One of the biggest triumphs of the Mahdi, who fought against British rule in Sudan (p56), was winning the trust of the Baggara. This achievement was all the greater for someone from Dongola due to mutual distrust.

But the Baggara, who were experienced slavers, had suffered greatly during British attempts to suppress the slave trade and were only too eager to take up arms against the colonial empire. Indeed, the Mahdi's second-in-command and eventual successor, Khalifa Abdulla ibn Mohammed, came from this tribe.

MISSERIYA

The Misseriya are closely related to the Baggara Arabs. However, due to the negative connotations that the name 'Baggara' has — often associated with cattle-raiding — they prefer to be called Misseriya instead.

The Misseriya are Arab pastoralists, practising many of the customs that are familiar to the Baggara.

Given their nomadic status, it is unclear how many Misseriya there are in Sudan but there may be as many as a million.

They are worth mention here because of the role that they have played in the North-South conflict, often unwittingly. The Misseriya live in the northern part of the contested Abyei region. Since they are cattle-herders, they often need to guide their animals to grazing pastures or water. As the summer heat arrives, and water in the north dries up, the Misseriya have to bring their cattle further and further south in order to find anything to drink. This has frequently brought them into conflict with the Ngok Dinka, a non-Arab tribe that lives in the South.

Non-Arab tribes

Non-Arabs mostly appear in South Sudan and in Darfur, to the west of the country. Identifying some tribes as 'non-Arab' is difficult, since their close association with Arabic groups of the North often means that they have picked up many Arabic traits, including religious beliefs and the language. This is particularly true in Darfur, where many of the tribes speak Arabic and practise Islam but are not generally classed as 'Arab'.

ZAGHAWA

Also known as the 'Beri', the Zaghawa is a semi-nomadic tribe found mainly on the border between North Sudan and Chad, although they are to be found in Niger as well. They are traditionally camel and cattle herders.

The Zaghawa dwell on ecologically-fragile lands in Darfur, where water is scarce and desertification is becoming a growing problem. The rains, when they come, usually last no longer than three months. In order to survive, many herdsmen drive their animals north to graze during the dry season, and return south when it rains.

The scarcity of water that the Zaghawa are now faced with in their homeland has contributed to ethnic fighting in Darfur. It has also led to the Zaghawa being branded as troublemakers and plunderers, although some argue that their increasingly desperate situation leaves them no choice but to fight for basic needs.

In the seventh century, the Zaghawa had their own kingdom, ruled by chieftains and divided into strict social classes and family clans. However, two factors have lead to the dilution of traditional beliefs. The colonial partitioning of Africa, which divided the Zaghawa tribe between Sudan and Chad, led to a weakening of the chiefs and the overall Zaghawa social system. The introduction of Islam around the 1600s also led to societal changes, and put an end to practices such as human sacrifice and ancestor worship

Yet some tribal beliefs persist, and many Zaghawa still wear charms and cover their babies' faces in public to ward off the evil eye.

Whilst the Zaghawa are not very powerful in Sudan, they dominate Chad politically, and many Chadian prime ministers, including the current one (Idriss Déby), come from this tribe.

MASALIT

Occupying a remote stretch of land that crosses the border between Sudan and Chad, the Masalit have been at the heart of the Darfur conflict for many years now, and have lost great numbers during the ethnic fighting.

The Masalit are a non-Arab people, although most adhere to the Islamic religion. Like neighbouring tribes, Masalit beliefs are influenced by their traditional customs, and they continue to pray to gods of the land and sky as well as to Allah. Many, though, are becoming increasingly conformist by abstaining from alcohol (which they famously make themselves), praying five times a day and asking for religious advice and instruction in important matters.

The Masalit have earned something of a reputation for being fiercely independent. They established an independent state between 1884 and 1921, which they called 'Dar Masalit' (this is still the name of a district within Darfur). For years, the Masalit remained relatively isolated from the world, preserving their own language and customs. Recently, though, this has started to change.

The Masalit make their living through growing crops and raising cattle, sheep and goats. They mostly live in village settlements that consist of several smaller compounds surrounded by fences made from millet stalks. Their round huts generally have conical thatched roofs.

NUBIANS

Nubians are a non-Arab Muslim people who once lived in the historic region of Nubia (p53), extending from Dongola in North Sudan up to Aswan in southern Egypt.

They are now concentrated in three main cities: Kom Ombo in southern Egypt, and Wadi Halfa and Khashm al-Girba in North Sudan. Nubians have much darker skin than the stereotypical Egyptian.

Once a Christian people, the Nubians succumbed to a gradual process of Islamicisation, starting in the 14th century. Today, the Nubians are virtually all Muslims, although some traditional beliefs (such as the idea that non-living objects have spirits) also influence their culture.

Nubian tribes have their own languages — Kenuzi-Dongolawi and Fedidja-Mahas being the most common — but many tribal members, particularly the men, also speak Arabic.

Archaeological discoveries have put the origins of the culture at least as far back as 3800 BC. Most of the customs of ancient Egypt are understood to have come from Nubian traditions.

THE ASWAN AND MEROWE DAMS

In the 1960s, the Nubian way of life was uprooted by a dam constructed across Aswan in Egypt, replacing the old one that had been built by the British. This created a 500-mile-long lake which permanently flooded many ancient temples and tombs, as well as many modern villages. Around 100,000 Nubians were forced to leave their homes.

More recently, Nubians again faced displacement with the construction of the Merowe hydroelectrical dam, which was inaugurated in March 2009 (p210). An estimated 70,000 residents were asked to leave the area, many of whom were given similarly-sized plots of land. However, there is some concern that the compensation did not adequately take account of nomadic tribes, which have no claim to land.

About Sudan

JAALIYN

Contemporary ethnographical thinking puts the Jaaliyn ancestrally close to the Nubian people of northern Sudan, although many of the tribe boast that they are direct descendents of Prophet Mohammed.

The Jaaliyn live along the banks of the Nile, not far from Khartoum. A number of the women, particularly the older ones, display facial scars in the form of a 'T' or an 'H', which are considered to be signs of great beauty.

Historically a farming people, many Jaaliyn families have now migrated to the major cities in search of work. Even so, tribal members are renowned for keeping close ties with their homeland, and return for frequent visits. Due to these close tribal links, marrying outside the tribe is often fiercely opposed by family members.

Most Jaaliyn are committed Muslims, although a few isolated groups have converted to Christianity.

DINKA

The Dinka are the largest ethnic group in South Sudan, with numbers estimated to be well over one million. The Dinka are a tall, thin and very dark-skinned people.

They have been major participants in the war that ravaged Sudan for many years. In fact, the celebrated southern rebel leader John Garang, who was killed in 2005 (p64), was himself a Dinka. He was succeeded by another Dinka, Salva Kiir, who is now the first president of an independent South Sudan.

Their involvement in the war has allowed certain Dinka tribesmen, such as Kiir, to enjoy the trappings of high office. But the fighting has also taken its toll on them as an ethnic group.

Many families have been torn apart by the conflict, and tribal customs have been eroded.

Despite the role that many Dinka now play in government, there is no over-arching hierarchical authority structure among traditional Dinka communities. Rather, their society consists of a series of independent but interlinked clans.

There has been certain speculation about whether their tribal religion can really be called animist in the true sense of the word. In its strictest form, animism is the belief that souls inhabit most objects. Whilst colonial-era anthropologists held off equating the Dinka word 'Nhialic' with God, contemporary thinkers now recognise the Dinka belief in a single God as a being who takes temporary possession of individuals in order to speak through them.

The Dinka are traditionally cattle herders. A great number still follow their traditional beliefs, although many have now adopted Christianity.

A particular tribal division of the Dinka — the Ngok Dinka — inhabit the disputed territory of Abyei and have often been in conflict with the Misseriya, to the north, when they bring their cattle down to graze.

NUER

The Nuer are the second largest ethnic group in South Sudan, after the Dinka. Their entire culture and way of life has traditionally been based around cattle and livestock.

Cattle are used for the payment of fines and debts, and offered as dowry payments in marriage. It is common for young children to fashion model cows out of clay or wood. Favourite cows in the tribe are often given names. Recent studies on the Nuer have found that they have now placed restrictions on the convertibility of money and cattle, in order to preserve the special status that cows have in marriage arrangements and in communicating with the divine.

Sudan's civil war has had a devastating effect on the Nuer and their traditional way of life, perhaps more so than on any other Sudanese tribe. Countless thousands of Nuer have been displaced by the conflict, many fleeing to neighbouring Ethiopia, Kenya or elsewhere. An estimated 25,000 have now resettled in the United States, and others have fled to Britain.

With the arrival of independence, a large number of these refugees have started to return home to help rebuild their war-torn country.

The Nuer are actually traditional enemies of the Dinka, although they served alongside during the rebel insurgency against the North and continue to share office in the new southern government. Riek Machar, South Sudan's vice-president, is from this tribe.

Although years of conflict have wreaked havoc on the traditional lives of the Nuer, most continue to adhere to animist beliefs. Many have converted to Christianity, though, and the number of Christian churches in the Nuer region is on the rise.

FUR

The Fur inhabit the plains and foothills of western Sudan, around the volcanic mountain Jebel Marra. It is from them that the name 'Darfur' comes, meaning 'land of the Fur'.

The Fur are a proud people, who remained independent from the rest of Sudan until 1916, when the ruling sultan was defeated by the British and the province was integrated with the rest of Sudan. The Fur subscribe to Islamic beliefs, although they are not Arabic and maintain some tribal rituals.

The attitude towards marriage in Fur society is unique among the tribes of Sudan. Once married, husband and wife operate as separate economic units, tending to their own fields and storage units. For example, whilst the wife might cook for her husband, she does so from his food storage and not a combined one. The food that she cooks for herself and her children comes from her reserves, and not her husband's.

Given their location in the country, it is not surprising that the Fur have become heavily embroiled in the fighting that has ravaged Darfur. In particular, the growing shortage of water and grazing land has resulted in direct clashes with the nomadic Baggara. A great number of Fur have reportedly fled to Chad and elsewhere in search of safety.

NUBA

The Nuba Mountains are situated on the border between North and South Sudan. They have had a tumultuous history, and have been wracked by fighting as the conflict in the South has spilled over into the region.

Many of the Nuba people who live in the mountains practice traditional animist beliefs, although a large number have converted to Christianity.

In many of the southern regions, ritual specialists and priests still hold much influence in the clans, for it is they who are thought to work the magic that is essential for controlling the rain, keeping the peace and ensuring the growth of crops.

Inhabiting such fertile land, the Nuba have traditionally been farmers and herders of livestock. They are also well-known for their love of competitive events, particularly traditional wrestling.

It is possible to see traditional Nuba wrestling in Khartoum (p129), but all competitors have to wear clothes, which is not the case in the original form.

SHILLUK

The Shilluk are primarily a farming community, who live on the west bank of the Nile just south of Kosti. They also fish and keep some livestock (mainly cattle, goats and sheep). The Shilluk land has recently become an important producer of gum arabic.

Traditionally, the Shilluk recognise the existence of a supreme being, who they call '*jwok ayimo*', although they also believe that ancestral spirits can be called upon in times of hardship. The Shilluk believe that the ghost of somebody killed or murdered haunts the perpetrator.

However, the location of the Shilluk kingdom on the banks of the Nile has made the tribe susceptible to outside influence, and much of the old belief system has now given way to Islam (in the North) or Christianity (in the South). The war has also displaced many Shilluk to North Sudan — and further afield, to the United States, Britain and Canada.

WILDLIFE AND NATIONAL PARKS

The relentless fighting across much of Sudan has taken a clear toll on its wildlife population. The war has meant that it has not been possible to put in place wildlife protection schemes, such as those found in other African countries.

Soldiers have cut down trees and slaughtered animals in order to feed themselves. Displaced people have set up camps within national parks, cutting down and burning large swathes of forest, and killing animals for food. Law enforcement has, to a large extent, ignored poachers, who have been eager to make some money in the midst of all the turmoil.

This means that a number of species in Sudan are now perilously close to extinction. Many parks remain inaccessible due to the poor security situation at the moment and so it is not clear what wildlife may yet emerge from the ashes of the civil war.

The most accessible wildlife park in North Sudan is Dinder National Park (p243) on the Ethiopian border, spanning some 10,000 km².

Refugees have exacted huge damage on the park, both those who have fled war within the South and those who have come across the border from Ethiopia and Eritrea. But things are starting to improve, largely thanks to conservation work being undertaken by the United Nations Development Programme (UNDP) and the Sudanese Environmental Conservation Society (SECS).

The park is now in a much better condition, and wildlife is starting to return. Baboons, deer, ostriches and warthogs are particularly common. There are even some lions in the park. The variety of birdlife is staggering, and it is quite common for ornithologists from Khartoum to come to the park to carry out research.

In the South, Nimule National Park on the Ugandan border remains the easiest wildlife reserve to get to. Spanning just 410 km² it is also one of the smallest.

Many of the animals were killed during the war but they are starting to return. Elephants and hippopotamuses are often spotted in the park. There have also been reported sightings of giraffes, oryx, antelopes, lions, leopards and gazelles — but these are rarer.

For now, the security situation in the South means that other parks are very difficult to get to, although some may open again to visitors if the situation improves.

There has been some talk of reopening the Southern National Park on the Congolese, but for now the area remains too volatile. Remnants of the Lord's Resistance Army, a Ugandan militia group, still operate in the area.

THE ECONOMY

In recent years, **oil** exports and an influx of foreign investment — mainly from China, Malaysia, India and the Middle East — has given a real boost to Sudan's economy.

But this economic boom, which has mostly been concentrated in North Sudan, has also created political unease and added greater weight to the voices of those calling for independence in what is now South Sudan.

Southern politicians have been quick to accuse the North of taking a disproportional share of the profits from the oil industry. Under the 2005 peace agreement, the oil profits should have been split 50-50.

Before independence, some 80% of oil exports came from the South.

Now that the country has finally separated, Juba is set to absorb the bulk of petro-dollars from the region.

On the other hand, the North retains much of the refinement technology and, crucially, the only access to the sea. Riek Machar, South Sudan's vice-president, has repeatedly said that he wants to explore ways of co-operating with the North, so that both sides can share in revenue from the oil industry. But southern politicians are also fond of reminding the North that they could use the facilities and distribution channels in Kenya instead.

Oil was first discovered in Sudan in 1981, by the US firm Chevron, which had been drilling in the country since 1975. Oil production, however, was halted in 1984 when rebels attacked the oil fields. It didn't start up again until the middle of the 1990s, when Sudan began to entice foreign investors into its oil industry.

In 1996, the Canadian oil firm Arakis arrived in the country. The construction of an oil pipeline from the South to the Red Sea began in 1997.

In 1999, Malaysia's Petronas, China's National Petroleum Company and Canada's Talisman also arrived in the country — with others following close behind.

Because of sanctions in place since 1997, US firms are not permitted to invest in the country's oil industry.

Sudan, taken as a whole, is the fifth largest oil exporter in Africa, but comes way behind Nigeria and Libya, who take first and second places respectively.

Politics make it exceedingly difficult to get hold of reliable oil statistics, but recent industry figures suggest overall oil production is 450,000 barrels per day, with five billion barrels of proven reserves.

By comparison, Nigeria produces 2.45 million barrels per day and has 36.2 billion barrels of proven reserves, whilst Libya has 41.5 billion barrels of proven reserves and, prior to the rebel uprising in the country, produced 1.8 million barrels per day. The African states of Algeria and Angola are also ahead of Sudan.

Sudan's other main exports are primarily agricultural and include cotton, gum arabic, sorghum wheat, sesame seeds and peanuts. The rearing of camels and sheep is also important to the economy. However, unpredictable weather conditions and inadequate transportation, especially in the South, place serious constraints on the agricultural economy.

Sudan is also thought to have large reserves of minerals under the ground — including gold, chromium, copper, iron, manganese, asbestos, gypsum, mica, limestone, marble, and uranium. Some mining ventures have begun in the country, with the collaboration of foreign firms, but the full potential of these resources has yet to be realised.

There remain some limitations to the **economic development** of Sudan. Like many other African countries, Sudan has had to endure years of economic mismanagement. In the 1970s and 1980s, cash from foreign donors flooded in, with the promise of an emerging stable country that was friendly to the West. However, many of the projects that the money was invested in were either too ambitious or poorly-managed, and so the initial optimism quickly gave way to disappointment.

The result of all this is was a huge **debt mountain** that Sudan has so far been unable to repay.

About Sudan

The current level of external debt is $38 billion, mainly owed to the World Bank and the International Monetary Fund (IMF).

At the time of South Sudan's independence, there was some uncertainty about what would happen to Sudan's debt — whether it would be shouldered by North Sudan or split between the two countries. After months of negotiation, North Sudan eventually agreed to take on the full amount of debt in return for being allowed to participate in a debt relief, the details of which are yet to be worked out.

US sanctions, which have been in place in the country since 1997, are also taking their toll. Although Khartoum has done its best to replace investment from the US with investment from elsewhere, such as China, many economists believe that North Sudan could grow even more if it did not have these constraints in place. Washington has promised to review sanctions in light of southern secession, although it has not yet given any firm commitment to lift them.

The sanctions do not apply to South Sudan.

POLITICS

Officially, **North Sudan** is a parliamentary democracy, with the country's president (currently Omar al-Bashir) serving as head of government as well as commander-in-chief of the armed forces. Whilst the country has had a multi-party system since 1998, the country has been criticised for being an authoritarian state and the ruling National Congress Party (NCP) has been accused of suppressing opposition voices.

Legislative power is vested in both the government and parliament. The National Legislature, as the parliament is known, has two chambers. The lower house is the National Assembly and consists of those parliamentarians who were voted into office during the last election. The upper house, the Council of States, is made up of members who are indirectly appointed by state legislatures. All members of the National Legislature serve six years.

The politics of **South Sudan** mirror those of the North. South Sudan is also a parliamentary democracy, with the president serving as head of government and commander-in-chief of the armed forces. Salva Kiir is the current incumbent.

South Sudan's Legislative Assembly was established in 2005, following the signing of the Comprehensive Peace Agreement (CPA). Like the North, it consists of a number of democratically-elected representatives (in the National Legislature, the lower chamber) and members that have been appointed by state legislatures (serving in the Council of States, the upper chamber).

Although the South has not yet elicited the same criticism that the North has seen, it is important to remember that the majority of the power remains in the hands of a single party — the Sudanese People's Liberation Movement (SPLM), the political wing of the former rebels. Other parties are represented in the National Assembly, but their influence is limited.

Now that the country has separated, the uneasy power-sharing alliance that the SPLM had with the NCP has ended. Those SPLM politicians who sat in the National Assembly in Khartoum have now returned to the South.

MAIN POLITICAL PARTIES IN SUDAN

North Sudan

The **National Congress Party (NCP)** is the country's main ruling party. It was founded in 1993 as the political face of the National Islamic Front (NIF), a fundamentalist political organisation derived from the Muslim Brotherhood, which was set up in 1986.

The **Umma Party** was founded in 1945, although it traces its origins back to Mahdist rule in the 1880s (p56). The Mahdi clan is still very much involved in the party, with Sadiq al-Mahdi, the great-grandson of the Mahdi, at its head. The Umma Party was the ruling party of Sudan between 1986 and 1989.

The **Democratic Unionist Party (DUP)** originates from the Khatmiyah sect, which opposed the Mahdist movement in the 1880s. Therefore, the DUP and Umma Party have traditionally been rivals. However, in 1986, the DUP was forced into a coalition with the Umma Party, after they each won a sizeable chunk of the votes.

The **Popular National Congress (PNC)** was created by Muslim hard-liner Hassan al-Turabi in June 2000, after he was expelled from the ruling National Congress Party.

The **Muslim Brotherhood** has been active in Sudan since 1949. It emerged from Muslim student groups in Egypt during the 1940s, and has gained something of a reputation for fostering extremism.

The **Sudanese Communist Party (SCP)** was formed in 1944, and quickly established a strong support base in universities and labour unions. Following a failed attempt to grab power in 1971, the SCP was disbanded, but it has since regrouped. It publishes a regular underground newspaper called Al-Midan.

The **Sudanese Baa'th Party** is a relatively small party, which aligns itself with the Baa'th Party of Iraq. Its central philosophy is the creation of a single Arabic nation state. It therefore advocates unifying North Sudan with either Egypt or Libya.

South Sudan

The **Sudanese People's Liberation Movement (SPLM)** is the political forum for the armed rebel struggle in the South. It was formed in 1983 by John Garang, out of the ashes of previous rebel groups. Garang died in 2005 and Salva Kiir is now head of the SPLM. The SPLM is now in power in the South.

The **United Democratic Salvation Front (UDSF)**, established in 1997, was the first legal political party established by the Southern Sudanese rebels since the beginning of the second civil war in 1983. It was initially led by Riek Machar, who is now the vice-president of South Sudan.

The **United Democratic Front (UDF)** was established in 2003 as a pro-independence political party in the South, and has been very vocal in calling for a divided Sudan.

HISTORY

Centuries ago, when Arab traders first ventured into Sudan from Egypt and across the Red Sea, they encountered a dark-skinned native people quite unlike any they had seen previously. They called the territory 'Bilad al-Sudan', which means, literally, the 'Land of the Blacks'.

The brief history that follows deals with Sudan as a single entity. Therefore, when we talk about `south` or `north` Sudan, we are generally referring to a geographical rather than political distinction.

One of the problems with writing about Sudanese history lies in the fact that, like so many other countries in Africa, Sudan is not really a single nation state, but rather a collection of independent entities welded together by a colonial past. Examining the border between Sudan and Chad provides a good idea of the slapdash way in which Africa's regions were drawn up by colonial powers, with no apparent regard for tribal culture and customs.

This results in different perspectives. Some historians focus on individual tribal cultures. Others look at how the Arabic culture has encroached on the country. Still others seek to examine the ancient Kushite Empire, with a number focusing largely on the Darfur conflict.

Early human activity

Whilst we have an abundance of knowledge about prehistoric man in the north of Sudan, little is known about the development of indigenous cultures in other parts of the country.

Part of this is to do with the precarious security situation in many regions, making excavations difficult. It also appears that, whereas countless treasures have been unearthed from the ancient tombs in the northern deserts, the past civilisations of the South have not chosen to preserve their heritage in this way.

Ironically, many recent archaeological discoveries in northern Sudan have come from the pressing need to preserve the country's heritage in the face of encroaching development.

In the 1960s, the construction of the Aswan Dam on the Egyptian border threatened to flood many important archaeological sites, prompting many archaeologists to rush in and preserve what they could. The same thing happened with the Merowe Dam, which was completed in 2009 (p210).

Rapidly expanding agriculture and housing are also putting pressure on archaeological sites and prompting renewed interest in the country's ancient heritage.

The first humans are thought to have appeared in what is now modern-day Sudan more than 200,000 years ago.

Climatic conditions were very different thousands of years ago. In 8000 BC, there is strong evidence to suggest that an ancient civilisation flourished across much of what is now the Sahara desert in the west of Sudan. Two thousand years later, though, the weather became markedly drier and the tribes appear to have retreated from desert conditions to settle on the banks of the Nile.

From about 3500 BC, at least two important cultures emerged in northern Sudan. One was centred between the First and Second Cataracts, and the other between the Third and Fourth Cataracts. Although the two cultures almost certainly had contact with one another, they differed in many respects. The remains of these people are also distinct from those of contemporary Egyptians, suggesting that the ancient people could have come from a different ethnic group

It was not long after this period that the emerging kingdom of ancient Egypt came into direct contact with the peoples of the south. Ancient Egyptian texts refer to the southern lands as 'Ta-Seti' ('Land of the Bow'), a testament no doubt to the fighting prowess of its inhabitants. These lands were subsequently known as Kush.

The ancient Egyptians are thought to have originally ventured south of the First Cataract around 3000 BC, in search of the riches of sub-Saharan Africa.

By 2300 BC, the Egyptians had firmly established themselves south of the Third Cataract, and what is now known as Kerma had developed into a flourishing metropolis.

Archaeological records show that, around 2000 BC, the ancient Egyptian kingdom started to fall apart. Although Egypt was booming culturally and commercially during this period, its system of government had become less centralised and therefore weaker. This prompted Egyptian withdrawal from Kerma and its surrounding lands, allowing the emergence of the Nubian culture.

Egyptian power started to resurface around 1550 BC, and lead to a power struggle between Egypt and Kush, resulting in the sacking of Kerma by Tuthmosis I. Rebellion ensued for the next 50 years before his grandson, Tuthmosis III, was able to continue the subjugation of Nubia, pushing south almost to the Fifth Cataract.

Egypt remained in control until the 11th century BC. When it withdrew, many of the indigenous cultural traits started to reassert themselves. By the 8th century BC, a new regime had emerged.

The Nubian dynasty

In 750 BC, the Kushite king, Kashta conquered Thebes, which was then capital of Egypt, and proclaimed himself Pharaoh. His successor, Piankhy, was responsible for reuniting Egypt under the 25th dynasty, also known as the 'Nubian dynasty'.

Under the reign of the Kushites, Egypt enjoyed a period of relative peace and prosperity, which reached its peak with the reign of King Taharqa (690 to 664 BC). Taharqa's expansionist ambitions — he had taken his kingdom to the edges of Libya and Palestine — were abruptly halted when his civilisation collided with Assyrian expansion from Babylon. The Assyrians swept into Egypt, pushing the Kushite rulers south. They eventually settled at Meroe near the Sixth Cataract.

Following the Kushites' expulsion from Egypt, the histories of the two countries start to diverge, leading to the emergence of a more indigenous culture in the south. The town of Meroe became increasingly more important and, during the height of its power in the 3rd century BC, extended over a region from the Third Cataract in the north to Soba, near present-day Khartoum, in the south.

The Pharaonic tradition persisted among a line of rulers at Meroe, who continued to erect pyramids and record the achievements of their reigns on tall stone plinths. They also continued to use Egyptian hieroglyphics.

However, by the 1st century BC, the use of hieroglyphics had given way to a Meroitic script that adapted the Egyptian writing system to the indigenous Nubian language spoken by the region's people.

Relations between Meroe and Egypt were not always peaceful. In response to Meroe's incursions into upper Egypt, a Roman army moved south and razed Napata in 23 BC. The Roman commander quickly abandoned the area, though, considering it to be too poor to warrant colonisation.

Christian Nubia

There is a great deal of speculation about the reasons for the decline of Kush. Archaeological evidence shows that, after the 2nd century AD, the royal tombs began to shrink in size and splendour, and the building of large monuments stopped — an indication that, by this point, the kingdom was already in decline.

The royal pyramid burials stopped altogether in the middle of the 4th century AD, giving rise to a popular theory that the kingdom was destroyed by an invasion from the Ethiopian kingdom of Axum around 350 AD.

By the 6th century, Nubia had become divided into three kingdoms. Nobatia in the north had its capital at Faras, in what is now Egypt. Makuria was centred at the old city of Dongola, 150 km from the town's present location. Alwa had its capital at Soba on the Blue Nile.

Missionaries introduced Christianity to the region in the 5th century AD. This helped put Nubia back in touch with the Mediterranean world. The church encouraged literacy in Nubia through its Egyptian-trained clergy and in its monastic and cathedral schools. The use of Greek in liturgy eventually gave way to the Nubian language, which was written using an indigenous alphabet that combined elements of the old Meroitic and Coptic scripts.

The rise of Islam

The Christian Nubian kingdoms prospered for several centuries, but they were constantly under threat by the establishment of Islam in the north. In 640 AD, shortly after the death of Prophet Mohammed, Muslim Arab invaders conquered Egypt, effectively severing Nubia's links with the rest of the Christian world.

Coveting riches in the south, the Arabs pressed on into Nubia, raiding as far south as Dongola. But the Nubians were strong fighters, and forced the Arabs into a stand-off. The Arabs, seeing little of value in the land, signed a treaty with the Nubians. This agreement, known as the *baqt*, lasted until the 14th century.

Despite the *baqt*, Nubia became increasingly Islamicised, largely because it was no longer directly in touch with the rest of the Christian world.

The south and the west

Whilst the Arabs were pressing south into Nubia, new powers were rising in the south and west of the region. The Funj was one of the most significant. Descendants of Arab immigrants, the Funj practised a combination of animist religions and Christianity. In 1504, they pressed north to Sennar, just south of Khartoum, where they united with the Nubian people to establish a kingdom that lasted until the Turko-Egyptian invasion of 1821.

Over the centuries, Islam gradually took hold in the area, and, in 1523, the Sennar monarchy officially converted to that religion, although many elements of the former belief system continued.

The expansion of the Funj kingdom threatened Ethiopia, and relations between the two nations remained tense. The Funj also endured conflicts with the Shilluk in the south, although these two powers were subsequently forced into an uneasy alliance to combat the growing might of the Dinka.

In the early 17th century, the Fur people in the west established the sultanate of Darfur, which eventually became a great power, extending as far east as the Atbara River. This sultanate lasted until 1875, when, beset by conflict between rival factions and external war with Sennar, it was destroyed by the Anglo-Egyptian government in Khartoum. The sultanate was re-established in 1898 and it lasted until 1916.

The formation of the Taqali state is inextricably linked to the history of Sennar and Darfur. Taqali was established in the Nuba Mountains around 1750, during the period of disorder in Kordofan, when the Sennar kingdom was in decline and Darfur was growing in power.

Despite its small size, Taqali remained independent of its more powerful neighbours. The kingdom of Sennar left the area alone, so long as Taqali paid annual tribute.

After destroying Sennar in 1821, Egypt launched three separate attacks against Taqali, but all of them failed. Eventually an agreement was reached whereby Taqali would remain *de facto* independent but would pay a nominal tribute and be officially included within the Egyptian Sudan.

The Turkiyah

At the end of the 18th century, the Mamluks were still a significant force in Egypt. The Mamluks had been in power in Egypt from 1250 until 1517, when they were overthrown by the Ottomans. After a brief period of repression, they eventually came to play an important role in government again.

By the middle of the 18th century, a delicate balance of power existed between the Ottoman rulers and the Mamluk forces in the country.

In 1760, Ali Bey, a Mamluk, gained control of the military and ousted the Ottoman governor. Assuming the post of governor general for himself, he sought to re-establish the medieval Mamluk empire.

Partially because of repeated clashes between Mamluk and Ottoman forces, Cairo was a devastated city by the time the French arrived in 1798. Napoleon Bonaparte was able to defeat the Mamluk forces with ease and assumed control of Cairo and Alexandria. But his position was precarious and, by 1801, he had been beaten back by an Anglo-Ottoman invasion force.

Napoleon's brief invasion of the country plunged Egypt into chaos. In an attempt to restore order, and to prevent a resurgence of Mamluk power, the Ottoman sultan appointed Mohammed Ali as governor of Egypt.

As soon as he had assumed power in Egypt, Ali sought ways of dealing with his main opposition: the Mamluks. During a period of severe repression, many Mamluks were massacred and their property confiscated. A great number fled south to Sudan.

In 1820, Ali wrote to the Sultan of Sennar, Badi VI, to ask him to expel the Mamluks who had settled at Dongola and who still posed a threat to Egypt. Badi VI was unable or unwilling to comply, and so Ali dispatched 4000 soldiers to conquer the country by force. Despite fierce resistance from Mamluk forces,

Egypt conquered Sudan without too much difficulty. When the invasion force arrived at the gates of Sennar, Badi VI immediately surrendered, without a single shot being fired. He was the last sultan of the Funj kingdom. Ali set about establishing a new regime in Sudan, which came to be known as the *Turkiyah*.

Ali's rule in Sudan is known for its repression and brutality. Tax was set at an exorbitant level by the governing forces. Furthermore, slave trading, already established in parts of Sudan, increased markedly. Many slaves were captured from the Nuba Mountains, as well as from the south and west of the country, and were enlisted in an army of foot soldiers known as the *Jihadiya*.

The heavy-handedness of Turko-Egyptian rule in Sudan lead to widespread resentment throughout the country, and many native Arabs rebelled against the new regime. The uprising was only quashed with the appointment of Ali Khurshid Agha as governor of Sudan in 1826. By granting a series of tax exemptions, and returning confiscated land, Agha was able to win the allegiance of many tribal and religious leaders.

The slave trade continued to flourish, though. As trade in ivory started to develop, so the demand for cheap labour increased.

Following Mohammed Ali's death in 1849, Egyptian interest in Sudan waned. It was revived, though, in 1863 when Ali's grandson, Ismail, took power. Ismail's greatest legacy was his determined efforts to end the slave trade once and for all. The slave trade had already been outlawed in Egypt by the time Ismail came to power, but this was not enforced and it continued to prevail throughout Sudan.

Under pressure from European anti-slave campaigners, Ismail enlisted the help of British explorer Sir Samuel Baker to suppress the slave trade in the White Nile basin — and to extend Egypt's borders south. Baker enjoyed some success in mitigating the slave trade, though he met with fierce resistance from the merchant class and Baggara Arabs, who had grown prosperous by selling slaves. The attempt to abolish slavery also caused unrest in the Egyptian army, as Ismail sought ways to reform his military forces without the need to depend on slaves for manpower.

In 1874, the anti-slavery baton was taken up by the renowned British officer, General Charles Gordon. Ismail made Gordon the governor general of the whole of Sudan in 1877, but he resigned just two years later, defeated by ill health and suffering immense frustration at being unable to completely stifle the slave trade.

The Mahdist uprising

Religion can be used as a powerful weapon, especially in the hands of a suitably charismatic leader. In 1881, when Sudan was firmly under the control of the British and Egyptians, Sudan found such a leader in Mohammed Ahmed, the son of a boat-builder from Dongola.

Ahmed became a devout preacher of Islam at a very early age, and it was said that he could recite the entire Qur'an flawlessly — no mean feat, even for the most studious of devotees.

In 1881, Ahmed proclaimed himself to be the Mahdi, the prophesied redeemer of Islam (p75). Historical accounts suggest that, whilst he had given some thought as to the existence of the Mahdi, he at first rejected the notion that he might be this man.

About Sudan

Perhaps the most remarkable achievement of the Mahdi was the way in which he managed to unite the many divergent tribes of Sudan against a common cause: the overthrow of Anglo-Egyptian rule. Even tribes that were historically hostile towards the Dongola tribes, such as the Baggara, were soon won over. The followers of the Mahdi became known as the 'Ansar', meaning 'those who follow'.

Some people followed the Mahdi because of the religious message that he preached. Others followed him because of dissatisfaction with the current regime in the country, particularly over efforts to end slavery.

At first, many doubted Ahmed's claim to being the Mahdi, dismissing it as either delusional or politically-motivated. But, as he was joined by more and more followers, the celebrity of the Mahdi grew. His status was boosted by a number of key victories over British and Egyptian troops, against seemingly insurmountable odds. Excitable followers also started to report miraculous occurrences and the appearance of the name 'Mohammed' in unlikely places. All of this added to the eminence of the Mahdi.

However, even with his growing band of followers, it remains doubtful whether he would have been successful in his campaign were it not for a number of serious blunders made by the ruling government.

In 1880, Mohammed Ra'uf Pasha replaced Gordon as governor general of Sudan. He was well aware of the religious activity of Ahmed, who at this time was preaching on Aba Island in the middle of the Nile, but did not consider that he posed any threat to the ruling class — until the proclamation that he was the Mahdi.

This public manifestation changed everything, and the authorities knew they had to act. Pasha wrote to the Mahdi, expressing the goodwill of the government and the desire to welcome him into the ranks of Sudanese loyalists. The Mahdi wrote a terse letter back, re-stating his claim to be the Mahdi and saying that "whoever does not believe in my Mahdia will be purified by the sword".

Unperturbed, Pasha decided that he had to meet this enigmatic sheikh, if for no other reason than to satisfy his own curiosity. He despatched a loyal adviser, Mohammed Bey, upriver to Aba Island to seek audience with the Mahdi and invite him to Khartoum.

First of all, the envoy expressed joy at the news that the long-awaited Mahdi had arisen at last, and then asked the Mahdi to lend his support to Pasha's government.

To this, the Mahdi is reported to have said: "You misunderstand. Who can be set above the Mahdi, personally selected by the prophet? It is Ra'uf who is duty-bound to obey me, along with the rest of the community of the faithful."

So Bey had no choice but to return to Khartoum to explain the failure of his mission and to prepare a more forceful response.

Deputy Governor General Carl Giegler later wrote: "In relation to the means of power at the command of Sudan government, this episode was an unpleasant, but not an important, far-reaching matter. Yet it became both important and far-reaching due to the stupidity with which the authorities in Khartoum handled the matter."

When government troops were sent to Aba Island, they met with stiff resistance from Mahdist forces and, despite their superior firepower, were quickly overwhelmed. The government lost 120 soldiers, but only 12 Mahdi followers were killed.

Meanwhile, London and Cairo were taking relatively little interest in the goings-on of Sudan. It was only when El-Obeid fell to Mahdi forces in 1883, leaving the Mahdi in control of much of the country, that the two nations sat up and took notice.

Even so, there was little appetite from either Egypt or Britain for direct embroilment in Sudanese affairs. By 1883, Egypt was a nation in financial turmoil, much of it brought about by Ismail's costly attempts to reinvent the country as a modern westward-looking state. Occupation of Sudan was also proving expensive.

As a result, Britain was more preoccupied with sorting out the affairs of Egypt than with staving off revolution further south. Due to the opening of the Suez Canal in 1869, which provided a convenient trade route between Europe and Asia, Egypt was of crucial strategic importance to Britain, whilst Sudan was just a financial burden.

Nonetheless, in spite of minimal assistance from Britain, the Egyptian government set about establishing a military force to recapture the town of El-Obeid. Colonel William Hicks was the officer chosen to lead the band of Egyptian soldiers into Sudan.

Woefully under-resourced, the mission was doomed to failure almost right from the start. Despite some early successes, Hicks's soldiers were eventually cornered by Mahdi forces in an inhospitable area of Kordofan known as 'Sheikan', named after the densely-clustered thorn bushes that populated the area. The entire army of 10,000 men was wiped out.

The annihilation of the Hicks mission reaffirmed the belief of William

Gladstone, the British prime minister, that defending Sudan was not worth the outlay in blood and money. He prepared for a complete withdrawal from the country, and decided to re-appoint General Gordon to carry this out.

Unfortunately for London, though, Gordon saw things rather differently. Shortly before leaving for Sudan, Gordon declared in an interview to the *Pall Mall Gazette*: "Whatever you may decide about evacuation, you cannot evacuate, because your army cannot be moved. You must either surrender absolutely to the Mahdi, or defend Khartoum at all hazards. The latter is the only course which ought to be entertained."

It is this dogmatic view, coupled with his own religious convictions, that was ultimately to lead to his execution at the hands of the Mahdi.

As the Mahdist forces marched on Khartoum, Gordon petitioned London to send a relief expedition. But, preoccupied with withdrawal rather than combat, Britain hesitated. Eventually, when the clamour to rescue Gordon became too great, the British did send a relief force along the Nile, under the command of Sir Charles Wilson. But it came too late. Khartoum fell on January 26, 1885, just two days before the relief force arrived.

As for Gordon, he was stabbed to death on the steps of his palace. The Mahdi's repeated calls to spare his life had been ignored.

The Mahdi's reign was short-lived. Just five months after capturing Khartoum, he became ill and died, probably from typhoid. He was succeeded by the Khalifa Abdulla, his second-in-command.

Whilst the Khalifa pledged to continue the campaign of the Mahdi against corrupt forces in the world, he lacked both the charisma and the religious self-belief of his former mentor. In fact, contemporary accounts document how he seemed more preoccupied with consolidating his own powerbase, and removing political opponents, than with spreading the message of the true Islam.

Without the unifying power of the Mahdi, the tribal alliances, which at best had been fairly shaky, started to fall apart.

The ousting of the Khalifa

The Khalifa's rule lasted 14 years, until a British invasion force was sent to reclaim the country.

There were two main things that re-ignited British interested in Sudan.

Although Britain had been slow to come to the rescue of Gordon when he was besieged by Mahdi forces, the British public did not quickly forget the tragic defeat of this man who was still revered as a hero back home.

Europe's 'scramble for Africa' also probably had a part to play in doing something about Mahdist rule in Sudan. In 1892, Belgium claimed part of southern Sudan for itself, which it integrated into the Congo. At the same time, the French claimed other regions of Sudan: Bahr al-Ghazal and the Western Upper Nile up to Fashoda.

Unlike previous British endeavours in Sudan, the campaign to depose the Khalifa was meticulously planned. General Herbert Kitchener was in charge of the operation. He arrived in Dongola in 1896, and set in place an elaborate plan to lay hundreds of miles of railway across barren desert in order to transport troops closer to Khartoum. The campaign also involved the haulage of several huge gunboats through

the Nile's notorious cataracts, as well as the deployment of 20,000 men.

The British troops met with the Khalifa's forces at Karari, just outside Omdurman, on September 2, 1898. The ensuing battle left 10,000 of the Khalifa's men dead. The Khalifa was forced to flee to Kordofan. Although pockets of Mahdi resistance continued in Sudan for many years, there was no doubt that Britain was now firmly back in control.

Many people welcomed the downfall of the Khalifa's regime. Sudan's economy had been all but destroyed during his reign and the population had declined by approximately one half because of famine, disease, persecution, and warfare. Moreover, most of the tribes had drifted back to their old tribal loyalties, and didn't display the same allegiances to the Khalifa as they had done to the Mahdi.

The Anglo-Egyptian condominium

In 1899, Britain and Egypt signed an agreement that established Sudan as a condominium, jointly ruled by the two powers. In practice, what this meant was that Britain would now take all the major political decisions and Egypt would retain a nominal role in the administration of the country.

A key article in the agreement specified that all responsibility for colonial administration would rest with the governor general, appointed by the British government and reporting to the Foreign Office via a resident officer in Cairo. A decision in 1910, however, curbed the powers of the governor general and made him accountable to an executive council for all legislative and budgetary matters.

Reginald Wingate became the first governor general of the new condominium in 1899.

His early years of ruling Sudan were devoted to quashing the remnants of Mahdism in the country, and establishing a programme of economic modernisation. New penal and criminal codes were drawn up. These were based on the ones already in force in India, although guidelines for *sharia* courts were also established. New tax codes were imposed and, for the first time in the country's history, there was a fixed taxation system.

Wingate also initiated a massive programme of construction and agriculture, which continued after he left office in 1916. Communication and rail links were extended across the north, and a dam was built near Sennar to improve irrigation. Work on this dam was completed in 1925, the same year in which the Gezira Scheme got underway. The idea behind the Gezira Scheme was to distribute water from the Blue Nile to farms lying between the Blue and White Nile rivers. This allowed several large agricultural projects to take hold in the region, and rapidly turned cotton into the mainstay of the country's economy.

The problem with the condominium administration was that all the modernisation programs were focused on economic development in the north, whilst the south was largely cut off from the modern world. The colonial administration barred northern Sudanese from entering the region, and gradually replaced Arab officials who were already working there. It also discouraged Islamic practices in the south.

Britain's idea for the south was that it should be allowed to develop along indigenous lines, which had been badly disrupted by the slavery trade, and eventually integrated into British East Africa (now Kenya, Uganda and Tanzania). Whilst this scheme led to some great anthropological studies during the 20th century, such isolation did little to alleviate growing poverty in the southern regions.

The struggle for independence

Egypt gained formal independence from Britain in 1922, thereby setting a precedent for self-rule in Sudan. However, early talks between Egypt and Britain on this matter quickly foundered, and any mention of Sudan's sovereignty was left out of the Egyptian constitution.

Even before the end of colonialist rule in Egypt, a nationalist movement was starting to emerge in Sudan.

In 1921, Ali Abdul Latif, a Dinka army officer, established the United Tribes Society, calling for an independent Sudan in which power would be shared between tribal and religious leaders. In 1924, this organisation was renamed 'the White Flag League', and started to organise mass demonstrations on the streets of Khartoum.

Solidarity protests also took place in Egypt, prompting accusations by British intelligence that the insurgency in Sudan was funded by the Egyptian Nationalist Party.

When Lee Stack, governor general of Sudan, was assassinated during a visit to Cairo in November 1924, Britain ordered Egypt to withdraw all troops and civil servants from Sudan.

Following the incidents of 1924, nationalism in Sudan was fiercely suppressed by the British. However, by the mid-1930s, two important nationalist factions were starting to emerge. One was led by the Mahdi's son, Sayed Abdul Rahman, who had regrouped the Ansar in a bid for independence. This later became the Umma Party. The other came in the form of an uneasy alliance between the National Unionist Party (NUP) and the Khatmiyah Brotherhood, led by Sayyid Ali al-Mirghani. Both groups favoured closer ties with Egypt, possibly leading to a formal union with the country.

Despite their differing viewpoints, the Ansar and the Khatmiyah Brotherhood lobbied the British government hard for independence. In 1942, an emerging group of educated Sudanese graduates, which spanned political boundaries, issued a memorandum calling for self-determination in Sudan and an end to north-south separation.

By the end of World War Two, British colonial administrators were starting to question the economic and political viability of keeping the southern and northern provinces separate. They were also enduring a significant amount of criticism from the Arab world for their northern policy.

However, not everyone was in agreement. Several key figures in government were worried that northern domination of the south could result in a southern rebellion against Khartoum. A landmark conference, convened in Juba in 1947, effectively ended separate administration in the country.

As predicted, many in the south were unhappy with the new arrangement. They feared northerners would overwhelm them and resented the imposition of Arabic as the official language of administration, which effectively prevented English-speaking southerners from entering the civil service.

In 1948, the pro-independence Umma Party won a landslide victory in national elections. The NUP, who favoured an alliance with Egypt,

boycotted the elections. In 1952, leaders of the Umma-dominated legislature negotiated a self-determination agreement with Britain, which would give Sudan responsibility in all areas except military and foreign affairs. Cairo, though, refused to recognise Sudan's claims to self-rule and, instead, declared Egyptian sovereignty over Sudan.

Anglo-Egyptian relations were patched up in a 1952 coup, during which Colonel Mohammed Naguib overthrew the reigning monarchy in Egypt. This paved the way for the signing, in February 1953, of an agreement between London and Cairo that allowed for a three-year transition period in Sudan, from condominium rule to self-government. Sudan got its first government following the parliamentary elections of late 1953.

Gradually, the government started replacing colonial officers with Sudanese from the north. The hostility of southerners turned violent in 1955, when southern army units were placed under the control of northern officers. Mutinous troops killed several hundred northerners — an ominous portent of what was to come.

Sudan finally achieved independence on 1 January 1956, under a provisional constitution. However, the nation's troubles were far from over.

The first civil war (1955-1972)

After independence, many southerners who had been involved in the military uprising of 1955 fled to Uganda to escape government reprisals. There they set up the Sudan African Nationalist Union (SANU). Its military wing, Anyanya (named after a poison made from snakes' venom), carried out a number of guerrilla-style raids against government targets, flitting back and forth across the Ugandan border.

However, it wasn't until 1958 — when General Ibrahim Abboud, commander-in-chief of the Sudan Defence Forces, overthrew the civilian government in Khartoum — that things really took a turn for the worse. Fiercely pro-Arab, Abboud embarked on a program of Islamicisation that was to ultimately lead to civil war and create divisions in the country for decades to come. Arabic replaced English as the language of education, and the missionaries, who were running most of the schools in the south, were hounded out of the country. The situation was exacerbated by economic mismanagement, which was what eventually led to Abboud's downfall in 1964.

At first, the Anyanya was a loose-knit group of tribes with seemingly little to hold them together. But, by 1969, the rebels had strengthened into a formidable fighting force, with strong foreign contacts that provided them with weapons and supplies. Many of the weapons were shipped from Israel, via Uganda or Ethiopia. Others came from Congolese rebels and arms dealers, or were captured from government troops. Much of the money for arms came from exiled rebels in Europe and America.

In 1971, Joseph Lagu, from the Madi tribe, became leader of the rebel movement, which he re-named the South Sudan Liberation Movement (SSLM). Despite persisting tribal differences, Lagu helped develop a tremendous sense of unity within the movement, and succeeded in driving the government from large areas of the southern territory.

Whilst the rebels were rebranding themselves, and trying to secure supply lines for their weaponry, Khartoum had its own problems. Following the demise of Abboud's military government, the country was plunged again into political chaos. The Umma Party and the NUP shared victory in the 1965 elections, but, due to irregularities at the ballot box, a number of smaller parties contested them. After a brief power struggle within the Umma Party, the great-grandson of the Mahdi, Sadiq, eventually emerged on top and formed a coalition government. However, his term didn't last long. Faced with insurgents in the south, political instability and economic turmoil, the government was soon forced to hand over to military rule once again.

Jaafar Nimeiri seized power in May 1969. At first, Nimeiri was welcomed by southerners, because he seemed to have a genuinely progressive and secular agenda. Nimeiri was also more concerned with consolidating power in the north than with confronting rebellious southerners. In 1971, fearing that the Ansar could contest power, Nimeiri decided to visit the group's leader on Aba Island.

Hostile demonstrations, though, prevented him getting near the island. Fighting eventually broke out between the Ansar and government troops, leaving thousands dead, including the Ansar leader. Despite his leftist leanings, Nimeiri also found himself locked in a power struggle with the communists, who staged an unsuccessful coup in 1971. In response, Nimeiri amended the constitution to outlaw all other political parties in the country. Sudan was now effectively a one-party state.

Turning his attention to the south, Nimeiri opened a dialogue with the SSLM in 1971. He believed that, by allowing independent regional governments in the south, he could bring stability to the region, thereby removing another potential threat to his powerbase.

The dialogue with the SSLM culminated in a 1972 conference held in Addis Ababa in Ethiopia. The two sides agreed on autonomy for three provinces: Equatoria (present-day Al-Istiwai), Bahr al-Ghazal and Upper Nile (present-day Aali al-Nil). The agreement also recognised English as the principal language of the south and established a 12,000-man southern command of the Sudanese army, consisting of an equal number of northern and southern officers.

Although many SSLM leaders opposed the settlement, Lagu approved its terms and both sides agreed to a cease-fire. The first civil war was at an end.

A brief respite (1972 to 1983)

Like many African states in the 1970s, Sudan soon became caught up in the confrontation between east and west: the so-called Cold War. Seeing the emergence of so many new democracies in Africa, both the United States and the Soviet Union sought to extend their influence into the region.

In the early 1970s, the Soviet Union was providing arms to Sudan. However, after the failed 1971 coup by the communists in the country, Nimeiri's relationship with the Soviet Union quickly soured. Gradually, the arms trade gave way to stronger ties with the United States, and development loans from the West started flooding in.

For a time, the Sudanese economy was booming and Sudan seemed destined to go down in history as an African success story.

Unfortunately, though, like so many other cases in Africa, many of the projects that development aid helped set up were doomed to failure. The projects were too ambitious and suffered from mismanagement or corruption. Throughout the 1980s, the Sudanese economy continued to decline, and was further hit by a severe famine in 1984. By the early 1990s, Sudan had become the world's largest debtor to the World Bank and the International Monetary Fund.

The worsening economy forced Nimeiri onto the back foot. With his powerbase significantly weakened, he could no longer spend time appeasing the southerners. Hard-line Islamic groups prospered on the back of a foundering economy. In 1977, Nimeiri brought two key Islamic figures into the government: Sadiq al-Mahdi of the Umma Party and Hassan al-Turabi of the Muslim Brotherhood.

In 1983, under pressure from fundamentalists both inside and outside of his government, Nimeiri tore up the Addis Ababa Agreement. The decision to do this was also inspired by the discovery, in 1981, of large amounts of oil in the south. The end of the Addis Ababa Agreement meant, among other things, that revenues from this newly-discovered oil would now accrue to central government and not the regional administrations.

In a final controversial move, Nimeiri decided to impose *sharia* law on the north of the country, which introduced harsh Islamic punishments such as amputations for theft and public flogging for possession of alcohol. In principle, the south was not affected by this new law. However, southerners living in the north were subjected to these punishments. Moreover, there was also a clause in the new law that

About Sudan

suggested it could be extended to the south at a future date.

The rebel response was unsurprising: an immediate and uncompromising return to war.

The second civil war (1983 to 2005)

In 1983, John Garang, a former rebel colonel from the Dinka tribe, appeared on the scene. From a rebel stronghold in Ethiopia, Garang launched the Sudan People's Liberation Movement/Army (SPLM/A) with the aim of overthrowing the military dictatorship in the country and assuming autonomous control of the southern regions.

Reeling from the country's economic crisis and hemmed in by Islamic opposition parties on all sides, Nimeiri was in no position to deal with this latest rebel insurgency. In 1985, whilst the country was still feeling the effects of a devastating drought, Nimeiri was swept from power in a military coup, led by Abdul Rahman Suwar al-Dahhab.

In 1986, elections were held as promised, and power was handed over to a civilian government under the leadership of Sadiq al-Mahdi. He formed a coalition with the Democratic Unionist Party (DUP), formerly the NUP, and the National Islamic Front (NIF), as well as a few southern parties.

Sadiq made some attempt to restore peace to the country, but his strong Islamic convictions made things difficult. In 1988, the SPLM/A and the DUP proposed a peace plan to suspend *sharia* law and end the state of emergency that had persisted in the country since 1983.

Meanwhile, the civil war in the south of the country was intensifying, and some hard-line elements in the coalition government — most notably, the NIF, which was headed

by the fiercely Islamic Hassan al-Turabi — saw little reason in compromising with the rebels. Consequently, Sadiq al-Mahdi refused to approve the peace plan. The DUP, in response, left the government.

In February 1989, the army presented Sadiq al-Mahdi with an ultimatum: either he moved towards peace or he would be kicked out of government.

In response to this threat, he moved closer to the DUP and approved the SPLA/DUP agreement. However, in so doing, he alienated the NIF wing of his government, who leant their support to a newcomer on the political scene: a military officer called Omar Hassan Bashir.

In 1989, Bashir staged a successful coup, with the help of the NIF, and replaced the government with the Revolutionary Command Council for National Salvation (RCC). Although the NIF leader, Turabi, didn't have an official role in the new government, he remained highly influential, calling for a *jihad* against rebel forces.

Both Bashir and Turabi believed that the only solution to the civil war was a military one, and they refused to negotiate with the SPLM/A.

The SPLM/A, meanwhile, was experiencing a number of problems with its armed struggle. In 1991, one of its main foreign supporters, Haile Mariam Mengistu of Ethiopia, was thrown out of power. Mengistu had been providing both training camps and arms for the Sudanese rebels.

The same year, the SPLM/A endured an even worse setback, when Riek Machar, an SPLA commander from the Nuer tribe, reignited tribal rivalries within the movement, in an attempt to displace Garang.

Garang clung on to his position, but the initiative succeeded in dividing the SPLM/A down the middle.

Living so close together, the Nuer and the Dinka tribes have traditionally been rivals. The region became increasingly split along ethnic lines.

With the southerners spending so much energy fighting among themselves, they had little left for the government, which launched a number of successful operations to recapture lost territory from the rebels.

In the 1990s, Sudan was perceived by many western nations to be a hotbed of fanaticism. In 1991, the late Osama Bin Laden, who subsequently gained notoriety as head of the Al-Qaeda terrorist group, moved from Saudi Arabia to Sudan, bringing with him ample cash and fundamentalist ideals. He ran a series of business operations in Sudan and organised a number of terrorist-training camps.

The government irked the West further when Turabi voiced support for Saddam Hussein during the first Gulf War in the early 1990s. There was also a failed assassination attempt on Egyptian President Hosni Mubarak, in which Sudan was implicated. In 1993, the USA placed Sudan high on the list of state sponsors of terrorism — a list from which the North has still not been removed, despite its best efforts.

The turning point in relationships between Sudan and the West came in 1998, when the US bombed the Al-Shifa pharmaceutical plant in Khartoum (p128), claiming that it was manufacturing chemical weapons. Although Bin Laden had been expelled from the country two years earlier, the US was convinced that Sudan was still harbouring Al-Qaeda sympathizers, and that the Al-Shifa plant had links to both Al-Qaeda and Iraq.

For all America's bluster, the Sudanese government was genuinely shocked that the US launched a missile attack on a target in the nation's capital. They were well aware of what had happened in other parts of the world when governments had incurred the wrath of America — and Bashir certainly didn't want the same fate to befall him. By the end of the 1990s, Sudan was ready to engage with the international community again.

It was not just the West that Bashir was worried about, though. In 1998, Turabi, Bashir's former ally, sought to appease the SPLM/A, in a bid to shore up his own powerbase. Al-Bashir responded by declaring a state of emergency in the country, and by seeking to suppress political dissent.

In 2001, Turabi's party, the Popular National Congress (PNC), signed a memorandum of understanding with the rebels. In the agreement, the PNC called for an end to the state of emergency that persisted in the country and for the government to end political repression. But the thing that troubled Bashir most was the call for peaceful resistance to his regime.

Turabi was arrested at his home in Khartoum later that year, and charged with being a threat to national security. Since then, his outspoken criticism of the current political framework in Sudan has seen him frequently in and out of gaol, or detained under house arrest.

Darfur

The north-south civil war is often confused with the separate conflict in Darfur. Although the rebels in the south do have strong ties with the rebels in Darfur, it is wrong to see the two wars as part of the same struggle.

A new rebellion erupted in Darfur in 2003. The rebels accused the government of neglecting the Darfur region, and called for a greater share of the wealth, as well as more of a say in the government of the country.

The Darfur crisis was further exacerbated by inter-tribal hostility, as neighbouring ethnic groups vied for increasingly scarce resources, such as water.

Khartoum has been fiercely criticised by the international community for providing support to the brutal *janjaweed* militia, in order to suppress the uprising. Latest UN reports suggest that the conflict has left as many as 300,000 people dead (which includes those who have died as a result of disease and famine), and displaced a further two million. The Sudanese government, however, insists that the actual number of people dying as a result of the war is just 10,000.

Peace

In January 2005, after two years of negotiation, the SPLM/A and the government finally signed a the Comprehensive Peace Agreement (CPA), which effectively brought an end to 21 years of war.

As one of the conditions of the CPA, John Garang, head of the SPLM/A, assumed the position of

---

KHARTOUM UNDER SIEGE

In May 2008, one of Darfur's most prominent rebel groups — the Justice and Equality Movement (JEM), led by Khalil Ibrahim — stunned the government in Khartoum by launching a surprise attack on Omdurman. The rebels were quickly beaten back, but the government was clearly shaken by this offensive: how had such a ragtag bunch of soldiers managed to penetrate so deep into the nation's capital?

JEM's motives for striking the capital were twofold. Their primary aim was to cross the bridges into Khartoum and storm the Presidential Palace. Their second purpose was to make it clear to the government that they are a sizeable force within Darfur and should be taken seriously. Many JEM members say that they are being ignored in favour of other Darfuri rebel groups, such as the Sudanese Liberation Army (SLA).

JEM is largely a non-Arabic militia with an Islamic agenda. In the 1990s, many senior JEM members held positions in the government, until they were forced out when President Bashir moved to consolidate his powerbase. Hassan al-Turabi, who was ousted from government at the same time (p65), is widely believed to wield considerable influence within JEM, although he denies such claims.

There is good evidence to suggest that JEM receive large amounts of support from neighbouring Chad. Most of JEM is made up of disenfranchised people from the Zaghawa tribe, which is a minority in Sudan but a very powerful political force in Chad. In fact, Idriss Déby, Chad's President, comes from this tribe. Whilst Déby was once a vocal supporter of Bashir, the two leaders have since fallen out with each other, and often provide support to rebel groups in each other's countries.

Following the JEM attack, hundreds of Darfuris were rounded up and questioned. More than 100 of these were subsequently sentenced to death for treason, although none of these sentences have yet been carried out and some have since been pardoned.

vice-president within the government. However, he was killed three weeks later, as the helicopter he was flying in flew into bad weather on its journey from Uganda to South Sudan.

Conspiracy theories abound as to whether Garang's death was really an accident. Some think that he was killed on the orders of President Bashir, who did not want to share power with such a charismatic and politically-ambitious man.

Others think that the Ugandan government may have had a hand in his death, since it was a Ugandan helicopter in which he was flying. Uganda has for some time supported the rebels in South Sudan, against the Islamic government in the North. However, Garang may have frustrated some members of the Ugandan government by being such an independent leader.

Still others think that Garang could have been killed by rivals within the SPLM/A, who also wanted a go at leading the movement. Upon Garang's death, Salva Kiir assumed his position as both head of the SPLM/A and vice-president of Sudan.

Another theory is that the US Central Intelligence Agency (CIA) had him killed, since Washington has always favoured secession of the south, whilst Garang stood for unity with the North.

The truth about Garang's death may never be known for certain, but the Sudanese never get tired of speculating about the theories.

On January 9, 2011, in line with the terms laid out in the CPA, South Sudan held a referendum on whether or not to separate from the North. Unsurprisingly, southerners voted overwhelmingly for secession and six months later — on July 9 — the Republic of South Sudan was born. Thus ends the history of the CPA, which is no longer a valid agreement.

Whilst the South and the North are now officially at peace with one another, skirmishes continue in some areas. Along the Congolese border in the South, remnants of the Lord's Resistance Army, a Ugandan militia group, continue to cause trouble. Cattle-rustling persists in many rural areas in the South, and there are periodic scuffles between different tribes.

The biggest problems, though, are seen in Darfur, where low-level conflict simmers, and in the border area between North and South Sudan.

In May 2005, the Darfur Peace Agreement (DPA), which should not be confused with the CPA, was signed by Khartoum and the Sudanese Liberation Movement (SLM), led by Mini Minawi.

The agreement was doomed from the start, since it did not have the popular support of the other rebel groups in the region, and, in February 2011, Minawi himself walked away from it.

Rebel activity still continues in large parts of Darfur, which remain off-limits to the casual traveller.

The biggest flashpoint between the North and the South is probably Abyei, which lies just to the South of the Nuba Mountains. There is still widespread dispute over whether the region should join the North or the South. The Ngok Dinka, who live in the region, would prefer to join the South. However, the Misseriya, a nomadic tribe from the North, relies on the green pastures of Abyei for grazing their livestock, and fear that such grazing rights would be denied if Abyei was to join the South.

Recently, violence broke out in Kadugli in the Nuba Mountains. Disturbances were reportedly caused by militia groups loyal to Abdul Aziz al-Hilu, of the SPLM, over claims that the May election in the region was rigged. As a response to the violence, Khartoum dispatched armed soldiers to the area.

War crimes

On March 31, 2005, the United Nations referred the Darfur case to the Hague-based International Criminal Court (ICC), which had been established in 2002 in order to investigate claims of mass atrocities.

On March 4, 2009, ICC judges agreed to indict the president for war crimes and issued an arrest warrant. Prosecutors pushed for genocide charges to be included in the arrest warrant, but judges threw this demand out, citing lack of evidence. However, at the start of 2010, the appeals chamber of the ICC overturned this earlier decision and said that there was enough evidence to include the genocide charge in the arrest warrant.

This indictment represents the first time that the court, established in 2002, has issued an arrest warrant for a sitting head of state.

North Sudan is not currently a member of the ICC and therefore does not recognise the validity of the court, nor does it see why it should give its president up. Feeling against the ICC is very strong and not just within the political elite. Ordinary people, many of whom oppose Bashir's rule, also fail to see why their country, as a sovereign state, should acquiesce to the demands of the ICC.

The counter-argument to this is that, since North Sudan is part of the UN, which referred the country to the ICC in the first place, the country has an international commitment to comply with the ruling.

Bashir's indictment comes close on the heals of ICC arrest warrants that have been issued for Ahmad Muhammad Haroun, presently the governor of South Kordofan, and Ali Kushayb, believed to be a leader of the government-backed *janjaweed* militia. Both of these people were indicted for war crimes in February 2007

Prospects for the future

Predicting what the future might hold for Sudan is not easy. When the government made peace with the rebels in 2005, there was a great mood of optimism in the country. Finally, concrete steps were being taken to tackle the civil war that had torn the country apart for more than two decades.

The peace agreement culminated with the secession of South Sudan from the North in July 2011. Independence was met with widespread jubilation in the South and a tacit acceptance in the North, both sides utterly wearied from the relentless fighting that has raged throughout the country ever since the end of colonial rule.

It remains far from clear how things will play out going forwards, and there remains much to be done to help get the world's newest nation state on its feet and make sure that it is able to enjoy some level of prosperity.

In amongst all the dust and the mayhem of the North-South conflict, it is easy to forget that the South is not an homogeneous country but, like so many states in Africa, a haphazard jumble of very diverse tribes. Even without interference from the North, many of these tribes share enmity that goes back generations. There continue to be reports of clashes among these tribes. Sometimes this has just been mere cattle-rustling. At other times, this fighting represents a power struggle between tribal leaders.

The country that has been born out of the ashes of Sudan's two civil wars is not a harmonious nation that is full of self-confidence and political unity. It is an economically and politically weak country, crippled by years' of fighting and now run effectively as a one-party state. Those that did not fight in the country's civil war struggle to make their voice heard politically, with questions asked about their loyalty.

South Sudan clearly needs help to get on its feet and to realise its potential. More than 80% of the Sudan's oil reserves are located in the South, and the agricultural potential of this fertile area of Africa is vast.

NGOs and aid workers may offer some help to the new country. The fact that the South will not have to take on any of the debt from the North — Khartoum has agreed to assume this burden in return for being able to participate in a debt relief programme — will really help the new country get up on its feet.

As for Khartoum, things look equally uncertain. With the separation of South Sudan, it has reputedly lost three quarters of oil revenue and must look for some way to replace this. Chinese oil companies, which had set up offices in Khartoum, are starting to relocate themselves to Juba.

The expectation of many that you talk to in the North is that the floodgates are now going to open for other forms of investment. Agriculture could help the North replace some of this lost revenue, as could tourism. Khartoum is still holding out hope that Washington will, at long last, lift sanctions on the country. The Barrack Obama administration has promised to review this.

Only time will tell what the North and the South can make of the future.

About Sudan

With nearly 600 recognised tribes spread across North and South Sudan, writing about a 'Sudanese' culture is not an easy thing to do.

It is this diverse blend of ethnicity that makes Sudan such a fascinating place to explore, for no two places are quite the same.

From the Beja of eastern Sudan, with their gold bangles and ceremonial swords, to the Kababish of the harsh northern deserts, with the daggers that they wear strapped to their arms. From the Zaghawa of western Darfur, with their amulets and charms to ward off evil, to the Nuer in the South, with their animist beliefs and reliance on witch doctors. Sometimes it seems that, when you speak about Sudan, you are actually talking about dozens of different countries.

Nonetheless, there are some cultural similarities, such as the famous Sudanese hospitality, that prevail in both the North and the South.

This section explores the main cultural customs that you will come across in Sudan.

Inevitably, a large part of the section focuses on Islam. This is in no way meant to diminish the importance of the other tribes, who subscribe to Christian or traditional belief systems. It is just that Islam has played such an important role in shaping the country that a certain amount of detail must be given about the faith.

The particular habits and customs of various Sudanese tribes have already been covered elsewhere in this book (p39).

ISLAM AND SUDAN

If you have spent time in other Muslim societies, you may notice some difference between what you already know about the religion and what is described within the pages of this book. The following pages concentrate purely on the faith as it applies in North Sudan.

One important distinction, which you'll notice if you spend any length of time with tribes outside the main cities, is that Islam in Sudan is not a single homogeneous set of religious principles. Rather, it has evolved into an intriguing blend of traditional Muslim teachings combined with pre-existing African customs.

For example, many tribes in the remoter regions of the country continue to carry amulets or talismans to ward off evil, whilst still reciting passages from the Qur'an (the Muslim holy book).

It is really worth making the effort to understand something about Islam before coming to North Sudan.

Besides helping to avoid the occasional *faux pas*, knowing a little about the fascinating religion will help you get that much more out of your trip to the country and really connect with the locals.

Within certain limits, ordinary Muslims in North Sudan are reasonably tolerant of other beliefs and traditions, although certain behaviour is likely to cause offence. For example, a man and woman kissing in public might be asked to leave a restaurant or a bus.

Dress is important in Islam and women should take particular care to dress modestly when out in public.

Culture

TEDDY BEARS AND TEACHERS

In November 2007, a British school teacher, Gillian Gibbons, was arrested for inciting religious hatred in Sudan.

Her crime had been to name a teddy bear Mohammed. She had asked her students to suggest a suitable name for the stuffed toy, and Mohammed was the one that they came up with.

According to the rules that govern Islam, no inanimate object can be named after Prophet Mohammed and so what she had unthinkingly done was akin to blasphemy.

For her crime, Gibbons could have received 50 lashes, but she was pardoned a week later by President Omar al-Bashir.

Perhaps more than anything, it is this apparent intolerance of other belief systems that sets the Western and Islamic worlds so far apart from one another.

Characteristics of Islam

The fundamental aspect of the Muslim faith, and the most important thing to remember when learning about Islam, is that there are certain things in the religion that cannot be questioned. In fact, the very word 'Islam' means submission to, and acceptance of, God. It is derived from the Arabic verb *aslama*, meaning to surrender or to submit.

Unlike the Bible, the Qur'an was narrated by a single man — Prophet Mohammed — rather than several men over a number of generations. Most of it was written down by his companions whilst Mohammed was still alive. Because of all this, the word of God, as told to the Prophet by the Angel Gabriel, is considered to be irrefutable. Anything within the revered Qur'an must, therefore, be followed by the devout Muslim, without exception. Unless one understands this essential facet of the Muslim faith, one cannot hope to comprehend the religion at all.

Another thing to remember about the religion is that, unlike the Western model of democracy, which is essentially secular, Islamic beliefs go hand-in-hand with government. They cannot be separated. Islam is intended to be a system of rules for all aspects of life, based on faith. Muslims believe that, since these rules originate from the direct word of God in the Qur'an, which cannot be questioned, it is not acceptable to create new laws that contravene them. This is where the belief in *sharia* law comes from, which still applies to North Sudan (although it has been relaxed for non-Muslims). In its true form, *sharia* (literally: 'the way') is a direct application to Muslim society of all rules found in the Qur'an.

It is this unwavering belief in God's will that makes the submission to *sharia* law so irresistible to the devout Muslim. But this close marriage of State and religion has also been used as a way for unscrupulous dictators to justify their ascension to power.

The different strands of Islam

Almost all Muslims belong to one of two major denominations of the Islamic faith — either Sunni or Shi'a. The schism was a result of a disagreement over who would succeed Prophet Mohammed after his death. Umar ibn al-Khattab, a prominent companion of Mohammed, nominated Abu Bakr, who was Mohammed's intimate friend and collaborator. Others added their

Culture

ISLAM'S DOS AND DON'TS

- Do not put anything on top of the Qur'an and make sure that the Qur'an is always at the top of your bookshelf. Nothing can be above the Muslim holy book.
- Try to understand the Qur'an, but do not refute its claims.
- Respect the Muslim prayer times.
- Dress modestly.
- Don't hold hands with a member of the opposite sex, or kiss in public.
- Do not name anything other than a person Mohammed.
- Never represent Mohammed in pictorial form.
- Do not joke about the Prophet Mohammed.
- Don't say that you are an atheist — it is better to practice a monotheistic religion such as Christianity than not to believe at all.

support and Abu Bakr was made the first caliph (leader of Islam).

But this choice was disputed by some of Mohammed's other companions, who held that Ali ibn Abi Talib, his cousin and son-in-law, had been designated his successor.

Those who recognised Umar as legitimate successor became known as 'Sunnis', whilst those who recognised Ali as the legitimate line were known as 'Shi'as'. Since Sudan is primarily a Sunni country, it is this aspect of the faith that we have concentrated on.

Sufism

Sufism is a formation of the Sunni faith that is widely practiced in Sudan. The name comes from the Arabic for wool (*suf*), a reference to the simple woollen garments that the original adherents wore.

Sufism developed in response to the evolution of orthodox Islam more than a millennium ago, which was becoming increasingly formulaic and based on doctrine rather than spirituality.

At the heart of Sufi belief is the pursuit of spirituality over and above material artefacts. Sufis believe that the key to ascension is learning to love God and one's neighbour, without consideration for any possible reward.

Sufi meditation and worship, known as *zikr*, is important in establishing a personal relationship with God. Communal ceremonies are widely used to bring devotees into a trance-like state, where they can communicate on a one-to-one basis with God.

There are different styles of Sufi worship, and it is well-worth trying to experience some of them if you get the chance. During some Sufi services, devotees rock backwards and forwards to a low chant. In others, worshippers spin frantically round in circles to the beat of a drum or other loud instrument.

The most famous example of Sufism in Khartoum is the so-called Whirling Dervishes, who hold their ceremony before sunset every Friday in Omdurman (p132).

Although Sufism is a noticeable part of Islam in North Sudan, only a minority of Muslims adhere to it. In fact, many of the more traditional adherents to the faith look down on Sufism, viewing it as contrary to the teachings laid out in the Qur'an.

The Five Pillars of Islam

In Sunni Islam, the devout Muslim must adhere to five principal duties, known as 'the Five Pillars of Islam'. The eight ritual practices which make up the Shi'a branch of Islam substantially overlap with the Five Pillars, and so are not covered here.

The **first pillar** of Islam is that there is only one true God, and that no other is worthy of worship. On no level does Islam recognise any man as being of divine origin. Although Jesus Christ features prominently in the Qur'an, he is viewed as a messenger, rather than as the son, of God. Mohammed is considered by Muslims to be the last and greatest of all prophets but, again, he is seen as a messenger rather than anything more celestial.

The **second pillar** is the ritual prayer, which must be performed five times a day. When praying, the devotee must face in the direction of the Great Mosque at Mecca, birthplace of Mohammed and centre of the Islamic world. In North Sudan, as in other Muslim countries, you will find that many of the local mosques loudly broadcast the call to prayer at the designated times — early morning, just after midday, between 3 and 3.30 pm, in the evening just before sunset and about one hour after sunset. Prayers are an essential part of a Muslim's life, but some flexibility can be given as to the timing of prayers, especially for those who are travelling.

It is interesting to note the prevalence of the prayer mat throughout North Sudan. Almost all companies — and many other organisations (such as hospitals and doctors' surgeries) — have a communal prayer mat, often hanging on a rail, so that a devout Muslim can make use of it if he or she has the need.

The **third pillar** of Islam is the practice of alms-giving, or zakat (p78). All Muslims who can afford it are expected to pay a portion of their income to help the poor and assist the spread of Islam. This usually amounts to 2.5% of the donor's post-tax earnings for the year, although it can be as much as 10%. In many countries, the zakat fund is administered by local mosques, but in Sudan it is managed by national government.

The **fourth pillar** of Islam is the practice of fasting during the holy month of Ramadan (p77).

The **fifth pillar** of Islam is the famous pilgrimage to Mecca in Saudi Arabia during the Islamic month of Dhu al-Hijjah. Every able-bodied Muslim who can afford it is expected to make the pilgrimage, known as 'the Hajj', at least once in his or her lifetime. Before arriving at the boundaries of Haram, the holy precinct of Mecca, the pilgrim performs a ritual ablution to wash away the impurities of the world. The pilgrim then dresses in Ihram clothing, which consists of two white seamless sheets. When the pilgrim dies, it will be these clothes that he or she is buried in.

Prophet Mohammed

Prophet Mohammed is considered to be the last and greatest of all of the religion's prophets. It was through him that the Qur'an was narrated. Despite this, many Muslims believe in the eventual coming of the Mahdi, a divinely-guided man who is destined to restore the true Islam (see following section). This apparent contradiction is explained in certain Islamic texts, which refer to the Mahdi as being subordinate to Prophet Mohammed. Others claim that the Mahdi is not a messenger of God, but simply the true

Culture

PROPHETS OF ISLAM

The following is a list of the main prophets mentioned in the Qur'an, with both their Islamic and Biblical names:

- **Adam** (Adam) was the first prophet of Islam and the first human.
- **Al-Yasa** (Elisha) continued the work of Ilyas (Elijah) after his death.
- **Ayub** (Job) reputedly suffered illness and misfortune for 18 years as a test of his patience and servitude to God.
- **Dawood** (David) is best known for his triumph over the Philistine warrior Goliath.
- **Harūn** (Aaron) was a brother of Musa (Moses).
- **Hud** (Eber) tried to convince his people to worship a single God rather than several Gods. When they refused, God wrought destruction upon their community, though Hud (Eber) was spared.
- **Ibrahim** (Abraham) is best known for almost sacrificing his son Ismail (Ishmael) for God in an event now commemorated annually by Eid ul-Adha.
- **Idris** (Enoch) lived during a period of drought inflicted as a punishment on people who had forgotten God.
- **Ilyas** (Elijah) tried to convince people of only one God. When they refused to listen, they were smitten with a drought and famine.
- **Isa** (Jesus) is one of the highest-ranked prophets in Islam, and certainly the most recognisable to followers of Christianity.
- **Ishaq** (Isaac) is the second-born son of Ibrahim (Abraham).
- **Ismail** (Ishmael) is the son of Ibrahim (Abraham) who was almost sacrificed.
- **Lut** (Lot) preached against homosexuality, as well as promoting the belief in a single God, but was mocked and ignored by the people he preached to.
- **Mohammed** is, of course, the most prominent prophet in Islamic belief.
- **Musa** (Moses) is most renowned for revealing the Ten Commandments, the Tawrat (Torah), to the Israelites.
- **Nuh** (Noah) was chosen to build the famous Ark.
- **Saleh** (Shaloh) left his people for their failure to spare the life of a special camel, as God had ordered.
- **Shoaib** (Jethro) was appointed by God to guide the people of Midyan and Aykah, who lived near Mount Sinai.
- **Sulaiman** (Solomon), according to Islamic tradition, was given power over all things, including the *jinn* (a race of spiritual creatures). He led a kingdom that extended into southern Arabia.
- **Yahya** (John the Baptist) captivated audiences with his powerful sermons.
- **Yaqub** (Jacob) is the son of Ishaq (Isaac).
- **Yunus** (Jonah) strived to lead the people of Nineveh towards righteousness.
- **Yusuf** (Joseph) was the son of Yaqub (Jacob) and became a prominent advisor to the king of Egypt.
- **Zakariya** (Zacharias) prayed to God for a son, since his sterile wife could not provide one. God granted his wishes.

Culture

descendant of the Prophet, who will lead Islam to triumph.

One of the gravest offences that anyone can commit in the presence of a Muslim is to insult the Prophet Mohammed or even to joke lightly about him.

The exact date of birth of Prophet Mohammed is not known for certain, but scholars suggest that it was around 570 AD. Mohammed's main line of business was as a trader.

He is reported to have received his first vision from the Angel Gabriel at the age of 40, and continued to receive visions until his death, aged around 62. Reportedly, he was unable to read or write and so dictated the visions for others to record.

The culture of the Mahdi

Woven into Islamic belief is the legend of the Mahdi — literally, 'the Guided One' — who will return to Earth before Judgement Day to redeem Islam. Shi'a Muslims tend to see the Mahdi as the so-called '12th Imam', a prophesied leader of Islam who went into hiding around the 13th Century. Among Sunnis, and therefore within Sudan, the notion of the Mahdi is rather different, and is not universally accepted by all members of the faith.

Mahdist philosophy is critical to understanding contemporary Sudanese history (p56). In 1881, a religious leader named Mohammed ibn Abdulla proclaimed himself to be the Mahdi. He led a successful campaign against British forces in the country, but died just five months after seizing power in 1885. Mahdist rule lasted until 1898, when General Kitchener's forces successfully reclaimed the country for the British Empire.

Opinion remains divided as to whether Mohammed ibn Abdulla really was the Mahdi, or simply used

HADITHS AND THE MAHDI

Although belief in the coming of the Mahdi is widespread throughout the Islamic world, it is interesting to note that his arrival is not foretold in the Qur'an. Rather, the details of who he is and what he will do are related in a series of *hadiths*, oral traditions relating to the words and deeds of Prophet Mohammed.

There is some debate surrounding the authenticity of many popular hadiths, but the following details extrapolated about the Mahdi are generally accepted by those who believe in his coming:

- The Mahdi will rule for five or seven years.
- The Mahdi will be descended from the Prophet Mohammed, with a broad forehead and prominent nose.
- The Mahdi's name will also be Mohammed, and his father's name will be Abdalla, just like the name of the Prophet's father.
- The Mahdi will appear in Medina.
- The Mahdi will protect the Muslims from destruction and restore Islam to its original position in the world.

Culture

this claim to take hold of power in the country. You will find that some Sudanese Muslims venerate the Mahdi, whilst others decry his campaign as nothing but politics.

Islam and Women

In order to understand how women are treated under Islam, it is important to appreciate the historical context under which the Qur'an was transcribed. The Qur'an was written at a time when women were very much suppressed in society, and the passages that relate to how they should be treated were actually included in order to improve their lot.

Many of the points that follow concern restrictions about how Islamic women should behave, but there are also benefits that they enjoy under the faith. Upon marriage, the man has to promise to provide for his wife. This includes paying for the wedding ceremony and providing a place for them both to live. The man is also expected to make a large investment in jewellery, which offers some security to the woman in the case of divorce.

In terms of dress, almost all Islamic women wear the *hijab* headscarf when out in public. In fact, in 1991, the Sudanese government introduced a Public Order Law that required this. Although the law has never been repealed, it is less strictly enforced these days — and foreigners will certainly be exempt from it.

Similarly, the rest of a woman's body will be fully covered, so that no skin, beyond their hands and faces, can be seen. The full black veil (the *niqab*), popular in Saudi Arabia and Yemen, is fairly rare in North Sudan. You will see it occasionally, though, especially in the east of the country.

Under Qur'anic law, a man can elect to have up to four wives at any given time. If he wants more wives than this, he first has to divorce his other wives. Women, on the other hand, are not permitted to take more than one husband. Technically, this is known as polygyny rather than polygamy, since only the man can take multiple partners and the woman cannot.

FEMALE CIRCUMCISION

Female circumcision is a classic example of traditional African customs fusing with a distorted interpretation of Qur'anic teaching.

There are two forms of female circumcision widely practiced in Sudan. One, known as infibulation or pharaonic circumcision, involves the complete removal of the clitoris and labia minora. This type of female circumcision is officially banned under Sudanese law, although still practiced in parts of the country. The other form, involving partial removal of the clitoris, is more common.

It is usually the older women in a family that advocate the circumcision of younger unmarried girls.

Several justifications are given for the unnecessary and exceedingly painful operation. Some say that it is done for hygienic reasons. A woman who has not had the operation is often not considered to be a proper woman. Another argument is that a circumcised woman is likely to be more faithful than one who has not undergone the operation, for she does not derive any pleasure from sexual intercourse.

Female circumcision carries with it a number of dangers, and can make childbirth exceedingly painful.

There is some disagreement among Islamic scholars about the practice. Many schools suggest that it is recommended though not mandatory and that, in cases where it is done, the cutting should be as little as possible.

The custom of polygyny is slowly dying out and you will see that many of the younger generation do not practice it.

Whilst such polygyny appals some in the West, defendants of it often claim that it avoids social problems by making sure children always have a number of parents around.

There are also strict stipulations placed on the man to treat all of his wives equally and to provide adequately for them. Admittedly, according to some schools of Islam, the bare minimum of what the man must provide seems fairly undemanding: two handfuls of the staple diet of the country a day, plus something to cook it in. In the case of Sudan, this amounts to two handfuls of the beans known as *fuul*.

Islamic women are not permitted to marry non-Muslims, but the same restriction does not apply to men. The argument goes that children are more likely to follow the path of their father than that of their mother. Similarly, it is often argued that women are more likely to adhere to the beliefs of their husbands than the other way round.

Divorce in Islam is a much easier, and more accepted, process than divorce in many other religions, including most branches of Christianity. A controversial way for a man to divorce a woman still exists in Sudan, although it is no longer recognised under the national legal system. Under this practice, the man must say to his wife '*talaq*' ('I divorce you') on three separate occasions. On the third time, the man and woman are no longer married.

Things are harder for a woman who wants to end a marriage under Islamic law. She must first seek the permission of her husband. If her husband refuses to give it to her, then she has some recourse through the Islamic courts and can seek a divorce via a *fatwah*, an edict handed down through an Imam. A common tactic employed by women who wish to divorce unwilling husbands is to start behaving badly and disobediently so that their husbands will want to leave them.

Women are expected to cook and clean in addition to their regular job (if they have one). In the cities, jobs involving heavy lifting are usually done by men. It is also often the men that go shopping in the markets.

It is expected that men riding on buses give up their seat for a woman, if not doing so means that the woman would be left standing.

Ramadan

Ramadan, which takes place during the ninth month of the Islamic calendar year, is considered to be the most holy and venerated time of year for Muslims. According to Islamic belief, Ramadan is the month in which Prophet Mohammed received his first revelation from God.

Since the Islamic lunar calendar year is 11 to 12 days shorter than the solar year, Ramadan migrates through the seasons.

During Ramadan, Muslims are obliged to reduce their dependence on material things and increase their awareness of, and love for, God. During daylight hours, Muslims must abstain from food, drink (including water) and sexual intercourse.

Under Sudanese law, during the month of Ramadan, workers are allowed to work an hour less each day, since they will have been up for a large part of the night.

Not everyone is obliged to fast during Ramadan. Children are usually exempt until their teenage years, or can choose to fast for only

Culture

RAMADAN BREAKFASTS

It is well worth experiencing a Ramadan breakfast if you get the chance. Fortunately, thanks to Sudanese hospitality, this is not a difficult thing to do — and many locals will be only too glad to have a foreigner join them.

Should you attend such a breakfast, here's what you can expect.

The meal usually starts with dates and dry fruits. This is followed by a hot soup, known as *shorba*, which is typically made with chicken. The other food is then presented on a tray, consisting of a variety of dishes, normally including: a cold salad with yogurt and cucumber (a little like the Greek *tzatziki*), the famous Sudanese *asida* (made from cooked wheat flour), spiced meat known as *kofta* and *fuul* (a stew made with fava beans). Next, you will be served with fruit. About one hour after breakfast, once the Muslim diners have returned from prayer, typical Sudanese sweets, known as *bastas*, will be offered round.

Throughout the meal, fruit juice, usually freshly-squeezed, will be provided. *Helomour* is a sweetened spicy drink associated with Ramadan, and will almost certainly be served, too. Another popular Ramadan beverage is *karkaday*, made from hibiscus, and useful for regulating blood pressure, which can drop during fasting.

half a day. The elderly and pregnant women are similarly excused. People who are ill and women who are menstruating also do not have to participate in the fasting — or they can choose to make up the days missed later in the year, usually during the month following Ramadan (called 'Shawaal'). If they are able to, women who do not fast are expected to give a tray of food to the poor, usually through their local mosque.

Ramadan is not only about fasting and abstinence from worldly needs. Throughout the month, Muslims are also expected to put more effort into following the teachings of Islam — such as refraining from lying, stealing, anger, envy, greed, and lust. Muslims are also encouraged to read the entire Qur'an during this time, and to give more generously to charity.

You will notice much greater activity at night in North Sudan during Ramadan. Places that are usually closed by midnight will stay open and busy well into the early morning.

In the last ten days of Ramadan, Muslims are expected to pay even greater attention to prayer and worship, sometimes praying for most of the night.

Ramadan ends with the religious holiday of Eid al-Fitr — which means, literally, 'the Festival of Breaking the Fast'. The celebration of Eid al-Fitr lasts three days, over which period the Sudanese will make a special effort to visit friends and relatives. Muslims who can afford it are expected to donate to the poor during this time — a process known as 'zakat al-fitr'.

Charity

Like anywhere, Sudan has its share of beggars. However, in North Sudan, you will notice that there are far fewer people asking for money than elsewhere in Africa (although increased immigration from non-Arabic countries means that their number is rising).

This is because of two key elements of the Islamic culture: the strength of the family unit under Islam and the practice of *zakat*, whereby the wealthier are expected to donate to the poor.

Zakat started as a voluntary contribution for the wealthy, at a time when Prophet Mohammed was a young preacher in Mecca. However, when Mohammed moved to settle in Medina, such was the poverty of emigrants there that it became a sort of tithe.

The method of calculating what percentage of their salary someone should give as *zakat* is laid out in the Qur'an, and interpreted by a special office that is dedicated to collecting the tax. The rate depends on how much individuals earn, but usually equates to between 2.5% and 10% of post-tax salary.

Muslims in North Sudan who earn a salary, and those who run a business, are obliged to pay *zakat*. In order to open a business, you have to get a tax-return statement from both the bureau of income tax and the *zakat* office.

For the giver, *zakat* is a form of purification, alleviating the guilt associated with accumulating wealth through the forceful relinquishing of something that the believer would rather keep.

For the poor, *zakat* serves a number of purposes. First of all, it makes the poor less envious of the rich, for the richer the rich become, the greater the windfall for the poor. Secondly, because *zakat* is administered through a mosque or central authority, the poor do not have to suffer the degradation of asking directly for charity themselves. It is, in their minds, as though Allah Himself has provided for them.

The system of *zakat* only applies in North Sudan — there is no similar system in the South, and so the needy usually have to rely on family support.

EATING AND HOSPITALITY

Outside of Ramadan, the Sudanese (in the North) generally take their 'breakfast' (*fatur*), which they consider to be the most important meal of the day, between 11 am and 2 pm. Dinner, taken in the evening, is far less important.

In the early morning, before their breakfast, the Sudanese typically drink tea and eat simple biscuits. If travelling, they might also partake in *zalabia*, sweetened balls of dough.

In the North, the Sudanese generally eat their main meals from a single tray (*sinaia*), on which several dishes are served.

For local traditional food, such as *fuul* or *asida*, the Sudanese (in both the North and the South) eat with their hands, using hunks of bread to scoop up the food. You should only ever eat with your right hand, the left one being used for ablutions.

Bear in mind that, if you arrange a dinner party for Sudanese friends, there are some foods that the locals find decidedly odd to eat without any utensils. Pasta is one such example.

In many families in North Sudan, men and women eat separately, although if you are invited to someone's house as a foreigner you can usually choose where you sit. The men are typically given the most comfortable dining positions (perhaps outside, in the cool), whilst the women tend to be relegated to a back room somewhere in the house. There is another benefit to eating with the men, too, since they are often served with the choicest parts of the dishes, and the women get whatever is left over.

Preparing family meals is still very much the concern of women in Sudan, and they will typically work together for many hours each day, especially during Ramadan, to prepare a variety of dishes for everybody.

Conversation is not as big a part of the meal in Sudanese culture as it is, for example, in Europe. Frequently, the meal is finished in silence, and at speed — and the conversation only resumes once the coffee or the *sheesha* (p100) are brought out.

If you invite the Sudanese for dinner, don't be surprised if they become restless once they have eaten. The Sudanese like to go out immediately after dinner — sometimes for an ice-cream or a coffee, or simply a drive.

The Sudanese don't generally bring anything when they are invited to dinner — and don't expect their guests to, either. If you do want to take anything, a box of chocolates is probably your safest bet (or flowers for a lady).

The family structure is extremely important to the Sudanese way of life. For family members who return after a long period of absence, a sheep or goat is often sacrificed in honour of their safe homecoming.

The Sudanese frequently turn up late for an appointment or a dinner invitation. There is some very good advice about time-keeping in Sudan, often offered by the locals to the foreigner. You should wait at least one hour for the Sudanese to turn up. If they have still not arrived after that hour, this is perfectly okay — continue waiting for another hour. By the third hour, if they have still not turned up, it is probably best to leave and come back the following day. Such tongue-in-cheek advice may be an exaggeration, but it does give a good illustration of the need for patience.

When visiting homes in North Sudan, take care not to express too much interest in your host's belongings. If you say that you like

something, then your host will feel obliged to give it to you.

Sudanese hosts will usually offer their guests freshly-squeezed juice and avoid packaged juices, despite the prevalence of them in the supermarkets. If you really can't provide fresh fruit juice, then offer a coke or water instead.

Most Sudanese use powdered milk at home, when offering tea or coffee.

DRESS

In **North Sudan**, women are expected to dress modestly, showing as little flesh as possible. Similarly, men should refrain from wearing shorts.

Although not as popular as it used to be, the colourful *tobe* is still used by many women in the North. A little like the Indian *sari*, this strip of long cloth is wrapped around the body and over the left shoulder although, unlike the *sari*, the woman's midriff is never exposed. Certain regions have a specific colour and pattern for this cloth. According to Islamic tradition, only married women should wear the *tobe*. These days, women generally dress in a long skirt and top, reserving the *tobe* for special occasions. Trousers are not normally worn except with a long tunic, or by young girls who want to imitate western dress.

Women who have just lost their husbands are expected to wear a white dress for around three to six months, as a sign of mourning. During this period, they are not allowed to leave their home. Nor can they see any men, apart from young children or very close relatives. At the end of this period, they typically have a big party with their female friends and plenty of food.

For men, a popular form of dress is the *jalabia*. This is a single white robe, usually stitched from two pieces of cloth, which slips over the head to cover the entire body. It is surprisingly comfortable in the intense Sudanese heat, which is no doubt why it is such a popular choice of dress.

In **South Sudan**, the clothes are much less conservative. It is unusual to see women wearing the Islamic head dress, and many have taken to wearing tighter Western-style trousers that would be deemed unacceptable in the Islamic North (although you can sometimes spot immodestly dressed southerners on the streets of Khartoum). Many dresses tend to be more flamboyant and colourful too, taking after the style of dress that is popular in other sub-Saharan countries such as Uganda and Kenya.

In remote tribal villages in the South, men and women still dress in exceedingly little — perhaps just a loin cloth and nothing more.

WEDDINGS AND MARRIAGE

As one might expect, wedding ceremonies in North and South Sudan are very different.

In **North Sudan**, it is common practice for family members of the betrothed to invite whoever they want to the wedding, even if the guests do not know the bride and groom. This means that, if you stay in the country for any length of time, you will almost certainly be invited to a wedding.

Food served at weddings in the North is almost always the same, and comes either wrapped in cling film or in a polystyrene box.

A typical tray consists of a bread roll, a piece of feta-like cheese, a few black olives, one pasty-like *sambuska* with cheese and another with meat, one *basta* (Sudanese sweet), some slices of pepper and a few wilting crisps.

THE DUKHAN RITUAL

Before a wedding, many Sudanese women perform a purification ritual, which is intended to make them fit for marriage.

Wearing nothing but a loose robe or towel, the betrothed will sit for up to an hour each day above a smouldering pile of perfumed embers. This daily ritual is usually performed for a whole month before the wedding, sometimes longer.

The aromatic wood used to make the embers is called *talih*. Souq as-Shigiara in Omdurman is famous for selling it (p185).

The *dukhan* smooths and tightens the skin. It is also believed to cleanse the woman in preparation for the new home into which she will enter.

Whilst serving such food at a wedding might appear frugal in other cultures, Sudanese guests expect such fare. If the arrangements are not as they anticipate, they may look unfavourably upon the families of the two who are being married.

A Sudanese wedding typically lasts for three days.

The first day ('*leilat al-henna*') is dedicated to the man and his friends and family. It is usually the man who invites all guests for this part of the proceedings. Although the woman is present, she does not choose who will attend the service. During this ceremony, the hands and feet of the groom are decorated with henna by his female family members. At the same time, the bride is anointed with perfume and creams. The hands and feet of the bride are also decorated with henna.

The second day ('*leilat al-dukhlia*') is the most important day of the nuptial rites and takes place in the bride's house. This ceremony is just for female guests. The only man that can attend is the groom.

In the evening, after a day of feasting and dancing, the bride is expected to perform a dance for her husband-to-be.

This gathering is an opportunity for the bride to show that she is pretty and worthy of marrying the man. Wearing relatively little, at least by Sudanese standards, the idea is that the woman should perform her dance in a sexy and slightly provocative fashion.

Traditionally, the next two days of the wedding were known as 'subhia and girtik', but now, for economic reasons, tend to be rolled into a single day. During the morning, the bride has to dance in front of her female guests whilst the groom receives good wishes from his male guests. In the afternoon, the couple begin their honeymoon.

The three-day wedding ceremony actually takes place roughly three months after the official and legal marriage of the couple. The groom and a male member of the bride's family (usually the father or a brother) will sign the registration document within the community mosque. In the past, this registration procedure could take place without the consent of the bride, providing that a male member of the bride's immediate family agreed. Nowadays, though, it is not possible to force a woman to marry against her wishes. Once the registration service is over, the couple are legally married, but Islamic culture dictates that they still cannot have sexual relations until after the official ceremony, three months hence.

If you attend a Sudanese wedding, a present is generally not expected. The proceedings will involve some form of live music and dancing, where both men and women click their fingers in the air as a sign of happiness for the couple.

As in most aspects of Sudanese life, men and women sit separately during the proceedings, although it is usually acceptable to sit together with the other side if you prefer.

Due to a noise curfew in place in North Sudan, all music stops around 11 pm and most guests will leave shortly afterwards, although some may stay on and participate in a further ceremony where both bride and groom, dressed in traditional clothes and surrounded by burning candles, sit and receive well-wishers. In some circumstances, a special permit can be obtained from the police to extend the noise curfew until midnight.

In terms of dress, the *tobe*, a colourful traditional dress, is popular with the ladies. They will also use the opportunity to apply copious amounts of make-up to their faces. Married women will generally wear some sort of henna design on their hands, as a sign of participation in the wedding. Many men will come to the wedding dressed in a white *jalabia*, or else wearing a smart shirt and trousers.

The bride will attend the proceedings wearing a white dress, similar to the one worn at Christian weddings. She will also use cream to make her face as light as possible. The groom will either wear a suit or a *jalabia* to the wedding.

In North Sudan, an Islamic marriage is more than just a union between husband and wife; it is also a marrying of the two families. For this reason, the families carefully study one another before the wedding. If they see problems in the family, or do not get on with key family members, they may choose to abandon wedding preparations.

This is one of the principal reasons why the marrying of cousins is so widespread in the country. Many families consider it ideal if they can entice two cousins to marry, as they then avoid the complications that unity between two different families can bring.

However, with divorce becoming more prevalent, there is another side to this: it can be far harder to disentangle a failed marriage within the family than between two different families.

Among **non-Islamic tribes**, and therefore within the South, marriage customs can vary quite significantly.

The dowry is a particularly important element of the marriage process among many tribes in the South, and before a man can entertain the notion of marrying the woman that he desires he must show that he (or his family) has sufficient means to pay the necessary price to the family of the bride. Among many tribes, the dowry is still specified in ‘heads of cattle’, although more urbanised families may now convert this amount into a monetary figure instead. A fairly typical dowry might be to part with a herd of 200 cattle, or the equivalent in South Sudanese pounds.

Most tribes in the South have their own specific traditions pertaining to the wedding ceremony. The Nuer, for example, divide a marriage into three parts. First of all, there is the betrothal, when the first instalment of the dowry is paid. This is usually accompanied by the sacrificing of an ox to honour the ancestral spirits. The ox is shared by the community and after this the couple are considered to be husband and wife. Then comes the formal marriage ceremony, with much local dancing and many festivities. The final part of the process is consummation of the marriage; it is only when the bride becomes pregnant that she is expected to move out of her parents' home.

These days, many wedding traditions in South Sudan, especially in urban centres, have been influenced by Christian habits that you might be familiar with in the West. These include the wearing of a white dress and the blessing by a priest. In cases where couples opt for a more Christian-style wedding, you will usually still find a heavy African influence in the proceedings, including colourful garments worn by the women and lively dancing based on tribal customs.

As in North Sudan, uniting the two families is usually as important as joining the bride and the groom. Therefore, if the two families do not get on, then it may be very difficult for the couple to continue with wedding preparations.

According to some tribal customs — such as among the Nuer and the Dinka — if the husband passes away, it is expected that a young sibling will replace him as the partner of the woman. Any children that are produced as a result of this union are considered to be the children of the deceased.

FUNERALS

As with weddings, funeral practices among tribes are markedly different from one another, depending on customary beliefs, although in the **North** there is some similarity between the way in which Islamic funerals are conducted.

Not all Muslims approve of the outpouring of grief at a Sudanese funeral, believing that this is tantamount to questioning the will of Allah.

Nonetheless, funeral ceremonies are an important part of the Islamic way-of-life in North Sudan and if a

Culture

community member has recently died, everyone in the community will be expected to stop by and at least pay their respects.

The outpouring of grief is most obvious among the female members of the family, where they will shriek shrilly, often for hours on end.

Before the funeral, the body is washed and then it is carried to the grave. Only the men are permitted to accompany the body to the grave, whilst the women stay at home and prepare hospitality for the many mourners that will descend on the home. The local sheikh will say a few words to the body, wishing it safe passage into the next life. Then everyone that has accompanied the body to the grave — usually close family members — will help cover it in earth.

PHONES

In general, the Sudanese love speaking on the phone and will often chat with their friends by phone for an hour or more each day, even though they live in the same city.

The Sudanese do not like to leave a phone unanswered. If they are in the middle of a meeting and their mobile phone rings, they will usually feel compelled to answer, even if it is just to say that they are busy and can't talk for the moment.

Text messages, on the other hand, are not so common in Sudan. If the Sudanese want to say something, they will, in general, call rather than send an SMS. If you send an SMS, then it is likely that the person who received it will phone you back instead of sending a reply.

SMSs are often used when someone does not answer their phone. "It's me, pick up!" is a common message to receive.

SUDANESE HOMES

The style of homes differs throughout the country, from square concrete blocks to conical thatched buildings.

In many homes in the **North**, beds are scattered throughout the rooms. The traditional Sudanese bed is known as the *angreb*, which consists of a lattice of ropes stretched across a wooden frame. In a country as hot as Sudan, the *angreb* offers a much more comfortable sleeping place than the modern foam-filled mattress. Many of the beds are used as sofas as well as places to sleep. Only in wealthier houses are you likely to find people sitting on sofas rather than beds.

North Sudanese homes frequently have a number of sitting rooms. One is usually reserved for guests and another for family members. It is also quite common to have separate sitting rooms for men and women, with the two sexes rarely mingling.

Recently, a flourishing flat culture has started to develop in Khartoum. Whilst most Sudanese still prefer living in a house with open spaces, many are increasingly attracted by the idea of living in flats.

Homes and houses in the **South** differ significantly from tribe to tribe. They may be the round *tukul* huts with thatched roofs or built from intertwined branches with a more tapered roof. Many of these traditional houses will have just a single room for sleeping, with a bed (possibly an *angreb* or sometimes just a mattress of straw). In many families, more than one person may sleep in the same room. Wealthier families, of course, will be able to construct much larger places.

GREETINGS

In **South Sudan**, a handshake is the commonest form of greeting — or a bear hug if you know the person very well.

Greetings in **North Sudan** are much more complex, and are given according to the level of familiarity between two people.

Men who don't know each other very well, or who have only just met, simply shake hands.

Men who know each other better will greet each other in traditional Sudanese fashion — by first touching the left shoulder with the right palm before shaking hands.

For men who know each other very well, a large hug is also acceptable.

Women usually shake hands with other women whom they don't know very well. Between friends, they may hug each other or kiss each other on the cheeks.

Public kissing between men and women is frowned upon in North Sudan and, therefore, kisses and hugs will never be exchanged between the two sexes (the only exception being if the two people are close family members).

Usually, men and women will just shake hands, however well they know each other. It is customary for the man to initiate this greeting. If you are a man, you will find that many women will not offer their hands unless you offer yours first. Some staunchly-traditional women will avoid touching the skin of a man at all. Therefore, if you offer to shake hands with them, they may wrap theirs in the sleeves of their clothes before returning the gesture.

TIPPING

There is not a big culture of tipping in Sudanese restaurants or cafés although, since many foreigners do, it is becoming increasingly expected of non-locals. In general, if you feel like tipping, it is up to you how much you want to leave.

Certain restaurants, particularly those aimed at foreign clientele, demand a service charge (usually between 5 and 10%). You can usually see if one exists by looking at the small print at the bottom of the menu. Since it is a service charge, this should replace the tip. Some restaurants also charge a 12% tax on top of this.

It is becoming increasingly common for guards of buildings to expect tips from foreigners who are staying there. However, you should not feel obliged to pay the guard any money. It is usually up to the owner of the building to take care of his salary.

PUBLIC TRANSPORT

There is a whole sub-culture concerning how to hail buses and other forms of public transport, but this is properly dealt with in the 'Transport' section (p86).

There are two things that are particularly worth knowing from a cultural point of view. Firstly, if two or more people know each other on the bus, it is courteous for the one nearest the money-collector to pay for the others. Secondly, men closest to the doors of the bus are always expected to give up their seats should women enter. If they don't, the man who collects the money may ask them to do so.

Culture

Many foreigners who move to Sudan have access to a private car for day-to-day travelling about. This car is often provided by the company or organisation for which they work. Sometimes, the employee will be able to drive the car, but more often than not the car will come with its very own driver.

A tragic consequence of this is that a great many expats who move to Sudan miss out on one of the greatest cultural experiences that the country has to offer — that of negotiating the infinitely bewildering public transport system.

Of course, many workers in the country — including UN staff and diplomatic representatives — are warned against using public transport, because of security fears.

Note that whilst public transport is relatively safe in the north and east of North Sudan, you should exercise much greater caution when moving about in the South or in Darfur. It is with good reason that the UN advises foreigners to only travel by private vehicle in these areas.

At their best, Sudanese cities can appear fairly daunting to get around in. Street maps are a rarity. Roads are not always clearly marked. There are few fixed bus stops on the streets, and locals use a complex series of hand gestures to flag public transportation down. Taxis are expensive and taxi drivers regularly put the prices up for foreigners. However, if you make the effort, you will find that things aren't quite as arduous as they first appear.

DRIVING

Most towns or cities in Sudan have places where you can buy or rent private vehicles, although prices can be relatively high.

In North Sudan, the government has recently raised import duties on cars, and stopped the import of second-hand vehicles. This is linked to the government's attempt to keep dollars within the country so that they can be used to buy primary goods (p177).

Note that you can hire vehicles with or without a driver, the latter option being the more expensive. However, under Sudanese law, if you want to hire a four-by-four vehicle (which is necessary for travelling in many parts of the country) then you must do so with a driver.

To get around by car or motorbike, you really just have to rely on your own knowledge of the area: there are few signposts or street maps to help you out. To make matters worse, many roads (particularly the smaller ones) are in a poor state of repair.

Night-time driving can be hazardous. In certain areas (such as near the Presidential Palace in Khartoum), the authorities have started to install street lighting, although the lights are not always turned on.

In North Sudan's major cities, new traffic light systems have been installed. Passing through a red light will invite an immediate 30 SDG fine and could result in you being arrested if the offence was deemed particularly dangerous. Some of the traffic lights have been poorly installed, so that it is

---

HITCH-HIKING

Hitch-hiking is still a fairly common way of getting around the northern part of North Sudan, and there are many travellers that choose to this way of getting from the Ethiopian border up to Wadi Halfa on the Egyptian border.

North Sudan is a very safe country in which to do this, and you will find the locals to be incredibly helpful to those travelling in this way. Some may even be able to offer or help find accommodation on the way.

The harshness of the landscape lends itself to getting a ride, as you can often look a bit deserted and desperate with your thumb out in the desert. For this reason, always head to the edge of towns. Some routes towards Port Sudan get the very large trucks which are usually happy to stop, albeit a kilometre down the road! There is a dearth of private vehicles on secondary routes, especially through the heat of the afternoon, so take plenty of water and snacks.

Drivers who pick up hitch-hikers in North Sudan usually look for a bit of verbal exchange and friendliness, and almost never ask for money. With such great roads, hitching can be a very rapid way to travel, and often drivers are going a long distance.

Although hitch-hiking is relatively safe, it can be made difficult by the police road-checks on the edge of almost every town in the North. The police will usually be friendly and welcoming, but completely mystified why a foreigner would choose this way of getting around. They may feel sympathetic towards your obviously impoverished state and flag down a bus on your behalf, telling the driver not to charge you.

Take much greater care if you are planning to hitch-hike in South Sudan or Darfur.

---

not clear to which road they relate. Take particular care at these junctions because the traffic police will almost certainly be watching.

If you are going to drive for more than three months in Khartoum, then you must get your national driving licence converted to either an international or a local Sudanese one. If you are already in Sudan, you cannot get an international driving licence without first leaving the country. You should speak to the relevant motoring organisation in your home country for more information about how to convert your licence to an international one.

The Sudanese Traffic Police handle all queries relating to local driving licences. In Khartoum, the Traffic Police headquarters are located on Jama'a Street — other cities have smaller offices.

It is not possible to make an appointment; you simply have to turn up and wait in line. Try to get there as early as possible, as the queues can be quite long and you risk being turned away if it gets too late.

In North Sudan, a local Sudanese driving licence (for non-Sudanese) costs 440 SDG and requires that you sit a test first. The test consists of four parts: a psychological evaluation, a test where you have to match road symbols on the computer, a test of simple road manoeuvres and an on-the-road test. Because there are so many different tests to sit, it can take up to a week or longer to get your licence. If things are not very crowded, you might manage to sit the whole test in a single day, but it will still take at least two days before you can collect your licence. You can usually ask to receive some explanations during the test in English.

The Traffic Police also handle the vehicle registration process. The yearly registration fee for a car is between 500 and 600 SDG. For a motorbike, the fee is around 240 SDG.

If you bring your own vehicle into Sudan, you may drive for up to three months without obtaining a local road licence, providing that it has comprehensive insurance cover. Car dealers in the country are unable to handle vehicle registration for you; you must turn up at the police yourself.

Although car insurance is compulsory in the country, remember that there are a large number of vehicles that don't have it. In case of an accident, you should call the police.

In North Sudan, under *sharia* law, if you accidentally kill someone whilst driving, you must pay 16,000 SDG in *dia* ('blood money') to the family of the deceased. South Sudan has similarly strict penalties for causing death by driving. You should make sure that your insurance adequately covers this eventuality.

In Sudan, it is illegal to use your mobile phone whilst behind the wheel, although most people seem to ignore this. It is also mandatory to wear seat belts whilst in the front — a rule that, once again, is only very loosely followed.

In the North, women are not allowed to drive motorbikes, although foreigners who ignore this restriction are usually tolerated.

CITY BUSES

The cheapest way to move around towns and cities is, without doubt, to use the local bus network.

Most inner-city journeys cost between 50 *piastras* and 1 SDG, depending on where the bus is heading and where you catch it from. In general, buses are more expensive if you catch them from a terminal point than if you catch them in the middle of the route.

Don't confuse the city bus with the minibus, which looks more like a van. The minibus runs along many of the same routes that the ordinary bus does, but generally costs twice as much. You might want to take a minibus, for example, if the route you are travelling along is particularly busy and all the ordinary buses are full. Moreover, minibuses sometimes serve destinations that ordinary buses do not.

HAND GESTURES

For those that want to get to grips with the local bus system, it is worth spending a little time to familiarise yourself with the hand gestures that are used.

A hand that is held out to the left or right and moved up and down indicates the direction that the bus will turn at the next main intersection.

If the conductor points downwards with his index finger, this means that the bus is heading to the town's centre.

An index finger pointing straight up means that only standing room is available.

If the conductor moves his finger in a small circle, this usually means that the bus is going to a place in town called 'Liffe', which means `roundabout´ in Arabic.

BUS ETIQUETTE

- When entering the bus, use the seats at the back or along the sides first. The central line of collapsible seats is used only when all others are full.
- If using the central line of collapsible seats, move towards the back first.
- If you are sat on one of the collapsible seats and someone behind you wants to get off, stand up and hold the collapsible seat for them so that they may pass.
- If you are sat near the door, you should be prepared to give up your seat if a lady enters and all the seats are full.
- When all the seats are full, standing room may be offered towards the front of the bus.
- The conductor collects the money only once all people are seated. He starts from the back of the bus and will usually request payment by clicking his fingers. The money is then passed between the passengers until it reaches the conductor.
- If you are travelling with a friend, or you meet someone on the bus that you know, the person who is closest to the door normally pays the fare.

In the last couple of years, sparkling new air-conditioned buses have been introduced into Khartoum. These tend to cost slightly more than the regular buses, but are noticeably more comfortable. Seats are not as cramped and there are proper handrails to hold onto if you are standing. When you get on the bus, you should move to the front and buy a ticket from the conductor. To get off the bus you still have to click your fingers — there is no 'stop' button. These new buses only serve a limited number of destinations

At first glance, the thought of navigating the chaotic and noisy bus system can be more than a little daunting. Few non-Sudanese use the bus system, preferring instead to travel by private vehicle or taxi. But it really is worth spending a little time to learn how the buses work, especially if you are going to be in the country for a while. It is an excellent way of seeing local life and will save you a great deal of money in the long run.

There are now a few official bus stops in the country, usually identified by a signpost that bears the symbol of a bus. Drivers will stop pretty much anywhere, but they are more likely to pick you up if you wait at one of these official bus stops or at one of the many unofficial congregation points where people tend to wait for the bus.

To catch a bus, simply flag it down at a convenient point and hop on, making sure that they are in a place where the bus driver can safely stop. Hand signals from the bus conductor indicate the direction in which the bus is heading, and allow the passengers to communicate their wishes (see box on p88). You can also guess at the direction in which a bus is heading by listening to the string of Arabic names that are blurted out, very quickly, by the conductor.

To request a stop, simply click your fingers or make a hissing noise through your teeth.

A coloured line around the bottom of the bus should also, in theory,

Transport

indicate the direction in which the bus is heading. However, these colours have become rather muddled, and you can now no longer be certain that two buses bearing stripes of the same colour are heading to the same place.

At the main bus stations in Khartoum, the bus bays are identified by unique numbers and the bus will always depart from the same designated spots.

BOKSIS

The *boksi* is a pick-up truck where seats have been added for passengers at the back. There will usually be two rows of seats facing one another, enclosed in a kind of metal cage.

The *boksi* used to be very popular in Khartoum, but the government has now banned its use within the city, although it is still used on Tuti Island. The *boksi* is much more popular outside of the capital, particularly in the east.

The *boksi* usually works as a form of shared transportation, where the costs are divided equally between all passengers. Simply sit on the *boksi* until it has become full, and then it will set off. It is certainly a memorable way in which to travel.

The *boksi* is more common in the North than the South.

TAXIS AND AMJADS

Taxis and *amjads* are the most convenient way of travelling around cities if you don't have your own vehicle, although they are also the most expensive. Taxis are usually yellow and look fairly beaten-up. *Amjads* are nondescript vans — most commonly blue or white, although they can be any colour.

To hail either a taxi or an *amjad*, simply raise your hand and indicate the way that you want to go. It is a good idea, and often cheaper, to hail a taxi or *amjad* that is already going in the direction in which you want to head.

Insistent beeping from an *amjad* or taxi often means that they are free and touting for customers.

Foreigners may have to fight over the price. It is a good idea to negotiate your fee before you get into the vehicle. However, if you are certain of the price for a particular route, you can just hand over the correct money when you get off. Since the driver may question the price that you think you ought to pay, it helps to go armed with some choice Arabic expressions. '*Ana ta-walee bedfa'a...*' (`I always pay...') is a good one to use.

If a taxi or *amjad* driver gets aggressive about how much he thinks you should pay, be firm. In the North, you should rarely pay more than 10 SDG for travelling to most places within a city.

In general, *amjad* drivers charge less than taxi drivers do.

Taxis are less common in the South, where the *boda-boda* (p91) has taken pride of place. Where taxi services do exist — such as in Juba — you usually have to telephone them in advance, and be prepared to pay a hefty fare (25 to 35 SDG is not uncommon for a single journey).

Make sure that taxi drivers know where they are going before they set off. They may ask you to pay more if they have to make a longer journey than they initially thought. Drivers generally speak little or no English, so it is a good idea to learn basic instructions in Arabic.

RICKSHAWS

Most of the motor rickshaws that rattle down city streets are imported from India. They are usually yellow in colour, and can seat two people comfortably in the back. Three can fit only with a bit of a squeeze.

Rickshaws are great for travelling short distances. Most journeys should cost between 3-5 SDG. On certain streets, you will also find shared rickshaws, which charge 50 *piastras* for a single journey (usually down streets where there are no buses).

In Khartoum, it is often not possible to take rickshaws between neighbourhoods because of restrictions on where they can travel. Rickshaws cannot, for example, cross Afriqia Street.

Again, as with taxis and *amjads*, you can either negotiate the price before you get in or just hand over the correct change when you leave.

Rickshaws are not so readily available in South Sudan as they are in the North, although many towns close to the North-South border have them. Rickshaws have also been banned from the streets of Kassala in eastern Sudan.

WALKING AND CYCLING

If you want to get some exercise whilst in the country, you might think about walking or cycling around town. This is sure to get some heads turning, as few Sudanese do either of these.

Walking is a great way of really experiencing the vibrancy of city life and helps to get your bearings. Once you have been walking in a city for a couple of weeks, you will really start to understand its layout.

There are bike shops in most main towns in Sudan, but it is still not easy to find a good-quality bicycle. You will probably have to make do with a second-rate one that needs a lot of maintenance. It is advisable to pick up a good set

TRAVEL PERMIT

Remember that a permit is needed for travel to many areas of the country. In Khartoum, this can be obtained from the Ministry of Humanitarian Affairs, just south of Qurashi Park in Khartoum 2, or from the Ministry of Tourism (🏠 Mashtal Street, Riyad in Khartoum). The permit will take at least a day to obtain from the Ministry of Humanitarian Affairs, but is usually immediate from the Ministry of Tourism. The permit is free, but you may have to pay a small tourism tax of 5 SDG. You do not need to get a separate permit for travel in the South.

of spanners and a bicycle pump, along with your bike, as you are certain to need them. A standard bike should cost you between 200 and 400 SDG/SSP.

Remember that Sudan is a very hot country — and it can be exceedingly tiring (even dangerous) to undertake too much physical exertion during the day.

Riding bikes is slightly more common in the South.

BODA-BODAS

In the South, the easiest and cheapest way to get round cities is to hop on the back of a bicycle or motorbike. These are known as *boda-bodas*, a corruption of the English word 'border' because of the fact that they are used to shuttle people between borders in Africa, especially the one between Uganda and Kenya.

A ride on a motorbike should cost you no more than 5 SSP, to most destinations within a city, whilst bicycles are usually a couple of SSP cheaper. Bicycles tend to be more

Transport

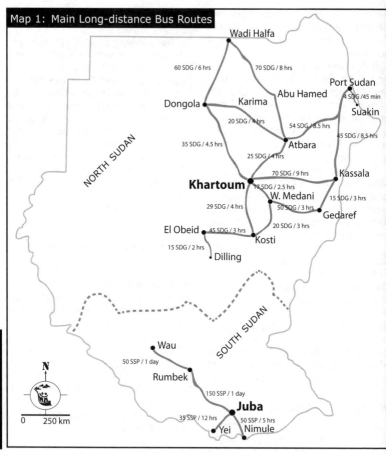

Map 1: Main Long-distance Bus Routes

Wadi Halfa
60 SDG / 6 hrs   70 SDG / 8 hrs
Port Sudan
4 SDG / 45 min
Dongola   Karima   Abu Hamed
Suakin
20 SDG / 4 hrs   54 SDG / 8.5 hrs
45 SDG / 8.5 hrs
35 SDG / 4.5 hrs   Atbara
NORTH SUDAN   25 SDG / 4 hrs
70 SDG / 9 hrs   Kassala
Khartoum   17 SDG / 2.5 hrs
W. Medani   15 SDG / 3 hrs
29 SDG / 4 hrs   50 SDG / 3 hrs
El Obeid   45 SDG / 3 hrs   Gedaref
20 SDG / 3 hrs
15 SDG / 2 hrs   Kosti
Dilling
SOUTH SUDAN
Wau
50 SSP / 1 day
N   Rumbek
150 SSP / 1 day
Juba
0   250 km   35 SSP / 12 hrs   50 SSP / 5 hrs
Yei   Nimule

popular in rural towns and may not be easily available in major urban centres. Boda-bodas are frequently used to travel between towns as well.

Be warned, though, that motorbike taxis have a tragically high rate of accident and injury. Motorcycle helmets are non-existent and many *boda-boda* drivers seem to have only a tenuous grasp on the concept of road safety. You should always make sure that you are comfortable with your driver, and don't hesitate to tell him to drive slowly if you feel in any way anxious.

The wisest thing to do, if you are going to stay in a city in the South for any length of time, is to find a *boda-boda* driver that you really trust and make sure you use him all the time. Take his number and remember to call him rather than hail a *boda-boda* in the street.

Boda-bodas are not used in the North.

TRAVELLING AROUND SUDAN

North and South Sudan are not the easiest countries to travel around and you should always be prepared for delays.

Roads are often in poor condition. Security is high in areas, which means it is not unusual to be stopped and questioned during your journey, especially if you travel by bus.

Distances between towns and cities are generally very large, which is why flying is such a popular way of getting around.

Whatever method of transportation you eventually choose, remember that patience is perhaps the most important attribute to bring with you.

Driving

It is possible to see much of Sudan by car or motorbike, although take care on some of the minor routes, which are poorly maintained and may consist of little more than a rough track in the countryside.

Roads in North Sudan — outside of Darfur — are generally very good, although many roads south of Khartoum become inaccessible during the rainy season.

The roads are less well-developed in the South, although a rapid construction frenzy is seeing many new ones being built. The best road in the South is still the route between Nimule and Juba. The state of the route between Juba and Wau is also improving.

Trains

Spanning 5500 km, Sudan's rail network is the largest in Africa. Unfortunately, though, it is also one of the most inefficient.

Mismanagement of the rail network has seen passenger trains almost completely stop throughout the country. The railways are now mostly used for the transportation

of goods, particularly agricultural produce.

At the time of writing, trains north of Khartoum had been completely suspended, although a new management team has been brought on board and so some sort of service may resume in the future.

Seat 61 (💻 www.seat61.com) is a forum that provides information about rail travel in different countries around the world, and regularly has updates about the state of Sudan's rail network. You could also check the website of **Sudan Railways Corporation** (💻 www.sudanrailways.gov.sd), but this isn't always well maintained.

Buses

Buses are a popular way of travelling between cities in North Sudan. They also serve some destinations in the South although, due to security concerns, don't travel everywhere. Long-distance bus travel in Darfur is also not that common due to the risk of banditry.

In the North, large air-conditioned coaches run along most of the more popular routes — such as between Port Sudan, Kassala, El-Obeid and Khartoum. Many of these serve food and drink during the journey. The food on such trips almost always consists of chicken and bread, with some white cheese and a syrupy sweet, all wrapped in cellophane. Toffees are generally proffered at the start of the journey, and you will always be served water. Onboard televisions frequently screen American movies subtitled in Arabic.

In South Sudan, the buses are far less comfortable and rarely air-conditioned. You may have to put up with a chicken or two flapping around your feet.

Transport

In both South and North Sudan, you can find more basic buses that do not run to a fixed timetable but simply leave when they are full. Such buses are not recommended for very long journeys.

Flying

If you want to hop between major towns or cities, the quickest option is to fly. Sudan Airways has domestic flights covering most of the country. Other popular companies include Marsland Aviation, Nova Air and Sun Air.

Bear in mind that, when catching a local domestic flight, the aircraft will not have been subject to the same safety controls as you would find in Europe and America. Nova Air is widely considered the safest option, since they have the newest fleet of aircraft, but they only fly to Port Sudan.

HUMANITARIAN FLIGHTS

In both North and South Sudan, the UN's World Food Programme (WFP) operates a Humanitarian Air Service (UNHAS). This air service is intended for UN personnel and NGO staff who carry out humanitarian work. Journalists can also sometimes use it, if they are working on a humanitarian-related story, although UN and NGO staff always get priority. You will need to pay a standard fare, though, which usually isn't all that much cheaper than a commercial flight. To reserve a place on a humanitarian flight contact the relevant WFP office. In Khartoum: ☎ 0183 248 001. In Juba: ☎ 0811 820 164)

Ferries

There are no passenger ferries running northwards from Khartoum, because of a series of shallow points (known as the Nile Cataracts) that make river travel difficult.

However, it is now possible to travel along the Nile between Kosti, south of Khartoum, and Juba. There are no official passenger services yet, but cargo merchants are usually fairly keen to earn a little extra by also carrying passengers. Remember that you will need an additional visa if you are travelling between North and South Sudan.

Since such services are unofficial, the prices that merchants try to charge vary quite widely. It is reasonable to expect to pay somewhere in the region of 100 SDG to travel between the two cities, although some will try to charge as much as 200 SDG. The best thing to do is put your best negotiating hat on when trying to secure passage, and remember that you're an extra source of income for them, not their primary source.

Travelling in this way is not for those that like their creature comforts. You will spend up to two weeks travelling from Juba to Kosti — possibly longer if you go the other way, since the Nile flows northwards. Sleeping arrangements will almost certainly be primitive and most of the journey will be spent surrounded by swarms of mosquitos. Make sure you bring your mosquito net, insect repellant and antimalarials.

ROUGH PRICE GUIDE FOR FLIGHTS
(BASED ON STANDARD FARES FOR ONE ADULT)

From Khartoum	Sudan Airways (return)	Marsland Aviation (single)	Nova (return)	Sun Air (single)
Wadi Halfa				
Dongola	460			
Port Sudan	480		550	
El-Fasher	600	365		300
El-Obeid	373			
El-Geneina	920	540		
Kassala	372			
Malakal	735			
Nyala	720	425		425
Juba	940	550		550
Wau	1100			
Kadugli	534			

With the arrival of independence, flight schedules and prices leaving from **Juba** are much less fixed. If you want to fly from here, there are a few companies that you can try. **Sun Air** (⌨ www.sunairgroup.com), **Feeder Airlines** (⌨ feederairlines.com) and **Fly 540** (⌨ www.fly540. com) between them have South Sudan fairly well covered. **Ethiopian Airlines** (⌨ www.flyethiopian.com) operates flights mainly to Malakal.

Eating & Drinking

In North Sudan, traditional cuisine has been strongly influenced by Middle Eastern cooking as well as some dishes from Ethiopia. Southern cuisine is more characteristic of African dishes found in Uganda and Kenya, as well as some that have worked there way over from Eritrea.

Beans and wheat form the staple diet of Sudan, in both the North and the South. The most popular dish in the North is known as *fuul* and consists of beans fried in sesame oil and usually sprinkled with white cheese. This dish is also eaten in some cities in the South.

Both the North and the South have a kind of sticky dough made with wheat flour, which is usually served with a spicy sauce. In the North, this is known as *asida*. In the South, it is called *baffra*.

The Sudanese are great lovers of meat, too, with lamb and mutton being the particular favourites. Chicken and beef are also easy to find. In the North, camel meat is widely available but pork is not. Pig meat is forbidden according to Islamic teachings and so imports are banned.

Both tea and coffee are popular in Sudan, and are available very cheaply from local roadside cafés. Spices, such as ginger and cardamom, are often added to the drinks.

In the North, *karkaday*, *helomour* and camel milk are widely drunk. Fresh fruit juice is popular in both North and South Sudan.

In towns and cities you will often find large earthenware pots by the side of the road. This is a particularly neat idea. The slightly porous pots have been ingeniously developed to keep water cool, allowing passers-by

LOCAL ALCOHOL

During your stay in Sudan, you may very well come across locally-brewed spirits. Two spirits that have become particularly popular in the main urban centres of the country are *aragi* and *marissa*. Both have their origins in the Nuba Mountains, where alcohol is an integral part of tribal culture.

Aragi is usually distilled from dates and can be extremely potent. *Marissa*, brewed from wheat, is more like a heady beer — not as strong as *aragi* but still fairly powerful. Among certain tribes in the Nuba Mountains, a very small quantity of this drink is still given to babies before they go to sleep so that their parents can get a restful night's sleep!

Be very cautious if you are offered these drinks whilst in Sudan. Not only can they be very strong for those that are not used to them, but they can also be contaminated with other substances such as methanol. Bear in mind that, in the North, alcohol is still illegal.

to refresh themselves as they feel the need to. Unfortunately, such communal pots aren't always very good at fending off the odd bug, and you might feel that it is safer to stick to the bottled filtered water that is widely available at most shops, costing between 1.50 and 2 SDG.

Although the purchase and consumption of alcohol has been illegal in North Sudan since 1983, such restrictions no longer apply in the South. The ban on alcohol in the North has simply pushed the industry underground and there is now a thriving trade in bootlegged liquor. Much of this illicit drink comes from the Nuba Mountains, which are mostly populated by non-Muslim tribes.

In Juba and Khartoum, the influx of foreign workers has led to an explosion of international restaurants. Pizzerias have become particularly popular, patronized by both the Sudanese and foreigners in equal measure. The pizzas, of course, are nothing compared to what you might find in Italy, and come with a unique range of toppings — such as the hotdog or sweet and sour pizza.

With the influx of Chinese and Indians into Sudan, it is unsurprising that Asian restaurants are also on the rise. Again, they tend to be nothing special and don't match the variety and quality that you might be used to in other major cities of the world.

Eritrean and Ethiopian restaurants are extremely popular. In the North, Syrian food is also gaining headway.

These days, many restaurants in Sudan try to offer many different styles of cooking in order to attract a broader base of clientele. This is a great shame and simply means that they end up doing everything poorly.

The reviews in this book endeavour to offer a comparison of restaurants within the country. Comparisons are made according to local, rather than international, standards.

TYPICAL FOOD

Ades is a popular staple dish of the North. Made with lentils and onions, and scooped up with bread, it is thoroughly delicious.

Agashay is a meat dish from Darfur. The meat, usually lamb or beef, is flavoured with spices and threaded onto skewers. These skewers are then stuck in the ground around a burning fire and slowly roasted — perfect for cooking in the desert, which is why the dish has become so popular in the remoter parts of North Sudan.

Asida is a sticky kind of dough, primarily made from wheat flour and water. It is usually served with a hole in the middle, into which is spooned some sort of sauce. *Mullah* — made with tomatoes, onion, meat and spices — is one of the most common types of sauce to have with *asida*.

Ayup, a popular dish in the South (especially among the Dinka and Nuer), is a type of dry bread usually made from sorghum wheat or millet flour. The dough is shaped into small round balls and then steamed. *Ayup* is often added to soups. Alternatively, it is mixed with a groundnut paste, which contains a lot of slow-release energy. The bread is popular with people looking after cattle or those travelling long distances, since it keeps for a long time.

Baffra is very similar to *asida*, but made with cassava flour rather than wheat and primarily eaten in the South.

Damaa is a popular meat stew, containing onions and other vegetables.

Fatira is an Egyptian-style pizza that is very popular in Sudan. The dough of the pizza is extremely thin, folded a few times and filled with various ingredients. It is cooked in a big wooden oven for several minutes. A sweet version of the *fatira* is also popular, typically containing cream, nuts and golden syrup.

Fatoush is a Middle Eastern salad that is becoming very popular in North Sudan. It is usually made with feta cheese, fried pieces of pita bread, olives and other vegetables.

Fuul (crushed up beans fried in sesame oil) is the staple of the Sudanese diet. There are a number of different *fuul* dishes — some served with grated cheese on the top, others cooked in

Eating & Drinking

Eating & Drinking

RECIPES

Damaa (serves four)

500 g mutton meat, chopped
4 red onions, chopped
4 tomatoes, chopped (or small tin of tomato purée)
3 garlic cloves, finely chopped
1 green chilli
salt and freshly-ground black pepper
2 carrots
2 potatoes
olive oil

Heat the oil in a large heavy-based saucepan. When the oil is hot, add the onions. When the onions are slightly brown, add the chopped tomatoes, if you are using these. (If you are using to-mato purée instead, don't add it yet). Add a litre of water to the pan, followed by the meat. Cook for about 20 minutes or until the meat is tender. Now is the time to add the tomato purée, if using. Season with salt and pepper. Add the garlic, green chilli, potatoes and carrots. Cover and leave to simmer for 15 minutes. Adjust sea-soning if necessary. Serve with bread or *gurrasa*.

Ades (serves four)

6 large onions, chopped
300 g lentils
small tin of tomato purée
1 tbs *dakua* (a little like pea-nut butter)
sunflower oil
salt and pepper

Heat the oil in a large heavy-based saucepan. Add the chopped onions. When the oil

is hot and the onion has started to lose its colour, add the lentils and one litre of water. Simmer uncovered for 30 minutes or until the water has been com-pletely absorbed. Keep stirring whilst cooking to prevent any lentils sticking to the bottom of the pan. Mix the tomato purée and the *dakua* with a little bit of water to form a smooth paste, and add to the pan. Serve with bread or *gurrasa*. Traditionally served as peasant food, this is a hearty meal, great for those win-ter evenings.

Gurrasa (make as much as you want)

flour
water
salt
yeast

Make sure the water is slightly tepid, so that the yeast will be enlivened, but not so hot that it will be killed. Mix the flour, wa-ter, salt and yeast together, until it forms a light, spongy dough. The trick is to add the water and flour slowly together, until you have obtained the desired quantity and consistency. Roll the dough out flat. Place the bread sheet in the oven and cook for 10 minutes. Turn the bread over and cook for a further 10 minutes.

spicy oil. *Fuul* is widely available in local Sudanese shops and eateries.

Gurrasa is a type of Sudanese bread, made with flour and water.

Kisra is the Sudanese adaptation of a type of sour flatbread widely eaten in Ethiopia and Eritrea, where it is known as *injera*. It is typically made with yeast and *teff* flour (*teff* being a particular type of African grass). The usual way of serving it is to drape it over a plate, a little like a large serviette, and then ladle quantities of food on top. The bread is used to scoop up the food and mop up the juices. The version served in Sudan tends to be browner, thinner and cooked for longer.

Kitcha fit-fit is an Eritrean and Ethiopian food often eaten for breakfast. It consists of shredded strips of bread, flavoured with a spicy sauce and often served with a scoop of yogurt. The bread may also be flavoured with tomatoes. It is popular in South Sudan.

Matuki is the African version of mashed potato, made from the inner pulp of a green banana. It is mainly eaten in South Sudan and not really popular in the North.

Menz is a little like a doughnut, made with flour and sugar but not as sweet. It is popular in the South.

Sha'urma is the Sudanese equivalent of the Turkish doner kebab. Strips of chicken or lamb are sliced from a roasting spit and either stuffed into a baguette or rolled up in a *fatira* wrap.

Sherri'a is a very thin and sweet type of pasta, served as dessert.

Tah'nlya is a sweet cake made from sesame seeds, often eaten for breakfast.

Tameeya is the Sudanese version of *falafel*, made with spiced chickpeas and served in baguettes or *fatira* wraps, often with humus or chilli sauce on the top.

Zalabia are balls of dough that are deep fried, coated in sugar and eaten with Sudanese tea or coffee. They are often served by local tea ladies.

TYPICAL DRINKS

Champion is the latest craze in North Sudanese soft drinks. Coming in a variety of different flavours, it tastes a little like shandy, although it is obviously non-alcoholic. When it first arrived in the country, people couldn't get enough of it. The fervour has since died down, but it remains astonishingly popular.

Gongleze is a refreshing white drink made from the fruit of the *tabaldi* (*baobab*) tree. It is a little sour, but sugar can be added according to tastes. It is an especially popular drink in the Nuba Mountains.

Helomour is another popular drink taken in the North during Ramadan. The name is derived from two Arabic words: '*helo*', meaning 'sweet' and '*mour*' meaning 'sour'. Combining syrupy sweetness with a unique blend of spices, the drink is a little difficult to adjust to. But, after the first few tentative sips, the taste becomes more enjoyable.

Jabana is the Sudanese variety of coffee, similar to that served in Turkey. Thick and strong, it is sometimes flavoured with cardamom or ginger and is guaranteed to keep you awake at night.

Karkaday is made from the hibiscus plant and is particularly popular in the North during Ramadan. It can be drunk as a sweetened cold drink, a little like grenadine, or as a hot tea. Hibiscus contains particularly high levels of vitamin C, which helps to strengthen the immune system. Hibiscus also helps to regulate blood pressure, which is one of the reasons why it is such a good drink to have during fasting

Sahlab is a thick and creamy hot drink, tasting a little like rice pudding. It is made from a white powder

---

TEA LADIES

There can be few Sudanese experiences as memorable as sitting on an upturned crate on the side of the street, sipping *shae* (tea) or *gahwa* (coffee) and munching on *zalabia* (sugar-coated fried balls of dough), whilst listening to the hum of Sudanese conversations all around you.

Most tea ladies are hard-working, friendly and welcoming. They will usually be burning sweet-smelling incense to chase away the flies. In any main town or city, you can be certain of finding a tea lady, no matter what the time of day. Remember, though, that not all tea ladies are the same. Some serve much better drinks, and others are in a more desirable location.

A tea from a tea lady costs 1 SDG and a coffee between 1.5 and 2 SDG. Tea can be drunk with milk (*shae bi laban*) or mint (*shae bi nana*). A generous plate of *zalabia* costs around 2 SDG. Many tea ladies also serve *karkaday* (hibiscus) and *ganzabeel* (ginger tea) — both extremely good for colds.

Coffee and tea are usually served with large amounts of sugar. The typical way of serving Ethiopian-style coffee is to hand you a cup half-filled with sugar along with a separate pot of freshly-brewed coffee. When you pour the coffee into the cup, swirl the sugar slightly to sweeten the coffee before drinking. Then repeat.

---

obtained from the dried tubers of a particular type of wild orchid. Sahlab is a popular winter drink in Egypt, but is also available in a number of the more established Sudanese cafés.

SHEESHA

Smoking *sheesha* has long been an important part of the culture in North Sudan. The chamber at the bottom of a *sheesha* pipe is filled with water, whilst flavoured tobacco is placed in the cradle at the top. This tobacco is then covered with aluminium foil, which is pierced with a fork. Burning coal placed on top heats the tobacco, which is then smoked by inhaling through a long length of pipe. The tobacco is filtered by passing through the water.

Many people who try *sheesha* find this way of smoking much milder than conventional cigarettes, though it remains an open point about whether it is any better for you.

Since alcohol is not readily available in the North, *sheesha* tends to take pride of place in Sudanese social gatherings. It is mostly the men that partake in the activity. Women are not generally invited to smoke *sheesha* although exceptions can be made for foreigners.

Sheesha cafés used to be hugely popular all over Khartoum, but the local authorities have recently banned smoking in public, claiming that it is a corrupting influence on the young. Khartoum's many *sheesha* cafés have therefore had to reinvent themselves as places to come for a drink.

Not everyone is happy with the ban and there are some signs that it could be lifted. But, for now, it remains in place. Smoking in private is still permitted, though.

Sheesha cafés are still widely available in towns outside North Sudan's capital, though.

Sheesha tobacco comes in a wide variety of flavours, including mint, pistachio, apple, melon and grape. For something a little bit different, you could try *jirak*, which is a kind of *sheesha* flavoured with honey.

Eating & Drinking

Although people have been living in the area for thousands of years, modern-day Khartoum has a relatively recent history.

Strategically-positioned at the confluence of the Blue and White Niles, the city was founded in 1821 as a military outpost by Mohammed Ali, who was then ruler of Egypt. Its name originates from the thin spit of land at the convergence of the rivers, which, with a stretch of the imagination, resembles the end of an elephant's trunk — or *khurtum* in Arabic.

Khartoum was the capital of Sudan from 1821 until 1885, when the Mahdi came to power and moved it to neighbouring Omdurman (p56). In 1898, when British forces recaptured the city, the capital was moved back across the Nile to Khartoum.

Khartoum is often referred to as the tripartite capital of North Sudan, because it is made up of three distinct parts. Khartoum proper extends south-west of the point at which the two Niles converge. Omdurman lies to the west of the city and Bahri (the nation's industrial hub) to the north.

From an aesthetic point of view, Khartoum can be a difficult city to get used to. Its beauty does not lie in grand monuments or glorious buildings that typify other nations' capitals. Khartoum's beauty comes from less overt characteristics: the friendliness and hospitality of the inhabitants, the unique blend of ethnicity harmoniously converging on the city, the charmingly relaxed way in which people carry on their day-to-day lives.

As the petrol dollars have poured into Khartoum, dramatic changes have been made to the city. This rush of foreign investment (mainly from China, India and Malaysia) has brought with it a fresh sense of optimism — a feeling that anything is now possible. The city is changing accordingly, with new glitzy buildings being thrown up in some quarters to replace the old architecture from the 1970s, when Khartoum experienced its last building boom.

KHARTOUM

Khartoum proper is broken down into a number of distinct areas, each with its own character.

Central Khartoum extends from Nil Street southwards to just past the old railway line, which is now used only to transport goods. The streets are laid out in the formation of Britain's Union Jack flag, a reminder of the nation's colonial past.

There are two main local bus stations in downtown Khartoum. Buses departing from the area around the football stadium — known as 'Stad' (p88) — mostly serve Omdurman. City buses for Bahri and elsewhere in Khartoum generally leave from the area around the old railway station, known as 'Jackson'.

Nil Street is lined with many old colonial-style houses, now used as government ministries. The Presidential Palace is also found here. If you walk west along the banks of the Nile, you will come to the **Mogran**, which is the point at which the two Niles converge. If you walk east, you will come to a lovely picnic area, where many families with young children gather in the evening or at weekends.

In the centre of the Nile sits Tuti Island, where members of a rural farming community still employ traditional farming practices to tend their fields. Stop-start efforts to develop the island have disrupted this way of life, but have not eliminated it completely (p133).

The districts of **Khartoum 2** and **Khartoum 3** are just south of the city centre, across the old railway line. There are a number of reasonable restaurants located in these areas.

Further south is **Amarat**, otherwise known as 'Khartoum's New Extension'. Many expats choose to live here and so it has a much more cosmopolitan feel to it. This is where many of the international shops and restaurants can be found. Amarat is laid out in a grid, with odd numbers denoting which road you are on.

To the east of this area, just across Afriqia Street, lies Khartoum's International Airport.

On the other side of the airport lies **Riyad**, the other major expat area in the city. Recently, rising property prices in Amarat have seen Riyad gain much more prominence as an area in which expats choose to live and spend time. As a result, many more restaurants and international supermarkets have opened in the district.

It is in this area that the UN's Mission In Sudan (UNMIS) used to have its headquarters. Now that UNMIS has left the country, it is not certain what will become of the building. A number of non-governmental organisations (NGOs) are also located in this area.

For completeness, it is worth pointing that, although UNMIS has now ceased to be, the UN continues to participate in an operation in Darfur, along with the African Union, which is known as UNAMID. A UN mission in South Sudan has also been established, known as UNMISS.

A distinctive feature of Riyad is a large park on its fringes, quite close to Afriqia Street, which houses a small fairground. Afra Mall, a shopping precinct popular with expats, nestles between Amarat and Riyad.

Not far from Riyad are the other neighbourhoods of **Manshea**, **Mamoura**, and **Arkowit**. **Garden City**, home to Burri Beach, lies a bit further out.

OMDURMAN

The origin of the name 'Omdurman' is not known for certain. Some say it is named after two small hills (*durman*) in the neighbourhood, so that the name would be 'mother of the two small hills'. Others suggest that the place could have been named after the mother of a man called Durman, who came from the west many years ago. He is reputed to have made a fortune, and his mother, an enterprising woman, is said to have started a ferry service between Omdurman, the island of Tuti, and the settlements of what is now Central Khartoum.

Omdurman is the historical and cultural capital of Sudan, and has an altogether different feel from neighbouring Khartoum. The Middle Eastern vibrancy that lends Omdurman its charm has caused some to deride the city for being less developed than the nation's true capital, but to take this view is to miss the very essence of the great city. The winding dusty alleyways that make up Omdurman are far more fascinating to walk around than the ugly grey grid that is Central Khartoum.

It is in Omdurman that you will find most of the historic attractions of the three cities, such as the Mahdi's tomb (p130) and the Khalifa's house (p130). Omdurman is also home to the fascinating Souq Omdurman (p183) and the camel market (p131) — both definitely worth a visit. You might want to take in the spectacular religious ceremony of the Whirling Dervishes, too, which takes place every Friday evening (p132).

It is worth going for a stroll along the Nile in Omdurman, to compare it to Nil Street in Central Khartoum. You will find it much quieter on this side, and you will not encounter ministerial security guards eyeing you suspiciously.

BAHRI

Opposite Khartoum, across the Blue Nile, is the third city making up the tripartite capital. Khartoum North, more commonly called 'Bahri' (meaning 'north' in old Egyptian), is often written off as an industrial wasteland where there is nothing much to see or do, but there are a number of reasons why you may end up in the area.

Whilst it may not have the glitz or shine of Khartoum proper, or the historical appeal of Omdurman, Bahri can be a pleasant place

to explore. There are a couple of good markets and walks along the Nile tend to be more relaxed than elsewhere.

Bahri is also the only one of the three cities to have remained relatively untouched over the last two decades of urban development that has transformed Omdurman and Khartoum.

Buses will drop you off at the central bus station. From there, you can head south towards the tallest building in Bahri — what used to be the five-star Friendship Palace Hotel — on the banks of the Blue Nile opposite Tuti Island. Here, you have a fantastic view of the Presidential Palace. It is fairly easy to wander down to the banks of the river, where there are huge expanses of white sand flanked by trees and fields. The setting is especially picturesque when there are traditional fishing boats nearby. This is also a popular place to swim.

The other attraction in Bahri is the huge clothing market, not far from the central bus station. Here you can pick up a traditional *jalabia* or *tobe* for relatively little money (p183). You can also watch weavers at work — adjusting or repairing clothes.

Bahri is also the place to come if you want to watch traditional Nuba wrestling, which takes place before sunset every Friday evening (p129).

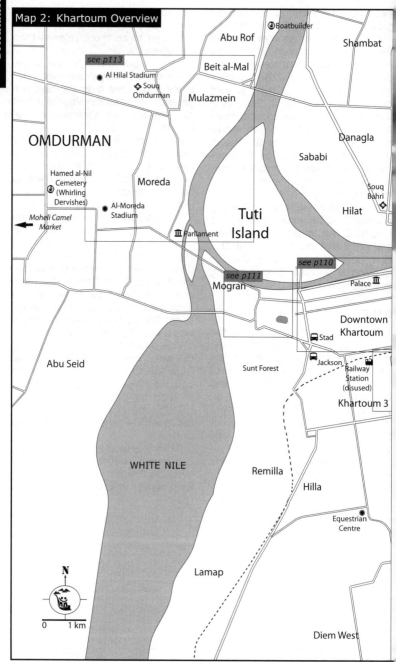

Map 2: Khartoum Overview

Boatbuilder

Abu Rof

Shambat

see p113

Al Hilal Stadium

Beit al-Mal

Souq Omdurman

Mulazmein

Danagla

OMDURMAN

Sababi

Hamed al-Nil Cemetery (Whirling Dervishes)

Moreda

Souq Bahri

Moheli Camel Market

Al-Moreda Stadium

Hilat

Tuti Island

Parliament

see p110

see p111

Palace

Mogran

Downtown Khartoum

Stad

Abu Seid

Jackson

Railway Station (disused)

Sunt Forest

Khartoum 3

WHITE NILE

Remilla

Hilla

Equestrian Centre

N

Lamap

0   1 km

Diem West

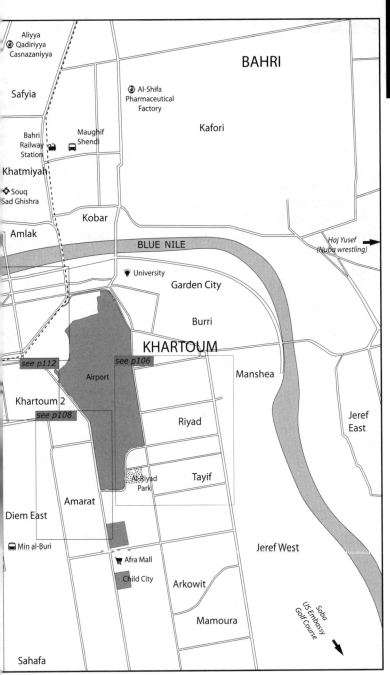

Aliyya
Qadiriyya
Casnazaniyya

Safyia

BAHRI

Al-Shifa
Pharmaceutical
Factory

Kafori

Bahri
Railway
Station

Maughif
Shendi

Khatmiyah

Souq
Sad Ghishra

Kobar

Amlak

BLUE NILE

Haj Yusef
(Nuba wrestling)

University

Garden City

Burri

KHARTOUM

see p112

see p106

Manshea

Airport

Khartoum 2

see p108

Riyad

Jeref
East

Tayif

Al-Riyad
Park

Diem East

Amarat

Min al-Buri

Jeref West

Afra Mall

Child City

Arkowit

Mamoura

US Embassy
Soba
Golf Course

Sahafa

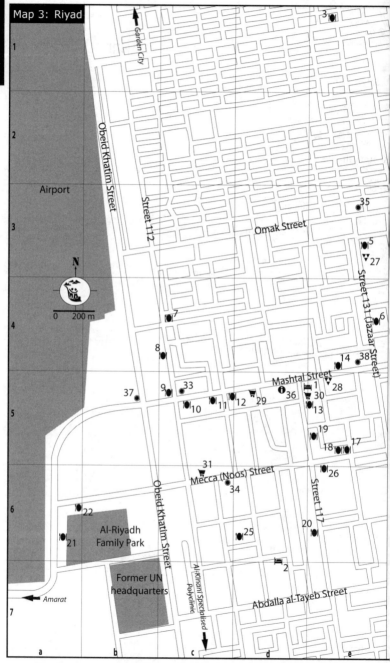

Map 3: Riyad

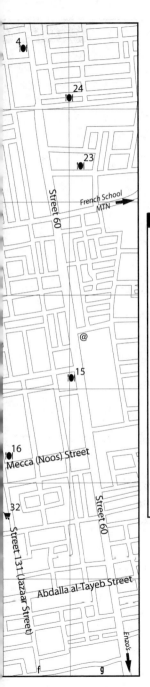

Riyad

Where to sleep 🛏
1. Lan Tian *d5*
2. Bougainvilla Guesthouse *d6*

Where to eat/drink 🍴 🍺
3. Mona Lisa *e1*
4. Syrian Fresh *f1*
5. Solitaire *e3*
6. Square *e4*
7. Oshin *c4*
8. Overseas *c4*
9. Havana *c5*
10. Syrian Gate *c5*
11. Dodi's *c5*
12. Debonairs *e5*
13. Beatles *e5*
14. Pizza Connection *e4*
15. Italy Pizza Centre *g4*
16. Laziz *f5*
17. Barista *e5*
18. M Burger *e5*
19. Smile *e5*
20. Time Out *e6*
21. Potato's *a6*
22. Tutti Frutti *a6*
23. Aroma Café *g2*
24. Panda *f1*
25. Thai restaurant *d6*

26. My Place *e6*

What to do ✌
27. Billiard Station *e3*
28. O2 *e5*

Shopping 🛒
29. Shamil House *d5*
30. Amarat Centre 2 *d5*
31. Sobtan *c6*
32. Shrimps *f6*

Services ◉
33. Memorial Photo *c5*
34. Mamlaka Laundries *c6*
35. Shams Dry Clean

Information ❶
36. Ministry of Tourism *d5*

Other ◉
37. Sudan Airways *b5*
38. Kawader Recruitment *e4*

Other symbols
@ Internet

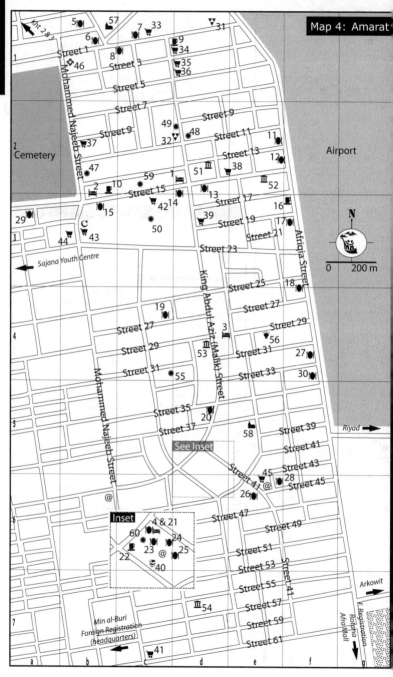

Orientation

Map 4: Amarat

N

0   200 m

Cemetery

Airport

Sajana Youth Centre

Riyad

Arkowit

Inset

See Inset

Min al-Buri
Foreign Registration
(headquarters)

Street 1
Street 3
Street 5
Street 7
Street 9
Street 9
Street 11
Street 13
Street 15
Street 17
Street 19
Street 21
Street 23
Street 25
Street 27
Street 29
Street 31
Street 33
Street 35
Street 37
Street 39
Street 41
Street 43
Street 45
Street 47
Street 49
Street 51
Street 53
Street 55
Street 57
Street 59
Street 61

Mohammed Najeeb Street
King Abdul Aziz (Malik) Street
Afriqia Street
Rotana
Afra Mall
E. Registration

Amarat

Where to sleep 🛏
1. Kanon *d2*
2. Al-Muhajir Hotel Flats *b2*
3. VIP *d4*
4. Safari *c6*

Where to eat and drink 🍴 🍷
5. Carnivore *b1*
6. Laziz *b1*
7. Lucky Meal *c1*
8. Al-Hana *c1*
9. Flash Fresh *c1*
10. Tropicana *b2*
11. Debonairs / Steers *e2*
12. Amwaj *e2*
13. Solitaire *d2*
14. Syrian Fresh Food *d2*
15. Laialy's *b3*
16. Lila Patisserie *f3*
17. Royal Broast *f3*
18. Momen / Napoli Pasta *f4*
19. Universal *c4*
20. Delak Pizza *d5*
21. Cedars *c6*
22. Star Cafe *c6*
23. Saaj al-Samak *c6*
24. Ice-Cream 41 *c6*
25. Dodi's *d6*
26. Osama Cafeteria *e6*
27. Gad *f4*
28. Tayba *e6*
29. Merkato *a3*
30. Cone Zone *f4*

What to do ⋎
31. German Club *d1*
32. Coptic Club *d2*

Shopping 🛒 ⬥ ✧
33. Amarat Centre *c1*
34. Nairobi Flowers *d1*
35. Wofa Flowers *d1*
36. Kranish for Flowers *d1*
37. Turkish Fashion Shops *b2*

38. Piano Piano *d2*
39. Home Care *d3*
40. Nile Bookshop *c6*
41. Jebel Owlia (fish) *c7*
42. Al-Hawi *c3*
43. Malhamat al-Khuti (meat) *b3*
44. As-Sharik al-Arabia Litmia Assarua al-Hauania (chicken) *b3*
45. Lipton *e6*
46. Small market area *b1*

Services ⬤
47. Kodak *b2*
48. MTN *d2*
49. Zain *d2*
50. Photo Style / The Studio Camera Artist *c3*

Embassies 🏛
51. French *d2*
52. Venezuelan *e2*
53. Saudi Arabia *d4*
54. Chad *d7*

Tourism ⬤
55. Italian Tourism Company *c4*

Courses ⚘
56. Catholic Language Institute Khartoum (CLIK) *e4*

Religion 📙
57. All Saints Cathedral *b1*
58. Peter & Paul's *e5*

Health and beauty ⬤
59. Queens *c2*

Other ⬤
60. Authors' Former House *c6*

Other Symbols
@ internet
☪ Mosque

Map 5: Downtown Khartoum

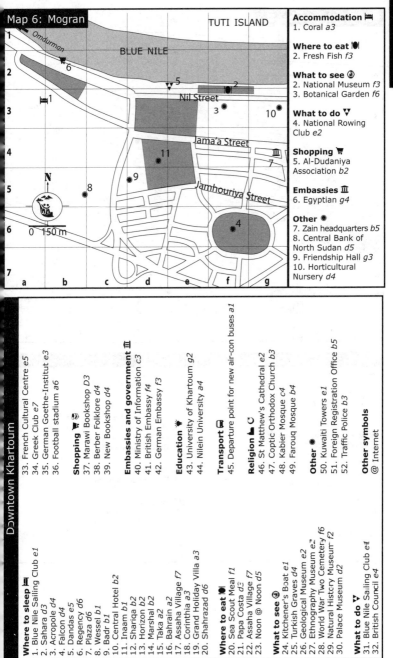

Map 6: Mogran

TUTI ISLAND

Omdurman

BLUE NILE

Nil Street

Jama'a Street

Jamhouriya Street

N

0   150 m

Accommodation 🛏
1. Coral *a3*

Where to eat 🍴
2. Fresh Fish *f3*

What to see ④
2. National Museum *f3*
3. Botanical Garden *f6*

What to do ⋎
4. National Rowing Club *e2*

Shopping 🛒
5. Al-Dudaniya Association *b2*

Embassies 🏛
6. Egyptian *g4*

Other ●
7. Zain headquarters *b5*
8. Central Bank of North Sudan *d5*
9. Friendship Hall *g3*
10. Horticultural Nursery *d4*

Downtown Khartoum

Where to sleep 🛏
1. Blue Nile Sailing Club *e1*
2. Sahara *d3*
3. Acropole *d4*
4. Falcon *d4*
5. Dandas *e5*
6. Regency *d6*
7. Plaza *d6*
8. Wessel *b1*
9. Badr *b1*
10. Central Hotel *b2*
11. Inaam *b1*
12. Shariqa *b2*
13. Horizon *b2*
14. Marshal *b2*
15. Taka *a2*
16. Bahrain *a2*
17. Assaha Village *f7*
18. Corinthia *a3*
19. Grand Holiday Villa *a3*
20. Shahrazad *d6*

Where to eat 🍴
20. Sea Scout Meal *f1*
21. Papa Costa *d5*
22. Assaha Village *f7*
23. Noon @ Noon *d5*

What to see ④
24. Kitchener's Boat *e1*
25. Turkish Graves *d4*
26. Geological Museum *e2*
27. Ethnography Museum *e2*
28. World War Two Cemetery *f6*
29. Natural History Museum *f2*
30. Palace Museum *d2*

What to do ⋎
31. Blue Nile Sailing Club *e1*
32. British Council *e4*

33. French Cultural Centre *e5*
34. Greek Club *e7*
35. German Goethe-Institut *e3*
36. Football stadium *a6*

Shopping 🛒 📚
37. Marawi Bookshop *D3*
38. Berber Folklore *d4*
39. New Bookshop *d4*

Embassies and government 🏛
40. Ministry of Information *c3*
41. British Embassy *f4*
42. German Embassy *f3*

Education 🎓
43. University of Khartoum *g2*
44. Nilein University *a4*

Transport 🚌
45. Departure point for new air-con buses *a1*

Religion ⛪ ☪
46. St Matthew's Cathedral *e2*
47. Coptic Orthodox Church *b3*
48. Kabier Mosque *c4*
49. Farouq Mosque *b4*

Other ●
50. Kuwaiti Towers *e1*
51. Foreign Registration Office *b5*
52. Traffic Police *b3*

Other symbols
@ Internet

Orientation

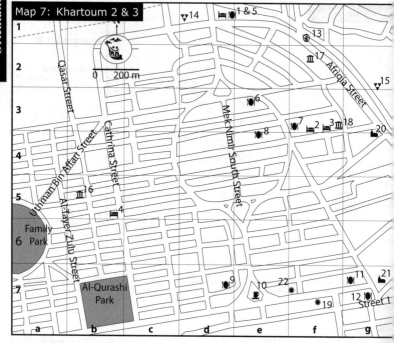

Map 7: Khartoum 2 & 3

Khartoum 2 & 3

Where to sleep 🛏
1. Alsaha Village *d1*
2. Al-Ahlam *f3*
3. Youth Hostel *f3*
4. 5M Hotel *b5*

Where to eat and drink 🍴 🍷
5. Alsaha Village *d1*
6. Pizza Corner *e3*
7. Chicken Shack *f3*
8. Real Burger *e4*
9. Italy Pizza Centre *d7*
10. Ozone *e7*
11. Carnivore *g7*
12. Laziz *g7*

What to see ◉
13. Fossilised Trees *f1*

What to do ☉
14. Greek Club *d1*
15. Tennis Club *g2*

Embassies and government 🏛
16. Ministry of Humanitarian Affairs *b5*
17. Canadian Embassy *f2*
18. Dutch Embassy *f3*

Education ♔
19. British Education School *f7*

Religion ⛪
20. Ethiopian Church *g4*
21. All Saints Cathedral *g7*

Services ◉
2. Ice Bear *f7*

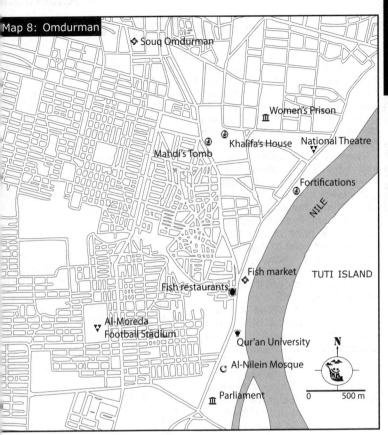

Map 8: Omdurman

- Souq Omdurman
- Women's Prison
- Khalifa's House
- National Theatre
- Mahdi's Tomb
- Fortifications
- NILE
- Fish market
- TUTI ISLAND
- Fish restaurants
- Al-Moreda Football Stadium
- Qur'an University
- Al-Nilein Mosque
- Parliament
- N
- 0   500 m

Getting Around

At first sight, Khartoum can seem like an impossible city to get around in, especially if you don't have your own car. However, once you get used to the city, you will find that things aren't as arduous as they first appear.

There is an abundance of taxis and *amjads* throughout the city. Khartoum also has an expansive bus network, which, if you spend some time familiarising yourself with, you will find not only efficient but also a huge money-saver. To help you get used to the seemingly confusing bus network, we have developed a series of innovative bus maps, which you'll find at the end of this chapter.

Most of the buses in Khartoum are fairly old, rickety things. However, recently, sparkling new air-conditioned buses have been introduced for certain routes. Views remain divided as to whether this was a wise use of money. The buses have become popular with some local Sudanese, but many traditionalists still prefer to bounce along in the back of one of the older-style buses than to pay twice as much for travelling in what might be seen as Western-style luxury.

Rickshaws are another popular way of getting around the city, although tend to be most suited for shorter journeys. Tighter regulations are increasingly limiting the routes that rickshaws can travel.

On Tuti Island, you can also experience the *boksi* pick-up truck.

RENTING AND BUYING CARS

If you want to have your own transport whilst in Khartoum, you need to decide whether you want to rent or buy a vehicle. The following companies can help with this decision.

Remember that, if you are going to rent a four-wheel drive vehicle for travel outside of Khartoum, then you must also pay for a driver. Rental prices usually depend on the type of vehicle that you want to rent, as well as where you are travelling. Prices do not normally include fuel, which can be surprisingly expensive in Sudan.

Car rental

5M (🏠 Cathrina Street, Khartoum 2; ☎ 0183 460 438 or 0183 462 962 or 0913 118 464 or 0912 010 385; @ mickey5m1@gmail.com; 💻 www.5mrentacar.com) offers a good service for foreigners and drivers usually speak English. The cheapest rate, for a small saloon car, is 120 SDG per day. For a high-end BMW, expect to pay 600 SDG. 5M also offers reduced monthly rates, which can be a big advantage if you are staying in Khartoum for a while. Prices are exclusive of tax.

Nice Limousine (☎ 0912 331 852; @ mano@nicelimousine.com) is a newcomer to the car rental scene. Run by a young Sudanese man, who has spent many years living in London, the company is clearly aiming at the foreign clientele market. However, prices are on the high side and you really have to be a tough negotiator to get the price that you want.

Europcar (☎ 0183 74661 or 0915 000 692; 💻 www.europcar.com), the international car rental chain, has a few offices dotted around Khartoum. The most convenient are probably the one at the airport, the one inside the lobby of the Coral Hotel and the one in downtown Khartoum, just off Mek Nimir Street. Prices are not unreasonable, starting at 120 SDG for a basic Skoda without driver, rising to 400 SDG for a Hyundai Veracruz, plus driver.

Abu Harba Limousine (☎ East of the Sudanese French Bank, Khartoum 2; ☎ 0912 345 227; @ nwaisa@abuharba.com; 🖥 www.abuharba.com) offers reliable cars at competitive rates.

Seven for Car Rent (☎ On the corner of Beu-Yokwan Street and Jazeera Street, Khartoum 3; ☎ 0914 450 024; @ malibs@hotmail.com or mohamed.alibs@seven.elnefeigroup.com) is another option worth trying.

Abu Tarha Car Rental (☎ Grand Holiday Villa Hotel, Nile Street; ☎ 0183 762 698 or 0912 359 743; @ contact@abutarha.com; 🖥 www.abutarha.com) offers good service and reliable vehicles, but prices are high. It's really aimed at short-term visitors to Sudan that have the means to splash out a little.

Car retail

Nefeidi Motors (☎ Barlaman Street, Central Khartoum; ☎ 0183 762 021; @ nefgroup@hotmail.com; 🖥 www.elnefeindigroup.com) is the official agent for BMW and Nissan.

Golden Arrow (☎ Afriqia Street, north end; ☎ 0183 579 481/87/97; 🖥 www.goldenarrowsudan.com) is the official agent for Toyota.

Dal Motors (☎ Afriqia Street, Soba; ☎ 0183 232 777) is the official agent for Mitsubishi and Mercedes.

Al-Safwa Motors (☎ Kafouri, Bahri; ☎ 0185 343 878) is the official agent for Audi and Volkswagen.

Spare parts

If you need any spare parts, the best thing to do is either to go to one of the dealers listed above, or to seek out a local mechanic. Local mechanics are not difficult to find and will probably be a lot cheaper than going to an official dealer. The best areas to look for a local mechanic are the old industrial area to the west of the city centre, the industrial area in Bahri (🌊 15°38'47"N 32°33'16"E) or the area around Al-Khor Street, just east of Khartoum 3 (🌊 15°35'16"N 32°31'21"E). If you want other services, such as darkening the glass or new covers for the seats, the western end of Street 15 in Amarat has a number of workshops.

TAXIS

Hailing a taxi or *amjad* in Khartoum is usually no problem. However, if you want to pre-arrange a taxi pick-up, then **Limo Trip** (☎ 0183 591 313 or 0123 003 488; 🖥 limotrip.net) comes highly recommended. The taxis are also slightly plusher than those you generally find driving around.

BUSES

Full details about bus travel in Sudan has already been given in the "Transportation" section of this book (p88). The bus network in Khartoum is exceedingly expansive, and for this reason is a very convenient way of getting around. Moreover, it is cheap, which makes it exceedingly attractive for those on a budget. To make negotiating the system that much easier, we have developed some innovative bus maps, which are included on the following pages. The box on the following page explains how to use them.

Many bus routes start and end in Central Khartoum. The area around the old railway station — which is now known as Jackson — usually serves destinations south of the Nile, as well as destinations in Omdurman. If you are travelling to Bahri, you will probably need to take a bus from the area around the football stadium, known as Stad.

The new air-conditioned buses tend to leave from just north of Jackson, around the Gandol roundabout.

The maps that follow assume that you are taking one of the normal buses. For the air-con buses, you will need to make appropriate adjustments

BUS MAPS

Our bus maps have been designed in order to allow you to follow your bus route by looking out of the windows and noting the landmarks to the left and the right. The bus routes can be followed in either direction, by turning the book around as necessary. However, you should be aware that the approach to the bus station sometimes varies slightly according to whether you are coming or going. This is not always reflected in the bus map. Moreover, the bus driver may sometimes alter the normal route according to weather conditions, road works and traffic.

The following diagram gives an overview of how the bus maps work.

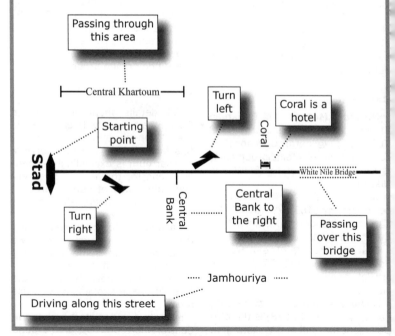

Getting Around

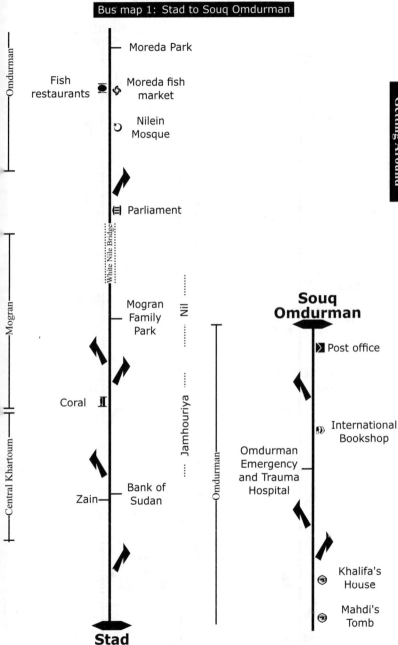

Bus map 1: Stad to Souq Omdurman

Omdurman

Moreda Park

Fish
restaurants

Moreda fish
market

Nilein
Mosque

Parliament

White Nile Bridge

Mogran

Mogran
Family
Park

Nil

Coral

Jamhouriya

Central Khartoum

Zain

Bank of
Sudan

Omdurman

Stad

Souq
Omdurman

Post office

International
Bookshop

Omdurman
Emergency
and Trauma
Hospital

Khalifa's
House

Mahdi's
Tomb

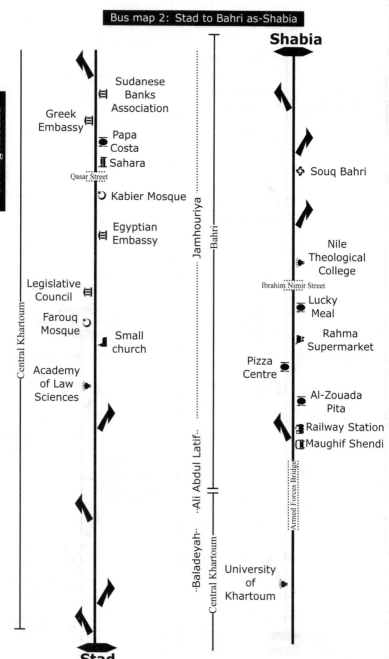

Bus map 2: Stad to Bahri as-Shabia

Shabia

Sudanese
Banks
Association

Greek
Embassy

Papa
Costa

Sahara

Qasar Street

Souq Bahri

Kabier Mosque

Egyptian
Embassy

Jamhouriya
Bahri

Nile
Theological
College

Ibrahim Nimir Street

Legislative
Council

Lucky
Meal

Farouq
Mosque

Rahma
Supermarket

Small
church

Pizza
Centre

Al-Zouada
Pita

Academy
of Law
Sciences

Railway Station

Maughif Shendi

Central Khartoum

Ali Abdul Latif

Armed Forces Bridge

Baladeyah

Central Khartoum

University
of
Khartoum

Stad

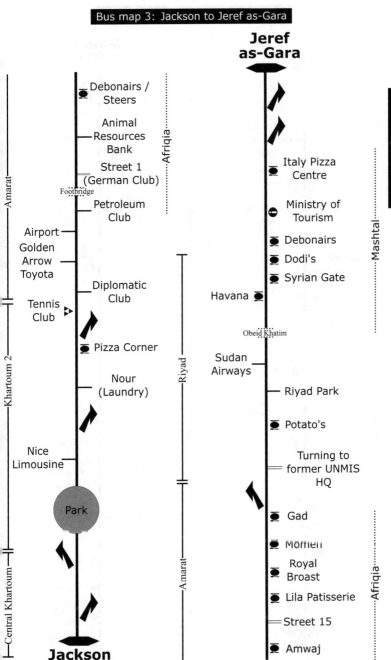

Bus map 3: Jackson to Jeref as-Gara

Jeref as-Gara

Debonairs / Steers

Animal Resources Bank

Street 1 (German Club)

Footbridge

Petroleum Club

Airport

Golden Arrow Toyota

Diplomatic Club

Tennis Club

Pizza Corner

Nour (Laundry)

Nice Limousine

Park

Jackson

Amarat

Khartoum 2

Central Khartoum

Afriqia

Riyad

Amarat

Italy Pizza Centre

Ministry of Tourism

Debonairs

Dodi's

Syrian Gate

Havana

Obeid Khatim

Sudan Airways

Riyad Park

Potato's

Turning to former UNMIS HQ

Gad

Momen

Royal Broast

Lila Patisserie

Street 15

Amwaj

Mashtal

Afriqia

Getting Around

Getting Around

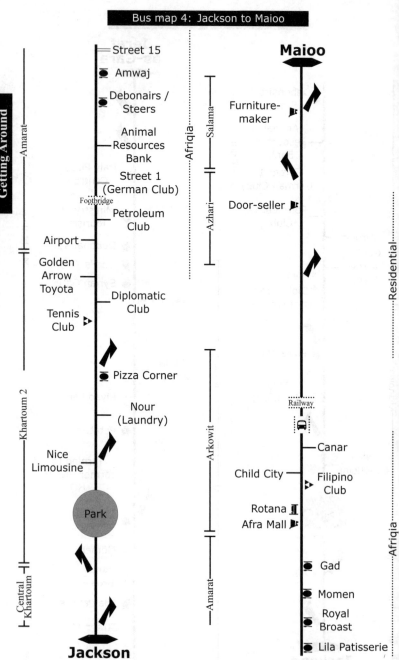

Bus map 4: Jackson to Maioo

Maioo

Street 15
Amwaj
Debonairs / Steers
Animal Resources Bank
Street 1 (German Club)
Footbridge
Petroleum Club
Airport
Golden Arrow Toyota
Diplomatic Club
Tennis Club
Pizza Corner
Nour (Laundry)
Nice Limousine
Park

Jackson

Furniture-maker
Door-seller

Railway
Canar
Child City
Filipino Club
Rotana
Afra Mall
Gad
Momen
Royal Broast
Lila Patisserie

Amarat — Khartoum 2 — Central Khartoum

Afriqia — Salama — Azhari — Arkowit — Amarat

Residential — Afriqia

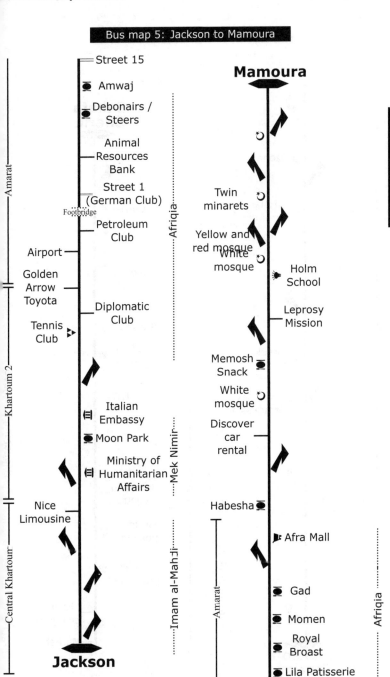

Bus map 5: Jackson to Mamoura

Street 15
Amwaj
Debonairs / Steers
Animal Resources Bank
Street 1 (German Club)
Footbridge
Petroleum Club
Airport
Golden Arrow Toyota
Diplomatic Club
Tennis Club
Italian Embassy
Moon Park
Ministry of Humanitarian Affairs
Nice Limousine

Amarat
Khartoum 2
Central Khartoum

Afriqia
Mek Nimir
Imam al-Mahji

Mamoura

Twin minarets
Yellow and red mosque
White mosque
Holm School
Leprosy Mission
Memosh Snack
White mosque
Discover car rental
Habesha
Afra Mall
Gad
Momen
Royal Broast
Lila Patisserie

Amarat
Afriqia

Jackson

Bus map 6: Jackson to Sahafa Sherik

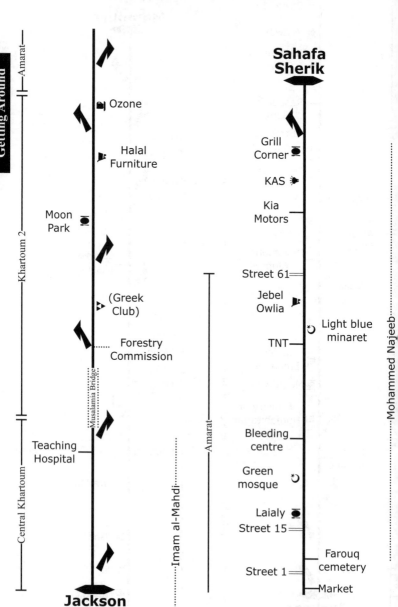

Getting Around

Amarat

Khartoum 2

Central Khartoum

Musalamia Bridge

Ozone

Halal Furniture

Moon Park

(Greek Club)

Forestry Commission

Teaching Hospital

Imam al-Mahdi

Amarat

Jackson Station

Sahafa Sherik

Grill Corner

KAS

Kia Motors

Street 61

Jebel Owlia

TNT

Light blue minaret

Bleeding centre

Green mosque

Laialy

Street 15

Street 1

Farouq cemetery

Market

Mohammed Najeeb

Bus map 7: Jackson to Sahafa Zalat

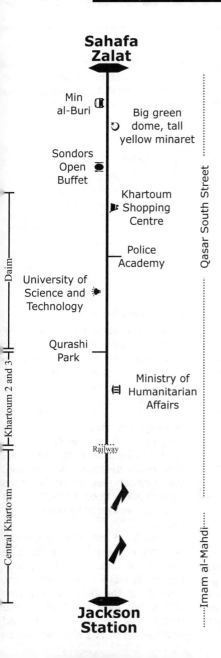

If you are looking to do a spot of sightseeing in the capital, you will probably find yourself dividing your time between Omdurman and Khartoum.

Omdurman contains many of the historical attractions — such as the tomb of the Mahdi and the house of the Khalifa — whilst the streets of Khartoum are awash with museums, grand religious buildings and old colonial houses stretching along the south bank of the Nile.

Bahri is less well known as a sight-seeing destination, although you can see the old Al-Shifa factory there and take in the weekly Nuba wrestling matches.

CENTRAL KHARTOUM

Botanical Gardens

Khartoum's botanical gardens are a relaxing place to come and get away from city life for awhile. A wide range of trees and plants flourish here, attracting a surprising variety of birds and butterflies.

The shade that the trees afford makes a welcome respite from the Sudanese heat but, unfortunately, there is a paucity of seating.

$ *Free.*

☎ *Varies.*

╪ *Just next to the Central Bank of North Sudan, east of the Coral Hotel. Take a bus from Jackson Station in Central Khartoum in the direction of Omdurman, along Jama'a Street, and get off when you see the shiny-blue Bank of Sudan building.*

Kitchener's Boat

General Herbert Kitchener's gunboat, the 'Melik', is most famous for its involvement in the campaign to reclaim Khartoum for the British, ten years after they were ousted by the Mahdi (p59).

After retiring from government service, the boat was handed over to the Blue Nile Sailing Club (p146) to be used as its headquarters. Badly damaged by corrosion, the gunboat was ironically saved by a massive flood in 1987, which washed it ashore to its current resting spot.

There is no indication of the importance of the gunboat at the Blue Nile Sailing Club, and no explanation of its history. Once inside the grounds of the club, you are free to clamber over the boat as you please. The vessel is fairly small and leaning to one side, which can make climbing the stairs rather interesting.

The Blue Nile Sailing Club also has a picnic pavilion and a fairly basic children's play area. There is even a small mosque for club members in the grounds, which was modelled on the larger Al-Nilein Mosque in Omdurman (p136).

💰 *Cost: 1 SDG.*

☎ *Varies, but usually between 9 am and 5 pm.*

🖥 *www.melik.org.uk*

☩ *On the banks of the Nile, about a 20-minute walk from Souq al-Arabi. Buses travel west along Jama'a Street, which is one street up, and east along Jamhouriya Street, which is two streets up. You can catch a bus from Stad in Central Khartoum, direction Souq Bahri.*

Friendship Hall

Along the banks of the Nile, west of the city centre, you will find a seventies-style concrete block. The building was constructed by Chinese architects and was intended as a symbol of peace between Sudan and the communist state, at a time when Sudan was briefly flirting with communism.

The architecture of the Friendship Hall is distinct from the colonial-style buildings nearby, or the much more modern Corinthia Hotel.

This building is now mainly used as a venue for political meetings and international conferences. There used to be a cinema in the complex, but it has recently closed down.

☩ *On the banks of the Nile, just next to the National Museum and opposite the departure point for ferries to Tuti Island. Buses run regularly east and west along Jama'a Street, one street up. You can catch one of these from Stad in Central Khartoum in the direction of Souq Bahri.*

Presidential Palace

This is where General Gordon used to live when he was Britain's man in Sudan. Now it houses the offices of the current President of Sudan: Omar al-Bashir. Unsurprisingly, high security surrounds the palace. It is not generally possible for members of the public to enter the main grounds, unless they have contacts or receive an official invitation.

☩ *On Nil Street, at the bottom of Qasar Street. Since you are not allowed to walk in front of the palace, the best way to get a look at it is from just across the Nile, in Bahri. Alternatively, you can drive in front of the palace at certain times of the day, when the President is not there.*

St Matthew's Cathedral

Don't expect the kind of grandeur you might see in many European cities. This cathedral, built between 1847 and 1907, is fairly small and looks rather more like a grand church than a cathedral. It is particularly worth visiting on Sundays or during Christian holidays, when lively African services are often held in the courtyard.

What To See

💲 *Free.*

☎ *Varies, services on Sunday.*

╬ *Nil Street, just opposite the Blue Nile Sailing Club. Simply catch a bus heading west along Jama'a Street, which is one street up, or east along Jamhouriya Street, which is two streets up. You can catch a bus from Stad in Central Khartoum, direction Souq Bahri.*

Turkish Graves

Two large beehive-shaped tombs, known as *qubbas*, mark the tombs of several notable Turkish and Egyptian soldiers, who died in the 19th century, when the two countries were in control of Sudan.

Isolated examples of *qubbas* are found all over Khartoum and the surrounding countryside, and are usually associated with Circassian or Ottoman architecture. They are typically linked to Islamic saints, and the fenced area enclosing them is traditionally a sanctuary where a traveller's goods can be left safely and without interference.

The Turkish tombs on Baladeyah Street are unique, though, because, whilst they might follow the *qubbas* design, they are essentially non-religious in nature, marking the burial spot of military men rather than sheikhs.

According to two small plaques, most of those buried within the tombs were originally Circassian slaves brought to Egypt, who rose to acclaim through the ranks of the military. Ahmed Pasha Abu Adhan was governor general of Sudan from 1839 to 1843 and Musa Pasha Hamdi was governor general

of Sudan from 1862 to 1865; both were previously Circassian slaves. An Egyptian writer, Ibrahim Bey Marzouk (who fought against government corruption in Khartoum) is also buried here.

It is something of a wonder that these tombs were not destroyed when the Mahdi came to power in 1881, as many similar buildings in Khartoum were. One theory is that the pre-Mahdi *qubbas* were used as architectural models for the tomb of the Mahdi, who died very shortly after the fall of Khartoum, and this tenuous association prevented their destruction, even as the rest of Khartoum's religious heritage was being dismantled.

💲 *Free.*

☎ *Any time.*

╬ *Just round the corner from the French Sudanese Bank, on Baladeyah Street (the same street as the British Embassy). Take a bus in the direction of Stad and get off at Qasar Street. Walk north for 20 minutes.*

The University of Khartoum

The University of Khartoum is the most prestigious and oldest university in North Sudan. In colonial days, it was known as 'Gordon College', after the British general who was killed by Mahdi troops whilst trying to defend the capital from invasion (p56).

The main campus houses the faculties of art, law, economics, history and science. Most of the other faculties are located in nearby buildings outside the main campus, although a few are as far afield as Omdurman and Bahri.

Walking around the university, you are likely to be stopped by curious students eager to practise their English.

The most impressive building on the campus is the university library: an ancient building resembling a castle.

- 💰 *Free.*
- ☎ *Any time during weekdays.*
- ⌖ *West of the city centre, on Jama'a Street. Buses travel west along this street and east along Jamhouriya Street, which is one street up. You can catch a bus from Stad in Central Khartoum, direction Souq Bahri.*

KHARTOUM 2 AND 3

World War Two Cemetery

There are no bodies buried in the World War Two memorial cemetery: simply white headstones to commemorate those who were killed in the fighting in North Sudan. The headstones are laid out in impossibly neat rows, in stark contrast to most Sudanese cemeteries that you will see around the city.

The garden of remembrance is extremely well-kept, with probably the neatest lawns in the whole of Khartoum. The cemetery is open all year round, although occasionally you may find the gate locked.

Although the cemetery was largely built to commemorate those who died in World War Two, a Remembrance Day service — which remembers the fallen soldiers of World War One — is held there every year on November 11. You will usually need a formal invitation to attend, though, which your

embassy should be able to provide you with.

- 💰 *Free.*
- ☎ *Varies.*
- ⌖ *East of the main bus station, just on the outskirts of Khartoum 3. Most buses, heading south from Afriqia Street, or north from the centre of town, pass close by.*

AMARAT

All Saints Cathedral

All Saints Cathedral is not a place you are likely to visit in search of aesthetic beauty, for it resembles little more than a dreary concrete block. Its main attraction, however, is the variety of African services that are held there

The cathedral chiefly caters for South Sudan's Christian community, living in Khartoum. It holds services in various tribal languages — such as Dinka, Nuba, Nuer and Zande — as well as in English and Arabic.

The services are particularly noted for their gaiety — both in the dress of the congregation and in their singing, clapping and dancing. The services are very social occasions, and everyone participates with great enthusiasm.

The best day to attend the services is on Sunday, when tribal gatherings occur one after the other, and there is always the opportunity to speak with members of the congregation.

As a foreigner, you will be warmly-welcomed to the services. Curious church-goers will almost certainly come up and talk to you.

What To See

ALL SAINTS CATHEDRAL SUNDAY SERVICES

Service	Time
English Homely Communion	8.30 am
Nuba Moro Congregation	10 am
General Arabic	12 noon
Zande	2 pm
Nuer / Dinka	4 pm
English	6.30 pm

All Saints Cathedral was built between 1979 and 1983, after the original cathedral, located near the Nile, was confiscated by the Sudanese government, which alleged that there was a tunnel from the cathedral to the palace. The old cathedral has since been turned into the Palace Museum.

💲 *Free.*

⏰ *Services throughout the week. Sunday services are particularly worth attending.*

☨ *Street 1, Amarat, just opposite Laziz restaurant. It is between Afriqia Street and Mohammed Najeeb Street. Buses run regularly down both streets. You can take a bus from Souq as-Shabi in the direction of Stad, or from Stad in the direction of Amarat.*

BAHRI

Al-Shifa Pharmaceutical Factory

The ruins of an old pharmaceutical factory that was bombed by the US in 1998 make for a slightly unusual tourist destination.

The US launched cruise-missile attacks on the site because of suspicions that it was being used to develop chemical weapons (p65). The Sudanese government has always insisted that it was a normal pharmaceutical operation and was an important producer of anti-malarial drugs.

The Al-Shifa ruins have been left exactly as they were after the US attack, which caused the building to collapse in on itself.

If the gate is open, you can let yourself in and take a stroll around this fascinating piece of Sudanese history.

💲 *Free.*

⏰ *Any time.*

📶 *15°38'47"N 32°33'41"E*

☨ *Where: Take a bus from Stad to Kafouri (direction: Samrab) and get out when you see some heaps of rubble on your left. Alternatively, take a bus to Souq Bahri and from there a taxi or rickshaw should cost no more than 5 SDG. You can walk from Souq Bahri if you have the energy, but it is quite a long way.*

Aliyya Qadiriyya Casnazaniyya

If you want to see a fascinating — albeit slightly disturbing — display of Sufism in Khartoum, you can try to locate the Aliyya Qadiriyya Casnazaniyya *tariqa* (sect). First established in Iraq, the religious order is named after Ali ibn Abi Talib, the husband of Prophet Mohammed's daughter Fatima.

During the show, the practising Sufis will inflict self-harm upon their bodies with seemingly no ill effect. They will stick skewers through their cheeks or their abdomens and hammer knives into their heads.

The idea is that their belief in Allah is so strong, and the support of their sheikh so solid, that they can accomplish anything and, unless Allah wills it, no harm will befall them. They also believe that, if anyone touches the hand of the saint, then, with his support, they will be able to perform similar feats. It is up to you whether you want to take this risk!

The *tariqa* performs such feats in order to demonstrate the power of the Qur'an, particularly to those who may doubt it. They believe that, by showing how their faith protects them from harm, they will inspire others to recognise and embrace the power of Allah.

Miracle-performing is officially prohibited according to North Sudanese law and so the Aliyya Qadiriyya Casnazaniyya sect do not always feel comfortable performing in public. Their *sufi* ceremony takes place every Friday and Monday evening, but they do not always perform the spectacle of sticking sharp objects into their body. If you are interested in seeing this, you should ask them about it. They are happy when foreigners take an interest in what they are doing.

💲   *Free.*

🕿   *Fri & Mon: 7 pm until late — but you may need to ask about the show.*

🔊   *15°39'36"N 32°31'37"E*

⊩   *The exact location is not easy to find. The nondescript mosque is rather tucked away, only identified from the side of the road by a discreet sign in Arabic. The easiest way to get there is to take a bus from the centre of Khartoum to the centre of Bahri. Then from there you can take either a bus or a rickshaw to Shambat. If you get off at the start of Shambat, the mosque is about a 10-minute walk away, along a network of winding streets. Ask the locals for directions; the sect is quite well known in the area.*

Nuba Wrestling

Traditional Nuba wrestling is one spectator sport that you should definitely try to see whilst in Khartoum. This competitive sport originated in the Nuba Mountains and is still practised in a number of the villages and communities there, particularly during festival days. Traditionally, male wrestlers fought naked in order to prove their fighting prowess to the tribesmen in other villages. In Khartoum, Islamic sensitivities mean that all Nuba wrestlers fight fully-clothed.

Although the fights may not have quite the same feeling as those that take place in the Nuba Mountains, the wrestlers still take them very seriously; you only have to look at the fierce expressions on their faces to see this.

There is a large police presence at the wrestling matches, In order to dissuade any troublemaking. Look out for the exuberant tribal dances that take place around the edge of the ring.

💲 *1 SDG (plus 50 piastras if you want a seat).*

☎ *Fri: before sunset.*

📶 *15°36'52"N 32°38'38"E*

✠ *Souq Sita, in the Haj Yusef district of Bahri. Regular buses run from Souq Bahri and Stad in Central Khartoum to this area.*

📶 *15°38'16"N 32°29'12"E*

✠ *Close to Souq Omdurman and just opposite the Khalifa's house. Take a bus from Jackson station in Central Khartoum, direction Souq Omdurman, and get off when you see the tomb to your right.*

OMDURMAN

The Mahdi's Tomb

The burial chamber of the Mahdi, who overthrew British rule in Sudan in 1885, is one of the top tourist destinations in Omdurman.

It is not the original tomb, which was destroyed by Lord Kitchener, who threw the Mahdi's ashes into the Nile. However, this is an item of trivia best kept to yourself, if you do not want to risk offending Muslims in North Sudan. Many people still revere the man who temporarily freed them from colonial rule.

Foreigners report that they have been refused entry to the tomb, on the grounds that they are non-Muslim. However, persistence can pay off. If you politely ask the guard outside to allow you into the tomb, there is a good chance that he will do so, although he may expect a tip of 1 or 2 SDG.

The interior of the burial chamber consists of a single room, with the tomb in the centre. On the walls around the chamber are various artefacts, including pages from the Qur'an that the Mahdi used to carry with him.

💲 *Free (plus optional tip).*

☎ *Varies.*

The Khalifa's House

The Khalifa was the Mahdi's second-in-command and eventual successor. The interior of the Khalifa's house is actually larger than it looks from the outside. Inside the house, you will find all manner of artefacts belonging to the Khalifa and relating to the period when he lived — including an assorted collection of *angreb* beds, some of the first wheeled vehicles to be used in Sudan and an interesting model of the original water system.

💲 *1.50 SDG.*

☎ *8 am to 6 pm; Mon & Fri: closed.*

📶 *15°38'19"N 32°29'18"E*

✠ *Close to Souq Omdurman, just opposite the Mahdi's tomb. Buses running from Jackson station in Central Khartoum drop you off nearby.*

Fortifications of Omdurman

In Omdurman, along the west bank of the Nile, you can see the old mud-fortress walls that were built by the Mahdi at the end of the 19th century to fend off British troops. An old gun-boat has also recently been placed in the area.

💲 *Free.*

🕙 *Any time.*

📶 *15°38'02"N 32°29'40"E*

✚ *There is no direct bus to the fortifications. From Omdurman's fish market, you can either walk for 30 minutes along the Nile or take a rickshaw (which should cost no more than a couple of SDG).*

Traditional Boatbuilding

Traditional boatbuilding, which used to flourish in the days of the Nubians, is in danger of dying out altogether in Sudan. There is now just one man in Omdurman who makes the beautiful wooden vessels, carved out of large tree trunks. The boatbuilder is extremely friendly. He is happy to talk about his work and show you around his workshop, and you can take pictures if you want. However, he doesn't speak any English. The boatbuilder works in the open air, from morning until sunset.

💲 *Free.*

🕙 *Most days, until sunset.*

📶 *15°39'24"N 32°30'23"E*

✚ *Abu Raouf quarter of Omdurman, 2 km after Shambat Bridge, along the banks of the Nile. You can take a bus to the bridge from Souq Omdurman or from Souq Bahri. The boatbuilder is then a short rickshaw ride (2 SDG), or a fairly long walk, away.*

Souq as-Shigiara

Not far from the boatbuilder is Souq as-Shigiara, a delightful handicraft market that sells small pieces of wood and wooden cups used for burning incense (p183). The market is particularly popular with Sudanese ladies who are about to get married; they come here to buy the sweet-smelling wood for use in the *dukhan* ceremony (p81). For this reason the market is popularly known as 'Souq al-Nissuan' ('women's market').

✚ *Follow the directions above for getting to the traditional boatbuilder.*

Moheli Camel Market

A few kilometres west of Souq Libya lies the biggest camel market in the region. It is fairly deserted most days of the week, but really comes to life on Wednesday and Saturday mornings, when traders come from all over the country, and even from abroad, to buy and sell camels. You will see hundreds of camels resting among the sand dunes, waiting to be sold or exported. Outside of these days, you are likely to see more cattle than camels, which causes some visitors to assume it is just a very large cattle market.

There are a couple of cafés not far from the market, where you can escape from the heat of the day.

You can't buy camel meat at Moheli. If you do fancy sampling some of this local delicacy, your best bet is to stop at Souq Naaga before you take the bus to Moheli.

💲 *Free.*

🕙 *Wed & Sat mornings.*

What To See

> ⊺ *A 30-minute ride from Souq Naaga in Omdurman, in an area called 'Moheli'. Souq Naaga is just a short walk or rickshaw journey from Souq Libya, which can be reached by direct bus from Jackson bus station in Central Khartoum.*

Karari Battlefield

Eight kilometres north of Bahri lies the famous Karari battlefield where, in 1898, British forces (led by General Herbert Kitchener) defeated the Mahdist forces that only 14 years earlier had taken control of the city of Khartoum (p59). This marked the end of Mahdist rule in the country.

The Karari battlefield is a fascinating place to visit. Here you can breathe in the remnants of history that are borne in on the arid breeze sweeping over the flat plains, now littered with rubbish.

A solitary plaque has been erected, to the left of the road, to mark the centenary of the battle. Its purpose is to give great praise to the courage of the Mahdi troops, who put up a brave fight in the face of insurmountable odds and firepower.

A telling quote of Winston Churchill, former British prime minister who also served under General Kitchener, is included at the bottom: "They were the bravest people who have ever set foot on the Earth. We did not defeat them in Karari. We only destroyed them with the power of weapons and fire."

To the right of the road, you will see a series of low-lying brick-and mud-buildings. In the distance, across the plains, one or two small hills break up the featureless landscape.

Whilst Karari can indeed be an historically fascinating place to explore, this what-to-see entry comes with a warning. On the other side of the road, not far from the plinth, is a military outpost where soldiers are highly suspicious of foreigners poking around in the area. On no account take any photos here — you will almost certainly be detained, and the pictures on your camera deleted. Even just visiting the area can raise suspicions and may result in you being brought in by the military. So only visit the area if you are prepared for a good deal of aggravation. You visit at your own risk.

💲 *Free.*

☎ *Any time.*

🔊 *15°44'23"N 32°30'20"E*

⊺ *A 30-minute bus ride from Souq Omdurman. Get off when you see a large open plain and a prominent memorial plaque.*

Whirling Dervishes of Omdurman

Every Friday evening, just before sunset, the site of Hamed al-Nil's tomb becomes the setting for the famous Sufi dance, popularly known as the 'Whirling Dervishes' because of the frantic way in which many of the Sufi worshippers spin around the ceremonial arena. This sight is not a tourist attraction but a genuine religious ceremony, so take care to be respectful.

Before the ceremony starts — between 4 and 5 pm, depending on the season — large numbers of Sufis gather within the tomb of Hamed al-Nil to pray. It is acceptable to peer inside. Outside, people start singing and chanting, and collecting money for the sect.

The ceremony doesn't properly start until a group of Sufis, bearing he green banner of the Hamed al-Nil *tariqa* (sect), begin marching from the graveyard to the beat of drums. The Sufis start dancing, chanting and clapping within a circle that is fringed by curious onlookers and other participators in the ceremony. Eventually, you will notice that the Sufi dancers start to break away and spin round — some of them really quite fast. Many of them chant 'la ilaha ill Allah' ('there is no God but Allah').

The purpose of the ritual is for the dervishes to reach a state of ecstasy and enlightenment that will make it possible for them to link directly to God.

A lot of disabled people attend this ritual, believing that they will be cured of their ailments.

The festival atmosphere is fantastic and watchers are actively welcomed. Bear in mind, however, that the area where the ceremony takes place is fairly poor and you may get pestered for money — or for impromptu English lessons!

There is no problem with taking photographs of the ceremony, but remember that, according to Islamic tradition, you should not photograph the surrounding cemetery. You can take photos of the tomb, though.

💲 *Free.*

⏰ *Before sunset.*

📶 *15°37'30"N 32°27'51"E*

✝ *Um Badda district, on the west side of Omdurman. Take a bus from Jackson Station in the centre of Khartoum or Souq Omdurman. Simply ask for Ghoob Hamed al-Nil.*

TUTI ISLAND

Tuti Island is a large expanse of farmland and lemon groves, interwoven with a network of dusty streets. It is located in the middle of the Nile junction between Khartoum, Omdurman and Bahri.

The fertile soil of the island is perfect for growing fruit and vegetables. During the summer rains, the Nile rises and covers half of Tuti, which makes getting around the island a little difficult. In September and October, once the waters have subsided, Tuti Island, draped in greenery, is a truly beautiful place to behold. Outside of the rainy season, a series of pumps around the island keeps the farmland irrigated with water from the Nile.

The only way to reach Tuti Island used to be by a ferry boat, which departed from just outside Friendship Hall. However, the opening of the new suspension bridge nearby means that you can now walk or drive directly to the island. This has made the ferry service redundant. Limited passenger boats run on Saturdays, which is the day that most people visit the island. You can also turn up at the mooring station and rent a boat — either to take you to the island or for a cruise on the Nile.

The easiest way to travel around the island is by rickshaw or *boksi*. A few buses also criss-cross through the island, but they are not particularly frequent. A rickshaw should cost you no more than 2 or 3 SDG for most destinations. *Boksi*s and buses should cost you around 40 to 50 *piastras*.

Tuti Island is not very big and it is not difficult to get your bearings there.

If you walk eastwards from the bridge or ferry terminal, you will eventually come across a large expanse of sand. Some years ago, this beach did not exist, but a change in the flow of the Nile washed the sand over from Bahri. From here, you can take in a fantastic view of the Presidential Palace and other buildings stretching along the river bank. To the north, Bahri is also very visible. The beach is a great spot if you are interested in birds. You will see many eagles wheeling in the sky and herons skimming across the water's surface.

If you head westwards from the ferry terminal, you will quickly find yourself walking through lemon groves and farmland. The farms on the island are privately owned by Tuti Island residents, although they are often worked by outsiders, many of whom come from Darfur.

It is not usually a problem to wander through the farms, as long as you are respectful of the land and remember to close all gates behind you. Many of the farm workers love to stop and chat, and may offer you a sample of fresh produce if you ask politely.

The farmland ends abruptly on the banks of the Nile, overlooking the Mogran area where the Blue and White Niles converge. Authorities plan to build another beach here, but there is local opposition to this.

Heading north from the ferry terminal, you will encounter more farmland, plus, on the banks of the Nile, a little-noticed defensive wall that was used by the followers of the Mahdi to counter British forces. This is similar to the one you will find in Omdurman (p130), only a little smaller.

Efforts to develop Tuti Island are altering the place irreparably. Initially, the beach on the east side of the island had been earmarked for development, but these plans have

now been shelved — partly because of strong opposition from the locals, but also because the ground was found to be unsuitable for building on. The centre for the development is now not far from the ferry terminal, where the new bridge from Khartoum enters the island.

💲 *Free.*

☎ *You can now get to the island any time you want to, by crossing the new bridge.*

🚢 *Tuti Island is located in the centre of the Nile. The easiest way to get to the island is via the new suspension bridge, which crosses the river from just next to the Corinthia Hotel. You can catch regular buses to Tuti Island from just outside Nilein University, next to Stad. Alternatively, occasional boats leave for the island on Saturdays, departing from outside Friendship Hall.*

THE NILE

There are two pleasant Nile-side walks to be had in the city: one in Central Khartoum and the other in Omdurman.

Central Khartoum

Nil Street is one of the oldest streets in Khartoum. Here, you will find many colonial-style houses now serving as ministry buildings, as well as the Presidential Palace .

A particularly pretty spot to visit is the Mogran area, to the west of the town centre, where the Blue and White Niles converge. There is a magnificent bridge here, but photographing it is prohibited. Police are here in droves and they will arrest you if they catch you. The area is famed for migratory birds. Nearby Mogran Family Park is also worth visiting.

A good point to start your walk along the banks of the Nile is east of the Mogran area, just in front of Friendship Hall (p125) and the National Museum (p138).

Heading east from here, you will enjoy some great views of Tuti Island (they are even more impressive if you climb on to the new bridge that is just before you get to Corinthia Hotel). Keep going and you will pass a number of the most important ministry buildings. These ministry buildings are slowly being relocated to less prestigious areas of Khartoum.

Armed guards patrol outside these buildings, so take care where you stop. If you sit for too long on the wall overlooking the beautiful Nile, you will start to look conspicuous and may be asked what you are doing there. If you pause to sit too

---

NILE CRUISE

If you don't fancy walking, an alternative way of experiencing the Nile is to rent a cruise boat. This is also a great way of seeing some of the Sudanese countryside, as riverside hotels and ministerial buildings quickly give way to wild scrubland and farms.

The Blue Nile Sailing Club can arrange chartered boats, but they usually work on the basis of renting out the whole boat and you will have to arrange the piloting yourself. A boat for up to 30 people typically costs 200 SDG per hour, whilst a smaller boat costs half that.

Alternatively, if you wander across to the marina next door, you will find a number of boats moored there. This is actually a private club for mooring boats, but you can also rent them, if you can find someone to speak to. These private boats typically cost 100 SDG an hour.

Another place where you can arrange a cruise is opposite the Grand Holiday Villa. A large boat is moored there most of the time, and is used to ferry workers from the Grand Holiday Villa to and from Tuti Island. When it is not being used for this purpose, it is possible to negotiate its use for a river cruise.

Close by is another marina, where private boats are moored. If you find the right person to speak to, you can arrange to rent these boats out, typically for 100 SDG per hour.

Alternatively, the National Rowing Club, not far from the Coral Hotel, rents out kayaks for 20 SDG an hour.

If you happen to pass under Bahri Bridge whilst on the Nile (to the east of the city centre), take a moment to look back at the prominent, though not particularly attractive, Kuwaiti Building. The building is made up of three separate blocks, leading away from the Nile. If you look at it from under Bahri Bridge, you should clearly see two ghostly crosses appearing between the interconnecting blocks, due to the way the top of the building indents slightly. Some say that this is a warning from God to the whole of Sudan. Others contend that it is just an accident of architecture. The crosses are only visible from this particular point in the Nile. They quickly fade if you head away from the bridge, in either direction. Because of the angles involved, you also cannot see them if you are standing on the bridge.

What To See

close to the Presidential Palace, you will almost certainly be waved on by the guards standing there.

Once you arrive at the palace, you will have to turn inland to continue your walk. Cars may pass in front of the palace, if the gate is open, but pedestrians cannot. Head over to Jama'a Street for one block and then you can cross back to the banks of the Nile.

Continuing further eastwards, the walk becomes much less governmental and rather more relaxing. It is along here that, in the early evening (especially during Fridays), you will find countless families sitting on rugs, enjoying their picnic dinners or playing cards. You will also find a number of street vendors selling cold drinks, crisps and sweets.

East of the palace, you can also take in the Blue Nile Sailing Club, where Kitchener's Boat is permanently docked (p124), and St Matthew's Cathedral (p126).

Omdurman

In many ways, a walk alongside the Nile in Omdurman is more relaxing than in Central Khartoum, since you are unlikely to encounter any armed guards eyeing you suspiciously.

If you start at the fish market on the southern side, just across the bridge from Khartoum, you will walk past the fortifications of Omdurman (p130), the Rivera Recreational Park and the National Theatre (p149). You will eventually end up, some kilometres down the route, at the traditional boatbuilder (p131).

If you walk this way at the end of the summer months, after the rains have stopped, you may see stooped men sowing new seeds in the fertile mudflats.

KHARTOUM'S MOSQUES

Khartoum is not particularly renowned for its architectural prowess.

If you do want to see a few remarkable buildings, you should think about a tour of some of the city's more impressive mosques. It is particularly worth visiting Al-Kabier Mosque, a sandstone coloured building rising up out of the chaos of Souq al-Arabi, and Al-Nilein Mosque in Omdurman, which is noted for its hedgehog-like exterior. Al-Nilein Mosque also houses the University of Qur'anic and Islamic Studies.

Other famous mosques in the city include:

- Al-Imam Rahman Mosque, Wad Nubawui, Omdurman.
- Al-Imam Al-Mahdi Mosque, Mulazmeen, Omdurman.
- Al-Sheikh Al-Dareer Mosque, Wad Urru, Omdurman.
- Al-Sheikh Ganad Al-Nil Mosque, Um Badda.
- Farouq Mosque, Jamhouriya Street, Khartoum.
- Sayed Ali Al-Mirghani Mosque, Shambat Street, Khartoum North.
- Khartoum University Mosque, Jama'a Street, Khartoum.

FOSSILISED TREES

In the desert to the north of Khartoum, towards Karima, the remnants of an old, petrified forest lie scattered across the sand. Some of these fossilised tree trunks have found their way into Khartoum and if you look hard enough, you can find them just sitting by the side of the road. The most obvious place to catch sight of them is at the south end of Afriqia Street, scattered around a sign for Omdurman Bank. You can also see them embedded in

EDWARD STANFORD LTD
12-14 LONG ACRE
LONDON

WC2E 9LP

TEL:020 7836 1321
VAT NO:512 5071 87

11-07-12 11:08 SALE 1 3600
Sigita

PRODUCT	QTY	VAT
Trail Guide To North And		
9780955927423	1	15.99 Z

ZERO RATE	15.99	15.99
TOTAL	1	15.99
CASH		20.00
TOTAL TENDERED		20.00
CHANGE		4.01

www.stanfords.co.uk

ENTERING MOSQUES

There is some disagreement among Muslims about whether people not of the faith should be allowed to enter mosques. The Qur'an expressly forbids polytheists — people who worship more than one God — from entering mosques:

"It is not for such as join gods with Allah, to visit or maintain the mosques of Allah while they witness against their own souls to infidelity. The works of such bear no fruit: in fire shall they dwell."

"O ye who believe! Truly the Pagans are unclean; so let them not, after this year of theirs, approach the Sacred Mosque. And if ye fear poverty, soon will Allah enrich you, if He wills, out of His bounty, for Allah is All-knowing, All-wise."

The Qur'an does not make the same stipulations for monotheists, although the Umayyad caliph Umar II famously barred non-Muslims from entering mosques.

These days, the decision on whether non-Muslims can enter mosques varies. You will be able to enter some mosques in Sudan without difficulty. Entrance to others will be denied to you.

If you are keen to see inside a mosque, the best thing to do is to respectfully ask people near the mosque whether or not it is alright to enter.

You will probably be unable to enter mosques during prayer time or while religious ceremonies are taking place. Women may also find it difficult to enter mosques. According to Islamic tradition, mosques remain the dominion of men and women usually pray at home or in private. However, foreign women may be tolerated in certain mosques, although only if they are fully covered (including their hair).

Remember to remove your shoes before you enter a mosque.

What To See

the wall of the National Forest Corporation, not far from Musalamia Bridge.

KHARTOUM'S MUSEUMS

There are several museums that are worth visiting in and around Central Khartoum.

Palace Museum

This museum is housed in a beautiful old Anglican church, which was built between 1904 and 1912.

As you enter the museum, you will see on your right a fascinating series of photos depicting the road to Sudan's independence from the British. On the left there is a collection of gifts made to various presidents of Sudan.

The museum also contains a number of memorials to various British nationals who died in Sudan during colonial rule, including Lee Stack, a previous governor general of Sudan who was assassinated in 1924 (p60). Interestingly, the sign acknowledging General Charles Gordon's successes in Sudan has been half-pulled-down.

The museum's star attraction lies outside the main Anglican Church building: a collection of presidential cars (including Rolls Royces, Lincoln Continentals and Humbers), which have been used at various times by different visiting heads of states — such as Queen Elizabeth of Britain, President Leonid Brezhnev of Russia and President Josip Tito of what was then called 'Yugoslavia'.

💲 *Free.*

☎ *Wed & Fri to Sun: 9 am to 1 pm, 4 to 8 pm.*

✢ *Just behind the Presidential Palace, on Jama'a Street. You can catch a bus west along this street, or one east along Jamhouriya Street, which is one street up. You can catch a bus from Stad in Central Khartoum, direction Souq Bahri.*

Natural History Museum

This museum mainly contains stuffed animals, pickled reptiles and birds' eggs. More interestingly, around the back, you will find a number of live animals — including a variety of snakes and lizards, some giant tortoises and a few birds. There are even two genuine crocodiles in the pond just next to the museum.

💲 *50 piastras.*

☎ *8.30 am to 6.30 pm; Fri: 8.30 am to 12 noon, 3 to 6.30 pm; Mon: closed.*

✢ *On the corner of Osman Digna Street and Jama'a Street. Buses head west along Jama'a Street and east along Jamhouriya Street, which is one street up. You can catch a bus from Stad in Central Khartoum, direction Souq Bahri.*

Geological Museum

Besides all manner of rocks, this museum also contains some very interesting fossilised sea life and dinosaur bones,

You must ask at the reception of the Geological Research Authority to see if you can get in. They will then summon a guard to unlock the museum. The museum isn't big but it is definitely worth a half-hour traipse around. It contains an impressive variety of rocks and fossils in quite a small area.

💲 *Free.*

☎ *8.30 am to 1 pm; Fri & Sat: closed.*

✢ *Housed in the Geological Research Authority on Nil Street, just to the east of the Presidential Palace. Buses run west along Jama'a Street, which is one street up, and east along Jamhouriya Street, which is two streets up. You can catch a bus from Stad in Central Khartoum, direction Souq Bahri.*

National Museum

Khartoum's National Museum houses a wealth of antiquities and artefacts from different periods of Sudanese history and prehistory, including glassware and pottery from the ancient kingdom of Kush and frescoes and murals from the Christian period of ancient Nubia.

The strong influence that Egypt has had on Sudan's history is evident within the museum. There are many items from ancient Egypt on display, including a mummified body and sarcophagi made out of both stone and wood.

The interior of the museum is divided into two parts: upstairs and downstairs. The upstairs area contains many UNESCO heritage artefacts. However, it is not always open and, quite often, you have to content yourself with browsing downstairs.

In the museum's gardens there are two reconstructed Egyptian

Don't miss

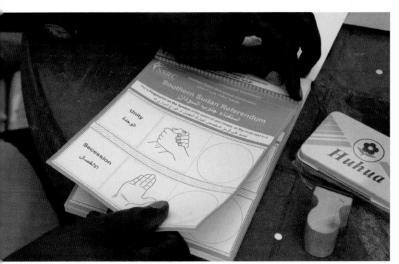

The building of the world's newest nation (p266) - JW

Ancient ruins in northern Sudan (p203) - AL

otos: Violetta Polese (VP), Blake Evans-Pritchard (BEP), Jenn Warren (JW; ww.jennwarren.net), Lara Palmisano (LP), Luke Addis (LA), Isabelle Sauser (IS), Audrey Olivetti (AO), Taha Sharif (TS), Antoine Luc (AL)

Sufi ceremony, Omdurman (p72) - VP

Ancient ruins in northern Sudan (p203) - AL

Moheli camel market (p131) - VP

Henna skin decoration (p76) - IS

Nuba wrestling in Bahri (p129) - VP

Rural life near Sinja, on the way to Dinder Park (p238) - VP

The serenity of the Red Sea (p224) - VP

The haunted town of Suakin and
the legend of its demonic cats (p235) - VP

The Whirling Dervishes of Omdurman (p132) - BEP

The panoramic view from the top of
Jebel Barkal (p213) - VP

The Sixth Cataract (p210) - VP

Wildlife in Dinder Park (p243) and in South Sudan (p266) - VP

The Khatmiyah Mosque in the Taka Mountains (p239) - V

Scenic mountainous view on the Gash River (p241) - VP

The ancient city of Kerma (p219) - AL

The traditional boatbuilder in Omdurman (p131) - VP

Hand-made boat on the banks of the Nile (p131) - VP

The frescos of tombs in El-Kurru (p215) - VP

The famous Lion Temple at Naqa (p221) - VP

Omdurman markets (p184) - VP

Market in the Nuba Mountains (p257) - BEP

The markets of Juba (p275) - LP

Fresh fruit juice (p96) - VP

The temples at Soleb (p211) - AL

The tribes of the South (p39) - JW

temples, which were salvaged when Nubian lands were flooded during the 1960s to make way for a new dam in North Sudan. These temples of Buhen and Semna were originally built by Queen Hatshepsut and Pharaoh Tuthmosis III respectively. A channel has been cut into the ground in front of these temples, to represent the Nile, but has not yet been filled with water.

At the entrance of the museum, still in the garden, are two enormous Pharaoh-style statues.

Look out for archaeological conferences and seminars that are regularly held in the museum.

💰 *2 SDG.*

⏰ *9 am to 6.30 pm; Mon & Fri: 9 am to 12 noon, 3 to 6.30 pm.*

✚ *On the banks of the Nile, just next to Friendship Hall, not far from the bridge that goes to Tuti Island. Buses run regularly east and west along Jama'a Street, one street up. You can catch a bus from Stad in Central Khartoum, direction Souq Bahri.*

Ethnographic Museum

If you are interested in learning more about the tribes of Sudan, the Ethnographic Museum is an excellent starting point.

It is well laid-out, with tribal artefacts grouped together in a logical order. Each artefact is clearly-labelled in both Arabic and English, giving just the information that you need, although you will probably get more out of your visit if you have some background knowledge of the tribes already — simply read the 'Culture' section of this book before you go (p70).

💰 *Free.*

⏰ *8.30 am to 6 pm; Mon & Fri: 8.30 am to 12 noon, 3 to 6 pm.*

✚ *On Jama'a Street, just opposite St Matthew's Cathedral. Buses run east to west along Jama'a Street and west to east along Jamhouriya Street, which is one street up. You can catch a bus from Stad in Central Khartoum, direction Souq Bahri.*

What To See

What To Do

Foreigners who arrive in Khartoum for the first time are often dismayed by how little there seems to be to do in the city.

However, those visitors who persevere will soon discover that, contrary to first appearances, there is actually quite a lot going on.

The imposition of *sharia* law in 1983 really narrowed down the entertainment options in the city. Until very recently, it wasn't even possible to find any live music other than music played at weddings.

Things are slowly changing, but only very slowly. You will find that many old-timers still hark back to the good old days in the 1970s and the 1980s, when the city buzzed with things to do.

These days, you have to make a bit more of an effort to really discover the hidden charms of the city. This section will show you how.

Note that different events are often held in the same venues. Below, all events and activities have been categorised according to their types rather than by venue. To avoid repetition, venue contact details are only included once (the first time that the venue is mentioned). After that, only the venue name is given.

EVENTS

Khartoum's **Flower Show** is held every year, either on the last Friday in February or the first Friday in March. The week-long exhibition is free to enter and is a great opportunity to see what local horticulturists are capable of growing.

Exhibitors from many different sectors are encouraged to participate, including commercial growers, government departments, universities, and private nurseries. Some foreign growers also usually show up.

Unfortunately, finding exact details about the Flower Show — such as where it is going to be held — can be tricky. The best idea is to keep your eyes open for posters and flyers around the town. The most popular venues for the Flower Show are Qurashi Park, Friendship Hall and Khartoum International Exhibition Centre.

Another event to look out for is the **Khartoum International Fair**, which is usually held in January. Companies from all over the world come to display their wares. Besides the exhibition halls, there are also food and drink stalls.

Look out for cultural events during Islamic religious festivals, particularly **Eid al-Fitr** and **Moulid al-Nabi** (p33). During both of these festivals, you will find live music and dancing going on amidst the devout praying.

CULTURAL CENTRES

Both the **French Cultural Centre** (🏠 Ali Dinar Street; ☎ 0183 798 035/36/37; @ ccf_khartoum@yahoo.fr) and the **German Goethe-Institute** (🏠 Mek Nimir Street; ☎ 0183 777 833; @ info@khartum.goethe.org; 🖥 www.goethe.de/khartum) run a series of cultural events, including art exhibitions, lectures, musical shows and film screenings. These events are in general free.

To find out more information about the cultural programmes of these centres, you can either consult the relevant websites or send an email and ask to be put on their mailing lists. A printed copy of the programmes is also available at each centre.

The **British Council** (🏠 Abu Sinn Street; ☎ 0187 028 000; @ info@sd.britishcouncil.org; 🖵 www.britishcouncil.org) has just started running a series of evening performances by local Sudanese musicians. The programme is known as WAPI, which stands for Words and Pictures, and has been extremely well-received by locals and expats alike. The British Council does not widely publicise these events but is happy to take inquiries about them. The British Council also organises film screenings every Thursday.

LIVE MUSIC

The opportunity to hear live music in Khartoum is still fairly limited.

Popular Sudanese singers are usually invited along to traditional **Sudanese weddings** (p81). In general, the more money the family can pay, the more famous the singer is likely to be. The singer may occasionally, though not always, be accompanied by a live band.

Outside of a Sudanese wedding, Thursdays are the best days to try and find live music.

The Blue Stars Jazz Band plays every Thursday evening at **Papa Costa** (🏠 Jamhouriya Street) from 8.30 pm. The place can get fairly busy, so it is best to reserve a table in advance (☎ 0915 060 350). Papa Costa also occasionally hosts other live music events — look out for the latest notices on its door.

Pizza Corner (🏠 Abdel Fadeel al-Faz Street, west of Italian Embassy; ☎ 0183 560 700) puts on live music shows every Friday night from 8 pm.

The **universities** often have live music concerts, too, and sometimes even invite really famous singers to play. Such shows will usually be advertised within the campus, so speak to university students or lecturers to find out what is going on. The best time to look out for such shows is during the universities' graduation period.

In Bahri, a group called **SWAP Open Mic** organises concerts and poetry readings. News of upcoming events is spread by word-of-mouth. Alternatively, you can take a look at their Facebook page (🖵 www.facebook.com).

The **Sajana Youth Centre** (🏠 West of Amarat; 📶 15°38'16"N 32°38'16"E) also holds regular music shows and events.

CLUBS

Social associations and clubs exist throughout Khartoum. Some of these, such as the Police Club or Officer's Club, are exclusive to a particular group of people, and run a little like an old-fashioned British gentlemen's club, popular in the late 19th and early 20th centuries.

Other clubs were initially established to serve the needs of a particular group of foreigners working in Khartoum, and are usually named after the countries of origin. It is in these clubs that people come to play sport, swim or just hang out.

There used to be a great many of these clubs in the city, but they have gradually been closed down. The latest one to go was the International Club, formerly the American Club.

Hellenic/Greek Club (🏠 Khartoum 2, near Musalamia Bridge and Assaha Village; ☎ 0183 467 577)

This club has a medium-sized swimming pool, two tennis courts, a volleyball court, basketball court and a football pitch. There is also a restaurant, with some tables around the pool. The prices in the restaurant are extremely reasonable — the club sandwiches are worth trying, and the fresh fruit juice is cheaper than you will get in many other expat places. As a member, you can use all facilities free of charge.

Free wi-fi is available. Regular sports activities are held at the club, such as volleyball on Wednesdays and Saturdays. The club often organises free swimming lessons for children — ask at reception.

Guests of members pay a daily rate of 10 SDG (without access to the pool) or 20 SDG (with access to the pool). A year's membership of the club, which gives you unlimited access to the facilities, costs 1500 SDG.

German Sudanese Club (🏠 Street 1, Amarat; ☎ 0183 462 438)

This club has a large swimming pool, a smaller swimming pool for kids, a basketball court, a basic weight-training hall and a reasonable restaurant. The poolside area is pleasantly green. Wireless internet is available at the club, free for members.

You must either be a member or be accompanied by a member to enter the club. The entrance fee for guests is 25 SDG. Guests who don't want to make use of the pool or gym pay 10 SDG.

The main problem with this club is that, although you can take out membership for a year, standard policy is to allow membership to run only from December to December. Therefore, if you join the club at the beginning of July, you will get just six months' membership for the same price that you would pay for a full year.

Family membership for the club costs 1550 SDG per year. There is now no individual membership.

The German Club regularly organises swimming and taekwondo lessons for children — just ask at reception for details. Occasionally, there are also water polo competitions.

Filipino Club (🏠 Off Afriqia Street)

This club can be very difficult to find and few local Sudanese seem to know that it exists. To get there, take one of the small streets leading off Afriqia Street, just opposite the Al-Salam Rotana Hotel.

The Filipino Club is rather different from other expat clubs in the city. It does not charge an annual subscription and there are only limited facilities within the grounds of the club.

The club's main activity is to organise social events and parties throughout the year, usually on Thursdays. Events include music shows, film screenings and basketball competitions. The biggest event of the year is Valentine's Day, involving party games, music and dance competitions.

On Friday evenings, the club is a good place to come and sample some traditional Filipino food.

It is definitely worth getting involved in the Filipino Club, if you can, as the events there are among the liveliest and most entertaining you can find in Khartoum.

Unfortunately, the Filipino Club is a little difficult to contact and does not have one permanent number. People usually hear about events through word-of-mouth. The best thing to do is take yourself down to the clubhouse one Thursday evening and try and ingratiate yourself with the people there. Alternatively, if you meet any Filipinos whilst in Khartoum, they are sure to let you know about events going on at the club.

Coptic Club (☎ Street 11, Amarat)

This club is exclusively for those of the Coptic faith. It organises social events and gatherings, but you can only attend if you are a Coptic.

SPORTS ACTIVITIES

Tennis

The Sudanese Lawn Tennis Association (☎ North end of Afriqia Street; ☎ 0912 650 480) is open every day between 4 and 11 pm. On Fridays, the entrance is sometimes through the café just next door.

Individual membership of the club costs 350 SDG for Sudanese nationals and 800 SDG for foreigners. Family membership is 400 SDG (Sudanese) and 1000 SDG (foreigners). Membership entitles you to use the tennis and squash courts at no cost until 6.30 pm. To play tennis after 6.30 pm, you must pay 10 SDG per hour for use of the lights.

You do not have to be a member to play at the club. You can simply turn up and pay 20 SDG on the door. This fee entitles you to the use of one court for an hour although, after 6.30 pm, you also

need to pay 10 SDG per hour for use of the lights.

Occasionally, the club holds national and international tennis tournaments.

The **Greek Club** has two tennis courts that are available for non-members (20 SDG per hour, and an extra 10 SDG for use of the lights).

Khartoum International Community School (KICS) (☎ Soba; ☎ 0183 215 000, @ principal@kics.sd; ☐ www.kics.sd) has one tennis court, but this is only available for teachers and students.

You can also find tennis courts at many of the more upmarket hotels, The **Coral** (☎ Mogran Street, Central Khartoum; ☎ 0183 774 100) charges 35 SDG for an hour's use of the court. Alternatively, you can buy a membership package (one month for 690 SDG, one year for 3450 SDG), which grants you access to the swimming pool as well as the tennis courts.

Grand Holiday Villa (☎ Nil Street, Central Khartoum; ☎ 0183 774 039) and **Corinthia Hotel** (☎ Nil Street, Central Khartoum; ☎ 0156 555 555) also have tennis courts, with the typical price being 20 SDG per person per hour.

Khartoum's **golf course** (p147) has two tennis courts.

Squash

Squash courts are available at many of the same locations at which you can play tennis: **KICS** (only for teachers and students), the **Sudanese Lawn Tennis Association** (20 SDG per hour per court for non-members) and at the **Corinthia Hotel**.

Gyms

Gyms are available throughout the city. Most of the bigger hotels

What To Do

in Khartoum also have gyms that non-guests can use for a fee.

ABBC Sports Centre (🏠 Afra Mall, first floor; ☎ 0120 837 632 or 0912 472 222) charges 100 SDG a month. There is also a 30 SDG one-off registration fee for joining. You do not get unlimited use of the facilities, though. The membership fee entitles you to use the gym three times a week, for no more than two hours each time. The gym has weights as well as several exercise machines.

Women can use the gym from 9 am to 9 pm on Sundays, Mondays and Wednesdays, and from 9 am to 1.30 pm on Tuesdays and Thursdays. Men can use the gym from 9 am to 11 pm on Sundays, Mondays and Wednesdays, and from 2 to 11 pm on Tuesdays and Thursdays.

The Sudanese Lawn Tennis Association has a well-equipped gym — one of the biggest in Khartoum. Membership is 150 SDG for women (use of the facilities 12 times a month) and 180 SDG for men (use of the facilities 15 times a month). You don't need to bring along any passport photos with you — just turn up and fill in the form.

Men have the option of paying extra money to use the gym more frequently; 50 SDG buys an extra five entrances to the gym.

Women can use the gym from 4.30 to 6.30 pm on Sundays, Tuesdays and Thursdays. Men can use the gym from 5 to 10 pm on Mondays, Wednesdays and Saturdays. For women only, a member of staff is on hand to help structure a fitness programme.

It is also possible to pay a single entrance fee of 20 SDG.

Al-Salam Rotana Hotel (🏠 Afriqia Street, Riyad; ☎ 0187 00 77 77) has a fairly small gym with only a few exercise machines, but the ones they do have are quite modern. The gym is open from 7 am to 10 pm, for both males and females. The daily entrance fee is 50 SDG during weekdays and 75 SDG during weekends and holidays. Prices exclude 15% tax.

The **German Club** has a disappointingly small gym with just a few weights and no exercise machines. Admission is free for members. Guests pay 25 SDG per session, which also includes use of the pool.

In Riyad, **O2** (Mashtal Street) has a well-equipped gym. The monthly fee for men is 170 SDG, whilst for women it is 150 SDG. The gym is open daily from 10 am to 10 pm, except Friday when it opens at 5 pm. Men can train four days a week — on Tuesday, Thursday, Friday and Sunday — whilst women can train on the other days.

Swimming

Most local swimming pools around the city have separate swimming arrangements for men and women. Hotels and expat clubs are more likely to allow mixed swimming in their pools, although many of them also organise female-only swimming sessions on certain days.

Grand Holiday Villa is one of the more expensive options (35 SDG per person during the week and 50 SDG at the weekend), although it is also one of the nicest. The pool is reasonably big and is usually not too crowded, even at peak times. The hotel has a separate pool, just for women.

Swimming at the **Coral Hotel** costs 35 SDG during the week, or 58 SDG on Fridays and Saturdays. Alternatively, you can buy a membership package (one month 690 SDG, one year 3450 SDG), which also gives you access to the tennis courts.

The **Al-Salam Rotana** has a very nice pool but, with admission for non-guests costing 100 SDG, you probably don't want to use it if you are on a budget. The swimming pool is open from 7 am to 10 pm.

Other options for swimming include: the **German Club** (25 SDG for non-members, female-only evenings on Mondays and Wednesdays) and the **Greek Club** (20 SDG for non-members).

Assaha Village (🏠 Off Afriqia Street, near Canadian Embassy, Khartoum 2; ☎ 0183 481 919; @ assaha.sud@assahvillage.com; 🖥 www.assahvillage.com) has a pool, but this is only available for guests.

Khartoum's **golf course** (p147) has a swimming pool.

Combat sports

The German Club regularly organises **taekwondo** lessons for children. Just ask at reception.

Classes for adults (☎ 0912 224 340) are held not far from the International University of Africa, near the south end of Obeid Khatim Street. Most of those who turn up are Sudanese. Classes take place on Mondays, Wednesdays and Saturdays between 5 and 7 pm. Each lesson costs 50 SDG. The style of taekwondo taught is that of the World Taekwondo Federation (WTF).

Self-defence classes take place every Tuesday, Thursday and Saturday at the Greek Club. A month of training costs 100 SDG.

Boxing classes take place at the Sajana Youth Centre — 40 SDG per month. The youth centre also runs regular courses in **karate**.

Football

Football is played everywhere in Khartoum; men just turn up in a big, dusty square and start kicking a ball about. Sudanese teams usually have their own areas where they play once a week. Foreigners are generally welcome to join in, although the game remains largely the pursuit of men.

If you have enough people, you can rent a football pitch at the **Greek Club** (150 SDG per hour with lights or 100 SDG without) or at the **Sudanese Lawn Tennis Association** (two pitches: cement 150 SDG, grass 200 SDG; prices are for two hours, light included).

A group of foreigners often play at the Greek Club on Friday and Monday evenings, from 8 pm, and you should be able to join in.

KICS also has a team of teachers and other foreigners who usually play once a week (Wednesdays 5 to 7 pm, 5 SDG each time). The venue changes from time to time, but most recently was at the Greek Club. All are welcome.

Touch Rugby

Khartoum Nomad's Rugby Club (@ khartoumnomads@gmail.com) has been temporarily suspended, but may start up in the future. The **Khartoum American School** (Mohammed Najeeb, south of Street 61; ☎ 0155 770 105) holds regular games.

Jogging

The **Hash House Harriers** (@ khartoumhhh@yahoo.co.uk; 🖥 www.africahash.co.za) is a social jogging club first established in 1938 by a group of British expats living in what is now Malaysia. It has since developed into something of an international phenomenon. The club has existed in Khartoum since 2003.

The idea behind the club is simple. Before the run, one person is

What To Do

nominated as the 'hare'. It is the hare's job to run ahead of everyone else and mark out a route, using bits of twig or chalk or whatever else is lying around. The 'harriers' then follow behind, picking their way through the signs that have been left for them. At certain places, the harriers may come across signs pointing in different directions. It is up to them to decide which way to head. The idea is that the ones in the front spend time looking for the correct path, giving the ones at the back a chance to catch up.

After the run, the length of which depends on the enthusiasm of the hare, a meal is organised at the house of one of the runners, who is the designated host for the evening.

The hosts and hares usually change each week, and there can be more than one hare setting the trail.

To participate in these runs, you need to be introduced to the organisation by someone. Otherwise, you could contact the Harriers directly in order to find out where their next meeting is going to take place. The location changes each week.

Be warned, though, that if it is your first time at a Hash event, you will normally be required to undergo an initiation procedure after the run. This typically requires the initiate to recite the Hash anthem and down a drink.

Runs take place on Monday evenings and start times vary according to the season. They usually begin around 5 or 5.30 pm in the summer and around 5.30 or 6 pm in the winter. Participation costs 10 SDG, including dinner.

Unfortunately, the club is no longer open to Sudanese nationals.

Volleyball

Volleyball sessions take place on Wednesday and Saturday afternoons at the **Greek Club**. Just turn up and play with whoever else is there. Members of the club can play for free, whilst non-members pay 20 SDG per session. You can play every Wednesday at **KICS** (5 SDG per game plus two passport photos for a membership card). **Sajana Youth Centre** also holds regular volleyball sessions.

Water sports

Membership of the **Blue Nile Sailing Club** (☎ Nil Street; ☎ 0912 207 565 or 0912 340 790) costs 1600 SDG for the first year and 400 SDG for each year after that. If you are going to stay for just one year, you can pay 1000 SDG for the whole year.

Club membership gives you free access to the club grounds (where there is a small cafeteria, a mosque and one of General Kitchener's gunboats), use of the club's sailboats and space to park your own boat if you have one.

The club can also arrange sailing lessons: 400 SDG for a month (three days a week, two hours each day).

Between November and April, the club organises regular sailing competitions and regattas on the Nile. These are held on Sundays and Wednesdays at 4.30 pm, and on Fridays at 9.30 am.

At the opposite end of town, near the Mogran, the **National Rowing Club** rents out kayaks for 20 SDG an hour. The club can also organise kayak lessons.

Golf

📶 15°30'47"N 32°36'44"E

Khartoum's golf course, popular with expats, is located a little way outside the city, on the road to Wad Medani.

A round of nine holes costs 30 SDG. If you just want to use the driving range, you can pay 10 SDG for a bucket of 40 balls. You can hire a set of golf clubs for 5 SDG. Caddies are also available at the course, usually costing about 10 SDG for one round.

Fridays and Saturdays are the most popular days to play golf. You can play outside these times, but it is best if you call in advance (☎ 0912 385 398) to check that the course is open.

To get to the course, follow the road out of Khartoum towards Wad Medani. Just before the Gezira checkpoint, veer off to the right. Immediately afterwards, turn left and continue following the railway track, which should be on your left. A few kilometres further on, you will come to the golf course.

The complex also has two tennis courts and a swimming pool.

SPECTATOR SPORTS

Horse racing

Horse races are regularly held at the **Equestrian Club**, not far from Souq as-Shabi. Tickets cost 2, 5 or 10 SDG (depending on where the seats are). Unfortunately, however, it is not easy to predict when such events will take place. Details of race schedules are usually spread by word of mouth. Races take place approximately once a month on a Friday, before sundown. If you are interested in attending, try and stop by the Equestrian Club to find out the latest race agenda.

Polo is also popular at the centre and usually takes place on Monday evenings, just before sunset.

Show-jumping occasionally takes place on Wednesdays but, again, the schedule is unreliable.

Big Sudanese companies often sponsor events at the race tracks.

Camel racing

Camel races take place on the outskirts of Omdurman every Friday morning very early (7 to 9 am in the winter and 6 to 8 pm in the summer). At this time of the morning, it is not possible to find any public transport going to the area, so you really need your own vehicle. The place is not easy to find. It is just off the road to Dongola, shortly after the police checkpoint.

Football

There are two football seasons in Khartoum: one runs from January until April, and the other from September until November.

During these months, games are regularly played in the main national stadium in Central Khartoum (otherwise known as Independence Stadium) or at individual clubs. The two most popular clubs in Khartoum are Al-Hilal and Al-Marikh. Both are located in Omdurman.

Premier division games usually take place on Fridays, with the less important games being played on Mondays. To find out exactly where games are taking place, look for details in the newspapers or on the television.

You can get in to watch second-division games for between 3 and 5 SDG, depending on how good the seats are. Major national games usually cost between 20 and 30 SDG, again depending on the seats. International games may cost even more.

Khartoum's national stadium is easy to get to; it is just outside Stad, the main bus station. To get to Al-Marikh's stadium, take a bus from Jackson station in Central Khartoum towards Souq as-Shabi in Omdurman, and get off at the town hall. The stadium is a 10-minute walk from there. To get to Al-Hilal's stadium, take a bus from Jackson towards Sadi al-Hilal and get off at the last stop.

MASSAGE AND SPA

The **Al-Kinani Specialised Polyclinic** (☏ Juba Station House 78, off Obeid Khatim Street, Mamoura; ☎ 0155 318 603 or 0915 262 163 or 0918 247 650) has both male and female masseurs who give nice, traditional Thai massages at reasonable prices. The place is clean and the Thai staff friendly. You have the choice of a Thai massage (30 SDG) or an oil massage (80 SDG). Thai massages take place in a big room, which you may have to share with other customers. Oil massages take place in private rooms.

There is also a **Thai physiotherapy clinic** in Riyad (☏ Between Mecca Street and Abdalla al-Tayeb Street; ☎ 0929 428 359 or 0929 428 358), which offers similarly-priced massages: 100 SDG for an oil massage, 50 SDG for a Thai massage and 50 SDG for a foot massage. The place also serves decent Thai food.

The **Al-Salam Rotana Hotel** offers a wider selection of different types of massage, including aromatherapy, *shiatsu* massage, reflexology and Swedish massages. Price start at 150 SDG per hour. It is open from 11 am to 8 pm.

Corinthia Hotel (☏ Nil Street, Khartoum centre; ☎ 0156 555 555) offers luxurious spa and massage facilities.

Queen Beauty Centre (☏ Street 15, Amarat; ☎ 0912 984 881 or 0155 102 762) offers oil massages for females only. Prices start at 60 SDG. Staff speak little English and all the masseurs are Sudanese.

The **Bahrain**, **Al-Salam Rotana** and **Coral** hotels both have saunas available for public use. The price is usually around 30-35 SDG.

LIBRARIES

The **British Council** used to have a very good library, but it has since been closed down.

The best foreign library in town is probably at the **French Cultural Centre** (@ bibliokhartoum@yahoo.fr). The library also has a good selection of DVDs available for borrowing, as well as internet access. Use of the library is free for those taking French lessons at the centre (p195). Alternatively, you can pay 75 SDG for a year's access, which entitles you to free rental of books, CDs and DVDs, as well as free access to the internet.

There are several Arabic libraries throughout Khartoum, such as the one just next to the **Palace Museum** on Jama'a Street.

CINEMA

Cinemas in Khartoum mainly show films in Arabic or sometimes in Hindi. There may be the occasional screening of an English flick, but such showings are few-and-far-between. Do not expect non-English films at cinemas to have subtitles in English.

There is a cinema in **Afra Mall** that shows movies in Arabic and

Hindi. The movies start at 1, 3, 5, 7 and 9 pm (Fridays to Wednesdays). Admission costs 10 SDG for adults and 5 SDG for kids.

The **French Cultural Centre**, **German Goethe-Institute** and **British Council** both regularly show European films, with subtitles in English. The times of the screenings vary, so the best thing to do is to take a look at their websites (p140) or pick up their latest cultural programmes. Screenings are generally free. The French Cultural Centre has a beautiful roof-top cinema, where you can watch movies in the open air.

The **Filipino Club** regularly shows films on Thursdays, with English subtitles.

DVD RENTAL AND SALE

DVD rental used to be very popular in Khartoum, but has declined in recent years due to the ease of downloading movies from the internet. There are a number of shops that sell DVDs and music CDs, but take care because, despite the high prices, most are pirated.

The more popular selection of DVD rental and sale places includes: **Java** (Mahuna Street, next to Ahmed Gasim Hospital, Bahri), **Piano** (📞 Mecca Street, Riyad; ☎ 0155 136 606), **Boys Shop** (📞 Street 131, Riyad), **Super Star** (📞 Shergi Street, Arknowit), **MB4** (📞 Next to Mekka Eye Hospital, Riyad) and **Evo Zone** (One branch in Bahri on Moasasa Street — ☎ 0912 270 395 — and the other in Riyad on the corner of Mashtal and Street 131 — ☎ 0912 968 758).

Al-Hawi (📞 Street 15, Amarat), has just started selling DVDs, many of which are in English.

THEATRE

Theatre is not all that common in Khartoum, although there are a few places that occasionally stage plays. The **National Theatre**, next to the Nile in Omdurman, is one such place — simply look out for posters around town or advertisements in the papers. Plays are usually in Arabic. A couple of times a year, international schools (such as **KICS** and the **American School**) also put on good performances.

BOWLING, POOL AND TABLE FOOTBALL

For a spot of ten-pin bowling, visit the first floor of **Afra Mall**. A game of 10 rounds costs 10 SDG per person.

You can find pool tables at a number of locations throughout the city. Games at **Tropicana Café** (📞 Street 15, behind where Sendyan Hotel used to be, Amarat) cost 15 SDG per hour. **Kronfil** (📞 Afriqia Street, just off Street 19 and next to Chicken Broast, Amarat) also charges 15 SDG per hour. **Billiards Station** (📞 Street 131, just next to Solitaire, Riyad) has a large number of pool tables for use. It is slightly pricier than the other places: 20 SDG for an hour or 15 SDG for half an hour. The **Coral** and the **Corinthia** hotels also have pool tables that the public can use.

Pool is also available at the **Sudanese Lawn Tennis Association**. **Afra Mall** has tables, but there is no air-conditioning. There is also a pool table at the **Blue Nile Sailing Club** — usually only available for members, but if it is not busy you might be able to negotiate the use of it.

You can play table football on the first floor of **Afra Mall** for 3 SDG per game. Unfortunately, though, the table is often woefully short of balls.

DANCING

Salsa classes are sometimes available in Khartoum, although they had been suspended as we were going to press. A two-hour session generally costs around 30 SDG and includes a salsa disco afterwards. For further information about when the classes might re-start, email **@** salsahavana@tiscali.co.uk.

A relatively new dance craze — **Zumba Fitness** — has just arrived in Khartoum. Inspired by Latin dance routines, the idea is to get participants to work up a sweat and burn off those excess calories. Hour-long Zumba Fitness classes are held three times a week, costing 30 SDG per session. For more details about the classes, including current location, contact **@** zumba.fitness@tiscali.co.uk.

African dance classes are given for women at Glamour (🏠 Street 21, Amarat). The dances are mostly Sudanese, although other African styles — such as Egyptian — are occasionally taught. This is a terrific way for women to gain an insight into the fascinating culture of Sudan. There will almost certainly be the opportunity to find out more about the Sudanese bridal dance (p81). A month's course, consisting of three hours per week, costs 130 SDG.

EMBASSIES

Many embassies in Khartoum organise parties and social gatherings. In order to go along to one of these events, you either have to know someone who works in a particular embassy or else you have to be working in the embassy yourself. Some embassies — most notably the Dutch, British and German ones — have become famous for regularly organising social clubs. The only way you can really find out about these, however, is to speak to people who work at the relevant embassies.

PICNIC SPOTS

There are a number of popular spots around Khartoum for hanging out with friends, playing cards and eating picnic lunches.

One of the best-known picnic spots is **by the banks of the Nile**, east of the Blue Nile Sailing Club.

Muzen Beach, just across the bridge that leads from Khartoum to Omdurman, is a particularly picturesque setting, and a very nice place to watch the sun set over the White Nile. There you will find a children's playground and a small cafeteria. You have to pay 2 SDG to enter the place, however.

Sunt Forest lies just to the west of the new bus station, on the banks of the White Nile. It's a little exaggerated to call the place a 'forest', but it can be a pleasant spot in which to relax.

Burri Beach lies further eastwards on the banks of the Blue Nile, just opposite Garden City. It is a very picturesque area and a popular place to swim.

Jebel Owlia is another option to consider. It's a little further than the other picnic destinations that have been mentioned — it takes almost an hour by road to get there — and you will have to take your passport with you, since you will be passing a security checkpoint. But the trip is worth it. Jebel Owlia is a great place for soaking up the sun in relaxing surroundings and eating fresh fish. There is even a campsite in Jebel Owlia, with proper camping facilities, where you can spent the night (p161).

Where To Sleep

There is a good and growing range of accommodation in Khartoum to meet your budgetary and comfort requirements. Prices are still a little on the high side, but they are starting to fall slowly, largely because of mounting competition.

Many hotels, particularly the ones at the top end of the market, will offer to register your passport with the authorities, which is something you are required to do within three days of arriving in Sudan (p28). This can save you a lot of inconvenience. However, bear in mind that, if you do register your passport yourself, you will only be charged around 117 SDG (the exact price varies depending on which registration office you use). By doing the registration for you, some of these hotels are making a lot of money. Remember that this is an optional service hotels offer and you should under no account feel obliged to make use of it.

For those on a budget, *lokandas* are worth considering. These are cheap and basic hotels, often with communal sleeping arrangements. There are *lokandas* all over Khartoum, but they are not always that easy to find. A few of the more popular ones are listed in this chapter. If you want to find any more, the best thing to do is to turn up in a suitable area (areas near marketplaces are usually best) and just ask around. Other cheap options include staying at the local youth hostel or pitching a tent at the Blue Nile Sailing Club.

Another important thing to consider, besides the size of your wal-

COUPLES

Under *sharia* law, it is forbidden for a man and a woman in North Sudan to stay in the same room in a hotel unless they are married. If you are a couple travelling in the country, many hotels will ask to see a copy of your marriage certificate before letting you stay in the same room.

let, is which particular area you wish to stay in.

Amarat and Riyad are both close to the airport, with some pretty decent restaurants and a large expat community.

Khartoum 2 and 3 are conveniently located between Central Khartoum and Amarat, also with some good restaurants.

Central Khartoum has an abundance of hotels to suit every budget, with the added advantage of being close to many sightseeing destinations. The cheaper ones are located in and around the market area, whilst the plusher hotels are found along the banks of the Nile. If you do opt for one of the cheaper hotels, remember to take particular care of your personal belongings, since theft is not uncommon in market areas.

Bahri and Omdurman have only fairly limited accommodation options.

HIGH-END

Grand Holiday Villa (☎ Nil Street, Central Khartoum; ☎ 0183 774 039; @ reservation@ holidayvillakhartoum.com; ☐ www.

holidayvillakhartoum.com) is housed in a lovely colonial-style villa on the banks of the Nile. This hotel offers many facilities, including: sauna, jacuzzi, pool tables, table tennis, table football, swimming pools and tennis courts. You can also find a barber, a travel agency, a souvenir shop and a cake shop on-site. The hotel's health centre provides massages for 115 SDG per hour.

There are three swimming pools in the hotel: one medium one, one big one and one that is only for women to use. At last visit, this third pool was undergoing refurbishment.

The hotel has wireless internet facilities, but they are not included in the price (12 SDG per hour).

There are two restaurants in the hotel, and a buffet organised every Friday.

It is worth asking for a room with a view of the Nile or one with a view of the swimming pool.

Grand Holiday Villa is definitely striving to capture the luxurious end of the market, with commensurate prices. A single room costs $230, a twin $260, a junior suite $500, an executive suite $600 and the presidential suite $2500.

Bahrain International Hotel (🏠 Sayed Abdul Rahman Street, Central Khartoum; ☎ 0183 746 873/4/9; @ info@ albahrainhotel-sd.com; 🖥 www. albahrainhotel-sd.com) is located along one of the main streets in the marketplace. Service is very friendly and rooms are comfortable. It has a very modern feel to it, with an efficient lift and electronic keycards to open doors. There are a number of different rooms to choose from. A single costs 200 SDG, a double 300 SDG, a suite (sleeping up to three people) 450 SDG and a flat (which includes a small hall and sleeps up to four people) 500 SDG.

All rooms come with air-con, fridge and TV. The suite has a bath, too. The hotel also has a meeting room that can host up to 120 people and a sauna (which costs an additional 30 SDG per hour). The hotel also provides free wi-fi for guests and there is an internet café on-site (one hour costs 5 SDG). The hotel has 58 rooms in total.

Corinthia (🏠 Nil Street, Central Khartoum; ☎ 0156 555 555; @ khartoum@corinthia.com; 🖥 www. corinthia.com), formerly known as Burj al-Fateh (management was trying to phase the name out as we went to press), is certainly the grandest hotel in town. The unique shape of the building is supposed to resemble the sail of a ship. The five-star hotel has 230 rooms and 55 suites, and caters particularly well for business travellers. Guests have free access to an indoor swimming pool, health centre, tennis courts, squash courts, and sauna rooms. The hotel also has a beauty salon, a fully-equipped business centre and six restaurants and cafés (including an Asian one on the top floor with fantastic views of the city). Although the hotel is right in the city centre, it is not within easy access of the airport and at peak times the airport run can take 40 or 50 minutes. Customer service is excellent and of international standards, as you would expect. There is wireless internet access throughout the hotel and there is an adjoining shopping mall. There is a handicraft stall at every Friday brunch in the 16th floor Mugran restaurant. Prices vary depending on demand, but expect to pay $270 for a deluxe room, $305 for an executive room, $435 for an executive suite, $1060 for the ministerial suite and the $3445 for the presidential suite. The hotel often runs promotions at weekends.

Coral Hotel (🏠 Mogran Street, Central Khartoum; ☎ 0183 774 100; @ info@coral-khartoum.com; 🖥 www.coral-khartoum.com),

formerly the Hilton, is one of the fancier hotels in Khartoum. Single rooms are around $180. Doubles (for two people) cost an extra $30. Suites cost between $325 and $400. Prices include breakfast but exclude 20% tax. Facilities at the hotel include swimming pool, gymnasium and free wi-fi access in the restaurant area and the business centre. In the rooms, there is cable internet access. The hotel has a souvenir shop, an ice cream parlour, a barber and a very good restaurant that is only open in the evening. There is also a separate buffet restaurant, open throughout the day, as well as a couple of cafés. Kids under six can eat free at the buffet, whilst those between six and 12 eat half price. The hotel has a Europcar office in the lobby where you can rent cars. The downside to this hotel is it is very difficult to get to by public transport and you really need to take a taxi, unless you enjoy walking long distances.

Al-Salam Rotana Hotel (🏠 Afriqia Street, Riyad; ☎ 0187 00 77 77; @ alsalam.hotel@rotana. com; 🖵 www.rotana.com/sudan/ khartoum/37) is one of Khartoum's best high-end hotels and is particularly good at taking care of business customers. It also has the added bonus of being very close to the airport. The best rooms to stay in during a business trip are on the fourth floor. For 650 SDG, you get a very decent room, but no breakfast. The executive rooms, costing 1000 SDG, are somewhat higger and include breakfast, as well as pre-dinner snack. Executive guests also get free airport pickup and drop-off, an hour's use of the hotel's internet facilities each day, an hour's use of the meeting room a day and unlimited beverages. The hotel also has two suites, which cost 1700 SDG and include all the facilities mentioned above. All

guests have free use of the swimming pool, the gym, the sauna and the Jacuzzi. There is also free wi-fi in the hotel. The Nuba restaurant offers daily buffets, with Wednesday night (seafood night) being a particular temptation. Monday is Italian night, Friday is Latino night, Saturday is international night and Sunday is Arabian night.

Assaha Village (🏠 Off Afriqia Street, near Canadian Embassy, Khartoum 2; ☎ 0183 481 919; @ assaha.sud@assahvillage.com; 🖵 www.assahvillage.com) has a lovely medieval look-and-feel to it. The hotel is close to the Canadian Embassy and not far from the Greek Club. The hotel has a small swimming pool (for guests only) and a café that serves delightful Ethiopian coffee. The hotel's restaurant serves international food (p172). A single room costs $150 and a double costs between $200 and $220, depending on how many people are staying in it. The hotel also has luxury VIP rooms ($225-250) and suites ($275-300). It is possible to put an extra bed in the room for $30. Prices include breakfast, airport reservation and drop off. The 20% tax is extra.

Lisamin Safari Hotel (🏠 Street 41, Amarat; ☎ 0183 595 815/17; @ info@lisaminsafarihotel.com; 🖵 www.lisaminsafarihotel.com) is a welcoming hotel with not unreasonable prices. A room with two beds costs $120 (for single occupancy) or $160 (for double occupancy). A junior suite costs $140 and a larger suite $160. Prices exclude 20% tax and breakfast. Guests can use the hotel gym for free, but facilities are extremely limited, comprising one running machine, one cycling machine and a few weights. There is a particularly good restaurant on the first floor — Cedars — which offers Lebanese fare (p169). All rooms have ensuite bathrooms. Each room has a TV, a phone and air-con. The hotel can help arrange travel and tours. It can also help with finding a more permanent place to live. At the back, there is a pleasant terrace and garden, which serve as an outdoor café in the summer. The staff speak very good English, and the manager also speaks some Danish and Swahili. The hotel can also arrange trips to see the Whirling Dervishes (p132) for $30, which some may consider pricey given that the ceremony is free to attend.

5M Hotel (🏠 Cathrina Street, Khartoum 2; ☎ 0183 462 962 or 0912 301 407; @ mickey5m1@gmail.com; 🖥 www.5mhotel.com) is a delightful place, with rather more of a European feel to it than you will experience in other hotels around the city. This may have something to do with the attention that is given to small details — such as hairdryers in the rooms and complimentary toiletry items. Rooms cost $120 for a single, $150 for a double and $180 for a suite. Discounts are available for UN workers. All prices exclude 20% tax, but include breakfast. The hotel offers free transport to and from the airport and two trips by car (with driver) into town. Guests also get free access to the internet on the first floor and there is wi-fi available. The hotel is owned by five brothers, whose names start with 'M' (hence the name). This is one of the few hotels in Khartoum that provides self-catering facilities; each room has its own kitchen, microwave, kettle and electric hotplate. You can also order food from nearby restaurants and have it brought to your room. The hotel has its own buffet lunch and dinner service for 30 SDG. English-language Sudanese papers are avail-

able in the lobby. Car hire services are available just next door.

Regency Hotel (🏠 Qasar Street, Central Khartoum; ☎ 0183 775 970/7; info@khartoumregencyhotel.com; 🖥 www.khartoumregencyhotel.com), formerly Meridian, was once one of the most popular and reputable places in town, but now has a rather faded and has-been look to it. The hotel has a medium-sized swimming pool (free of charge for guests) and a sauna (50 SDG). There is also an internet centre on the first floor (free for guests, 5 SDG per hour for non-guests). Rooms come with free wireless internet, hot water, TV and ensuite bathrooms. The hotel has 108 rooms. A single costs $130 and a double $150. The hotel also offers a free pick-up and drop-off service.

VIP Al Basair International Hotel (🏠 Street 29, near Afriqia Street, Amarat; ☎ 0183 566 470; @ vipalbasairhotel@yahoo.com) is rather tucked away and difficult to find, but it offers good service and staff that speak at least some English. The standard price for a single is $100 and $120 for a double, including breakfast and tax. Rooms are clean and reasonably big, each having either a shower or a bath. Free wi-fi is available for guests.

Acropole Hotel (🏠 Zubeir Pasha Street, Central Khartoum; ☎ 0183 772 860 or 0183 772 518; @ acropolekhartoum@gmail.com or acropolekhartoum@yahoo.com; 🖥 www.acropolekhartoum.com) claims to be the oldest hotel in Khartoum. It certainly has that dusty, olde-worlde charm about it. The Greek-owned hotel is a popular place for journalists to stay when they come to Khartoum. The staff are very friendly and great at fixing up things for you to see and do, if you just ask. The hotel even has a doctor on call (although guests must pay for this service). There is a good selection of English books in the lobby, plus internet terminals (free for guests) and reasonably up-to-date copies of magazines such as *The Economist*, *Time* and *Newsweek*. There is wi-fi throughout the hotel. Every room has air-con, a phone, a balcony and a TV. Rooms cost $115 for a single, $160 for a double and $210 for a triple. Prices include tax and breakfast. If you want full board, a single is $136, a double $203 and a triple $257. The Acropole is one of the few places in Khartoum where you can find postcards.

Dandas International Hotel (🏠 Abu Sin Street, Central Khartoum; ☎ 0918 220 132 or 0183 741 932/3; @ dandas2006@hotmail.com) is a comfortable hotel that offers good-sized rooms at reasonable prices. There is a certain queasy kitschness to the decor, but that aside there is much to recommend the hotel. It is also located conveniently close to the town centre, but not so close that you can hear the commotion of the *souq*. A standard single room costs $100, a king-sized room $120 and a suite $135. Prices include breakfast but exclude 20% tax All rooms come with a TV, air-con, fridge and ensuite bathroom. It is one of the few hotels where you can find a bath in many of the rooms. Everything is spotlessly clean. Free wi-fi is available. The hotel can help arrange a visit to the deserts, including the Merowe dam, as well as excursions on the Nile (850 SDG for the rent of a big boat for one hour, or 385 SDG for a smaller one).

MID-RANGE

Bougainvilla Guesthouse (🏠 House 339, Block 21, off Abdalla al-Tayeb Street, Riyad; ☎ 0123 883 390 or 0922 615 445; @ mail@ bougainvillaguesthouse.com; 🖥 www.bougainvillaguesthouse.com) is a quaint little place owned by a Norwegian and Danish couple. All rooms have air-con, TV, and wi-fi (5 SDG per day). There is also hot water. The hotel has a rooftop bar and restaurant, which is open every day of the week apart from Friday. The restaurant is just for guests and is only open in the afternoon and evening. A meal costs between 30 and 35 SDG, depending on the menu. The hotel has 17 rooms. A small single room, with shared bathroom, costs $60. For a larger room, with ensuite bathroom, expect to pay $80. A business suite, including office facilities, costs $100. For double occupancy, add 40% to all prices. Prices include breakfast, served on the roof, but exclude 20% tax. The hotel offers transportation to and from the airport (30 SDG), although this is far more than you would pay for a taxi. A meal at the restaurant costs around 30 SDG. A discount on accommodation is available for UN staff.

Plaza Hotel (🏠 Sayed Abdel Rahman Street, Central Khartoum; ☎ 0183 792 986 or 0183 793 898 or 0183 772 197; @ sudanplazahotel@ yahoo.cn or shima200909@yahoo. cn) has single rooms for $80 and double rooms for $100. Prices include breakfast and tax. Service is friendly, but the English of the mostly-Chinese staff is fairly limited. There is also a small shop in the hotel that sells souvenirs, postcards, books and stationery. Wi-fi internet is available and the hotel can help organise international and domestic flights.

Taka Hotel (🏠 Abdul Monim Street, Khartoum; ☎ 0155 256 950 or 0912 616 231; @ info@ takahotel.com; 🖥 www.takahotel. com) has 42 ensuite double rooms, and two rather poky single rooms. If you are on your own, it is worth asking for one of the double rooms for the same price — if they are not too busy, this might be possible. Rooms cost 200 SDG for a single and 280 SDG for a double. All prices include breakfast and tax.

Every room comes with a fridge, a TV and wireless internet. There are also internet terminals in the lobby that guests can use free of charge. The hotel has free parking and can organise tours to the Merowe Dam for groups upon request.

Falcon Hotel (🏠 Off Baladeyah Street; ☎ 0183 774 641 or 0183 772 195; @ falcon@alokgroups.com) is conveniently-located between Baladeyah Street and Jamhouriya Street. The rooms are nice and clean and all have air-con. Unfortunately, they are fairly small and so is the bathroom. The hotel offers a free laundry service for guests. A single room costs 181 SDG, a double 217 SDG and the suite 285 SDG. Breakfast, tax and wireless internet are included in the prices. There are 18 rooms. The hotel fills up quite quickly, so it is better to book in advance. Each floor has a pleasant common area with chairs and tables.

Al-Muhajir Hotel Flats (🏠 Street 15, next to Tropicana Café, Amarat; ☎ 0183 483 020; @ almuhajiir.flats@almuhajiir.sd) is well-located in the centre of Amarat. Rooms cost 150 SDG for a single and 200 SDG for a double, including tax and wireless internet. It is best to ask for the bigger rooms, since they cost the same as the smaller ones. A big attraction of this hotel is the free supervised parking at the back.

Shahrazad Hotel (🏠 Jami Street, Central Khartoum; ☎ 0183 770 965 or 0183 783 577 or 0183 775 967; @ shahrazad_hotel@hotmail.com) is a fairly characterless and noisy hotel. It seems to be particularly popular with local Sudanese, but hosts few foreigners. Rooms cost 226 SDG for a single and 306 SDG for a double. There are also family rooms, which sleep four people, for 520 SDG. However,

these rooms are disappointingly basic, each containing little more than four beds and a small TV.

Al-Ferdous Hotel (🏠 Jami Street, Central Khartoum; ☎ 0183 747 200/1; @ info@alferdoushotel.com; 🖥 www.alferdoushotel.com) opened in 2006. Rooms cost 300 SDG for a single and 354 SDG for a double, inclusive of tax and breakfast. All rooms have air-con and a fan. Some rooms have small balconies. There is a laundry service available and free wireless internet in the rooms. Outside, computer internet terminals cost 7 SDG per hour.

Inaam Hotel (🏠 Sayed Abdul Rahman Street; ☎ 0183 786 635/40; @ inaam@yahoo.com) has a number of fairly small rooms. Each one has an ensuite shower and hot water, plus a TV. Singles cost 110 SDG and doubles cost 126 SDG. There are 40 rooms in the hotel. There is also a fairly basic restaurant on the sixth floor and a café on the ground floor.

Aharga Hotel (🏠 Central Khartoum; ☎ 0183 747 278/79/80/81) has single rooms for 372 SDG and doubles for 408 SDG. Prices include breakfast and tax. Every room has air-con, TV and a bath. There is an internet connection (6 SDG per hour) in the restaurant on the ground floor. The hotel has 35 rooms in total.

Horizon Hotel (🏠 Malik Street, near Qandoul Roundabout, Central Khartoum; ☎ 0155 151 144; 🖥 www.horizonhotel-sd.com, @ horizon@horizonhotel-sd.com) is customer-orientated with decent-sized rooms at reasonable prices. A single room costs $150, a double costs $200, a triple costs $250 and a suite costs $300. The hotel often gives discounts at off-peak times. There is a rather nice little south Indian restaurant on the ground floor (p163).

Where To Sleep

Al-Ahlam (Street 47, Khartoum 2; 0155 779 901/2 or 0123 503 636; info@alahlamhotel.com; www.alahlamhotel.com), which means 'the world' in Arabic, is conveniently located not far from the airport, just down the road from Khartoum's youth hostel. It is one of the newer hotels in town and business remains correspondingly slow. Still, service is very friendly and prices are reasonable. A single costs $100, a twin $150 and a suite $200, including breakfast and tax. The manager used to work for Palace Hotel in Bahri, which has since closed down. The place has 34 rooms including suites, and all come with satellite TV. It has two restaurants — the regular one for guests and a VIP one, which those not staying at the hotel are free to use. Like many places in Khartoum at the moment, the restaurant tries to cater for all tastes, boasting that it will cook whatever the guest wants — with the result that dishes can be disappointing. The hotel has free wi-fi for guests and a stand-by generator. It also offers free pickup and drop-off to the airport. Management have grandiose plans for the hotel — including building a gym, sauna and massage parlour — but you shouldn't expect them to be ready any time soon.

Shariqa (Off Jami Street, near Qandoul Roundabout) is one of the more upmarket places to stay around the *souq* area. It's rather hidden away down one of the backstreets, but most people in the area should be able to point you in the right direction. A single room costs $50, a double $60 and a triple $70. Prices included breakfast and tax. The hotel has wireless internet but you have to pay (5 SDG for one hour). The hotel also offers a laundry service (one item for 2.5 SDG). There is a lift in the hotel. Rooms are clean and come equipped with TV, air-con, fan, fridge and ensuite bathroom.

Kanon Hotel (Street 15, Amarat; 0183 59 59 59; mail@kanonhotel.com; www.kanonhotel.com) prides itself on its customer service, which is really very good. Located in Amarat, it is one of the newer additions to Khartoum's accommodation scene, but has already started to attract a steady stream of business. Most of the staff speak good English. The hotel has a gym, sauna and massage parlour. It also offers laundry and car rental services.

Sahara (Off Jamhouriya Street) is conveniently located in the centre of town, but rather tucked away with a nearly impossible-to-find entrance. When you finally do work out how to get in, it feels as though you are entering a secret, underground place that doesn't belong in Khartoum. Scattered around the entrance way to the hotel are a number of folkloric shops, selling all manner of interesting knick-knacks.

GHOST HOTELS

Beware of hotels that no longer exist!

Arak Hotel (Souq al-Arabi) used to be one of the biggest hotels in Khartoum, with surely one of the largest signs announcing its presence. The sign still exists, which can prove fairly frustrating for those weary travellers wanting to find a bed for the night. The hotel, you see, closed in 1985, following the implication of some of its staff in a crime in Khartoum.

Ditto for Africa Hotel on Afriqia Street, which closed down more recently.

We haven't included any of these hotels in our reviews simply because they no longer exist.

Another hotel which you probably won't be able to stay at is Sudan Hotel on the banks of the Nile. If you try to get a room in this establishment, you will be told that the hotel is reserved exclusively for Chinese oil workers.

Rooms are basic but clean, consisting of a fridge, air-cooler, fan, TV and ensuite bathroom (with bath). The hotel also has a lift. Singles cost 120 SDG and doubles 150 SDG.

Lan Tian International Hotel (☎ Street 117, off Mashtal Street, Riyad; ☎ 0183 526 789 or 0906 277 779 or ☎ 0912 350 739 or 0910 167 578; @ ltih@sina.ch or 1479719377@qq.com) is a Chinese-owned hotel located in the heart of the Riyad district. The hotel is a classy place with good customer service. All rooms are ensuite and come with high-speed internet access, air-con, digital TV and a fridge. A single costs between $60 and $90, and a double $120. Prices include breakfast. There are a number of international shops in the locality, many selling a good range of spices from India and China. The hotel has a good, though somewhat pricey, restaurant where a meal can easily cost 80 to 100 SDG..

BF Hotel (☎ Street 37, near Afriqia Street, Amarat; ☎ 0912 360 966 or 0183 488 204 or 0183 484 195; @ hamza.gad2010@yahoo.com) is a small tucked-away little place in Amarat. Not the cheapest place but rooms are decent: $75 for a single and $150 for a double. Prices include breakfast. Staff speak limited English.

Al-Faisal Hotel (☎ Koliyat Altib Street; ☎ 0183 789 999) is a big hotel with 40 rooms. All rooms come with air-con, fridge and ensuite bathroom. The rooms are extremely clean. A single costs $50 and a double $75. An hour's use of internet costs 3 SDG. The hotel also has a laundry service — a single item costs between 1 and 4.50 SDG.

Dubai Hotel (☎ Abdel Rahman Street / Isbitalya Street; ☎ 0183 790 800/1/2) is a clean and comfortable place to spend the night. Each of the hotel's 25 rooms come with air-con, fridge and ensuite bathroom. Guess also have free access to the gym and can make free local phone calls. Free wi-fi is avail-

able. A single room costs 170 SDG and a double 185 SDG.

LOW-END

Central Hotel (☎ Malik Street, just on Qandoul Roundabout, Central Khartoum) is a somewhat dilapidated option in the centre of town, which doesn't appear all that clean. Prices are a little on the high side for what you're getting — 75 SDG for a single and 95 SDG for a double. Rooms come with an air-cooler, fan, TV and rather rough-and-ready ensuite bathroom.

Wessel (☎ Sayed Abdul Rahman Street, Central Khartoum) also in the centre of town, is slightly downmarket but good if you want to save a few bucks. The hotel could do with a little sprucing up, but at least the rooms have air-con (although they don't have a TV). The hotel is fairly small and is often full. A single costs 40 SDG and a double costs 70 SDG.

Badr (☎ Sayed Abdul Rahman Street, Central Khartoum) offers fairly basic rooms for 70 SDG (single) or 90 SDG (double). There is no difference in the rooms, only the number of people that can stay there. Rooms include a TV, air-con, fan and ensuite bathroom (usually with bath). The hotel has 40 rooms in total.

Youth Hostel (☎ House 66, Street 47, Khartoum 2; ☎ 0183 480 385; @ info@sudaneseyha.net; 🖵 www.sudaneseyha.net) is a nice, cheap and clean place to stay, with a lovely enclosed outdoor area. People are still surprised to learn that Khartoum has a youth hostel, but it is easy enough to find; it is just down the road from the Dutch Embassy and not far from the Ethiopian Church. There are 65 beds in the hostel. Staying in a room with two beds costs 35 SDG per person. A night's sleep in a room with more than two beds costs 25 SDG. If you don't mind sleeping in a dorm with up to 25 people, then you can pay as little as 10 SDG. You must have a YHA card to sleep at the hostel, which can be purchased on-the-spot for 20 SDG. The hostel is closed between 10 am and 2 pm for cleaning. There is an 11 pm curfew.

Dama Hotel (🏠 Abdul Monim Street / Isbitalya Street, Central Khartoum; ☎ 0183 743 583/4/5; @ scad@dama.com) is a pretty low-cost option, but expect to get what you pay for. A single costs 50 SDG and a double 70 SDG. This is worth thinking about, considering the price, but some of the *lokandas* offer better value for money. Each room has an ensuite bathroom, an air-cooler, a fan and a TV. There are 32 rooms in the hotel. At last visit, its restaurant was undergoing renovation.

Abdel Dayim Hotel (🏠 Hashim Beh Street, Central Khartoum) is a small *lokanda* with only eight rooms. A bed in one of these rooms costs 10 SDG. You can also rent a whole double room for 20 SDG or a triple room for 30 SDG. Each room has a fan and a separate bathroom.

Wadi Halfa Hotel (🏠 Central Khartoum; ☎ 0183 776 054) has single rooms for 15 SDG, double rooms for 25 SDG and triple rooms for 30 SDG. You pay for the whole room. Each room has a fan, a plastic table, a chair and a cupboard. The bathroom is separate.

Al-Nahrain Hotel (🏠 Isbitalya Street, Central Khartoum; ☎ 0183 780 315) is a pretty basic *lokanda* with 11 double rooms. A bed for the night costs 15 SDG. Expect to share the room if you are alone, unless you want to pay 30 SDG for the whole room. The bathroom is outside, but it is very clean.

Omnia Tourism Hotel (🏠 Hashim Beh Street; ☎ 0911 248 063 or 0121 979 450) is a *lokanda* with

basic single rooms costing 24 SDG. If you want a room with a cooler and a fridge, this will cost 35 SDG. The bathroom is outside. Sleeping in a dorm costs 8 SDG.

Marshal Hotel (🏠 Off Malik Street), just opposite Horizon Hotel in the centre of town, is just about as cheap as they come. Expect to pay 25 SDG for a rather pokey two-bed room, which looks as though it hasn't been cleaned in a while. Besides the beds, the only amenity in the room is a clunky fan. The toilet and shower are separate.

CAMPING

Blue Nile Sailing Club (🏠 Nil Street, Central Khartoum; ☎ 0912 207 565) has spaces where you can pitch your tent for $5 a night. You must have your own tent, however. The club is a great spot for watching the sun set over the Nile, although the place is a lot less tranquil since the nearby Mek Nimir Bridge opened, just to the west of it. The site also has some parking space. Motorcycles are free. Cars and trucks cost $15. Buses cost $20.

A campsite at Jebel Owlia (☎ 0900 914 148 or 0917 623 036) a 45 minute drive out of town, offers plots to pitch your tent for $40 per person (kids can stay half price). Alternatively, you can stay in one of the tents already on the site for $160, which includes three meals. Cheaper rates are available for half-board and simple bed-and-breakfast. Barbecue facilities are available on the campsite. Kayaks can be rented for $10 an hour. If you want to make use of the camping facilities, including the barbecue, but don't want to sleep there, then you can just pay the entrance fee of $20 per person (half price for kids).

INDEX OF RESTAURANTS

Most of the international-style restaurants are located in the Riyad and Amarat districts of Khartoum. Khartoum 2 and 3 also have a handful of such restaurants.

Afriqia Street, the road that runs alongside the airport, has the lion's share of the city's fast-food restaurants.

For something more local, check out some of the places around the *souq* in Central Khartoum. The best local restaurant, though, is without a doubt Mona Lisa (p166).

If you want to visit an area that has a bit more buzz to it, try Street 41 in Diem. Here you'll find dozens of small local cafés and restaurants, staffed by female waitresses and patronised exclusively by men. If you have just come from another capital city in Africa, you might find it strange to describe this area as the height of Khartoum's nightlife. But live for a while in the city and you'll start to understand the appeal of Diem.

CENTRAL KHARTOUM

Noon @ Noon (🏠 Qasar Street, in front of Regency Hotel; 🍴 Sudanese; ☎ 0912 559 429 or 0912 209 603; 💲 Cheap) is one of the few places where you can eat cheap Sudanese food in comfortable surroundings, rather than perched on the edge of upturned drinks crates. There are many tables in the restaurant, but they often fill up quite quickly. Very good value for money; expect to pay around 3 SDG for a basic meal. There is an internet café on the premises.

Horizon (🏠 Malik Street, near Qandoul Roundabout; 🍴 Indian / Chinese; ☎ 0155 151 133/44; 💲 Moderate), a hotel in the centre of town, offers very good curries (mostly from southern India) at reasonable prices. The service is

excellent and the waiters are very knowledgeable about the food they are serving. Food is cooked fresh and can be adjusted to your tastes. The restaurant also serves Chinese food, but this is more hit-and-miss.

Papa Costa (🏠 Jamhouriya Street; 🍴 Greek / Sudanese; ☎ 0915 060 350; 💲 Moderate) offers the usual grilled Sudanese fare, as well as sandwiches and pizzas. Disappointingly, it has lost its Greek influence for which it had become so well known, even though a note on the menu still heaps praise on the restaurant's founder, who it claims is still remembered for his freshly baked Greek bread. However, the food is not bad, especially the sandwiches, although prices are a little on the high side. A particularly nice feature of the restaurant is the outside terrace, where live music is performed every Thursday evening. Papa Costa does home delivery, takeaway and catering. There is also wireless internet.

Sea Scout Meal (🏠 Nil Street; 🍴 Sudanese; ☎ 0183 795 125; 💲 Cheap) is an unattractive place not far from the banks of the Nile, but the food is surprisingly good and the prices low. The burgers, served with fried egg, won't disappoint.

Rickshaw (🏠 Corinthia Hotel, Nil Street; 🍴 Indian / Chinese; ☎ 0187 155 155; 🕐 7 to 11 pm, closed Friday; 💲 Expensive) is probably the best Asian-style restaurant in town. Set on the 18th floor of Khartoum's most distinctive hotel, it offers fabulous views of the Nile and Mogran area. Food is very tasty and uses fresh ingredients. Dishes are adjusted depending on the season, and the friendly waiters are on hand to give advice about what to order according to tastes. As might be expected, prices are high, but not outrageously so —

a three course meal, with coffee, might cost around 80 SDG.

Fresh Fish (🏠 Nil Street; 🍴 Fish; 💲Cheap) is a reasonably decent place to come and eat fried fish on the banks of the Nile. There are places that serve better fish, but perhaps not in such a nice setting — a lovely little terrace garden overlooking the water. A portion of fish costs 14 SDG.

RIYAD

Italy Pizza Centre (🏠 Ustaz Ahmed Khair Street, near Ozone; 🍴 Italian; 💲Moderate) — see Italy Pizza Centre in Khartoum 2 & 3. The one in Riyad is bigger, with better service.

Aroma (🏠 Off Street 60, near Mashtal; 🍴 Café) is a relaxing place to come for a coffee, with cool air-con, free wi-fi and soft lighting. For something different, they also serve the traditional Sudanese drinks *tabaldi* and *karkaday*. European-style meals are available for between 22 and 30 SDG.

Time Out (🏠 Street 117, near Abdalla al-Tayeb Street; 🍴 Café; ☎ 0912 315 155) is one of the many new cafés that have sprung up in Riyad recently, with very nice tables and chairs and extremely good air-con. A TV in the café shows music and films. The menu includes a range of mocktails (12 SDG), fresh juice (10 SDG) and frappés (14 SDG). These prices are exclusive of 20% tax and service charge. Upstairs, there is even a computer arcade and Play Station room (10 SDG will buy you four games). The café also serves ice-cream. Drinks are good but not exceptionally so.

Tutti Frutti (🏠 Next to Riyad Park; 🍴 Italian café / Ice-cream parlour; ☎ 0122 542 493; 💲Moderate; ⏰ Sat-Wed: 9 am to 11.30 pm, Thu: 9 am to 12 midnight, Fri: 10 am to 11.30 pm) is another of those places in Khartoum where quality and service has tragically gone downhill. The ice-cream is still okay, with an extensive range of flavours, but it used to be one of the best places in the city. The café also serves some typical Italian specialities such as *affogato al caffé* (vanilla ice-cream garnished with hot espresso). There is a pleasant terrace outside. Tutti Frutti can also provide catering for big parties.

Barista (🏠 Mecca Street, near Street 117; 🍴 Café; ☎ 0183 596 599; 💲Expensive) is an American-style café with excellent customer service (this seems to be one of their top priorities). The café is very spacious inside, and has a large outside garden. The cakes and other snacks they serve are very good, and it has an excellent range of iced coffees (great for those hot days). Worth visiting just for the aroma of freshly-ground coffee lingering in the air. Of course, the quality of coffee, food and service is all reflected in the price.

M Burger (🏠 Mecca Street, just next to Barista; 🍴 Fast-food; 💲Cheap) serves arguably the best burgers in town. A fairly hefty burger costs around 7 SDG. There is no formal seating — customers (usually Sudanese men) simply eat whilst sitting on upturned drink crates.

Potato's (🏠 In front of Riyad Park; 🍴 Fritterie; 💲Cheap) advertises itself as the first Belgian-style fritterie in town, and the novel idea seems to be gaining popularity. The chips are beautifully cooked and served with an exotic range of sauces, including honey mustard mayonnaise, barbecue and green chilli mango. Portions cost between 4 and 9 SDG and come with one free sauce.

Oshin (🏠 Street 112, near Mashtal; ☎ 0183 520 226; 🍴 Japanese;

Expensive) is the only Japanese restaurant in town and has become incredibly popular among Sudanese and foreigners alike. The Japanese grill, where the food is cooked right in front of you, is exceptional. Less good is the sushi. The restaurant has a nice outdoor area where you can dine.

Syrian Gate (🏠 Mashtal Street; ☎ 0901 231 007 or 0123 330 005 or 0120 788 727; 🍴 Syrian; 💲 Moderate) serves very good food at extremely reasonable prices. The salads are excellent — 8 SDG for a good portion. They have a great range of Syrian food, and it is quite common to order a number of different dishes and share among friends. They do a particularly delicious *fatoush* salad, which is a typical Syrian dish made from fried pita bread and vegetables. Juices are also very good here (10 SDG each) and the restaurant is one of the few places to serve kiwi juice. For something a little bit different, ask for a strawberry and pineapple juice. It is lovely to dine in the outside garden, although it can get hot since no cooling water-jets have yet been installed.

Debonairs (🏠 Mashtal Street; 💲 Cheap) — see branch in Amarat.

Smile (🏠 Street 117; 🍴 Sudanese; ☎ 0155 242 020; 💲 Cheap) is a basic and rather unexciting sandwich and pizza restaurant, but it does have a cute name that is bound to put you in a good mood. A basic margarita pizza costs between 7 and 19 SDG, and a chicken sandwich between 8 and 14 SDG.

My Place (🏠 Mecca Street, near Street 117; 🍴 International; ☎ 0120 885 500 or 0120 770 055; 💲 Moderate) is one of the newer additions to Khartoum's international dining scene, but it is certainly not one of the fanciest. Appearances are scruffy and service is disappointing; it can take ages to attract the attention of a waitress to serve you, even when the place is clearly not very busy. But the food is decent and not as pricey as some of the posher places in Riyad. The free wi-fi is an added bonus. The place also does home delivery (3 SDG).

Beatles (🏠 Street 117; 🍴 International; ☎ 0913 337 338 or 0923 368 261; 💲 Moderate) is a Western-style restaurant that used to be pretty decent. These days, though, it suffers from terrible service and mediocre food — a tragic shadow of its former days. The mocktails (8 SDG) are worth trying, though, and the restaurant does a decent plate of chips, too. Although the name is spelt as above, the restaurant is dedicated to the Beetle car, rather than to the pop group: there is part of one mounted just over the entrance. The inside of the place is furnished with attractive wood panelling. Expect to pay between 10 and 18 SDG for sandwiches and 25 to 30 SDG for chicken or beef main courses. The restaurant also serves fish (20 to 24 SDG).

Star Moon (🏠 Mashtal Street; 🍴 General) is one of those restaurants that is trying to do too many things to please too many people, rather than doing one thing well. It serves posh Sudanese food — such as stuffed pigeon for 25 SDG, although this isn't always available — whilst at the same time offering Moroccan tagine, Turkish cuisine, Indian curries, Chinese dishes and Thai food. Mains are all more-or-less around 25 to 30 SDG. Service is extremely friendly, but the food is nothing exceptional. The place seems to be crying out for customers and it might start attracting some if it could only work out what kind of restaurant it wants to be.

Havana (🏠 Mashtal Street; 🍴 Lebanese; ☎ 0155 180 405; 💲 Moderate) offers an assortment of grilled meat and fish, as well as good Lebanese humus. The prices are pretty high and the service leaves a little to be desired, but the quality of the food isn't bad. Home delivery is free for orders above 30 SDG.

Dodi's (🏠 Mashtal Street; 🍴 Egyptian; ☎ 0155 775 777; 💲 Cheap) — see Dodi's in Amarat.

Square (🏠 Street 131; 🍴 Indian / Chinese; ☎ 0912 919 417 or 0912 114 017 or 0183 231 100 or 0183 231 200; @ info@square.int. com; 💲 Moderate to expensive), formerly Little Asia, is a pretty decent restaurant serving fairly authentic Indian and Chinese cuisine. Main courses start at 20 SDG. Portions are a good size, although rice and naan bread are extra (10 SDG for plain rice and 3 SDG for plain naan). Dining in the open-air garden is particularly pleasant.

Solitaire (🏠 Street 131; 🍴 International; ☎ 0155 770 003) — see Solitaire in Amarat. This one is much bigger, though, and has many more plugs for recharging your laptop if you come here to work.

Laziz (🏠 Mecca Street / Street 131; 🍴 Sudanese; ☎ 0912 433 042; 💲 Cheap) — see Laziz in Amarat.

Pizza Connection (🏠 Mashtal Street; 🍴 Italian; ☎ 0155 183 330; 💲 Moderate to expensive) has a rather faded has-been look about it these days. The pizzas are not bad, and the service friendly, but the prices remain high (24 to 30 SDG for one pizza). The rise of a number of other decent pizzerias has left this particular restaurant struggling for customers. Pizza Connection also serves other Italian dishes (such as bruschetta and lasagne) as well as a selection of sandwiches and fried chicken. They do home delivery — 2 SDG for Riyad and 4 SDG for Amarat.

Mona Lisa (🏠 Off Street 60, northern end; 🍴 Sudanese; 💲 Cheap) is unquestionably the best place in Khartoum to come for sampling traditional Sudanese fare. Not just because of the price (very low) and the quality (extremely good), but also because of the wide range of different dishes. It is a really great place to experiment with different styles of Sudanese cooking. The drawback to the place is that the menu is only in Arabic and things can get very chaotic when the place is crowded (which is always). Thankfully, the people serving are very helpful and patient. Simply point at a dish you want, say "*da shinu?*" and they will tell you its name. You pay the cashier for whatever dish you want and he will give you a series of coloured tokens, which you exchange for the food at the relevant counter. The place is exclusively for men, although foreigners (male or female) are always welcome. The place, which is only open in the evening, is particularly popular with bus and rickshaw drivers, who come here after a day's work. Some dishes that are especially worth trying include *agashay* (roasted meat on skewers), *shaya* (barbecued meat) and the excellent *kawaree shorba* (beef soup).

Enzo's (🏠 Southern end of Street 60; 🍴 Italian; ☎ 0912 331 416 or 0912 331 417; 💻 enzo@enzo-pizza.com; 🕐 Sat-Thu: 11 am to 12 midnight, Fri: 5 pm to 12 midnight; 💲 Moderate) is one of the newer restaurants in town, serving pizzas and other Italian-style dishes. Service and quality of food tends to be somewhat variable, but on the whole is a reasonably decent place to eat. It used to be a popular place for UN staff to come, when they were stationed in the city.

TAYIF AND ARKOWIT

Habesha (🏠 Off Obeid Khatim Street, east of Afra Mall; 🍽 Ethiopian; ☎ 0912 302 410 or 0912 606 869 or 0912 366 616; @ habesha_restaurant@hotmail.com; 💲 Moderate) is an excellent place to go to if you are after an authentic taste of Ethiopia. The décor is delightful, with low stools around romantically-lit circular tables, on top of which are straw table covers. The Ethiopian staff are very friendly and the food is excellent: an enjoyable variety of spicy vegetarian and meat dishes to match all tastes, accompanied by traditional Ethiopian *kisra* bread. The coffee is pure heaven. It costs 7 SDG for a *jabana* that easily does four cups. Prices are extremely reasonable.

Afra Mall Food Court has a range of restaurants serving burgers, pizzas, Chinese dishes, sandwiches and ice-creams. Quality is generally disappointing and prices are not as low as they ought to be. It is inexplicably popular with Khartoum's middle class youth, who like to come and hang out with their friends. The only reason for coming here is if you are in the area anyway, since there are no other choices nearby. At 30 SDG a dish, the Chinese restaurant is outrageously expensive.

There is a wonderful little **Thai restaurant** (🏠 Between Mecca Street and Abdalla al-Tayeb Street; 🍽 Thai; ☎ 0929 428 359 or 0929 428 358), tucked out of the way and almost impossible to find unless you know where to look. It is identified only by a sign saying "Physiotherapy" outside. The centre offers Thai-style massages as well as very good food. Dishes cost between 25 and 35 SDG. Portions are

small, but quality is exceptional. And, like the food in Bangkok, they don't hold back with the spices. You can eat at the centre — there are some tables and chairs, both inside and out — or take your order away.

GARDEN CITY, BURRI AND MANSHEA

Garden City Café (🏠 Sharif al-Hindi Street, Garden City; 🍽 Café; 💲 Moderate) is a pleasant outdoor café, with a big screen showing various video clips. It is one of the few cafés in town that serves flavoured coffee. The hazelnut variety is particularly worth trying.

Spark Café (🏠 Gasim Hashim Street, western end; 🍽 Café; ☎ 0124 890 777 or 0124 890 888; 💲 Cheap) is a relaxing café with nice outdoor space that includes cooling water-jets. The restaurant also offers Syrian-style food, including *fatoush salads* and soup. Fresh juices are available.

Syrian Fresh Food (🏠 Street 60, north of Omak Street; 🍽 Syrian; ☎ 0918 119 624 or 0923 023 807; 💲 Moderate) — see the one in Amarat.

Topkapi (🏠 Gasim Hashim Street, eastern end; 🍽 Turkish; ☎ 0183 268 888/9 or 0183 260 000 or 0909 500 700; 💲 Moderate) takes its name from a famous palace in Istanbul, which was once the official residence of the Ottoman sultans. Food is very good and the service is even better. Despite Sudan's strong links with Turkey, there are not all that many Turkish restaurants in Khartoum and so eating here makes a refreshing change. Even better, the food is very typically Turkish, featuring such stars as Turkish pizza, *lahmacun* and *pide*. The restaurant also offers the more easily-recognisable durum kebabs. The aromas coming out of the restaurant are exquisite. There is a nice garden attached to the place, with water-coolers. Prices are around 20 to 30 SDG for a main.

Panda Restaurant (🏠 Near Chinese Embassy, Riyad; 🍴 Chinese; ☎ 0912 987 718 or 0183 483 770; 💲 Moderate) is a reasonable Chinese restaurant. The food is nothing special, but the portions are huge and the price is generally not excessive. The seafood dishes can be a little expensive, though. The restaurant does takeaway, which you can order by phone.

AMARAT

Star Café (🏠 Street 41; 🍴 Café) used to be a *sheesha* place, with a lovely outdoor space to chill in. It is still a relaxing place to come, only minus the *sheesha*. There is also an air-conditioned inside area in case the Sudanese heat gets too much for you. The place serves a range of pizzas (18-20 SDG) and sandwiches (13-19 SDG). Its range of ice-cream (9-11 SDG) isn't bad either.

Ice-Cream 41 (🏠 Street 41; 🍴 Ice-cream parlour; 💲 Cheap) has become something of a legend among local Sudanese. It is often said that most of the couples whose romances blossomed in Khartoum have, at some time, passed through here. On any given afternoon or evening, you will find amorous couples sitting outside the parlour, lost in each other's company, enjoying ice-creams. The aroma of freshly-baked cornets is delightful. The shop only has two flavours — vanilla-and-chocolate and strawberry-and-pineapple — although you can add honey or nuts as a topping. Prices are very cheap — between 1 and 3 SDG, depending on the size of the ice-cream.

The shop doesn't have any formal seating, but, if you don't mind dirtying your clothes a little, there are some blocks of cement that you can perch upon outside.

Dodi's (🏠 Street 41, near Lisamin Safari Hotel; 🍴 Egyptian; ☎ 0155 775 777/8; 💲 Cheap) makes good pizzas at very reasonable prices. They also serve *sha'urma* and *fatiras*. Try the vegetarian pizza. There are several branches of Dodi's: in Amarat, in Riyad, in Bahri and in Omdurman. The ones in Bahri and Riyad also serve *kusheri*, an Egyptian noodle dish, and some of the best burgers in town. Ask for a double cheeseburger and you will not be disappointed. The restaurant has also started selling a range of tempting Arab pastries and desserts. There is a nice outside garden to eat in.

Osama Cafeteria (🏠 Street 41; 🍴 Sudanese; ☎ 0918 105 185 or 0912 354 144; 💲 Cheap) serves cheap but good traditional Sudanese food, such as *fuul* and *tameeya*. The name of the place is not written anywhere, but it is quite easy to find. Food and décor are simple, but the place has become very popular among the Sudanese. Prices used to be very cheap, although they have gone up recently. A *tameeya* sandwich costs around 3 SDG and a meat one around 5 SDG. Other dishes cost between 5 and 9 SDG. Kofta and shish kebabs cost slightly more — around 30 SDG each. They're nice, but perhaps not worth the extra money given what else is on offer.

Saaj al-Samak (🏠 Street 41; 🍴 Fish; ☎ 0922 222 242; 💲 Moderate) is probably the best place in Khartoum to come and eat fried fresh fish. The aromas pouring out of the low-thatched building are delightful, and the food is even better.

The place is very Sudanese — the name of the restaurant is written only in Arabic — and cheap. The restaurant is almost always busy, and it can be quite difficult to find a table, especially if you are a large group. The fish is served on large platters, with salads and sauces. The dining experience is made all the more pleasant by the décor and ambience. Low tables, huddled together beneath a thatched roof and within a dimly-lit interior, remind the diners that they are in Africa after all.

Cedars (🏠 Street 41; 🍴 Lebanese; ☎ 0183 595 815; 💲 Expensive), on the first floor of the Safari hotel, is extremely popular with local Sudanese and foreigners alike. The restaurant is a little pricey, but the atmosphere is very relaxing and the food delicious. Particularly worth coming for the spicy potatoes.

Delak Pizza (🏠 Street 35, near Malik Street; 🍴 Syrian; ☎ 0155 106 633 or 0183 491 912; 💲 Cheap to moderate) specialises in pizzas and pies. Try the calzone and the Syrian pie for something different. The restaurant also sells a small selection of cakes. Home delivery is available: 2 SDG for Amarat, 3 SDG for Khartoum 2 and 4 SDG for Riyad. Delak Pizza has been in operation for more than 15 years, but previously you could only order by phone — the shop is brand new. Prices are not unreasonable; a basic pizza costs between 12 and 20 SDG, depending on the size. The restaurant also has a Facebook group — search for "delakpizza" (all one word).

Cone Zone (🏠 Afriqia Street, near Street 35; 🍴 Ice cream parlour; ☎ 0912 643 409; 💲 Moderate) has good ice-cream, though at comparatively higher prices than many of its competitors. It doesn't

have a terrace outside, but there are a few tables on the street where you can sit. Cookies-and-cream flavour is recommended.

Gad (🏠 Afriqia Street, near Street 33; 🍴 Egyptian; ☎ 0183 460 856 or 0183 480 055; 💲 Cheap to moderate) is an Egyptian chain. The restaurant is very big, with a buffet on the first floor and the main restaurant, plus a café, on the ground floor. Gad sells Egyptian food, *sha'urma* and some international dishes. It also has a good selection of sandwiches. There is a covered terrace area with cool water-jets.

Universal (🏠 Street 27; 🍴 Italian; ☎ 0912 307 796; 💲 Expensive) used to be one of the most popular pizzerias in town. It still offers decent pizzas (the vegetarian one is particularly recommended), but has lost some of its edge over the competition. The restaurant is spacious and has a very pleasant garden terrace where you can dine. The bruschetta is well worth trying.

Pasta Napoli (🏠 Afriqia Street, near Street 25; 🍴 Italian; 💲 Moderate) sells thick American-style pizzas. The four-cheese one is particularly nice. It has a salad bar but, unfortunately, the salads are not always fresh.

Momen (🏠 Afriqia Street, near Street 25; 🍴 Fast-food; ☎ 0183 590 950; 💲 Moderate) is your fairly standard burger joint. As well as the usual burgers and fried chicken, it also offered some rather tasty Sudanese and Greek-style sandwiches. The combo menu starts at 11 SDG.

Merkato (🏠 Street 15, west of Mohammed Najeeb Street; 🍴 Ethiopian ; 💲 Moderate) is a very nice Ethiopian place, especially worth coming for the coffee. The place also does fresh mango and orange juice (5 SDG). The food is nothing exceptional, but it is traditional, including dishes such as *zigni* and *tibsi* (both spiced meat) for around 17 SDG. The restaurant hasn't really done itself justice with the décor, though, and Habesha (p167) feels much cozier in this respect.

Laialy (🏠 Mohammed Najeeb Street / Street 15; 🍴 Turkish; 💲 Cheap to moderate) offers some of the best chicken *sha'urma* in town for very reasonable prices. Ask for the meat in a *fatira* wrap, which is definitely preferable to having it in a baguette. The whole roasted chickens, at 15 SDG each, are particularly reasonable. They also serve fresh Nile fish for 15 SDG each, although this is pricier than you can get in many other local places. The restaurant serves freshly-squeezed orange juice for 5 SDG a pop.

Tropicana Café (🏠 Behind Street 15, near Al-Muhajir Hotel Flats; 🍴 Café; 📞 0183 474 914; 💲 Cheap to moderate) serves fresh fruit juice. There are only a few tables for sitting at. Its main attraction is that it has a few pool tables (15 SDG per hour) and an adjoining internet café (3 SDG per hour).

Syrian Fresh Food (🍴 Syrian; 🏠 Street 15, opposite Kanon hotel; 📞 0926 948 950 or 0927 427 864; 💲 Moderate) does excellent Syrian-style cuisine, including *sha'urma* and a range of grilled meat dishes. A meal costs around 22 to 25 SDG. Portions are generous and they do take-away. You can also order grilled meat by the kilogram. They do very nice salads, including the Syrian-style *fatoush* (5 SDG), and pizzas (12-15 SDG for a small one).

Solitaire (🏠 Street 15; 🍴 International; 📞 0155 770 002; 💲 Moderate to expensive) is symptomatic of the 'new Khartoum' that has been evolving over the last five years: new, modern and flashy. It serves as both a café and a restaurant. A variety of European-style dishes are available, including grills, sandwiches and salads. The quality of the food is outstanding and the service is excellent, but expect to pay correspondingly high prices (the 12.5% tax is only added on to your bill at the end). Solitaire offers free wi-fi and ample plugs for recharging your laptop. The place can get quite busy, especially at peak times, but there is a bigger branch in Riyad. Copies of the *International Herald Tribune* and *Figaro* are available for customers to read. Recently, the restaurant has introduced a loyalty card entitling customers to a 10% discount on all items purchased. The card costs 100 SDG for one year.

Royal Broast (🏠 Afriqia Street, near Street 15; 🍴 Fast-food; 📞 0183 573 334; 💲 Moderate) serves chicken burgers and fried chicken dishes. The food is a little disappointing, though, and there are better places to go in the city if you are after chicken. Try nearby Amwaj, for example.

Lila (🏠 Afriqia Street, near Street 17; 🍴 Bakery / café; 📞 0157 908 994 or 0902 973 246) is a nice and friendly Turkish-owned place, serving a delicious range of pastries, cakes, tarts and ice-cream (although the ice-cream isn't always available, presumably owing to a lack of demand). Lila also caters for birthdays and weddings, and there is a café on-site. Prices are not unreasonable.

Steers (🏠 Afriqia Street, near Street 13; 🍴 Fast-food; 💲 Moderate; 📞 0183 358 548) serves decent burgers but prices are high (15 SDG for a basic burger combo meal, plus 1 SDG if you want to eat in). It looks more like an American diner than a typical fast-food joint

— your food will be brought to your table if you choose to eat in.

Debonairs (🏠 Afriqia Street, near Street 13; 🍴 Italian; ☎ 0183 585 484, home delivery 0157 999 898; 💲 Moderate) is a South African restaurant chain serving American-style pizzas. There are two branches in Khartoum: one in Amarat and the other in Riyad. Small pizzas start at 11 SDG. There is a small extra charge (1 SDG) for eating in the restaurant rather than ordering take-away. Of particularly good value is the family menu, where you get any two pizzas, a pasta salad, chicken strips and garlic bread for 60 SDG. The sweet-chicken pizza is interesting.

Amwaj (🏠 Afriqia Street, near Street 13; 🍴 Sudanese; ☎ 0912 368 308; 💲 Moderate), which means 'waves' in Arabic, may look like a classic school canteen, but it is actually one of the best and most popular eateries in town. It certainly does the best fried chicken that you will find anywhere in Khartoum. Main courses come with a soup, salad and some bread (unless you take away — in which case you just get the main course). It isn't cheap, but the quality is excellent and the portions are huge.

Lucky Meal (🏠 Street 1; 🍴 Fastfood; 💲 Moderate) is a somewhat unremarkable fast-food joint, good if you're nearby and want a quick bite but not worth seeking out especially. It is strong on chicken burgers, but also does other types of meat and sha'urma. Slightly cheaper than other fast-food places: 11-13 SDG for a meal.

Al-Hana (🏠 Street 1; 🍴 Egyptian; ☎ 0922 125 747; 💲 Cheap to moderate) mainly serves Egyptian fatiras. There is a good range to choose from, at fairly reasonable prices (12-15 SDG). The nice thing about this place is that it has

an upstairs, from which you can discretely look down on the fatira preparation. The menu is only in Arabic.

Laziz (🏠 Street 1; 🍴 Sudanese; 💲 Cheap; ☎ 0912 309 607), meaning 'delicious' in Arabic, serves decent Sudanese food at reasonable prices. Unfortunately, in recent years quality has declined and prices have gone up. The sha'urma and tameeya sandwiches are particularly popular. The restaurant also has a good ice-cream parlour. There are two branches of Laziz: one in Riyad, the other in Amarat. The one in Amarat is bigger and has a proper seating area, whilst the one in Riyad is just a take-away.

Flash Fresh (🏠 Street 1 / Malik Street; 🍴 Café) is a small kiosk, with limited seating space outside. It serves very nice fresh fruit juices. If you want to try something different, ask them to mix the juice with milk.

KHARTOUM 2 & 3

Ozone (🏠 Ustaz Ahmed Khair Street; 🍴 Café; ☎ 0183 575 500; 💲 Moderate to expensive) is a little oasis of green in the drab dustiness of Khartoum. Bizarrely, and a little inconveniently, it is situated in the centre of a roundabout, which can make getting there (especially during rush-hour) somewhat hazardous. The café is owned by Dal Group, Sudan's largest private company. It has recently been renovated, and now has an indoor area for eating and drinking, as well as a very nice garden with efficient water-cooler system. The place can get extremely crowded, especially in the evening, and finding a spare table is sometimes an ordeal. Ozone serves snacks — such as quiches and sandwiches. The ice-creams and milkshakes are particularly enticing. Surprisingly, there is no table service for the ice-creams; you have to order them yourself. They have a selection of excellent pastries and freshly-baked bread, including ciabatta.

Carnivore (🏠 Street Zero, near Mohammed Najeeb; 🍴 African; ☎ 0917 936 670 or 0905 834 446; @yahoo.coml; 💲 Expensive) probably needs no introduction. It is a branch of the very famous Carnivore restaurant based in Nairobi, although why one has suddenly appeared in the intensely hot and dusty city of Khartoum is something of a mystery. The restaurant was initially located on the banks of the Nile, but the high cost of renting in such a desirable location forced it elsewhere. The restaurant is still struggling to build up a name for itself, and to pack the walls in the same way that its namesake in Nairobi does. The problem may be that people are not always after meat in such a hot climate. Unlike the one in Nairobi, which is strictly regulated about what it can or can't serve (lions are now off the menu, for example), no such restriction has yet been imposed on the one in Khartoum. Gazelle, crocodile, camel, ostrich and even pigeons are all served (although availability depends on supply). There is a nice outside terrace to eat in. A typical meal might cost 85 SDG. It remains to be seen whether this restaurant, which has an excellent reputation in Nairobi, can succeed in such a different environment.

Sweet & Sour (🏠 Khartoum 2, near 5M Hotel; 🍴 International; ☎ 0155 140 525 or 0919 404 029; @ sweet-and-sour1@hotmail.com; 💲 Moderate) is another one of those countless Western-style

coffee houses that have sprung up recently all across Khartoum. The café also offers a range of sandwiches (around 17 SDG) and main courses (30-35 SDG). A nice, comfortable and cool café to relax or work in. Free wi-fi is available.

The Chicken Shack (🏠 Khartoum 2, between Mek Nimir Street and Afriqia Street; 🍴 Fast-food; 💲 Moderate) has the best batter of any fast-food place in Khartoum. Unfortunately, the chicken can be a little dry. Its dining room is small and comfortable and service is friendly.

Pizza Corner (🏠 Abdel Fadeel al-Faz Street, west of Italian Embassy; ☎ 0183 560 700) has three restaurants under one roof — a pizzeria, a New York deli and a fancy café. The prices are extremely reasonable. You can get a basic pizza for around 13 SDG. The restaurant also offers somewhat novel items, such as pizza in a cone (for between and 10 and 14 SDG). This is smaller than the regular pizza, with more crust and less cheese. The range of pizzas served is very broad, and you can choose from a thick or a thin base. There are several options for vegetarians, too. Drinks are more expensive than you might find in other similar restaurants — 3.50 SDG for a soda and 3 SDG for a small bottle of water. You can get a wide range of exotic drinks from Coffee World, with smoothies and frappés starting at 10 SDG. The place is fully air-conditioned and has free wi-fi, with ample plugs for computers. It is very large, spread over two floors with a nice outside space. The New York deli also serves burgers (9 SDG) and *sha'urmas* (8 SDG).

Assaha Village (🏠 Off Afriqia Street, near the Canadian Embassy; 🍴 Lebanese; ☎ 0922 946 469 💲 Expensive) is a beautiful hotel that has a great little Lebanese restaurant attached. You can choose to dine inside or in the garden, where you can admire the medieval look-and-feel of the establishment. Prices are high but the food is worth it.

Italy Pizza Centre (🏠 Ustaz Ahmed Khair Street, near Ozone; 🍴 Italian; 💲 Moderate) has a wide selection of pizzas and a salad bar. It has a nice space outside with fans and water coolers, and air-con inside. The pizzas are reasonably good, but service can be slow, even on quiet days.

Al-Albawdi (🏠 Abdul Latif Street; 🍴 Sudanese; 💲 Moderate) mainly serves barbecued and fried chicken. The place is extremely popular and gets very busy. Try the grilled chicken served with bread and salad. It costs 19 SDG and is enough for two.

The Real Burger (🏠 Abdul Latif Street; 🍴 Fast-food; ☎ 0183 468 211; 💲 Cheap) is a rather disappointing fast-food restaurant, although it is inexplicably popular with local Sudanese. There is no seating inside, but there are a few benches to sit on outside. The place is cheap — but, unless you have a particular yearning for a cold burger in a dry bun, it's best to take your money elsewhere. The restaurant also serves pizza, which is just as bad.

BAHRI

Syrian House (🏠 Sayed Ali Street, just past Petronas petrol station; 🍴 Bakery; ☎ 0123 121 123) 💲 Cheap to moderate) has a well-deserved reputation for its exceedingly good cakes and biscuits. Syrian House also has a restaurant on the other side of the road, where you can order savoury food such as *sha'urma* and sandwiches.

Dodi's (🏠 Mahna Street; 🍴 Egyptian; ☎ 0155 775 775; 💲 Cheap) — see Dodi's in Amarat.

OMDURMAN

Dodi's (🍴 Egyptian; ☎ 0155 775 774; 💲 Cheap) — see Dodi's in Amarat.

Gigi (🏠 Moreda Street; 🍴 Egyptian; ☎ 0914 284 349; 💲 Cheap) is an Egyptian restaurant popular for its *kusheri* (an Egyptian dish with rice, noodles, a vegetarian sauce and caramelised onion). It only costs 3 SDG and is certainly one of the best in town. The restaurant also serves pizzas, but not much else.

Shopping

Shopping

Khartoum is unlikely to beat New York or London at any time in the near future as a destination for shop-until-you-drop weekend excursions. There are bargains to be had, if you look hard enough, but many products sold in the city are pricey and not always of very good quality.

Foreign goods are particularly hard to come by, although there are growing numbers of international supermarkets that specialise in importing products from overseas. Expect to pay well over-the-odds for these items, however.

For your daily household needs, you will find small local shops throughout the city. Most of these do not display prices on items; the shopkeepers just remember them

all by heart. Most shop-owners are quite honest and won't rip you off just because you are foreign, although the same can always be said of traders in the market or taxi drivers (see the section 'Bargaining' on the following page). Local shops stock similar items, although prices can vary slightly.

Khartoum isn't a great city for fruit and vegetables; prices are quite high and the variety is not as great as you will find in most large American and European cities. Prices can also fluctuate quite dramatically according to the season. Markets are the best places for fresh produce.

If you are looking for souvenirs you should spend a few hours wandering around some of the

ROUGH PRICE GUIDE FOR COMMON ITEMS	
Product	**Price**
1 small box of tea	3.50 to 4 SDG
100g jar of coffee	3.50 SDG
1 kg apples	8 SDG
1 kg aubergines	3 SDG
1 kg bananas	1 to 1.50 SDG
1 kg carrots	2 SDG
1 kg flour	3 SDG
1 kg green peppers	4 to 6 SDG
1 kg lentils	3.50 SDG
1 kg onions	2 to 3 SDG
1 kg potatoes	2.50 SDG
1 kg rice	3 SDG
Litre of petrol	1.90 SDG

city's *souqs* (markets). However, in your quest to take home something memorable, make sure you steer clear of certain items such as stuffed crocodiles, crocodile-skin purses and ivory trinkets. Although these items are still sold in Khartoum, they are illegal and you face a hefty fine if you are caught trying to take them out of the country. Animals are dying in large numbers to provide such knick-knacks; think twice before you lend your support to this industry.

Most shops are open daily from fairly early in the morning until 11 pm. The exception is Friday when, in certain areas, many shops open only in the afternoon.

SUPERMARKETS

Local shops are good for basic food needs but, if you are looking for something slightly more particular, then your best bet is to try one of the growing number of supermarkets that are springing up throughout the city. More and more supermarkets are also starting to sell basic medicines, such as paracetamol.

The best-stocked supermarkets are found in Riyad, Amarat and the centre of Khartoum 2.

In Amarat, **Amarat Centre** (🏠 Street 1, Amarat) is a little pricey, but has a good range of international products. It regularly runs promotions, advertised in

Shopping

BARGAINING

You only have to spend a few minutes in one of Khartoum's many markets, listening to the locals squabbling, to realise how much the Sudanese really do enjoy a good bargaining session.

The art of negotiation is a skill that takes time to learn. It also helps if you know roughly how much goods should cost. When you arrive in the city, you are almost certainly going to end up paying over-the-odds for many items. The longer you spend looking around local shops and markets, the harder it becomes for traders to pull the wool over your eyes.

The important thing about bargaining is to remain as cheerful as possible, and never to get agitated. Treat the whole exercise like a game; this is exactly what the Sudanese do. If a price is too high, just smile politely and say *'la'* ('no'). Another good phrase to remember is *'ana bedfa'a tawali...'* ('I always pay...') Going to the markets with a local Sudanese friend is not a bad idea. Not only is your friend likely to know the prices and some bargaining tricks, but traders are also more inclined to lower the price for a local person.

Whilst bargaining is extremely common in the *souqs*, it is not so common in the local shops or supermarkets around the city.

It is also usual to haggle with *amjad*, taxi, and rickshaw drivers. Again, this is a situation in which foreigners are more likely to get overcharged. It helps to know the price that you should pay on certain routes. Even so, many drivers can be fearsome arguers, insisting forcefully that you should pay the price they quote because that is the standard price (even if you know it isn't). It is a good idea to agree on a price before you start the journey. That way, you can avoid a heated argument at the end. Also, try to have the correct change available. Some drivers claim not to have any change on them when you try to pay, in the hope that you will let them keep the change.

Shopping

English so, occasionally, you can find items that you might be missing from back home at real bargain prices. The shop also has very convenient opening hours: 8 am to 11 pm most days, even during Ramadan. On Fridays, the shop opens slightly later (9 am). Another branch of the supermarket has recently opened in Riyad (see below).

Another good choice is **Al-Hawi** (🏠 Street 15, Amarat), which even has a French delicatessen. This supermarket has also just started selling DVDs, many of which are in English. **Sefco** (🏠 Mohammed Najeeb Street, in front of the cemetery, Amarat) is particularly good for aluminium containers and plastic products. **Mugiama al-Nujum Lel Tasuig** (🏠 Mohammed Najeeb Street, opposite Street 27, Amarat) has many international items at reasonable prices.

Over the past couple of years, Riyad has surpassed Amarat as the centre for Khartoum's expat community, with the result that many more supermarkets have been opened in the district. Mashtal Street is the place to look for them, and you can't walk much more than a couple of blocks before stumbling upon one.

Alanfal (🏠 Eastern end of Mashtal Street, Riyad) is a large Western-style supermarket, containing a good range of foreign produce. It also has a well-stocked delicatessen that sells cuts of meat. You have to leave your bags with the security before you enter the shop.

Just off Mashtal Street, next to Lan Tian hotel, you will find **Amarat Centre 2** (🏠 Street 117, Riyad), a branch of the supermarket in Amarat that bears the same name. This supermarket is particularly good for its range of spices, as well as an impressive selection of olive oil and olives. It also has a range of

---

FROZEN MEAT

Be aware that, when buying frozen meat, most butchers will charge you for the weight of the meat when it is frozen. This means that you are paying for the locked-in water too!

---

food flavourings and colourings that are difficult to find elsewhere.

Two other international supermarkets that you can find on Mashtal Street are **Latif** and **Shamil House**.

The supermarket in **Afra Mall**, which lies between Tayef and Amarat, is good value for cleaning and toiletry products. It also has a good bakery, as well as a range of items for the house and for sport. But, for other items, it is rather overpriced. Afra Mall's supermarket is the first in Khartoum to introduce a loyalty card for its customers. This is free to apply for and entitles you to regular discounts when shopping there.

Farouk (🏠 Market area in Khartoum 2) is a particularly well-stocked supermarket, noted for its wide range of spices. **Another one** close by, which covers its shop front in words from the Qur'an rather than a name, is also good.

Maruwa (🏠 Manshea) has a good selection of foreign products, including some well-known ice-cream brands, but is generally a bit pricier than its competitors.

Macro Supermarket (🏠 Malik Street / Street 15, Amarat) is another reasonable option.

MEAT

It is not difficult to find meat in Khartoum, but cuts vary significantly in quality. Always be careful when choosing where to buy your

NORTH SUDAN'S DOLLAR POLICY

In order to stabilise the local currency, the government has imposed restrictions on carrying out trades in dollars, to prevent them going abroad. This has made it harder to import certain goods that would ordinarily be paid for in foreign currencies — such as fish caught from outside of Sudan and chocolate. This is limiting the supply of these goods, and many chocolate bars that you find in the shops (for example) may have been there for some time. Check the 'best before' date!

meat, as it is not always stored in the most hygienic conditions.

Chicken, lamb and mutton are the most popular kinds of meat that you will find in the city. Beef is common, too, and is used a lot in sausages and imitation mortadella (an Italian delicacy, typically made with pork). Due to Islamic beliefs, pork is not sold in Khartoum.

A reliable, albeit pricey, place to buy meat is **Hakeem** (🏠 Street 15, Amarat; ☎ 0183 491 927).

The supermarket in **Afra Mall** also has a good variety of fresh meat, particularly chicken breasts. It is slightly cheaper than Hakeem.

Malhamat al-Khuti (🏠 Mohammed Najeeb Street, near to the green mosque) is quite a small butcher's shop that sells the best beef fillet and minced meat in town, according to the locals. It is fresh and much cheaper than elsewhere. The butcher's shop is located in a bigger supermarket called Muggiamma al-Khuti al-Istilakh.

The butcher doesn't sell chicken though, because on the other side, there is a shop selling extremely cheap

chicken: **As-Sharik al-Arabia Litamia Assarua al-Hauania**. Here, you can buy a whole chicken for 9 SDG a kilo or chicken legs for 13 SDG a kilo.

Next door, the **Arabic Company for Livestock and Development** sells fresh eggs.

Khartoum 2 is well-known among local Sudanese as a good area for buying meat. There are a couple of decent butchers next to each other in the market area, selling meat at reasonable prices. The chicken is good, but is generally only sold whole and frozen.

FISH

Nile fish is very popular in Khartoum and is usually quite cheap. In some places, it is also possible to buy fresh fish from the Red Sea, flown to Khartoum specially each day. However, this trade has been a recent casualty of Khartoum's policy over the dollar (see box).

When buying frozen fish, be careful that fishmongers do not refreeze the fish once it is defrosted. Some may do this if there is a power failure and they do not have a generator; always check that the fish is not soft and that it does not have an overly-strong smell.

For fresh Nile fish, the best option is **Jebel Owlia** (🏠 Mohammed Najeeb Street / Street 61, Amarat; @ sales@jeff.co.sd; ☎ 0902 490 999). There is not a big variety, but you get the chance to choose Nile fish that are still alive. The prices are very reasonable (around 8 SDG for two whole fish).

Shrimps (🏠 Street 131, just after Mecca, Riyad; ☎ 0912 345 850 or 0912 131 441 or 0183 233 409) is good for Red Sea fish and other imported sea food. Here you can find treats such as salmon, swordfish and prawns — among others.

Shopping

Expect to pay around 20 SDG per kilo. Fresh Nile fish is also available.

Omdurman's fish market (🏠 Moreda Street) sells extremely fresh fish caught from the Nile; you can even watch fishermen bringing it in. You will also find some Red Sea fish for sale. Surprisingly, the market is more expensive than many other seafood retail outlets. Still, if you have managed to hone your bargaining skills, you may be able to come away with a good deal.

Smoked salmon is available in Khartoum but, disappointingly, it is only sold frozen. You can find it in **Amarat Centre** (🏠 Street 1, Amarat) or **Al-Hawi** (🏠 Street 15, Amarat) for 20 SDG. It is sold in smaller quantities in **Lipton** (🏠 Street 41, Amarat) for 15 SDG.

FRUIT AND VEGETABLES

Much of the fruit in Khartoum is exceedingly delicious and mouth-watering. The best local fruits to try are mango and watermelon. Small bananas are also available, as well as papaya, although these can be slightly tricky to find.

Common vegetables for sale include green peppers, courgettes, aubergines, onions, garlic, carrots, potatoes and okra. Bell peppers and mushrooms are also available, but only in international supermarkets

Markets are the best places to search for fresh fruit and vegetables. **Souq al-Merkhazi** (p184) has the best selection of fruit and vegetables, both local and imported although, as a foreigner, be prepared for some tough bargaining.

There are many little stalls throughout the city that sell fruit and vegetables. These are typically a bit more expensive than the markets, because most of the time the traders buy their wares from the markets in the first place and simply resell them.

One **small collection of stalls** (🏠 Mohammed Najeeb Street, next to Street 1, Amarat) is worth a mention here, for the variety of produce that it stocks. Here, you can find rarities such as papaya, fresh coriander and fresh pineapples.

Despite the high prices that international supermarkets charge, the quality of their local fruit and vegetables is often disappointing. However, if you want imported vegetables, you have no choice but to go to these international shops — and to be willing to part with large amounts of money.

HERBS AND SPICES

Do not expect to find a tremendous range of herbs and spices in Khartoum. Certain dried spices are relatively easy to find here (such as coriander, cumin, nutmeg, turmeric and chilli) and, if you go to the right places, the quality can be really quite good. Many local shops sell these spices. You can also find them in the markets.

Fresh herbs are much harder to come by: mint, parsley and coriander are the commonest in the city. Others — such as rosemary, thyme, basil and sage — are only occasionally available in fancier supermarkets, and are usually over-priced.

The best place for picking up dried Indian spices is in **Omdurman**, which has a large community of Indian immigrants. There are a number of small local shops selling a good variety of spices and some well-stocked market stalls.

CAKES, BISCUITS AND CHOCOLATE

Syrian House (Sayed Ali Street n Bahri, just past Petronas petrol station; ☎ 0123 121 123) has a well-deserved reputation for its excellent cakes and biscuits

Tayba (🏠 Between Afriqia Street and Street 41) started off as a typical Sudanese bakery, selling the usual white baguettes, but has since expanded its shop to sell a rather tempting range of European-style cakes and buns.

Al-Abdel (🏠 Nadi Al-Dubat Street, between Amarat and Khartoum 2) sells very good-quality Egyptian and Sudanese pastries and *bastas* (Sudanese sweets).

Ozone (🏠 Ustaz Ahmed Khair Street, between Amarat and Khartoum 2; ☎ 0183 575 500) also has a very good bakery, with an excellent selection of cakes and fresh pastries.

Lila (🏠 Afriqia Street, Amarat; ☎ 0157 908 994 or 0902 973 246) is a Turkish bakery that serves a delicious range of pastries and cakes. The place also caters for birthdays and weddings.

You can find good chocolates n **Amarat Centre** (🏠 Street 1, Amarat), **Afra Mall** and **Al-Hawi** (🏠 Street 15, Amarat).

CLOTHES AND SHOES

Good-quality clothes and shoes are expensive in Khartoum. The main places to look for designer labels are on Mohammed Najeeb Street and Afriqia Street in Amarat, where you can find some of the big international branded shops such as **Adidas** and **Cons**.

J'adore (🏠 Street 35, off Malik Street, Amarat) and **Crystal** (🏠 Malik Street, just next to Nastwood) have some reasonable suits and evening dresses. In Riyad, try **A La Mode** (🏠 Street 131).

For bags and shoes, try **Al-Maestro** and **Fantasia** (🏠 Street 15, Amarat).

If you are after less expensive items, and are not too worried about the quality, some good options are the markets **Souq as-Shabi** (🏠 South-west of Amarat) and **Souq Bahri**. Remember that branded goods sold in the market are, more often than not, counterfeit. Nevertheless, you can still find some decent clothes imported from Turkey, China and Saudi Arabia, without paying too much money.

HOUSEHOLD APPLIANCES

Amarat House (🏠 Street 1, in front of Amarat Centre, Amarat) and **Home Care** (🏠 Malik Street, close to Street 21, Amarat) are both good for household appliances. The supermarket in **Afra Mall** is another option. **Nastwood** (🏠 Malik Street, Amarat; ☎ 0183 466 770 or 0183 460 934) has a good range of electronic and sports equipment, but prices are steep.

In the market area around Khartoum 2, **Zero 9** sells well-known brands of electronic products, from external hard drives to the latest models of digital cameras.

Recently, a number of **Samsung** stores have sprung up all over Khartoum, offering slightly more reliable goods at reasonably competitive prices.

DIGITAL AND PASSPORT PHOTOS

With the number of official forms you'll have to fill in during your stay in Khartoum, it is useful to know where to get passport photos printed.

Shopping

There are several **Kodak** shops around the city: Mohammed Najeeb Street (🏠 Near Street 13) Souq al-Arabi and Afra Mall.

The one in Mohammed Najeeb Street does passport photos of very good quality.

The one in Afra Mall (☎ 0912 306 900) is usually only open between 4 and 10 pm, although these times can be unreliable. Expect to pay 10 SDG for six passport photos. Digital photo printing costs around 1 SDG per picture, although the studio requires that you print a minimum of six pictures.

A **Fuji** shop in Afra Mall, just outside the supermarket, offers digital printing only. It is slightly cheaper than the Kodak one a few meters away.

There are a number of photo-processing stores just off Street 15, in the area behind Al-Hawi supermarket.

Photo Style and **The Studio Camera Artist** (☎ 0122 377 893) offer similar printing and passport photo services. Expect to pay 10 SDG for six passport photos. The Studio Camera Artist no longer offers cheap single prints of photos, which used to be one of the main attractions of the place.

If you want single prints, the best place to go is **2N Photo Lab**, just north of Qurashi Park (☎ 0912 148 135) in Khartoum 3. Here they offer digital printing for around 50 *piastras* per photo.

LAUNDRY

When the local Sudanese want to have their clothes cleaned, they usually find a local woman that can do this for them. This is far cheaper than going to one of the official laundry places that have sprung up in recent years. A local washerwoman will typically charge 80 or 90 *piastras* per garment, compared with 2 or 3 SDG at an official laundry.

The problem is finding such a woman to do this cleaning for you, especially as a foreigner. The best thing to do is to ask the locals where they go and follow their lead.

If you can't find a local washerwoman, or don't want to go down this route, then there are plenty of other options. Many of the larger hotels offer laundry services, although these tend to be more expensive than stand-alone ones.

Khartoum doesn't yet have any self-service laundromats. You have to hand your clothes to one of the people in the shop and they do it all for you.

In Khartoum 2, you can try **Ice Bear** (🏠 Near Ozone; ☎ 0912 126 869 or 0912 951 655 or 0123 884 777), **Officer Club Laundries** (🏠 Abdubat Street; ☎ 0122 094 671) or **Panda Dry Cleaner** (☎ 0155 130 122 or 0916 153 801). In Amarat, try **Ghasan Automatic Laundry** (🏠 Street 15; ☎ 0154 954 460 or 0917 987 711). **Goldstyle Cleaning Services** (🏠 Baladeyah Street, ☎ 0183 797 207) is in the centre of town. A growing number of laundries are springing up in Riyad. Try **Shams Dry Clean** (🏠 At the top of Street 131) or **Mamlaka** (🏠 Mecca Street).

Prices and service are pretty standard, at around 2 or 3 SDG for each item of clothing and between 14 to 17 SDG for a suit.

SOUVENIRS AND GIFTS

There are several good souvenir shops operating between Jamhouriya Street and Barlaman Street in Central Khartoum. If you poke around in the area just to the west of Marawi bookshop, you'll quickly discover a range of shops selling traditional crafts

The marketplaces are also worth a visit, particularly **Souq Omdurman** and **Souq as-Sabit**.

Souq Omdurman's main souvenir shops are all located in Khateen Street. **Sudan Folklore** (☎ 0912 472 402 or 0912 642 049) is the best to try, but you might also want to visit a few others: **Folklore Omdurman** (☎ 0912 809 689; @ amgad_1986@hotmail.com), **Hashim Abdalla Ata** (☎ 0912 286 916), **Abanosa Craft** (☎ 0911 226 733) and **Folklore Sudani** (☎ 0122 409 893). All have fairly similar merchandise.

If you are looking for a nice present to give to someone, **Homecare** (🏠 Malik Street, Amarat) has a good range. The shop also sells a selection of greeting cards. However, the shop isn't particularly good for souvenirs.

Natural Looks (🏠 Near to the market area in Khartoum 2) is a good place to shop for body-care products.

There are also a few shops along Street 15 in Amarat, near Mohammed Najeeb Street, which offer some good ideas for presents. The shops around the market area in Khartoum 2 are also worth a browse; look out in particular for **Mondial** and **Al Basha**.

Piano Piano (🏠 Street 15, Amarat; ☎ Sat-Thu: 9 am to 10 pm) is a new souvenir and gift shop, selling a range of intriguing artefacts that come principally from China, Malaysia and Egypt. In amongst the antiques and miscellaneous curiosities, you'll also find somewhat overpriced goods such as a wide-screen TV for 3200 SDG

Contemporary Sudanese arts and handcrafts can be found in **Rashiddia Centre** in Jeref West (🖥 www. rashiddiabartscentre.net; ☎ 0155 180 058 or 0122 800 060).

Al-Sudaniya Association for Handicrafts, opposite the Coral Hotel in the Mogran area, also sells local Sudanese handicrafts. It is a very friendly place staffed by women who love to talk about their trade. Prices are not that cheap, but at least you'll be supporting local Sudanese industry if you shop here, rather than Chinese or Indian businessmen.

BOOKS

If you are looking for English books in Khartoum, then your options are limited. In the marketplace, you can find many classic works from authors such as Oscar Wilde and Joseph Conrad. These are most likely to be dusty old volumes that once had a place in the syllabi of Sudanese secondary schools. The places to look for such bookstores are in the area around **the universities** and in **Souq Omdurman**, just next to the post office.

More modern English books are generally very expensive. This is largely because of the perception that such books are extremely costly to import and therefore should be expensive. The mercantile booksellers are making fairly hefty profits through the proliferation of this half-truth.

The best place to try for foreign books is **Marawi Bookshop** (🏠 Barlaman Street, Central Khartoum), which has the largest collection of up-to-date titles. The owner of the bookshop has recently opened a branch in the new **Corinthia Hotel**.

New Bookshop (🏠 Zubeir Pasha Street, near Souq al-Arabi, Central Khartoum; ☎ 0183 774 425) has a good selection of books for teaching and learning English, as well as a small range of fiction and some other titles.

Other possibilities include **Sudan Bookshop** (🏠 Tayar Murad Street, Central Khartoum, ☎ 0183 772 089) and **Sudanese House For Books** (🏠 Baladeyah Street, Central Khartoum; ☎ 0183 780 031). A few of the bigger supermarkets also stock English books.

In Amarat, try the **Nile Bookshop** (🏠 Street 41, Amarat; ☎ 0183 463 749; @ info@thenilebook.com; 🖥 www.thenilebookshop.com), which also has back issues of some foreign newspapers and magazines.

Some of the hotels, including the **Acropole** and **Lisamin Safari**, also sell a small range of foreign books.

If you are looking for language books to help you learn Sudanese Arabic, the best place to try is the **Catholic Language Institute of Khartoum** (🏠 Street 29, near Afriqia Street, Amarat). Here you can find a good Sudanese grammar book (45 SDG), plus an exercise book (15 SDG) and a phrase book (5 SDG).

Al-Hawi supermarket (🏠 Street 15, Amarat) has a selection of dictionaries and grammar books, but they are fairly pricey. The supermarket in **Afra Mall** stocks some Arabic dictionaries and old books in Arabic, with cassettes.

BEAUTY AND HAIRSTYLING

Traditionally, Sudanese women use a particular mix of essences and sandalwood (called *khumra*) in order to please their husbands.

Recently, conventional perfumes and beauty products have started to give way to more international brands, although such beauty products remain pricey and there is still not a great range.

Natural Looks (🏠 Near the market area in Khartoum 2) has a wide selection of soaps, shampoos and creams. **Oriflame** (🏠 Afriqia Street, near Street 3, Amarat 🖥 www.oriflame.com) is a members-only beauty shop. Membership costs 15 SDG per year. Once you have joined, you can ask for a catalogue and choose products from this catalogue or from Oriflame's website.

Glamour (🏠 Street 21; Amarat) offers a full range of beauty treatments for women at competitive rates.

In Khartoum, most of the small barber shops will charge between 5 and 8 SDG for a simple cut. If you want something a bit more special go to **Grand Holiday Villa** on Nil Street (men only), **Coral Hotel** in the Mogran area or **Plaza Hotel** in the centre of Khartoum.

In Khartoum most of the female hairdressers also offer services such as waxing, henna, manicures and pedicures (sometimes even a massage).

For religious reasons, men are not allowed to enter female hairdressers, and the employees in such places are women only. In most of the centres, the machines and techniques are still old and traditional (for example, hair is ironed with a proper iron and waxed with a cold mixture of sugar, honey, lemon and water).

If your budget doesn't allow you to go to international hotels you can try the following centres:

- **Queen Beauty Centre** (🏠 Street 15, Amarat; ☎ 0912 984 881), is a hair salon and a beauty centre. Expect to pay between 20 and 100 SDG for a haircut, depending on what you need. An arm or leg wax costs 50 SDG and an hour's oil massage 60 SDG.

- **Plaza Hotel** (🏠 Qasar Street, Central Khartoum) has a beauty centre and hair dresser. The lady speaks only a little English, but service is friendly.
- **Ms G Beauty Salon** (🏠 Mufty Street, Khartoum 2, ☎ 0183 580 075/6) offers a range of beauty and hair-styling services.

PRINTING

Access (☎ 0183 573 661/62; @ access@interunivers-ltd.com; 🖥 access.interuniverse-ltd.com) offers printing for advertising, business cards, and company gadgets. They even offer a free design service.

GARDENING AND FLOWER SHOPS

For your gardening needs, **Plants** (🏠 Street 131, Riyad; ☎ 0155 126 000; 🖥 www.plantsco.com; @ info@plantsco.com) is good. Although the **Garden Centre** (Street 1, Amarat) is a gardening centre, it doesn't have any seeds for sale. It is also very expensive.

If you're looking for flowers, try **Nairobi Flower** (🏠 South end of Malik Street; ☎ 0155 292 700; @ nairobiflowerssudan@yahoo.com). However, staff are not particularly friendly and prices change quite dramatically depending on who is serving you.

Just next door, you'll also find **Karanish Flowers** (☎ 0912 364 859 or 0912 601 811) and **Waffa Flowers and Decorations** (☎ 0912 673 253).

Other options are **Sobtan Flowers** (🏠 Mecca Street, Riyad; ☎ 0912 370 140; @ sobtan@canar.sd), **Fresh Flowers** (🏠 Nil Street, under Cobra Bridge,

Central Khartoum; ☎ 0183 784 101) and **Gardenia** (🏠 Khartoum 2; ☎ 0183 497 979).

THE MARKETS

Khartoum has a good variety of marketplaces. Each one is worth visiting for different reasons, depending on what you are looking for.

Souq as-Shabi, meaning 'the people's market', is located southwest of Amarat, not far from the main bus station for long-distance coaches (Min al-Buri). It is a general market, selling everything from vegetables to items of clothing. Clothes and shoes are particularly cheap. Buses from Jackson station in the centre of Khartoum run direct to Souq as-Shabi.

Souq as-Sabit is a fairly small Ethiopian market in Khartoum 2, just off Afriqia Street, not far from the Dutch Embassy and UNICEF. The market is only held on Sundays, between 9 am and 3 pm. It is a great place to come for unusual souvenirs and sells many things imported or made by Ethiopians, such as the coffee pots (*jabanas*) and incense holders.

Omdurman's **fish market** in Morada not only sells fresh Nile fish but also offers a variety of imported fish, including those from the Red Sea. Unfortunately, it isn't as cheap as one might expect. Just behind the market, you can see the Nile fish being caught. Opposite the market are some reasonable fish restaurants and it is a particularly beautiful place to come and eat at night. Getting to the market is easy. Simply take a bus from Jackson station in Central Khartoum, heading in the direction of Souq Omdurman. Get off when you see the market on your right and the fish restaurants on your left.

Shopping

Souq Omdurman is the biggest market in Sudan. It is a general market where you can shop for pretty much anything you might need. The market is well-organised and is divided into different sections for different items.

Even if you do not want to buy anything from this colourful and lively market, it definitely warrants a visit. You will see a whole variety of people from many different walks of life, buying and selling goods. There is a vibrant mix of ethnic groups and nationalities.

Of particular interest is the area called **Khateen**, dedicated to souvenirs and handicrafts from around Sudan and other parts of Africa. As well as the macabre and illegal crocodile-skin and ivory products, you can also find unusual musical instruments, hand-painted plates, ebony-wood carvings of animals and shoes made of animal skin.

These shops are definite traps for foreigners, and it can be tough to negotiate a significant reduction in the prices, which you will find to be quite high.

Be careful when buying souvenirs here. Increasing numbers of such items are imported from China, so examine goods very carefully if you want to purchase something authentic.

Souq Libya has an interesting history. Established by tribal groups fleeing the fighting in Darfur, many believe it to be a conduit of illegal arms for the war-torn region. It is also believed to do a flourishing trade in drugs. The market is reputedly a little less safe than other areas in the capital, and so you should take extra care of your belongings. The market is open-air and generally very crowded. Unfortunately, most of the items sold are imported and of quite low quality. To get to Souq Libya, you can take a bus direct from Jackson station in Central Khartoum.

Just next to Souq Libya, behind the Con Corp petrol station, there is a smaller clothes market: **Souq Abu Zeid**. This is where many Sudanese come to sell items belonging to family members who have recently died. Clothes here are extremely cheap.

Souq al-Naaga, just next to Souq Libya, is a good place to come if you want to purchase camel meat (although the market doesn't, in general, have any live camels). In Arabic, a *naaga* is a female camel. The market is fairly small, and is populated by hordes of butchers hacking up meat (not just camel meat, but other types of meat as well, such as beef and mutton).

You can purchase meat from any butcher and take it to one of the local restaurants in the market, where it will be cooked for you in a variety of spices, although this can be expensive.

Camel meat costs around 10 SDG per kilogram. Expect to pay the same again for the cooking and the use of the restaurant.

Souq al-Arabi used to be one of the main markets in Khartoum: crowded, noisy and dirty. Prior to November 2007, it was the main hub for minibuses in the city. Now that public transport has been taken away from the area, the market has changed dramatically. These days, it is pretty empty and many of the shops and eateries have relocated to the new bus depot, near Stad. The main attraction of this market today is to see the sand-coloured Kabier Mosque (p136) in the centre.

Souq al-Merkhazi, in Bahri, is probably the best place to go in Khartoum for cheap fruit and vegetables. This is where many Suda-

...ese families buy their greens once a week, at a considerable saving.

The market is divided into two main areas: one for fruit and the other for vegetables. There are some stalls selling fruit at the edge of the market but, to get to the fruit market proper, you need to walk for about 10 minutes.

The market is open every day, from morning until sunset. Here you will be able to find many vegetables that are hard to find elsewhere, including pumpkins, sweet potatoes, a variety of salads and fresh herbs. Products should be much cheaper than you would find elsewhere in the city but, being a foreigner, you really have to bargain quite firmly.

There is a **small fruit and vegetable market** at the bottom of Mohammed Najeeb Street in Ama-rat, just off Street 1. Here, you can find rarities such as papaya, fresh coriander, and fresh pineapples. The produce is usually clean and well-displayed. In general, only seasonal fruit is sold here, although you can get some imported items, such as apples and grapes. Watermelons and honeydew melons are particularly worth sampling. Some excellent varieties of mango can be found here, although watch out for the occasionally stringy and fibrous ones. The market's location means that the stallholders are very used to dealing with foreigners. They are always friendly and helpful, but you will have to negotiate quite hard to get the price you want.

Souq Bahri is a large, covered market that can get fairly crowded.

The market is particularly well-known for the wide range of clothes that are on display there. The stalls selling traditional Sudanese clothes are especially good for a browse. You can even see tailors, hunched over sewing machines, stitching together the clothes that are then sold in the market. Shoes and sandals are also made locally. Souq Bahri is a bit pricier than some of the other markets in Khartoum, but the quality is also a little better.

A direct bus runs from Stad, in the centre of Khartoum, to Souq Bahri.

Bahri also has a separate market for clothes and perfumes — **Souq Sad Ghishra** — but the prices are very high. Buses from Stad run direct to this market (direction Shabia).

Souq as-Shigiara in Omdurman is a small handicraft market, located just next to the traditional boat builder in Abu Raouf (p131). The market is particularly well-known among Sudanese ladies, as this is where they buy the material to perform the *dukhan* (p81). The market is 2 km east of the Shambat bridge. You can take a bus to the bridge from Souq Omdurman or Souq Bahri, and then a rickshaw (2 SDG) to the market.

Souq al-Moheli, to the west of Omdurman, is the biggest camel market in the region. The best time to visit it is on Saturday mornings. For more details of this market, see p131.

Shopping

Living & Working

As foreign investment capital has flooded into North Sudan, opportunities for living and working in the capital have sky-rocketed.

Voluntary and non-governmental organisations have permeated the country. There has also been a growing influx of international corporations, particularly in the oil and telecoms sectors. This has all had a knock-on effect for other areas of the economy; Khartoum's hospitality sector has really started to pick up and tourism in the country is developing fast. As a result, there is a pressing need for workers who can speak English, fuelling a demand for English teachers in the country.

It is true that, with independence, many sources of income for North Sudan have drifted elsewhere. The UN mission in the capital has now left, with many personnel being relocated to Juba in the South. A number of oil companies, also, have uprooted their staff and headed South, where the majority of oil fields now lie.

However, the hope is that a peaceful North Sudan will attract other sources of private foreign investment. Therefore, opportunities haven't disappeared altogether — they have simply been replaced with new ones.

Since North Sudan is an Islamic country, there are inevitably cultural differences between how things are done in the West. The purpose of this chapter is to try to bridge some of these divisions, and to help you navigate your way through some of the red tape that you will almost certainly encounter whilst in the country.

VISAS AND PERMITS

If you are coming to North Sudan for business purposes, either on a short trip or to work here, you will first need to find an organisation to sponsor you. Your chosen organisation should send a letter of invitation to the Sudanese Embassy in your home country, indicating which visa it is prepared to sponsor you for.

A standard business visa for North Sudan usually lasts one month, and is renewable a maximum of three times whilst you are in Sudan. The cost of this visa depends on your country of origin.

It is normal to come to the country on a temporary visa and then if you are going to stay longer than three months, apply for a residence permit.

Residence permits are available from the Department of Aliens in Diem, just next to Sudan University for Science and Technology. To get there, take a bus towards Mir al-Buri and Sahafa Zalat. The office is open from Sunday to Thursday (9 am to 4 pm), and on Saturday (9 am to 2.30 pm). The permit should only take two working days to obtain, but it is best to apply well in advance.

There are two types of residence permit that you can get, depending on your needs. Both last a year. The **single-entry residence permit** costs 257 SDG. Although the permit is relatively cheap, the downside to it is that, if you want to leave the country during your stay, you will have to apply for permission to do so and pay additional costs (see below). The **multiple-entry residence permit** costs 1200 SDG and allows you to enter and leave the country as many times as you like during its period of validity.

Both of these permits require you to submit the following: a document proving your sponsor to be a registered and legal business, a letter from the company indicating that you are going to work there, a copy of your university certificate and two passport photos. If you are going to arrange the visa yourself, you will also need a letter from your sponsor authorising you to do so.

For a residence permit, you will also be asked to take an AIDS test, which is performed behind a shabby screen in the Department of Aliens. It usually takes three working days to get the results back. The results of an AIDS test from outside of Sudan will not be accepted. The test is fairly expensive: 250 SDG. If you are married to a Sudanese, you are exempt from the test.

In 2008, a law came into force that means a residence permit is only valid between January and December of a particular year. Therefore, if you come to Sudan in July, for example, and want to stay a year, you will have to apply for two residence permits: one when you arrive in the country and the other in the January of the following year.

If you have a single-entry residence permit, each time you wish to leave the country temporarily during your stay, you must apply for an **exit and re-entry visa** from the Department of Aliens. This costs 255 SDG and requires a letter from your sponsor granting you permission to travel.

If you stay in Sudan for longer than three months, the business must provide a release letter in order for you to leave the country. This proves, among other things,

that you have done the job you were required to do and that your tax payments are up-to-date.

Even travelling outside your city of domicile can be difficult, without approval from your sponsor. Whenever you wish to apply for a travel permit, your sponsor will need to provide a letter.

All this gives your sponsor a lot of control over you whilst you are in the country, so it is a good idea to make sure that you are getting a fair deal, and the best possible visa, before you arrive.

Do not forget to *register* at the Foreign Registration Office when you arrive in the country (p28), although your sponsor or the hotel where you are staying may agree to do this for you.

The website 🖳 www.passport.gov.sd has up-to-date information (in Arabic only) about the requirements for each of the various types of visas and permits.

LABOUR LAW

Before signing up to work in North Sudan, you should spend some time familiarising yourself with the country's labour law. This is also a good idea if you are going to be running a business in the country and will need to recruit local staff. The most important points are given below:

- Male Sudanese must prove that they have completed National Service (duration: 12 months) or else show that they are exempt from this. Foreigners, Sudanese with dual nationality and people above a certain age are exempted from National Service.

- Sudanese are not given their university certificates or diplomas until after they have com-

POINTS TO CONSIDER BEFORE COMING TO KHARTOUM

- There have been reports of some companies trying to hold onto the passports of foreigners whom they employ, because they do not want workers to leave. This is usually done subtly, with the employer claiming that it is normal procedure to keep your passport for a long time. Do not let companies get away with this.

- You need an authorisation letter from your sponsor every time you want to leave North Sudan or your city of domicile.

- To work here for more than three months, you must undergo an AIDS test within the country.

- If you are married to a North Sudanese, every time you want to leave the country or travel outside your city of residence, you must have authorisation from your spouse.

- The country is not cheap to live in.

- You will not be able to change employer once you are in North Sudan, unless your sponsor agrees to this — or unless you leave the country and wait for another business visa from your new company.

- Alcohol is strictly forbidden.

- North Sudan is an Islamic country and you should make sure you know as much about the culture and religion as possible, to avoid any unpleasant surprises.

- If your residence permit is cancelled in Sudan, for whatever reason, you will not be able to re-enter the country for at least six months.

pleted national service.

- Women are entitled to claim one day off work on the first day of their period each month.

- Many workers now enjoy two-day weekends (Friday and Saturday). However, this is still at the discretion of the company and many continue to give their employees just one day off a week (Friday).

- Normal working hours are 48 hours a week. Workers are entitled to a minimum of a half-hour paid break each day (one hour for women and children).

- During Ramadan, the working week is reduced by one hour a day.

- Women are not generally allowed to work between 10 pm and 6 am (apart from in certain professional, administrative and social-care jobs).

- Overtime must be agreed by both parties, and cannot exceed four hours a day or 12 hours a week.

- Workers are entitled to annual leave of 20 days once they have worked one full year at a company. After eight years, this goes up to 25 days. After 15 years, holiday entitlement is 30 days. Workers are also entitled to all official holidays in the country. Holidays are taken on full pay.

- Women are entitled to paid maternity leave (four weeks before expected delivery and four weeks afterwards), provided that they have worked at the company for at least one year.

- Sick leave is paid according to length of service (either on full-pay, half-pay, or quarter-pay). However, you cannot take sick leave until you have exhausted all of your annual leave.

- A woman who has just lost her husband is entitled to four months and 10 days of bereavement leave.

- The notice period for termination of an employee's contract depends on how long the individual has worked at the company. If he or she has worked there for more than five years, the notice period is one month. Otherwise, the notice period is the same as the frequency with which the worker gets paid: one month, two weeks or one week.

COMMUNICATION

Internet

If you are staying in Khartoum for a while, you might want to think about getting a permanent ADSL connection at home. ADSL broadband services were only introduced in 2004. Sudani continues to be the largest broadband provider, but others, such as Canar, are becoming more popular.

If you do not want to go through the trouble of setting up an internet connection at home, there are a number of other options.

Sudani, MTN and Zain all offer internet packages through a dongle that plugs into your computer's USB port. To access the internet, you insert an ordinary SIM card into the dongle. You need to make sure

---

TELECOMS COMPANIES

Sudani: 💻 www.sudani.sd

Canar: 💻 www.canar.sd

Zain: 💻 www.zain.com

MTN: 💻 www.mtn.com

---

that the SIM card has an internet subscription first. For subscriptions longer than a month, you usually have to arrange this through the offices of your chosen telecoms company. However, internet providers have now started offering the possibility of accessing the internet on a daily, or sometimes even hourly, basis. This shorter-term access can be arranged directly from your phone, by sending an SMS to a particular number that is given by your telecoms provider. Paying an hourly or daily basis can save you money, compared to taking out a monthly subscription, but the service is usually slower.

These days, there is not very much difference between the rates that the different companies offer for mobile internet access. The USB dongle costs 99 SDG with Sudani and 100 SDG with Zain. MTN charges slightly more — 149 SDG — but this does come with 15 days free internet access.

A month of internet access costs 95 SDG with Sudani, 99 SDG with MTN and 100 SDG with Zain.

Daily internet access usually costs between 60 *piastras* and 1 SDG, depending on the company.

These prices are intended as a guide only and are subject to change — you should consult the individual websites of the telecoms companies for the latest deals.

Canar is slightly different, in that it is principally a provider of fixed-line telecom services rather

Living & Working

than mobile phones. It is able to provide mobile internet packages, combined with telephone services, through the use of Wireless Local Loop (WLL) technology. This works well in big cities like Khartoum, but is not so useful if you are going to be travelling to smaller towns in North Sudan.

Canar packages tend to be most suitable for those who do not require much use of the internet each month, and who like the idea of combining an internet package with the ability to make cheap calls.

The typical cost for Canar line rental is 35 SDG per month. This includes 200 minutes of free domestic calls plus five free hours of dial-up internet access. After that, internet is charged at the rate of 1.30 SDG per hour.

A Canar package comes with what looks like a conventional phone. This can be carried around and plugged into the computer's USB port in order to connect to the internet. You use Canar by buying prepaid top-up phone cards, available from many grocery stores and other shops throughout the city. In order to subscribe to the Canar service, you must be able to provide a work permit, a residence permit and a letter from your employer.

There are growing numbers of wireless internet hotspots in Sudan, where you can surf using your own laptop (see box).

There are many other internet locations in the city where you can use computers. These are not always immediately visible but, if you ask around, you'll soon find that they are in pretty much every neighbourhood. Internet cafés tend to cost between 2 and 3 SDG per hour.

WI-FI HOTSPOTS

Restaurants

Aroma (p164)
My Place (p165)
Papa Costa (p163)
Pizza Corner (p172)
Solitaire (p170 & p166)
Sweet & Sour (p162)

Hotels

5M Hotel (p156)
Acropole Hotel (p156)
Al-Ahlam (p159)
Al-Ferdous Hotel (p158)
Al-Muhajir Hotel Flats (p158)
Al-Salam Rotana Hotel (p155)
Bahrain International Hotel (p153)
Bougainvilla Guesthouse (p157)
Coral Hotel (p153)
Corinthia (p153)
Dandas International Hotel (p157)
Dubai Hotel (p160)
Falcon Hotel (p158)
Grand Holiday Villa (p152)
Plaza Hotel (p157)
Regency Hotel (156)
Shariqa (p159)
Taka Hotel (p157)
VIP International Hotel (p156)

Other

Afra Mall (p167)
Khartoum International Airport (p18)

Telephones

Most people who come to Sudan, even those staying for a long time, opt for a mobile phone rather than a fixed line. In this respect, Sudan has followed the phenomenon of most countries in Africa and the developing world. Because mobiles hit Africa just as the continent was trying to straighten out its land-based phone network, many people ended up bypassing land phones altogether in favour of these new portable wonders.

Although people do have landlines in Khartoum, it can be quite an ordeal getting one set up and usually not worth it in terms of time and money spent. If you want to persist in this course of action, your best option is to contact Sudani, the country's national telecoms provider, who can give you all the latest details, including prices. Canar offers good packages for businesses, combining both internet and telephony services (see previous section).

There are three main mobile phone providers in Sudan: Zain, MTN and Sudani. MTN was the first company to offer per-second billing, but a recent regulation passed by the National Telecommunication Corporation (NTC) means that all companies must now bill their customers in this way.

Many Sudanese claim that MTN is the more reliable of the networks. Because it has fewer users, one doesn't tend to get the 'congested' signal that is a particular problem with Zain. MTN also tends to be better for making international calls.

However, Zain offers a greater level of coverage outside Khartoum, which can be useful if you plan to do a lot of travelling around the country. A particularly neat feature of Zain is the company's One Network facility. No matter what package users choose, they are not subject to high roaming charges when they take their phone to almost any other country that has the Zain network.

When choosing a mobile phone, bear in mind how often you are going to need to top it up. Zain and MTN require the phone to be recharged fairly frequently (depending on the type of package purchased) whilst, with Sudani, crediting the phone with 10 SDG is enough to last a year.

You can buy prepaid mobile-phone packages in many outlets, including the airport, shopping malls and the market. Packages can cost anywhere between 5 and 30 SDG, depending on the plan that you choose and where you buy them. These packages come with a SIM card, which may or may not include a certain amount of credit already loaded. You can usually get a better deal in the market than you can in shops.

All packages offer different tariffs and other benefits, so it is wisest to check the latest deals when you get to the country.

Top-up cards can be purchased all over the place. Most local shops sell them, as well as kiosks in the street or at the market. Cards usually come in denominations of 2, 5, 10 or 20 SDG.

Some shops now use electronic point-of-sale top-up machines, where they will type in your telephone number and top-up your phone without you needing to buy a scratch card. However, if the shop offers such a service, make sure you ask for a receipt. There have been a few isolated cases of vendors only pretending to type in the number, so that your phone does not actually get topped up.

Postal and delivery service

There is no door-to-door postal service in Sudan, so if you are going to be living in the country for some time it might be worth thinking about opening a PO Box.

This can be done at one of the main post office branches in Khartoum, Omdurman or Bahri. A PO Box costs 35 SDG per year for private usage and 300 SDG per year for businesses. Sudapost's new website (🏠 www.sudapost.com) has the latest details. To open a PO Box, simply take along a photocopy of your passport — along with a copy of your business registration card, if you are opening a PO Box for business purposes. Access is not 24 hours, but is usually between 8 am and 6 pm, depending on the post office where you open your PO Box.

There are also a couple of major international-delivery companies that operate in Sudan:

- TNT International Express (🏠 Mohammed Najeeb Street, Amarat; ☎ 0183 472 203/4/5/6).

- DHL Express Sudan (🏠 Nihimi Street, House 10; ☎ 0183 777 500).

BUSINESS ETIQUETTE

If you are coming to North Sudan for business, you should try to familiarise yourself with the business customs that exist in the capital.

In terms of dress, more and more businessmen are replacing their traditional *jalabia* (p80) with a more Western-style, namely: smart trousers, shirt, jacket and tie. The jacket is usually optional, but only consider wearing a shirt without a tie if you want to dress informally.

Business acquaintances greet each other according to their levels of familiarity. People who don't know each other very well usually just shake hands. The handshake should be firm and confident, exhibiting trust and goodwill towards the other party. However, people in positions of power, or very wealthy people, may offer a limper handshake to those beneath them, as a sign of superiority. People who know each other better normally touch one another on the shoulder as well as shaking hands. Business associates embrace if they are very

BUSINESS CARDS

The business card is an important accessory for the businessman in Sudan, especially as contact-building is so important. When designing your business card, it is worth having Arabic text printed on one side and English on the other.

There are generally three types of business card that you can opt for. One type that is particularly popular is printed on a standard set of glossy cards. These cards are generally black, blue or white and have a small decorative border (usually gold or silver) around the outside. The cards look and feel cheap, as indeed they are, and will cost you between 15 and 20 SDG per 100.

The more luxurious cards are a little pricier — around 30 to 35 SDG per 100 — but are definitely worth thinking about. The texture and finish to the cards is much more professional and, most of the time, you can choose whatever design you want.

You can also get a thicker, waterproof type of card. This card is more expensive than the others because it uses the offset printing method, and therefore you have to order them in large quantities. However, the quality is incomparable.

A note of caution. If you are thinking about printing business cards in Sudan, the professionalism of many printing companies is disappointing. They frequently make mistakes or omissions on cards, even if you have provided them with a soft copy of the text. Therefore, it is advisable to either bring business cards from abroad or make sure you carefully inspect a sample card before arranging for all the cards to be printed.

close friends. Sudanese business-women also shake hands, although it is usually up to the man to initiate this. See p85 for more information on greetings.

However you greet a business contact, always try to engage in some small talk before moving on to the real purpose of the meeting. It is considered rude to plunge straight into business matters, without making some attempt at conversation on other subjects. A good starting point is to inquire about the health of the other person's family.

Personal contacts are particularly important in Sudanese business transactions. Business managers are far more likely to take into consideration the fact that they know the person who is offering them their services than to weigh up the quality or price of services being offered.

If you want to integrate yourself into the North Sudanese business community, it is imperative that you approach networking in the right way. Although business associates often meet for a drink or *sheesha* at a club or a hotel, an invitation to dinner at home is considered more intimate and personal. It is a sign that you are really interested in developing a good relationship with them. Inviting business contacts for lunch at a restaurant is far less common in North Sudan than it is in Europe or America.

Personal contacts are also extremely important when it comes to job hunting. If you know the person offering the job, you stand a far better chance of being hired than if you just apply with no personal connection.

Most offices in Khartoum have a mat for employees and visitors who wish to pray. Remember that you should never walk over this prayer mat with shoes on, nor should you touch it with dirty hands. Also, do not talk to people who are praying or take any photographs.

When scheduling meetings, try as far as possible to consider the Islamic prayer time. In this day-and-age, many Muslims — particularly businessmen — accept that their time for praying can be moved when necessary. However, they will still appreciate a non-Muslim who gives this due consideration.

Also, when arranging meetings, you should clearly state in advance whether or not the visitor is female.

And don't forget that old Sudanese adage: punctuality is far less important than patience and politeness. So, try to be on time yourself for scheduled appointments, but don't be frustrated or annoyed if the person you are meeting is late.

In terms of language, English is widely-spoken in business circles, although a few words of Arabic will be well-received and will help put the other party at ease.

See p298 to brush up on some Arabic.

SCHOOLS

If you have a young family, choosing a school will probably be a priority for you once you arrive in Khartoum. There are some good options as far as private schooling for expats goes, but expect to pay quite a lot for the top schools in the city.

The **International Standard English School** (🏠 Street 33, near Mohammed Najeeb, Amarat; ☎ 0155 170 446 or 0122 757 686) only has a fairly small number of students. Most of the teachers are either British or Sudanese-American.

The **British Educational School** (🏠 Street 1, near

Living & Working

Mohammed Najeeb, Amarat; ☎ 0183 583 703/4/5 or 0912 148 502; @ britishinstitutes25@ yahoo.co.uk) employs teachers from a wealth of different backgrounds, including British, Filipino and Sudanese (with international experience). Although the school has branches throughout Khartoum, the headquarters is the only place where they teach in English.

The **Khartoum American School** (🏠 Mohammed Najeeb, south of Street 61; ☎ 0155 770 105/7; @ kas@krtams.org; 🖥 www.krtams.org) is a large school with a very good reputation in Khartoum. The school has around 225 students, coming from more than 40 different countries. Class sizes range from 15 to 20 students. The school follows an international curriculum and operates programmes for children from two years old through to high-school students. The school also provides English as a Second Language (ESL) training for those students who need extra support. The school is accredited by the Middle States Association of Schools and Colleges (🖥 www.middlestates.org) in the USA and is a member of the Council of International Schools in the UK. Nursery and pre-school fees are currently $7,550. For primary pupils the fees are $16,900, and for high-school pupils they are $21,000

The **Khartoum International Community School (KICS)** (🏠 Soba; ☎ 0183 215 000; @ principal@kics.sd; 🖥 www.kics.sd) also has a very good reputation in Khartoum. It is part of the DAL group, which is the largest privately-owned company operating in Sudan. The American-styled campus is impressive and has a beautiful football pitch and tennis court. This is a school that has plenty of resources: not surprising when they charge annual fees of between 20,000 and 30,000 SDG.

The school operates the International Baccalaureate system, starting at age three. Class sizes are between 15 and 20 students. Classes are taught by one International Baccalaureate Organisation (IBO) certified teacher and one support teacher (only in the younger age groups). Teachers are mainly American or American-Sudanese.

Unity High School (🏠 Qasar Street; ☎ 0183 786 585; @ principal.uhs@hotmail.com; 🖥 www.unityhighschool.org) was originally established as a Christian school in 1902, but has since expanded to incorporate people of all denominations. It prides itself on the proportion of Islamic teachers that it employs, and now offers Islamic and Arabic classes as well as Christian studies. The school's syllabus is based on the English National Curriculum. Pupils at the school are aged between four and 18. The school is situated in the heart of Central Khartoum, not far from Souq al-Arabi, and has a beautiful garden within the grounds.

Ecole Française de Khartoum (🏠 Riyad; @ ecolefrancaisekhartoum@ yahoo.com; 🖥 www.efk-sd.com) is a French-speaking school, where everything is taught in French and they follow the French curriculum. The classes are reasonably small. Fees are €4,470 for pre-school, €5,040 for primary and €6,900 for secondary.

The **Sudanese Academy International School** (🏠 Kafouri, near the Vatican Embassy; ☎ 0912 378 964) is located in a residential area of Khartoum and offers primary and secondary schooling. The school is financed by Sudan's Ministry of Foreign Affairs and its employees. There are two sections: one where students are taught in Arabic and the other where they are taught in English. In the English-teaching section, teachers are from different nationalities. The school is very new and was built in 2007.

Holm English Medium School (☎ Mamoura; ☎ 0183 248 614/5/8; 🖥 www.holmschool.com; @ hemsedu@yahoo.com) began as a pre-school that prepared children for entry into the British primary education system. It has since expanded into a fully-independent school, preparing students for higher education. The school caters for children of all nationalities between the ages of three and 16. The curriculum follows the International General Certificate of Secondary Education (IGCSE) syllabi. Classes are taught in English, with Arabic language and religious studies forming an integral part of the curriculum. The school is quite large and is owned by an Indian lady and her daughter.

Khartoum Diplomatic School (☎ Malik Street; ☎ 0183 468 003; @ info@khartoumdiplomaticschool.com; 🖥 www.khartoumdiplomaticschool-edu.com) teaches children from 30 different countries. Most classes are taught in English, although Arabic and French are offered as additional languages. The school takes children from the age of two all the way up to 16. Annual fees are £3,000 for pre-school, £4,000 for primary and £4,500 for secondary.

COURSES

Arabic

The **Catholic Language Institute of Khartoum (CLIK)** (☎ Street 29, near Afriqia Street; ☎ 0183 483 972/3/4) offers a number of courses in both Sudanese and Standard Arabic. Lessons begin throughout the year, with a minimum of five students. CLIK has produced its own book of Sudanese grammar (45 SDG), plus an exercise book (15 SDG) and phrase book (5 SDG). The standard course costs 450 SDG and consists of four hours of teaching a week over a two-month period. Private lessons and intensive courses are also available. The school is closed on Fridays and Sundays.

Spanish and Italian

Comboni College for Science and Technology (☎ Qasar Street, near Meridian Hotel, Central Khartoum; ☎ 0183 780 260 or 0922 399 544; @ info@combonicollege.com; 🖥 combonishortcourses.com) regularly runs courses of Spanish and Italian — check their website for news of upcoming courses, plus latest prices. Their ability to run these courses is very much dependent on being able to find suitable teachers.

French

The **French Cultural Centre** (☎ Ali Dinar Street, Central Khartoum; ☎ 0183 798 035/36/37; @ ccf_khartoum@yahoo.fr; 🖥 www.ccfkhartoum.info) offers 42 hours of French teaching for 180 SDG. Conversational courses are also available — 110 SDG for 24 hours. Classes take place between 10 am and 12 noon, between 4.30 and 6.30 pm or between 6.30 and 8.30 pm.

The **Catholic Language Institute in Khartoum (CLIK)** (☎ Street 29, near Afriqia Street, Amarat; ☎ 0183 483 972/3/4) runs classes for small children in French. Teachers are mainly French nuns.

German

The **German Goethe-Institut** (☎ Mek Nimir Street, Central

Living & Working

COURSE LIST FOR GERMAN GOETHE-INSTITUT

Course	Duration	Hours per week	Price
Extensive Course	11 weeks	5.15 hours	165 SDG
Intensive Course	11 weeks	10.30 hours	330 SDG
Intensive Course Plus	11 weeks	12 hours	385 SDG
Preparation Course	4 weeks	3.45 hours	80 SDG

Khartoum; ☎ 0183 777 833; @ info@khartum.goethe.org; 🖳 www.goethe.de/khartum) offers a range of courses in German (see box). Fees do not include teaching materials.

Business and management

The **British Council** (🏠 Abu Sinn Street; ☎ 0187 028 000; @ info@sd.britishcouncil.org; 🖳 www.britishcouncil.org) regularly hosts management and business seminars, plus courses in business leadership. Contact them for the latest details.

WHERE TO WORSHIP

If you are a Muslim, you will have no problem finding a place to worship in one of the city's many mosques. Options for Christians are slightly more limited, but there is still a good range of churches in Khartoum. Denominations include: Catholic, Orthodox and Anglican.

- **Anglican Church** (🏠 East of Omdurman General Hospital, Omdurman).

- **Coptic Orthodox Church** (🏠 Mek Nimir Street / Nil Street, Central Khartoum).

- **Episcopalian Orthodox Church** (🏠 Jamhouriya Street, Central Khartoum).

- **Eritrean Orthodox Church** (🏠 Tayif).

- **Ethiopian Orthodox Church** (🏠 Afriqia Street, Khartoum 2).

- **Greek Orthodox Church** (🏠 Jamhouriya Street, Central Khartoum).

- **St Matthew's Catholic Cathedral** (🏠 Nil Street, Central Khartoum).

- **St Mary's Roman Catholic Church** (🏠 Riyad).

- **The Catholic Language Institute Khartoum (CLIK)** (🏠 Street 29, Amarat) holds Mass once a month in French, as well as special services during Christmas and Easter.

- **All Saints Anglican Cathedral** (🏠 Street 1, Amarat).

- **Khartoum International Church** (🏠 Near the Italian Embassy, Khartoum 2).

- **St Peter and Paul's** (🏠 Street 33, near Afriqia Street, Amarat).

HOW TO FIND A JOB

The most popular sectors for foreigners to be employed in are: teaching/training, engineering, management and humanitarian or NGO work. Due to the absence of catering schools in the country, many international restaurants also seek good chefs from abroad. If you can speak some Arabic, the opportunity for employment in the country markedly increases.

To find a job in Sudan, you can either apply directly to the organisation that you want to join or go through a recruitment agency that is used to dealing with foreigners (see box).

Bear in mind that, under Sudanese law, only foreigners educated to degree level can obtain work permits.

Working as a journalist

All journalists in the country must be registered with the authorities. Journalists who operate without permission run the risk of being arrested.

Short-term permission (usually limited to a month) is easy to obtain. All you have to do is take 150 SDG and two passport photos along to the **Ministry of Information and Communication** (🏠 Jama'a Street, Central Khartoum; ☎ 0183 779 042; @ info@ minic.gov.sd; 🖥 www.minic.gov. sd). A temporary photo ID will then be made up for you on the spot.

More permanent accreditation is available from the **National Press Council (NPC)** (🏠 Osman Digna Street; ☎ 0183 779 816). This accreditation is usually granted to news outlets permanently stationed in the city, such as the BBC and Reuters, but others should be able to get it, providing that they can provide a letter of introduction from a publication they regularly contribute to.

The Secretary General of the NPC has the final say about whether accreditation can be awarded to an individual, on a case-by-case basis. Permanent accreditation costs around 1,000 SDG for a year.

RECRUITMENT AGENCIES

Recruitment agencies are a relatively new concept in Khartoum, so there are still not all that many. A few of the more popular ones are:

- **Lutfi Self Development Centre** (🏠 Tayif, just next to the Kenana building; ☎ 0183 252 661; @ info@lutfisdc. net; 🖥 www.lutfisdc.net).

- **Qurtoba Recruitment and Management Training** (🏠 Obeid Khatim Street, Riyad; ☎ 0914 148 931 or 0155 166 311; @ info@qurtobasd. com; 🖥 www.qurtobasd. com).

- **Kawader for Recruitment and Training** (🏠 Mashtal Street, Riyad; ☎ 0183 237 933 or 0120 868 661; @ info@kawader-sd.com; 🖥 www.kawader-sd.com).

Two popular websites that list jobs in North Sudan are:

- 🖥 **www.sudanjob.net**

- 🖥 **www.sudazone.com**

Working as a teacher

Working as a teacher in Sudan can be a great experience, but you should also be aware of Muslim sensitivities. Teachers have got into trouble in the past for causing offence.

You should not be overly-worried about this — most Muslims are fairly understanding and make allowances for people who are not of the same faith — but you should make an effort to familiarise yourself with the Islamic culture if you are going to teach in the country.

Some things you should be aware of as a teacher in Sudan:

- Be very careful what you say about Prophet Mohammed. Jokes cannot be made about him and he cannot be represented in any form other than in words.

- You may not give the name of any Islamic prophet to any animal or inanimate object.

- Many stricter Muslims refuse to look at a woman who is not their wife or a family member and, therefore, will not want to be taught by a woman.

- Be careful if you are thinking of playing music in class. Some Muslims are reluctant to listen to it, believing that it interferes with their communication with God.

- Always allow a break during prayer time and never start talking to someone who is praying.

- Be careful when asking a man to describe a woman or her clothes. Some Muslims feel uncomfortable with this.

- The best time to look for work as a teacher is just before the start of the school year (from June to August).

OPENING A BUSINESS

In recent years, investment opportunities have really taken off in Sudan. Foreigners who wish to open a company in the North should find the process relatively straightforward, although local taxes can be a little off-putting.

Although foreigners do not need to have a local partner in order to open a business in North Sudan, many choose to do so for local support. It can be great to have

LAWYERS

- El Tigani El Karib (🏠 Mek Nimir Street, Central Khartoum; ☎ 0183 779 998 or 0183 781 991).

- Ahmed Mohamed Fadl (☎ 0183 780 243 or 0183 771 220).

- Wanni & Wanni (🏠 Jamhouriya Street, Khartoum Insurance Co. Building, First Floor, Central Khartoum; ☎ 0183 777 517 or 0183 778 086).

- Sudan Bar Association (☎ 0183 783 845).

- House of Legal Consultancies & Services Ltd. (🏠 Nil Street, Kuwaiti Building, 4th Tower, Central Khartoum, ☎ 0183 785 704 or 0183 790 378/9 or 0183 777 751; @ awahab@hlcs-law.com).

- Sudanese Commercial Law Office (🏠 Near Chinese Embassy, Manshea; ☎ 0922 530 704; @ wael.abdin@sudaneselaw.com; 🖥 www.sudaneselaw.com).

- Omar Abdel Atti (🏠 Baraka Tower, 7th floor, Central Khartoum; ☎ 0183 776 400 or 0183 781 268; 🖥 www.omerabdelati.com).

someone who can help navigate the mesh of rules and regulations in the country, especially if they also have an understanding of local market conditions. Trading with a local partner, rather than on your own, may also help you to get favourable tax treatment.

There are some restrictions to the companies that can invest in North Sudan. Under US law,

American companies may not invest in the country. Under Sudanese law, international companies that trade with Israel are prohibited from establishing themselves in the country.

The steps involved in registering a business in North Sudan depend upon whether you are just planning on trading with the country or whether you will be setting up a more permanent initiative.

Government policy is very much geared towards promoting sustainable investment in the country. Therefore, if you are simply a trading company, you are likely to be hit by very high taxes. If you are establishing a more permanent base — ideally employing local staff — then your application will be treated more favourably and taxes will almost certainly be lower.

Companies investing in Sudan must first register with the Company Registrar. If the company is a subsidiary of an international corporation, the relevant documents of the parent company must also be provided. Company registration is not expensive, although it can be a good idea to consult with a local lawyer (see box on p198).

Companies must also provide two copies of a visibility study, detailing what their involvement will be in the country. One must be sent to the Ministry of Investment and the other to the Ministry of Industry.

The Ministry of Investment favours strategic companies over non-strategic ones. Strategic businesses are those that seek to provide a product or service not already available locally. Such companies can set up with greater ease and enjoy various tax concessions. Non-strategic companies provide products or services that already exist and get less tax breaks.

USEFUL BUSINESS CONTACTS

Sudan Development Corporation (SDC) (🏠 Amarat; ☎ 0183 472 186/95) is involved with investment and the provision of finance for development in Sudan.

Sudan Chamber of Commerce (🏠 Jamhouriya Street / Huria Street; ☎ 0183 772 346 or 0183 776 518; @ info@ sudanchamber.org.sd; 🖥 www. sudanchamber.org.sd).

Sudanese Chamber of Industries Association (☎ 0183 471 717/8/9 or 0183 471 761 or 0912 306 524; @ sudinass@hotmail. com; 🖥 www.sudanindustry.org) is the representative of the Sudanese industrial private sector.

British Businessman's Association (☎ 0912 627 480; @ dpmart@hotmail.com) can offer advice for British expats wanting to set up a business in Sudan.

UK Trade Invest (☎ +44 20 7215 8000; 🖥 www.uktradeinvest. gov.uk) is a British government body that provides free advice for citizens looking to invest in other countries around the world. For a fee, they can also provide a more detailed analysis of a particular country, tailored to your requirements.

Ministry of Foreign Trade (🏠 Jama'a Street, not far from the palace in Central Khartoum; ☎ 0183 772 973 or 0183 770 940 or 0183 774 853).

Ministry of Investment (🏠 Nil Street, near National Museum, Central Khartoum; ☎ 0183 787 199 or 0183 760 848).

Ministry of Industry (☎ 0183 778 940 or 0183 789 641).

Trading companies have slightly different procedures, and are generally subject to high levels of tax and custom duties. They must register with the Ministry of Foreign Trade and the Ministry of Commerce.

OPENING A BANK ACCOUNT

It is possible to open a bank account in North Sudan as a foreigner, providing that you can prove you are working in the country. Do not expect to earn much interest on your money, however (see box below).

To open a bank account in Khartoum, you need to submit to the bank a copy of your passport and visa, a copy of your residence permit, two passport photos and a letter from your employer to prove that you are working there. You can either open a savings account, which is free, or a current account, for which there is a monthly charge. Both types of account come with a Sudanese ATM card, but only the current account gives you a cheque book.

Don't take it for granted that your Sudanese banking card can be used abroad. The Sudanese banking system is slowly becoming more integrated into global financial networks, but it is still lagging behind in some respects. If your card is

Living & Working

ISLAMIC BANKING

Islamic banking, as defined by the Qur'an, operates on a slightly different basis from banking in other countries. In particular, Islamic law prohibits the collection and payment of interest, which is the most common way for banks and savers to earn their money in other banking systems.

However, some people have criticised modern Islamic banks for simulating interest rate payments, even if they do not refer to them as such. Although Islamic law prohibits the collection of interest, it allows a seller to resell an item at a higher price than it was bought for, as long as there are clearly two transactions.

This idea is widely employed in the Sudanese banking system, using a concept known as *murabahah*, meaning 'profit'. Under this scheme, the bank offers a fixed-income loan to a third-party borrower, who agrees to pay a certain amount back at a date agreed in the future, which is the amount of profit that the bank owns for the transaction. The bank cannot charge additional interest on late payments, but generally retains some collateral (such as real estate) until the loan is repaid in full.

This system has the bizarre effect of generating a different rate of return for each transaction, which requires a dedicated team of actuaries to make sure everything balances out.

All of this means that, if you are a customer of an Islamic bank, you should not expect to receive any interest on your current account. Certain savings accounts do yield some profit above what you have paid into the bank, but such pseudo-interest tends to be quite variable. For example, you might receive a rate of 3% one year, 4% the next and nothing the year after that. It is best to check specific details of saving rates with banks in Sudan, but don't expect the process of saving money in the country to be more profitable than the process of saving money abroad.

All banks in the North have to operate according to Islamic law.

compatible with the 123 ATM network, you should be able to use it in neighbouring countries, including Egypt, Kenya and Ethiopia. Sudanese banking cards will not be accepted in Europe or America.

Things are slightly more complicated if you wish to open a bank account on behalf of a foreign-owned company in Sudan and it may be better to simply go to the bank as an individual. If you are nonetheless determined to open a bank account in the company's name, then, in addition to the requirements stated above, you will also need an official letter from head office, detailing your responsibilities to the company. This letter has to be translated into Arabic by a certified translator and then formally approved by the Ministry of Industry.

In January 2008, North Sudan's Central Bank stopped holding its reserves in US dollars and switched over to the euro instead, in order to minimise the risk of US sanctions against the growing economy. This means that it is now not possible to open a Sudanese bank account in US dollars.

The Central Bank says that you can still open a bank account in the euro, the British pound, Saudi Arabia's riyal and the United Arab Emirate's dirham. You may need to obtain formal permission from the Central Bank in order to open a bank account in a particular currency — check with the local branch of your chosen bank first.

Banks are open Sunday to Thursday, from 9 am to 1 pm. They are closed at weekends.

MEETING AND CONFERENCE ROOMS

Many of the high-end hotels in Khartoum have conference and meeting rooms available for hire, including the **Grand Holiday Villa**,

Al-Salam Rotana, **Corinthia**, and the **Coral**. Prices and facilities vary, so it is best to call in advance to check what is available. Full details for each of these places can be found in the 'Where To Sleep' section of this guidebook (p152).

ACCOMMODATION

Recently, Khartoum's over-inflated rental-property market has started coming down. This is largely because the UN and other foreigners, which had been keeping rental prices so high, have had to leave the country. Prices still aren't what you might call cheap, especially in the highly desirable areas such as Riyad and Amarat, but at least they have become more reasonable.

Prices vary significantly according to location, property condition and whether or not the property is furnished. The more expensive areas to live in are: Riyad, Khartoum 2, Garden City, Manshea and Kafouri. These are also the ones with the greatest concentration of expats.

In these areas, very basic, two-bedroom studio flats start at around 1,000 SDG a month. For this price, expect to get fairly tatty-looking furniture and, in most cases, no hot water. More attractive two-bedroom apartments cost between 2,000 and 2,400 SDG. For larger flats, with more than two bedrooms, expect to pay between 3,000 and 5,000 SDG. A house with a garden should cost between 4,000 and 8,000 SDG. If you want to find a house with a swimming pool, budget for at least 6,000 SDG although, in practice, the price may be much higher. Charges are usually extra on top of the rent. Remember, if you look beyond the popular expat areas, you can often find better deals, although the location may not be quite so convenient.

Living & Working

Be aware that many estate agents and independent landlords try to charge foreigners a great deal more money than the market dictates, especially those who are new in town. Therefore, it pays to spend some time shopping around.

You should make sure that the rooms in the place you are renting come fitted with air-conditioners or air-coolers — essential in the summer. Air-conditioners are great for chilling the room to the desired temperature, but air-coolers have the advantage of letting some fresh air into the place. Power cuts are rarer than they used to be but still happen, so checking if the place comes with a generator might not be a bad idea either.

You will find that many flats and houses have very small windows and shutters that are closed for most of the day. Although this makes things a little dingy, it also helps keep the house as cool as possible.

The length of the lease varies, but usually lasts between six and 12 months. You will usually be asked for a refundable deposit of three to six months' rent.

Finding a property to rent at a decent price can be tricky, especially with so many people keen to make money out of foreigners. The best thing to do is to ask other expats if they've heard about any places that are available for rent, or which estate agents they used to find their place. In many cases, a good estate agent can just be a man with a phone.

One estate agent that is used to dealing with foreigners is **Easy-move Property** (☎ 0183 486 363; @ info@easymoveproperty.com; 🖥 www.easymoveproperty.com). Others can be found in Amarat, along Street 37, towards Mohammed

Najeeb Street. **Lisamin Safari Hotel** can also help with flat-hunting.

You can also find notices about places to rent on the Khartoum Klub Facebook page.

ELECTRICITY, WATER AND WASTE

Sudan's electricity supply is 220 volts. Most accommodation in Khartoum uses a pre-pay system for the electricity bill. The metre, normally located outside or in the basement, can be recharged with a coupon bought from your local National Electrical Corporation centre.

Before the completion of the hydroelectrical dam at Merowe in 2009, North Sudan was struggling to meet its energy needs and power outages were a common occurrences. These days, things are much better and power cuts are far rarer.

They do still happen from time-to-time, though, so it always pays to be prepared.

You should keep an ample supply of candles and matches (or flashlights) around your house or flat. It is also a good idea to have a power generator, both at home and at work. Voltage stabilisers are recommended, to reduce wide voltage fluctuations and protect electronic equipment against sudden power surges.

There is a monthly charge for water and waste removal, which is usually collected at the door. Charges vary according to where you live.

Water costs 40 SDG for first-class areas (including Amarat, Riyad and Central Khartoum), 20 SDG for second-class areas and 10 SDG for third-class areas.

Waste collection costs 15 SDG for first-class areas, 10 SDG for second-class areas and 5 SDG for third-class areas.

The North
Ancient cities of the deserts

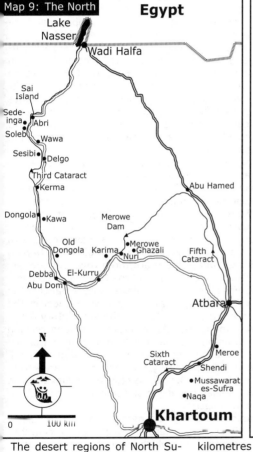

Map 9: The North

Egypt

Lake Nasser

Wadi Halfa

Sai Island

Sede-inga
Soleb
Abri
Wawa

Sesibi
Delgo

Third Cataract
Kerma

Abu Hamed

Dongola
Kawa

Merowe Dam

Old Dongola
Karima
Merowe
Ghazali
Nuri

Fifth Cataract

Debba
Abu Dom
El-Kurru

Atbara

N

Sixth Cataract

Meroe

Shendi

Mussawarat es-Sufra

Naqa

Khartoum

0   100 km

Highlights

- Enjoy the scenic views of the Sixth Cataract.

- Stay in Atbara, heart of Sudan's railways.

- Visit the remarkable Lion Temples of Naqa and Mussawarat es-Sufra.

- Climb the cobra-headed mountain of Jebel Barkal.

- Visit the ancient pyramids of Merowe.

- See the 16th century Ottoman settlement on Sai Island.

- Admire the vivid pharaonic wall paintings of El-Kurru's tombs.

- Discover the ancient Christian fortress of Old Dongola.

- See the remains of the oldest urban civilisation in Africa.

The desert regions of North Sudan yield some of the country's most impressive archaeological treasures.

Whilst many of these sites are accessible by bus from Khartoum, others can only be reached by private transport. To get to some of the remoter areas, which lie some kilometres away from the main roads, a four-wheel drive vehicle may be necessary.

There is some confusion about whether a travel permit is needed for the north or not. Officially it is, but in practice such a permit is rarely checked. The best advice is to get one before you go, just

SUDANESE ARCHAEOLOGY

The following is kindly supplied by Derek Welsby, who is responsible for the Sudanese and Egyptian Nubian collections in the British Museum in London.

The earliest archaeologists to work in Sudan invariably came from an Egyptological background and they assessed Sudan's ancient cultures in relation to those of Egypt. Their conclusions often reflected sentiments expressed by the powerful ancient Egyptian propaganda machine when Sudan was termed vile, wretched and miserable.

Now, however, the balance is changing. Many archaeologists are concentrating solely on Sudan's heritage and the importance of the region is being highlighted as never before. North Sudan, like Egypt, has an incredibly rich heritage. As well as temples to rival those in Egypt itself, there are vast numbers of pyramids. To these can be added innumerable cemeteries of many different periods, along with settlements containing houses, palaces and on occasion churches. There are also mighty fortresses, particularly from the Egyptian Middle Kingdom, the Kushite, Medieval and Islamic periods.

Three periods of Sudan's history stand out. The first of these, named after the town at Kerma near the Third Cataract, was the first urban civilisation in sub-Saharan Africa by millennia. Indeed, the development of urbanism here is almost as old as it was in Egypt. Kerma, the metropolis of the state known to the Egyptians as the Kingdom of Kush, retains its central temple, called the 'western *defuffa*' by the locals, and is surrounded by the remains of other temples, palaces, store-rooms and houses. The capital of this massive Nile Empire was originally at Napata in the region of Jebel Barkal where there are three royal cemeteries, massive temples and palaces. By the middle of the first millennium BC, the main royal residence was at Meroe, where extensive remains of the capital can be seen as well as the pyramids under which most of the rulers were buried from the 3rd century BC until the 4th century AD.

The Kushites, borrowing many aspects of ancient Egyptian religion and culture, continued to worship the old gods long after their worship was abandoned in Egypt. The final collapse of paganism in northern and central Sudan came in the 6th century AD when missionaries from the Byzantine Empire converted the kingdoms of Nobatia, Makuria and Alwa to Christianity, extinguished paganism and brought to an end the 5000-year tradition of human sacrifice.

Fighting off Arab incursions in 642 and a decade later, the medieval kingdoms flourished for 1000 years. There are many towns, churches and monasteries dating from this time which testify to the rich and vibrant culture of the Middle Nile. Old Dongola has the most impressive remains — of churches with granite columns, of a monastery with large numbers of wall paintings as well as what may have been the royal throne hall of the Makurian kings.

Several kilometres to the south, recent excavations have unearthed numerous churches at Banganarti, again with impressive wall paintings and a large amount of graffiti left by pilgrims. The capital of the

SUDANESE ARCHAEOLOGY (CONT.)

southern kingdom, Alwa, has not fared so well. Its proximity to Khartoum meant that it was prey to systematic looting for building materials in the 19th century.

Islam was introduced at a very early date to the Red Sea coast, but the Christian Nile kingdoms were able to hold out against increasing pressure from the north until the 14th century. The royal throne hall at Old Dongola was converted into a mosque in 1317 and the dedication inscription remains *in situ*. In the south, Alwa succumbed by around 1500 to pressure from the Abdallab Arabs and the Funj sultans of Sennar. When the Ottomans advanced up the Nile in the 16th century, Christianity had vanished. The Ottomans established their frontier on Sai Island, building a fortress on top of the Egyptian New Kingdom town while the Funj controlled much of the area to the south.

Anglo-Egyptian control in the 19th century opened up the country to archaeologists and fostered a local interest in the heritage of Sudan, leading to the founding of the first National Museum in 1904. Sudan now has a very active antiquities service, the National Corporation for Antiquities and Museums, a fine national museum and a number of regional museums.

Today, Sudan is a rapidly-developing nation and this is placing its heritage under increasing threat. New road projects abound, irrigation is being extended and urban centres are expanding. The greatest threat, however, is coming from dams on the Nile. As construction began on the Merowe Dam (p210), an international effort from archaeologists was initiated at the Fourth Nile Cataract to preserve the artefacts that would be flooded by the 170 km reservoir.

in case. The Ministry of Tourism (🏠 Mashtal Street, Riyad in Khartoum) can issue you one free-of-charge. The Ministry of Humanitarian Affairs (🏠 South of Qurashi Park, Khartoum 2) also issues permits, but the process will probably take longer and you may have to pay 5 SDG in tax.

The standard entrance fee for visiting archaeological sites is 20 SDG, payable on arrival. If you plan to visit a number of sites, try to negotiate the entrance fee. If you pay 20 SDG for every site that you visit, your trip can quickly become very expensive. A good trick is to retain the receipt for the first ticket that you purchased, and use that to negotiate entrance to subsequent sites. Often, the officials in charge

of entrance to the other sites will agree to a discount.

SHENDI

🔝 16°41'23"N 33°25'49"E

Some 150 km north-east of Khartoum lies the bustling market town of Shendi. Once a major trading and agriculture centre, its most salient point these days is that President Omar al-Bashir was born in a village nearby. It was once a highly prosperous town, thriving on the back of the slave trade. Now though, there is precious little sign of this former wealth.

The town was founded in around 350 AD by the Daju tribe, which came south from Meroe. The name of the town is believed to be derived from the old Daju word for sheep ('*chenday*') — an indication, perhaps, that the original settlers of the town were nomadic herders, who shepherded their flocks between the north and south in search of fresh grazing land.

There is not a great deal of immediate interest to see in the town, but it makes a good stopping-off point for travellers eager to visit the archaeological sites further north. Shendi is not very far from Naqa, Mussawarat es-Sufra and Meroe. However, you will need your own transport to get to these places.

The local market has a good vibe and there are plenty of bargains to be picked up, if you are in the mood for haggling.

Where to eat and sleep

If you want to get something to eat in the town, the market is your best bet: *fuul*, grilled meat kebabs and stews are widely available.

If you plan to spend the night in the town, your options are rather limited. There are a couple of fairly grotty *lokandas* around the marketplace, charging between 5 and 10 SDG for a dorm bed or a little more if you want your own room. **Al-Kawther Hotel** (☎ 026 172 364) is a slightly nicer place on the banks of the Nile, charging 120 SDG for a single. Comfortable but not outstanding.

How to get there

Getting to Shendi is relatively straightforward. The main Khartoum-to-Atbara highway, which runs quite close to the town, is in good condition. If you don't have your own transport, public buses regularly shuttle people between Shendi and Khartoum. The town has a train station, although at last visit trains were not running.

NAQA

🔊 16°16'47"N 33°16'44"E

Not far from Shendi lies the important Kushite site of Naqa, possibly one of the best-preserved settlements from the era. The site contains the remains of a huge **palace**, from where Queen Amanishakheto ruled during the 1st century BC. There are also two impressive Meroitic temples: the **Temple of Amun** and the **Lion Temple**.

The **Lion Temple** is a beautiful sandstone structure, with walls decorated with the images of prominent gods and kings. The temple is dedicated to the Kushite god Apedemak, who is depicted with the head of a lion. King Natakamani, who ruled Kush from the 1st century AD, is also vividly depicted in some of the pictures, standing proudly with Queen Amanitore over his vanquished enemies. Lions are shown devouring the slain.

The **Temple of Amun** lies on the western outskirts of the settlement. It was commissioned in the 1st century AD by King Natakamani as a tribute to the god of air. The temple was once a glorious structure, possibly one of the most prominent in ancient Kush. But time has been harsh on it, and now only the doorways, built out of sandstone, remain. The rest of the walls, built of fired bricks, have collapsed.

The god Amun is represented on the temple walls in both human and ram-headed form.

Just in front of the Lion Temple is a small kiosk known as **Temple B**, which incorporates both Roman and Nubian architectural styles. The kiosk would have been connected to the Amun Temple by an avenue lined with sphinxes.

Near to the site is a deep well still used by the nomads.

How to get there

You really need your own vehicle to get to Naqa, which can easily be reached from the Khartoum-to-Atbara highway. It takes around three hours to get to the site from Khartoum. The ruins are located around 3 km into the desert from the main road. There are no villages along the way, which makes it quite hard for travellers to get a lift from the main road. Entrance to the site costs 20 SDG.

The nearest town to the site is Shendi, but don't expect to be able to catch any public transport from here. You may be able to rent a car from the locals, though.

MUSSAWARAT ES-SUFRA

📶 16°25'13"N 33°19'35"E

Just north of Naqa lies Mussawarat, which is similar in style and design. There are two principal points of archaeological interest: the **Great Enclosure** and the **Lion Temple**.

The Great Enclosure is the largest set of Meroitic ruins in Sudan, consisting of a rambling structure of low walls and toppled columns. The site may have been a training ground for elephants, which were often used for military purposes. Large numbers of elephant images are carved into the walls.

The Lion Temple lies roughly 1 km to the east of the Great Enclosure and is dedicated to the lion headed god Apedemak. King Arnekhamani ordered the building of the temple around 230 BC. Its distinguishing feature is the massive pylon at the entrance, which depicts the king making offerings to the god. There are also some beautiful carvings of elephant processions at the rear end of the temple. In the 1960s, the Lion Temple was restored by

Humboldt University in Berlin, and it is now one of the finest Meroitic structures in Sudan.

A single ticket to visit the entire area costs 20 SDG and can be purchased on arrival.

How to get there

You need to have your own vehicle to get to Mussawarat, since public transport does not go here. The nearest main town is Shendi.

If you are en-route to Meroe, it is possible to visit both Mussawarat and Naqa with a few hours' detour.

MEROE

📶 17°01'02"N 33°43'49"E

North of Shendi lies the ancient Kushite capital of Meroe. It is unclear exactly when it was founded, but it probably became the capital of Kush around 750 BC, when King Kashta started pushing south into what is now modern-day Sudan.

The site is most famous for its **pyramids**. In the past, there may have been as many as 200 pyramids located at the site, but many have since been reclaimed by the desert. There are now less than 20 still standing. Archaeological finds show that, in the 3rd century BC, many tombs were moved to the town from Nuri, further north.

Meroe is a popular destination for those wanting to see a little of Sudan's archaeological heritage, and it is often the first name that springs off the tongues of those advising you where to travel in the north. This may have something to do with its close proximity to Khartoum and its ease-of-access, or because of the archaeological significance of many of the finds at Meroe.

Whilst Meroe is definitely interesting to visit, don't expect to be

The North

blown away by the pyramids, which lie low among the sand dunes. They are certainly nothing as grand as the pyramids of Giza in Egypt.

As you approach from Khartoum, the pyramids are a little way off to your right. On the other side of the road, to the left, is the **Royal City of Meroe** — also definitely worth taking an hour or so to walk around.

Officially, you need to buy separate tickets for visiting the pyramids and the Royal City, although you may be able to negotiate with the officials on duty.

Where to sleep

Meroe works well as a day trip from Khartoum, with a stop-over in Naqa and Mussawarat and possibly the 6th Cataract. However, you can also choose to spend the night just north of the pyramids, which may be a good option if you planning to head on to some of the other archaeological sites further north.

Accommodation is not cheap, though. The only place available is the **Tented Camp at Meroe** (☎ 0915 124 871 or 0907 978 532) which belongs to the Italian Tourism Company in Khartoum (🏠 Amarat, Street 31; ☎ 0183 487 961; @ info@italtoursudan.com; 🖥 www.italtoursudand.com). Double tents at the camp cost 600 SDG per night and singles cost 550 SDG per night. Prices are for half-board — breakfast and dinner — and exclusive of 20% tax. The camp is clean, well-run and relaxing. It is only a short distance from the pyramids, and you can pay for a camel to take you there if you want.

If you do not wish to pay for staying in the luxury Tented Camp, it is permissible to pitch your own tent in the desert. However, you should make sure that you are a reasonable distance (at least 100 metres) from both the pyramids and the Tented Camp. Bear in mind that

there are no shops or other facilities nearby, so you will need to bring all the food and water that you need.

Souvenirs are sold just outside the pyramids. Such products are mainly handmade and cheaper than those you will find in the gift shops of Khartoum. It is also better to part with your cash here, rather than in Khartoum, since you will be benefiting the local craftsmen rather than the wealthy owners of retail outlets.

ATBARA

🔊 17°42'17"N 33°59'08"E

Atbara is a dusty little town in the northern deserts where many travellers end up by accident rather than design, caught on their way to somewhere else.

It is located at the point where the Atbara River, flowing in from Ethiopia, joins the Nile — its last tributary before rushing on to Egypt.

There is little to hold the wayfarer here beyond an idle curiosity in locomotives — although, to be fair to the place, the story of the railways is a fascinating one.

Atbara is the historic heartland of Sudan's railway system. It is also the headquarters of the country's Communist Party, the history of which is closely linked with that of the railway — a relationship that, to a large extent, explains the decline of the rail industry in Sudan.

As trade unions started to emerge in the 1940s and 1950s, fanning the flames of Sudanese nationalism, Atbara's railway industry became the focus of industrial unrest. Over the decades, the power of the trade unions grew to become a formidable political force in the country. Sudan's Communist Party grew out of this trade union movement.

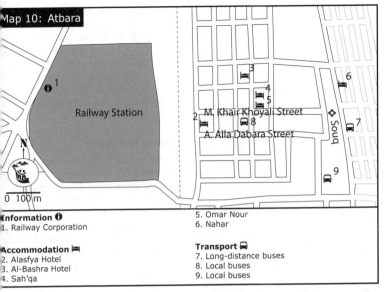

Map 10: Atbara

Railway Station

0 100 m

Information ❶
1. Railway Corporation

Accommodation 🛏
2. Alasfya Hotel
3. Al-Bashra Hotel
4. Sah'qa

5. Omar Nour
6. Nahar

Transport 🚍
7. Long-distance buses
8. Local buses
9. Local buses

Jaafar Nimeiri, the military leader who took power in 1969, feared the influence of the unions and therefore sought to move against them. In the 1980s, he took the decision to decentralise the country's rail system, and thus break the political hold that Atbara had on the country — an initiative that was to have a devastating effect on Sudan's railway infrastructure.

Another significant historical event linked to the railway took place in Atbara in 1898. At this time, Anglo-Egyptian forces, under the leadership of General Herbert Kitchener, were engaged in a campaign to reclaim Sudan for the British flag, having lost the country to the Mahdi more than a decade earlier.

Kitchener knew that, for his campaign to be successful, he had to secure the railway lines, which would provide an important channel for arms and supplies and, most crucially, a way of transporting his gunboats past the shallow stretches of water known as the Nile Cataracts.

The crippling attack on Mahdist forces stationed in the town, which took place on April 8, marked a turning point in Britain's fortunes in Sudan.

These days, Atbara is much like any other town in the northern deserts. There is a **small market** to browse around, including a good number of stalls selling spices.

If you have an hour or so to kill in the town, the best thing to do is wander down to the **old railway station**, where stationary passenger trains huddle together like dead bodies in a crypt.

Poor management of the railway put an end to passenger trains some months before we went to press, although cargo trains still run. A fresh management team is reportedly looking at relaunching passenger services from Atbara, but, this being Sudan, it is probably best not to hold one's breath.

The North

Just next to the railway station is the **Railway Corporation**, where you can usually find someone that speaks a little English and is eager to opine about Sudan's rail industry.

Where to eat and sleep

Eating options are extremely limited in the town. You will find **a few places selling *fuul* and grilled meat** around the market and near the bus stations. None of these particularly stand out. Just try and find a place where it looks as if the food has been freshly prepared.

There are a range of accommodation options in town. By far the fanciest place is **Alasfya Hotel** (☎ 0120 766 760), just across from the railway tracks. Here, ensuite rooms come with a fridge, TV, air-con and hot water in the bathroom. Rooms are large and very clean. Staff are friendly and speak some English. A double-room costs 135 SDG and a triple room 180 SDG. Wi-fi is available throughout the hotel.

A cheaper option, still with reasonable rooms, is **Al-Bashra Hotel** (☎ 0114 579 099 or 0211 725 446), not far from the market. Here, a large single room costs 75 SDG. All rooms are clean and come with air-con as well as a TV. The hotel has 11 rooms.

There are a couple of more downmarket *lokandas* in the centre of town, for those on the budget, although prices tend to be higher than you might expect for *lokandas* elsewhere.

Sah'qa (☎ 0905 354 444) is a friendly place, with cleaner rooms than your average *lokanda*. Prices are a little steep, though — 60 SDG for a fairly basic room with fan.

Next door, **Omar Nour** (☎ 0126 082 738) offers rooms for less — 40 SDG. However, the place is pretty vile and looks as though it hasn't been cleaned in decades.

In both of these *lokandas*, you can get a bed in a dorm for 10 SDG.

Nahar, slightly outside the centre, is the place to come if you want to sleep outside. Rooms cost 40 SDG whilst an outside bed in the courtyard costs 10 SDG.

How to get there

The easiest way to get to and from Atbara is via coach. Coaches to Khartoum take 4 to 5 hours and cost 25 SDG. The journey to Dongola cost 20 SDG and take 4 to 5 hours. The journey to and from Port Sudan takes seven to eight hours and costs 50 SDG. To Wadi Halfa, the bus costs 70 SDG and takes eight hours.

MEROWE

🔊 18°29'18"N 31°48'57"E

Just south of the Fourth Cataract lie the ancient remains of Merowe. There isn't a great deal to see in the town, beyond a few crumbling pyramids, and there are far richer sights in the settlements to the north and the south.

These days, the reason why most people have heard so much about the area is because of the controversial hydroelectrical dam that was constructed there, just 40 km from the old settlement, between 2004 and 2009.

The noble idea behind the project was to find an efficient way of meeting North Sudan's growing energy needs. Prior to the dam going live, power shortages around North Sudan, including in the country's capital, were a regular occurrence. The demands on the national grid had become so high that the government was forced to ration energy, switching off the supply of electricity to certain districts for a number of hours each week.

Now that the dam has been completed, things are much better and power cuts are a rarity. However, such energy security has come with a price.

In order to construct the massive 174 km-long reservoir, the surrounding lands had to be flooded, displacing an estimated 70,000 people. Many of these have been resettled and received compensation. However, a number of nomads in the region have lost out, since they do not have any formal entitlement to land and therefore it has been unclear what compensation they should receive.

It is worth driving past Merowe, just to see the impressive 9 km serpentine dam glistening in the midday sun.

GHAZALI

18°26'53"N 31°55'91"E

Ghazali, 20 km east of Merowe, is another relic of Sudan's ancient Christian kingdoms. The most distinguishing mark of the town is the **monastery**, which was probably founded around the 9th century AD. It was abandoned 200 years later, as the advance of Islam resulted in the decline of Nubian Christianity.

At its peak, as many as 50 monks may have lived within the monastery, in cramped conditions. The ancient walls of the monastery are impressive — a metre thick in places to ward off possible invaders. Now, of course, they lie in ruins, eroded by the passing of time. The remains of a **medieval church** lie within the confines of the monastery.

The remote location of Ghazali means that getting to the town is not easy, and you really need your own vehicle to reach the site.

The standard entrance fee to the site is 20 SDG.

KARIMA

18°33'24"N 31°50'57"E

If you are looking to immerse yourself in ancient Sudanese history, one of the best places to start is probably the ancient market town of Karima, a six-hour drive north of Khartoum.

Whilst the old market-town doesn't, in itself, make for a particularly interesting destination, it is surrounded by a glorious wealth of ancient treasures — including royal cemeteries, religious temples, pyramid ruins and the famous cobra-headed mountain of Jebel Barkal (p213).

Whilst in Karima, it is worth checking out the town's own archaeological museum, which contains many ancient and beautiful treasures that were rescued from Lake Nasser on the Egyptian border when it was flooded with water.

If you want to use the internet, **S-Magic** (⌂ Hosbitalia Street, next to the post office; ☎ 0122 064 133) has a good connection for 3 SDG per hour.

If you are going to stay in Karima, you must register with the local authorities. The registration office is situated in the north part of the market, in an area known as Souq al-Foqh. To get there, face away from the hospital and walk to the right. In the distance, you should see a tall tower. Continue walking in this direction and you will find the market just before the tower. If this proves too tricky, a rickshaw from the main square should cost no more than 3 SDG and will be able to take you straight to the office.

The North

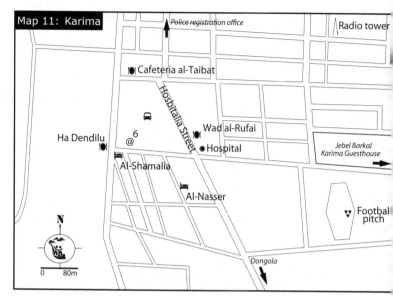

Map 11: Karima — Police registration office, Radio tower, Cafeteria al-Taibat, Hosbitalia Street, Wad al-Rufai, Ha Dendilu, Hospital, Jebel Barkal Karima Guesthouse, Al-Shamalia, Al-Nasser, Football pitch, Dongola, N, 0 80m

Where to eat

There is a significant shortage of good-quality restaurants in Karima. The best place to try is the **Nubian Rest House** (☎ 0231 820 368 or 0907 456 029), just in front of Jebel Barkal, though prices aren't cheap. A simple lunchbox costs around 60 SDG. A restaurant meal costs 110 SDG at lunchtime and 120 SDG in the evening. Drinks cost roughly ten times the prices charged in regular shops. A small bottle of Coca-Cola costs an astonishing 6 SDG.

In the main square of the town, you will find several small restaurants, including **Cafeteria al-Taibat** (☎ 0121 635 301). The place serves only fairly basic food, such as boiled or fried eggs and *tameeya*, but the prices are low. Greater variety can be found at **Wad al-Rufai** (🏠 Hosbitalia Street; ☎ 0910 922 170), including grilled fish and chicken. Walking up the street, you will see several other restaurants, all fairly similar. **Ha Dendilu**, in front of Haramen

Pharmacy, has fried fresh fish for 5 SDG and liver for a similar price.

Where to sleep

If you are looking for a bit of luxury during your stay in Karima, you had best check into the **Nubian Rest House** (☎ 0231 820 368 or 0907 456 029). Set in beautiful surroundings at the foot of Jebel Barkal, this really is a welcome oasis from the uncouth desert all around.

The guesthouse is owned by the Italian Tourism Company in Khartoum (🏠 Amarat, Street 31; ☎ 0183 487 961; @ info@italtoursudan.com; 🖥 ww.italtoursudan.com) and prices are the same as for their Tented Camp at Merowe. A double room costs 600 SDG, whilst a single costs 550 SDG. Prices exclude tax. The hotel also has a couple of so-called villa rooms, which are a little cheaper and more basic than the others. The hotel doesn't usually rent these unless all other rooms are full, but you may

The North

be able to persuade them to make an exception.

The hotel is in good condition, clean and relaxing. There is a nice garden area outside, which houses a couple of local cafés.

Al-Nasser Hotel (🏠 Next to Sinaiya al-Kahraba al-Gawamay School; ☎ 0915 024 195) is little more than a *lokanda*. It is conveniently located, not far from the town's hospital and the main square. A night spent sleeping on a bed outside costs 10 SDG and a double room costs 20 SDG. Rooms are simple and the mattresses are reasonably comfortable. Unfortunately, the toilets are rather dirty and the showers next to them have a strong, rather unpleasant smell.

Al-Shamalia (🏠 Hosbitalia Street, near Al-Nipras Bookshop, ☎ 0915 171 629) charges 4 SDG for beds outside and 5 SDG for beds in a four-person dormitory. If you are the only person sleeping in the dormitory, you will be charged 10 SDG per night. All rooms have a fan. The rooms are reasonably clean and the outside shower is decent. Thankfully, the shower is set apart from the toilet, which has the same lingering odour as the one at Al-Nasser Hotel. The mattresses in the rooms, unfortunately, are not so comfortable.

How to get there

A good asphalt road runs between Khartoum and Karima, and the town is served by regular buses from the nation's capital. The six-hour trip between the two cities costs 25 SDG, one-way. Regular buses also run to and from Dongola in the west. The journey takes two-and-a-half hours and costs 25 SDG. Luxury buses depart from Karima very early in the morning. If you want to leave the town later than

this, you will have to make do with sharing a minibus, which costs a similar price.

There is no public transport running to the nearby towns of Nuri and El-Kurru. A taxi ride to these places will cost you 25 SDG (for Nuri) and 15 SDG (for El-Kurru). You can also take a ferry over to Nuri, which departs from the little port at the end of Hosbitalia Street (50 *piastras*).

JEBEL BARKAL

🔊 18°32'18"N 31°49'20"E

The first thing that you see when approaching Karma is the looming silhouette of Jebel Barkal, a great flat-topped mountain of sandstone rising up out of the desert floor. On its south flank is a distinctive needle-shaped pinnacle, standing at a height of 74 metres. Ancient Egyptian texts describe this pinnacle as a rearing cobra (or *uraeus*), which was the symbol of the king. Others have suggested that the pinnacle resembles a giant statue of a pharaoh.

Jebel Barkal actually means 'Holy Mountain' in Arabic. Ancient Egyptian and Kushites believed that Amun, the god of air, dwelt within the mountain. Since air is associated with life, Amun eventually became known as the 'creator god' and was labelled father of gods, one of the most important and powerful deities in Egyptian mythology. Hence Jebel Barkal became a key religious cornerstone for Egyptian and Kushite beliefs.

Jebel Barkal also appears to have been the primary centre for royal coronations and rituals and, for centuries, each new king of Kush would come to the mountain to be confirmed and crowned in the presence of Amun.

The North

The area continues to attract a lot of archaeological interest from all over the world. In the 1990s archaeologists discovered a number of important wall paintings, depicting the military campaigns of Taharqa, one of the most notable kings of Egypt and Kush. At the beginning of 2003, Swiss archaeologist Charles Bonnet discovered the mask of the effigy of Tanoutamon, Taharqa's successor.

At the foot of the mountain, not far from the pinnacle of the rearing cobra, lie the ruins of the **Temple of Amun**. Founded in the 15th century BC during the reign of the Egyptian King Tuthmosis III, the temple was later expanded by a series of Kushite rulers, turning it into the largest temple in the kingdom. The temple is now little more than rubble, but some intriguing plinths remain and its former glory is clearly discernible beneath the thick layers of sand and dust that have blown in from the desert.

Not far from the Temple of Amun lie the ruins of a **smaller temple**, dedicated to Amun's wife, Mut, the Egyptian goddess of the sky.

If you climb a little way up Jebel Barkal, you will have a fantastic aerial view of the Nile and of the green fields surrounding Karima. The climb will take around an hour. There is no clear path nor any indication of where you should start. The easiest route begins on the side of the mountain furthest away from the pinnacle. Getting down the mountain is much easier — simply slide down the sand at the edge of the mountain. This should take no more than 10 or 15 minutes.

Near to the temple ruins are a few sculptured **granite rams**, the lonely remains of a long avenue that once stretched all the way down to the Nile.

On the western side of Jebel Barkal is a small **royal cemetery** of several pyramids, which was briefly used by Napatan kings around the 3rd century BC.

How to get there

Jebel Barkal lies only a few kilometres outside of Karima's town centre. A short rickshaw ride to the mountain should cost around 5 SDG. A taxi may cost slightly more: between 7 and 10 SDG. Getting back, though, is slightly harder, since there are no taxis or rickshaws regularly leaving the mountain. To return, the best thing to do is walk in the direction of the Karima Guest House (clearly visible from the mountain). The main road lies just beyond this guesthouse, and there you can find plenty of taxis and rickshaws to take you back into town.

NURI

18°33'38"N 31°52'51"E

The pyramids at Nuri, just upstream from Karima, are slightly older than those at Jebel Barkal. The Napatan king Taharqa was the first ruler to be buried here, in around 664 BC. Over the next few centuries a further 19 kings and 54 queens were also interred in the great cemetery, but none of the pyramids subsequently built on the site were quite as large — a testament, perhaps, to Taharqa's prominence as a warrior and a leader. The second-largest pyramid belongs to Aspelta, Taharqa's great-grandson.

Taharqa's tomb was excavated in 1917, but many of the original treasures had long since been plundered. The tomb was also flooded with water. After pumping the water out, archaeologists discovered over 1200 carved funerary figures, which would serve the king in the afterlife.

The pyramids at Nuri are slightly less well-preserved than those at the foot of Jebel Barkal, although this probably has as much to do with the young lads who scurry up and down them as it does with their age.

There are also some rather splendid sand dunes to look at.

There is no place to stay in Nuri and you probably won't want to spend much more than an hour in the town.

How to get there

Nuri is easily reached by road or by ferry from Karima. The port in Karima is around 20 minutes' walk from the hospital, in the direction of Al-Nasser Hotel. The short ferry ride costs 50 *piastras*.

If you come by road from Karima, head back towards Khartoum before turning left onto the new bridge. The exit to Nuri is immediately after this bridge. During the drive, take a moment to look around at the wonderful countryside, where you can see farmers tilling the land using traditional farming methods.

Once you are in the town of Nuri, the pyramids are easy to reach from the main road: either a 10-minute walk across the sand or a short ride in a four-wheel drive vehicle.

EL-KURRU

🔊 18°24'68"N 31°46'51"E

The royal necropolis at El-Kurru, 15 km south of Karima, dates from the 8th century BC and is the oldest collection of Nubian pyramids in Sudan. It is believed to have been established by Piye, the son of Kashta, the powerful ruler of Egypt and founder of the Kushite kingdom.

Kashta and Piye are both buried at El-Kurru, along with seven other kings and 14 queens of the Kushite dynasty. It is interesting to note that Taharqa broke with tradition and opted instead to have his tomb erected at nearby Nuri. However, Tanoutamun, his successor, returned to the site of El-Kurru for his burial.

There are no pyramids at El-Kurru now. These collapsed long ago, and all that now remains amidst the rubble is a series of low-lying tombs set into the rock.

Only two tombs are open to visitors and both are kept locked. A local guard has the key. You should be able to find him in the town or along the road leading to the site. He can be identified by the lantern that he carries at his side and uses when showing visitors around the tombs.

Tanwetamani, the nephew and successor of Taharqa, is buried in the tomb nearest the entrance. The second tomb belongs to that of Tanwetamani's mother, **Qalhata**.

The most stunning features about the tombs are the impressively-preserved wall paintings. Strong colours are used to depict scenes of pharaohs and gods, surrounded by Egyptian hieroglyphics. Some other paintings, though, have been badly damaged by flood water, allegedly when British excavators left the tomb open following an exploration of the site. These are now barely discernible on the tomb walls.

In order to visit the tombs, you should first obtain a permit from the police station in the centre of town. This is free for Sudanese, but costs 20 SDG for foreigners. You may be able to procure this permit at the site itself, but don't count on it.

How to get there

If you are coming from Karima, El-Kurru is reached by continuing straight past the new bridge, rather than turning left onto it. The initial part of the road is in good condition, but after a kilometre or two the asphalt road ends and it becomes a dirt track. There are no signs leading into El-Kurru, but the road is straight so it is difficult to get lost. The drive along the Nile is extremely pleasant, with some interesting buildings on your right.

Once in El-Kurru, you can get to the main archaeological site by turning right into a small road just before the main square.

There is no public transport going to El-Kurru. However, there are regular, shared taxis from Karima that can take you there: 15 SDG per person when the car is full, or 20 SDG per person when there are just two or three people.

OLD DONGOLA

📡 18°13'12"N 30°44'12"E

Not to be confused with the modern-day town of Dongola, 80 km to the north, the medieval town of Old Dongola is set on a hill overlooking the Nile

Most of the town is now little more than ruins, but you may see some signs of life when you enter it: a sprinkling of local cafés and the occasional group of Sudanese men playing cards.

Old Dongola was chosen as the capital of the Makurian kingdom because of its strategic position along the Nile, from where the region could easily be defended against invaders. It was the capital of the region between the 4th and 14th centuries, until the influence of Islam undermined the town's Christian roots.

It is well-worth visiting Old Dongola to appreciate one of the few remaining examples of Sudan's ancient Christian heritage, before the arrival of Islam. It was here that the early missionaries made their first forays into Sudan, seeking to teach the local population a new religion to replace the polytheistic one that they had been used to.

Over the years, more than a dozen churches have been excavated in Old Dongola, although many of these have since been plundered to provide building material for local homes.

The most prominent building still standing is that of the **Throne Hall**, which was built in the 9th century. It has probably survived so well because, in the early 14th century, it was converted into a mosque (which was still in active use until 1969). The original purpose of the hall is unknown, but it may have served as an audience chamber for the ruling monarch of the time.

Not far from the Throne Hall is the **Church of the Granite Columns**, which was built on top of an earlier church to serve as the seat of Old Dongola's bishops. The church is so-named because of the 16 granite columns that supported the building, each measuring 5.2 metres in height.

You don't need a permit to visit the main sites of Old Dongola, but you do need one to visit all of the town's archaeological treasures. The **Monastery of the Holy Trinity**, which is still being excavated, requires a permit.

Old Dongola is listed as a UNESCO World Heritage Site.

How to get there

Old Dongola is on the opposite side of the river from Dongola. You can take a ferry across to Old

Dongola from Ghaba, a small village just south of Dongola. Driving up from Khartoum, the asphalt road leading to Ghaba will be on your right, just after a small police checkpoint.

If you are travelling by public transport along the Khartoum-Dongola road, simply ask the bus driver to drop you off after the checkpoint. You can then walk the short distance down the asphalt road. Alternatively, shared minibuses run from Dongola down to Ghaba. The 90-minute journey costs 15 SDG.

It is possible to take your car on the ferry, but make sure that it is a four-wheeled drive vehicle. On the other side, you will be driving on dirt tracks and sand.

The ferry costs 1 SDG per person and 7 SDG for a car.

If you are travelling from Karima, then you will be on the correct side of the Nile already and there will be no need to take a ferry. The journey from Karima to Old Dongola takes around an hour-and-a-half by road.

How to get around

Old Dongola is quite spread out so the only way to really get around is with your own vehicle or by renting a car.

There is no official rental car company in the town, but the locals can usually help with arranging things. Abdul Gadir (☎ 0122 913 727) and Dafa Allah (☎ 0129 088 798) are good people to try. They can help organise a quick tour of the site for around 15 SDG. Alternatively, you might like to rent a pick-up (with driver) to make a wider tour of the area. If you just want to drive to Karima, expect to pay 200 SDG. A tour of all the sites between Old Dongola and Karima will cost 350 SDG.

DONGOLA

🔖 19°11'35"N 30°28'28"E

The modern town of Dongola, the capital of North State, lies 80 km north of Old Dongola, on the opposite side of the river.

It is a relaxing enough place to spend a day or two in, with some reasonable places to stay and cheap eateries. It doesn't have the archaeological allure of other towns and cities in the northern deserts, but by the time you reach Dongola you might feel like taking a break from all this fabulous Sudanese heritage.

The North

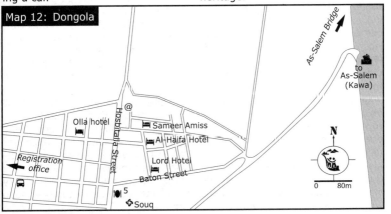

Map 12: Dongola

The city is an interesting blend of Nubian and Mamluk origins. When Mohammed Ali came to power in Egypt in the 19th Century, he expelled the Mamluk rulers from the country. It was in Dongola that they sought safe haven.

Moreover, Dongola is the birthplace of Mohammed Ahmed, the acclaimed Mahdi, who successfully ousted the British from the country at the end of the 19th Century (p56).

The only archaeological site worth visiting from the town is Kawa (p219), which can be reached by taking a ferry from the eastern port to As-Salem on the opposite bank. There is now also a new bridge that links the two banks together.

In the town, you will find a market, a few basic shops and some restaurants. The only internet café in town is **Rwan.com** (☎ 01261 937 450), which is open daily from 8 am to 3.30 pm and from 5 to 9 pm. The proprietor of the place is often not there. If this is the case, just call and let him know you are waiting.

Where to eat

There are several small restaurants in the market area, serving local Sudanese dishes. At the corner between Baton Street and Hosbitalia Street, **Cafeteria al-Multaka** (☎ 0918 838 819) is a big blue structure that is popular for *fasulia*, *ades* and a few other vegetable dishes. It is one of the best and cleanest places to eat in town. The potato-based dish that they cook is particularly tasty. Each dish costs around 3 SDG. They also have homemade mango and guava juice for only 50 *piastras*. Be warned, though, that this is made with unpurified iced tap water

Where to sleep

Remember that you should register with the local authorities before checking into the hotel. The police station is next to the Military Hospital, around 2 km from the ferry in the direction of Souq as-Shabi. It can be recognised by a distinctive black-and-white gate on the left.

Haifa Hotel (🏠 Hosbitalia Street, north end; ☎ 0911 203 838) is by far the best option in town. There are 12 rooms in the hotel, each containing two double beds, an air-cooler, and an ensuite bathroom. A room for the night costs 50 SDG. The hotel also has two communal living rooms, with tables and TVs. The hotel is conveniently located near the internet café and is 10 minutes' walk away from town.

Olla Hotel (🏠 Next to Abdul Ahal High School; ☎ 0241 821 848 or 0912 143 369 or 0923 917 561) is a bit more ramshackle, but it is slightly quieter and there is a nice courtyard, where trees provide some welcome shade. There are a few tables and chairs in the courtyard. A double room with bathroom and air-cooler costs 30 SDG. Dormitory-style beds cost 6 SDG each. The interior of the hotel really needs some work. The shared bathrooms look particularly bad and, frequently, nothing works. Don't expect running water from the taps.

Lord Hotel (🏠 Entrance on Hosbitalia Street; ☎ 0241 822 405 or 0915 586 808) is a good place to stay on a budget. A room with an ensuite bathroom costs 20 SDG and a room with an external bathroom costs 30 SDG. There are a couple of ensuites available for 40 SDG. If you just want a bed outside, then this will cost 10 SDG. The hotel sells a range of basic toiletry products, such as toothpaste, soap and razors.

Sameer Amiss Hotel (🏠 Hosbitalia Street) is located just a few metres from Lord Hotel. It has a nice courtyard and a few rooms. A bed in a shared dorm costs 6 SDG.

How to get there

Dongola can easily be reached by car from Khartoum or Karima. The road out of Khartoum will take you to a junction, where you can decide if you want to continue your journey to Karima (to the right) or to Dongola (to the east).

The journey from Karima to Dongola takes around two hours. Make sure that you bring enough water and food for the journey to the town, since there are few places to stop along the way.

A new bridge now makes crossing to the other side of the river easier, and there is no need to take the ferry that used to be there.

Souq as-Shabi is the main bus station in the town. It is located on the way to the police station and registration office, about 15 minutes' drive from the ferry. Buses to and from Khartoum cost 35 SDG. Travelling between Dongola and Port Sudan costs 74 SDG. There are no buses heading directly north from Dongola. If you wish to continue your journey northwards, you first need to cross the river and take a bus from there.

KAWA

📡 19°07'48"N 30°33'05"E

Just across the river from Dongola lies Kawa, the historical centre of the Kushite kingdom. The ancient settlement is about 5 km from As-Salem, on the east bank of the Nile.

You can walk to Kawa from As-Salem, by keeping the Nile on your right. However, this is only recommended for those accustomed to desert conditions, since it is quite a long way. If you do choose to walk, remember to take plenty of water. Walking will take you past some lovely villages and green vegetation before the track turns into the desert and becomes much more arid. You may be able to persuade one of the villagers to give you a lift in a donkey cart (it is reasonable to pay 10 SDG for such a ride).

There is not a great deal to see in the windswept town, and much of the ancient treasures have now been eaten away by the harsh desert winds or obscured by layers of sand.

The town was most famous for a Temple of Amun, which was built under the command of the famous Egyptian pharaoh Tutankhamun. Little remains of the temple, though, and what treasures it once held are now largely in the museums of Cairo and London.

Kawa is a two hour drive from Karima. Simply turn into the desert 2 km before the turning to As-Salem Bridge.

Officially, you don't need a permit to visit Kawa. However, this doesn't always stop some of the locals trying to make a quick buck out of the unsuspecting foreigner, by insisting that a permit is necessary.

KERMA

📡 19°40'00"N 30°25'04"E

The ancient city of Kerma was possibly one of the earliest urban centres in Africa, with a civilisation in the town emerging around 2400 BC. The city rapidly developed into a sprawling metropolis, becoming the first capital of the ancient kingdom of Kush in around 2000 BC.

Sitting just south of the Third Cataract, Kerma was perfectly located along the banks of the Nile to control the important north-south trade route. The land around Kerma is also highly fertile, making it likely that Kerma's prosperity developed on the back of agriculture as well as trade.

The site remains one of the most popular places for archaeological excavations, and continues to yield a wealth of treasures that provide an insight into Sudan's ancient past. Many of these finds can be viewed in the National Museum in Khartoum.

The most prominent landmark in the town is a massive mud-brick building known as the 'Western Defuffa', which is 5 km south of the town centre. 'Defuffa' is a Nubian word that means, literally, 'large brick building'. It was a name usually given to buildings of some religious importance.

Now worn with age, the structure once stood over 18 metres tall, with a floor surface of 50 metres by 25 metres. The building was originally at the heart of the town, surrounded by a number of houses, public buildings and workshops. It probably served as the main religious building in Kerma.

A second *defuffa* is located 2 km east of this site. This second building occupies a similar area, but is not quite as tall. Given its proximity to the town's cemetery, this building was probably important in providing funeral services.

The nearby necropolis is expansive, containing evidence of as many as 30,000 burials. The site contains four large royal burial chambers, where Kushite kings were interred with their retainers. These tombs are marked by large mounds of earth and stone, known as *tumuli*.

There is a large market within Kerma's town centre, which is at its busiest on Mondays. This market is also a good place to seek out cheap local eateries.

Where to sleep

There is only one official place to stay in the town: **Hotel Kerma**, which is fairly basic but particularly clean. A bed for the night costs 7 SDG. You can either choose to sleep in a shared dormitory or take your bed outside and sleep beneath the stars. Female travellers may have some problems staying here, since there are no private rooms.

Although this hotel is the only official place to stay, a number of enterprising villagers have started hosting travellers in their homes, in exchange for a sum of money. They often provide meals as well. Such places tend to have better standards than *lokandas*, although the price is a little more expensive.

How to get there

Direct transport runs weekly between Kerma and Wadi Halfa in the north. It takes around 10 hours and costs 55 SDG to get there. Travelling to Kerma from Khartoum is slightly harder, and you usually have to make your way to Argo or Dongola first, before heading south. Shared taxis serve these destinations (7 SDG to get to Dongola). A number of buses coming from Khartoum do pass close to the town, however, and you can usually ask to be let off there.

Expect to pay 150 SDG for a private taxi to take you from Dongola to Kerma. Usually, you can persuade a taxi driver to take you back without having to pay much extra. However, this will probably only give you quite a short stay in Kerma, since the taxi driver will be anxious to get back once you arrive.

SOLEB

🔖 20°26'10"N 30°20'00"E

On the western bank of the Nile, not far from the Third Cataract, stands what is perhaps one of the best-preserved temples of the region. The Temple of Soleb was established in the 14th century BC by Amenophis III, an ancient king of Egypt and ruler of the 18th Dynasty. The temple was dedicated to Amun, the god of air.

Amenophis III is perhaps best known for commissioning the famous temples at Luxor, in Egypt. It is therefore of no surprise that, architecturally, the Temple of Soleb resembles these great structures. The temple was built with two pylons, a large temple court dominated by columns (known as a 'hypostyle hall') and a sanctuary. Altogether, the building measures 130 metres in length.

The density of the columns within the temple is a distinctive feature of the era, since this was the only way that architects knew how to design large buildings that could support the weight of the roof.

Within the temple complex, there is an arena dedicated to the ancient Egyptian festival of *heb-sed*, which was held to celebrate a pharaoh's continued rule. The name of the festival means 'feast of the tail', and refers to an animal tail that was often attached to the back of a pharaoh's clothes. Historical finds suggest that the *heb-sed* festival was held to mark a pharaoh's 30th year on the throne, and then every three years after that. *Heb-sed* festivals included elaborate temple rituals, offerings made before the gods and acts of religious devotion. Such festivals may have evolved as a way of staving off the habitual assassination of pharaohs who were deemed to be too old to rule any longer.

There are some well-preserved wall carvings in the temple depicting the *heb-sed* festival taking place.

Soleb is located on the west bank of the Nile, 40 km south of Abri. There is no transport from the east side since all the villages are located in the west. The easiest way to reach Soleb is by taking a ferry from Wawa.

There are no proper hotels on the site, but locals often offer a place to stay at the ferry port. Expect to pay between 15 and 25 SDG for this.

Other temples, not far from the one at Soleb, are also worth exploring: Sesibi to the south and Sedeinga 12 km to the north.

SAI ISLAND

🔖 20°42'11"N 30°19'59"E

In the centre of the Nile, between the Third and Fourth Cataracts, lies one of the largest islands in the Nubian stretch of the river. The island has been inhabited since early times, but didn't become a major settlement until the 16th century, when the Egyptians pushed forth from the north.

There are four villages on the island, containing numerous archaeological sites, including large burial grounds, ancient settlements and a medieval church.

To get to the island, you can take a ferry from Tabaj, 10 km south of Abri. If there is space, you can also take a car on the ferry.

WADI HALFA

🔖 21°49'00"N 31°22'21"E

North Sudan's northernmost town is perched on the southern edge of Lake Nasser, which was created when the Aswan Dam flooded the surrounding lands. The main reason for coming to Wadi Halfa is because it is a transit point to and from Egypt.

Ferries leave Wadi Halfa for Aswan, in Egypt, on Wednesdays. They leave Aswan for Wadi Halfa on Mondays. The crossing takes around 16 hours. See p19 for prices.

Wadi Halfa is not in its original location. Prior to 1963, the town was located several kilometres further north. However, the citizens were forced to relocate when the Aswan Dam was completed. The buildings of the old town are now submerged beneath several feet of water.

Wadi Halfa itself is a fairly grey and drab place to visit, with none of the spirit, charm or beauty of towns further south. However, the town is surrounded by a wealth of ancient Egyptian antiquities so it can be a good place in which to base yourself if you want to do a tour of archaeological sites in the far north. Wadi Halfa is a good-sized town, with the advantage of having all the local amenities that this entails.

One of the nicest things to do in the town is take yourself off to the lake-front and watch fishermen bringing the daily catch in, some of which is dried in the searing sun. The old boats, lying beached and forgotten along the water's edge, are particularly photogenic.

Wadi Halfa also has a special place in Sudan's history. Between 1895 and 1898, the town served as the headquarters for the British-led forces, seeking to reclaim the country from Mahdist rule.

Where to sleep

It is not difficult to find places to stay in Wadi Halfa. There are a few reasonably-priced *lokandas* in the centre of the town (about 7 SDG for a night). Try **Nile Hotel**,

near where the buses are, or **Wadi al-Nil**, a little closer to the market.

For a more established place, **Al-Sha'ab** or **Boheires Hotel**, both not far from the centre of town, are good options. Both are clean and friendly, with prices for a room starting at 40 SDG.

How to get there

Getting to the town is fairly easy. Regular buses run from Khartoum and Atbara in the south. A train from Khartoum used to run to Wadi Halfa once a week, to coincide with the departure of the ferry. It has been discontinued for the time-being, but may resume in the future. The journey used to take two days — worth it for the experience, but not if you are in a hurry.

THE NILE CATARACTS

Between Khartoum and Aswan on the Egyptian border lie a series of shallow stretches of water known as the Nile Cataracts, 'cataract' being a word derived from the ancient Greek for 'waterfall'. Referring to these shallow parts of the Nile as 'waterfalls' is a little over-zealous when, at their fiercest, they are little more than fast-flowing rapids.

Nonetheless, for centuries these rapids have thwarted river passage between southern Egypt and Sudan. Even now, this means that no long-distance river transport exists in the northern part of the country.

The Cataracts are most easily navigated just after the rainy season (in September or October), when the Nile is swollen with fresh water and the Cataracts are deep enough for some boats to pass.

The Cataracts were a particular hindrance to Britain's attempts to reclaim Sudan from the rule of the Mahdi in the late 19th century — a struggle that is vividly captured by

Winston Churchill in his book The River War (p320).

There are six cataracts in total.

The **First Cataract** (🐾 24°04′40″N 32°52′40″E) is not far from Aswan, just across the Egyptian border.

The **Second Cataract** (🐾 21°28′48″N 30°58′11″E) which used to lie in Nubia just south of the Egyptian border, was submerged beneath the waters of Lake Nasser when the Aswan Dam was built in the 1960s.

The **Third Cataract** (🐾 19°45′36″N 30°22′12″E) lies midway between Dongola and Soleb. This is a lovely spot to stop and take some photos, and maybe enjoy a picnic lunch.

The **Fourth Cataract** (🐾 18°54′36″N 32°21′35″E) used to lie not far from Merowe and Ghazil, in the Mansair Desert. It was flooded when the Merowe Dam was constructed.

The **Fifth Cataract** (🐾 17°40′37″N 33°58′11″E) is north of Atbara, not far from where the Atbara River meets the Nile.

The **Sixth Cataract** (🐾 16°17′16″N 32°40′15″E) south of Shendi, is the closest to Khartoum and is a very picturesque place to escape the city for half a day or so. Unfortunately, it is not easy to reach this area by public transport — you really need your own vehicle.

People from Khartoum often come here to have barbecues or parties. Consequently, locals are very accustomed to tourists and the various tricks that can be used to extract money from them. They will frequently claim that the Sixth Cataract is on private land that belongs to them. This is not true. If you are just going to visit the Sixth Cataract, then you do not need to pay. However, if you wish to stop at the café overlooking the Nile, then you are obliged to purchase drinks there. You may be asked to pay extra money if you bring your own food to the café.

Renting a small boat from the local villagers is a pleasant way to explore the Nile Cataract, and you can also stop on some of the small secluded islands, where you may be lucky enough to see salamanders sunbathing.

If you want to come to the area to have a party with loud music, you will first need to obtain permission from authorities in Khartoum.

The North

The Red Sea
Port Sudan, Suakin, Arkowit

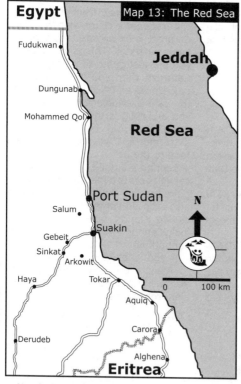

Egypt

Map 13: The Red Sea

Fudukwan

Jeddah

Dungunab

Mohammed Qol

Red Sea

Port Sudan

Salum

Suakin

Gebeit

Sinkat

Arkowit

Haya

Tokar

0   100 km

Aquiq

Carora

Derudeb

Alghena

Eritrea

N

Highlights

- Go diving and snorkelling off the coast of the Red Sea.

- Explore the famous underwater wreck of the Umbria.

- Discover the underwater experiments of Jacques Cousteau.

- Relax in a luxury resort overlooking the Red Sea coast.

- Learn about the legend of the demon cats at Suakin.

- Cool off by heading for the hilltop town of Arkowit.

- Relax by the docks over a strong cup of Sudanese coffee.

- Dine on fried fresh fish in the markets of Port Sudan.

North Sudan's only point of contact with the sea is the narrow strip of coastline that runs along the north-east of the country, from Egypt down to Eritrea. The capital of Red Sea State, Port Sudan, is roughly equidistant from the two bordering countries and remains a vital gateway for goods into and out of North Sudan. Even though it has split with the North, expectations are that the South will continue to use the Red Sea port for some of its trade, although an increasing amount is likely to be routed through Kenya.

The Red Sea area is hot and humid for most of the year. The weather is most pleasant between November and January, whilst the summer months can be very hard to adjust to if you are used to colder climes.

Fortunately, along the coast, regular sea breezes bring welcome relief from the heat, whilst inland the

Red Sea hills offer greater altitude and therefore cooler weather.

British soldiers, who used to be stationed in Port Sudan before independence, would often escape the stifling heat by retreating into the hills for short breaks. Arkowit (p236) was a particularly favourite place to go.

The Red Sea coast has a lot to offer the traveller in Sudan. Whilst the country's tourist industry has been slow to catch on to this potential, things are starting to change.

DIVING IN THE RED SEA

Some of the best scuba diving in the world is to be found in the Red Sea. However, Sudan (unlike its northern neighbour) is still relatively unknown as a diving destination.

Part of the reason for Sudan's apparent unimportance in the world of scuba is the difficulty and cost of getting to the good diving spots. Whereas tour companies in Egypt ferry diving enthusiasts out to sea by the boatload, lack of demand in Sudan keeps the number of tour operators to a minimum and the prices fairly high. However, more and more tour operators are starting to enter the market. As they do, expect to see prices come down and customer services go up.

The lack of other divers has its advantages, of course. It means that you get to explore many of the dive sites almost entirely on your own.

There are two ways to approach diving off the coast of Port Sudan. One is to organise a tour on a live-aboard. This has become a particular popular option, but the downside is that you often have to book the tour in advance and may have to allocate a number of consecutive days for the diving trip.

JACQUES COUSTEAU

It was in the Red Sea, just off the coast of Port Sudan that Jacques Cousteau, French naval officer and scientist, undertook some of his most important research into life underwater, such as the effects of long-term immersion on the human body.

In the 1960s, he arranged the construction of a giant underwater village, which he named 'Précontinent 2'. His first Précontinent experiments had taken place off the coast of Marseilles, in France. Précontinent 2 housed eight men for a month, allowing them to spend many hours each day carrying out underwater research and experiments.

The pioneering research carried out off the coast of Sudan was the main subject of Cousteau's famous documentary film, *Le Monde Sans Soleil* ('The World Without Sun'). Forty years on, you can still swim through the remains of his village, just off the Sha'ab Rumi Reef (p227).

An alternative way of seeing the wonderful underwater world of the Sudanese Red Sea is to arrange day-trips from the mainland. Such a diving centre has yet to properly develop in the country, but one new establishment that does offer such trips is the Red Sea Resort (p228). Such excursions are becoming increasingly popular with weekend-trippers from Khartoum, who do not have the time to arrange a tour on a live-aboard boat.

Out of season and during the Islamic month of Ramadan, arranging a dive can be difficult, since many of the tour operators in the area will be closed. The Red Sea Resort remains open throughout the year, although offers less services between July and September..

The Red Sea has three distinct zones of depth: the shallow reef-studded shelves of less than 50 metres, the deep shelves of between 500 and 1000 metres and the central trench of more than 1000 metres. The Red Sea is at its deepest (3040 metres) just off the coast of Port Sudan.

The magnificent coral reefs that run along the coast of the Red Sea attract a wonderful array of marine life. Among the most common fish that can be spotted in the area are tarpon, giant herring, milkfish, soldier fish, goggle-eye, angelfish and rock cod. Sharks are regularly seen, the most prevalent being the hammerhead, grey-reef, white-tip and tiger sharks. Turtles and dolphins are often spotted in open-water.

There are a couple of good wrecks to explore off the coast of Port Sudan, too: the Italian warship Umbria, which sank in 1940, and the enchanting Blue Bell, which capsized in 1977 whilst transporting a cargo of Toyota cars.

Unusually, the temperature of the Red Sea does not vary significantly at different depths. The surface temperature near Port Sudan is between 26.2°C and 30.5°C. At a depth of 150 metres it is between 23.9°C and 25.0°C.

Salinity levels in the Red Sea are particularly high, so you should adjust your buoyancy accordingly when diving.

Visibility is almost always good, due to low levels of plankton and algae in the water.

The dives in Sudan are suitable for beginners as well as more experienced divers.

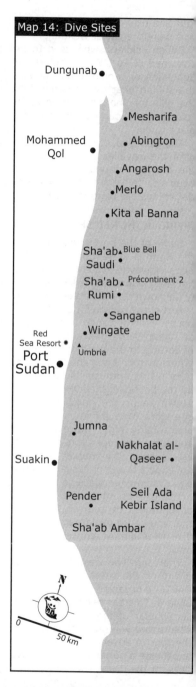

Map 14: Dive Sites

Diving Itineraries

THE CLASSIC DIVES

Wingate Reef is the place to visit if you want to see the famous Umbria warship, sabotaged by its Italian crew in 1940 to prevent capture by the British. The warship had been transporting weapons and ammunition to support the military campaign in Abyssinia, and still holds more than 300,000 unexploded rounds of artillery shells and bombs.

The Umbria does not lie that far beneath the surface and the shallower parts can even be explored by snorkel. Light and visibility are good in these waters, so most parts of the ship can be visited safely.

Sanganeb Reef is particularly well-known for its British-built lighthouse, which you can spend time looking around during intervals on the surface. The site also offers some of the richest coral displays in the Red Sea.

The reef rises from 800 metres to the surface, and you do not have to dive particularly deeply to appreciate the opulence of sea life.

There are three diving points off the reef. The south plateau (25 metres) is a fabulous dive with both soft and hard corals. The fish you can see there include jackfish, barracuda, tuna and snapper. Look out for grey-reef and white-tip sharks.

The northern point has two terraces. The first is at 20 metres over pink corals. The second starts at 40 metres with a forest of black corals, where schools of hammerhead sharks are common. When the sea is very rough, it is not possible to make this dive.

Sha'ab Rumi Reef is the most famous reef in Sudan and is where Jacques Cousteau (see box on p225) built his *Précontinent 2* underwater village. It is still possible to see the hangar that Cousteau and his men lived in, ten metres down and now encrusted with corals.

At 27 metres lie the remains of shark cages and other equipment that the diving team used for their experiments. The south plateau (25 metres) boasts a particularly colourful reef, where it is possible to see schools of barracudas, jackfish, and hammerhead sharks. North Point is a very colourful reef wall where white sharks often come with their young.

Sha'ab Saudi is famous for the wreck of the Blue Bell that crashed into the reef in December 1977, carrying Toyota cars, which are now scattered in a wide area across the sea bottom. The ship is upended, with the bow 15 metres below sea level and the stern at 80 metres.

THE NORTHERN DIVES

Angarosh, **Merlo** and **Abington** are reefs that are all very close to one another, teeming with marine life and full of colourful corals.

Angarosh means 'Mother of Sharks', an apt name for the area. It has two plateaus, at 25 metres and 45 metres, and is famous for sightings of manta rays.

A mile or two south-west of Angarosh lies Merlo, surrounded by soft and hard corals and sloping down to about 450 meters. White-tip, grey-reef and hammerhead sharks are common here. You can also see the wreck of a live-aboard boat called The Freedom.

Marked by a lighthouse, the reef at Abington only just breaks the surface. It is a popular breeding ground for turtles, and schools of hammerhead sharks are frequently seen. Watch out for strong currents, though.

The Red Sea

Kita al-Banna is a reef just in front of Mayetib Island ('Snake Island') and can offer a great quantity of colourful fish.

Mesharifa is in shallow waters, protected by two reefs. It is popular for sightings of manta rays, which come here to breed between August and November, when the water is particularly warm. At dusk, the bay becomes bathed in a wonderful pink light. The beaches here are white with fine sand and it is a good spot to do some bird-watching, too.

THE SOUTHERN DIVES

Jumna is a fairly small yet very colourful reef, which attracts a great wealth of tropical fishes.

Sha'ab Ambar is a sheltered reef, often used for mooring by liveaboard boats. The reef is a popular spot for dolphins.

Nakhalat al-Qaseer are pinnacles rising from depths of between 60 and 65 metres in surrounding waters that drop to 630 metres. The main cone-shaped pinnacle starts at five metres and is a good spot to see hammerhead sharks, manta rays and larger oceanic sharks. Its diameter is around 30 metres, and can easily be explored in a single dive.

Pender Reef is similar to the main pinnacle at Nakhalat al-Qaseer, but has a wider top. The marine life at Pender is prolific: schools of jackfish, tuna and occasional sightings of hammerhead sharks.

Seil Ada Kebir Island is a good place to come and see turtles during your dive.

Tour operators

Red Sea Dives (☎ 0912 341 282 or 00882 1631 111 139; @ arnesen@bodmiscombe.demon.co.uk; 🖵 www.redseadives.com) operates dive excursions from the Don Questo live aboard ship. Trips usually last for one or two weeks.

The company has offices in Italy (🏠 19 Via Borodin, Pisa; @ info@sudandiving.it; 🖵 www.sudandiving.it), but there is no office in Port Sudan. Therefore, you should book your diving trip on the Don Questo before you get there.

A diving trip costs €820 per person for one week and €1600 per person for two weeks. A trip to the far southern end of the Red Sea costs slightly more — €1800 per person.

Prices include full board and unlimited dives, but equipment hire is extra — 90 SDG per day.

The Don Questo covers all the major dive spots from Egypt to Eritrea, depending on the season and weather conditions.

Courses can also be arranged once you are on the ship: €300 for basic PADI certification, €200 for an advanced open water course, €250 for an underwater rescue course and €450 for a PADI Divemaster course.

Diving World (☎ +44 20 7407 0019; @ info@diving-world.com 🖵 www.divingworld.co.uk), a British company that offers diving excursions around the world, including off the coast of Sudan. Dives in Sudan are from a live-aboard ship, and only for those that hold advanced PADI certification and have logged at least 50 dives. A week's diving costs around £1750 (€2000), including flights.

Resorts on the Red Sea

Sudan Red Sea Resort (☎ 0912 465 650 or 0122 293 427; @ imanosmandekock@yahoo.com, 🖵 www.sudanredsearesort.com) is an eco-camp that lies 30 minutes drive north of Port Sudan. Accommodation is in bungalows, although there are plans to re-introduce bedouin tents into the resort. The resort is now completely powered by solar energy. Prices start at 150 SDG per person per night for bed-and-breakfast. Half-board is 200 SDG and full-board is 250 SDG. All prices include taxes.

The spot is a beautiful place to come and relax for a few days, and the mud flats leading down to the sea are a great foraging ground for a variety of birds.

The resort offers both diving from the shore and from boats. From the shore, prices start at €50 for one day, rising to €190 for four days. Boat dives start at €60 for a single day, rising to €290 for five days. The resort also offers PADI courses. Open water certification costs €399, an advanced course costs €299 and a PADI Divemaster course costs €699. Prices exclude equipment rental, which is around €35 per day for a full set. Snorkelling is also possible from the shore — €13 to rent the mask, snorkel and fins.

The advantage of booking a dive course with the Red Sea Resort, rather than one of the liveaboards listed previously, is that it is fairly easy to make arrangements whilst in the country. The resort even has offices in Port Sudan.

A permit is required to travel up to the resort, but this can be arranged on the-spot. Just bring three copies of your passport and visa. The permit is free.

Arous Resort, about 30 km north of Port Sudan, has recently been closed due to poor management. It may reopen in the future, but there are no signs of this happening any time soon. The resort is owned by Sudan's Ministry of Tourism.

SAUDI ARABIA

Regular ferries from the coastal port of Suakin leave for Jeddah in Saudi Arabia.

The 12-hour journey costs between 200 and 400 SDG, depending on the company that you travel with and whether you want to travel first or second class. Many of the ferries make the crossing overnight — leaving in the early hours of the morning and arriving in early afternoon the following day.

Two shipping companies that have offices in Port Sudan are **Sobat** (☎ 0311 829 634 or 0311 829 359/356) and **Baaboud** (☎ +966 262 700 00; @ info@baaboud.net; ⌨ www.baaboud.net). The offices aren't always open, though. They are usually open to coincide with sailings, which often occur in the evenings.

Two other companies that run regular services to and from Jeddah are **Wadi Al-Nil** and **Namar**, although they don't have offices in Port Sudan.

Getting a visa to Saudi Arabia is not an easy thing to do. In general, you have to have a formal invitation from a Saudi citizen living within the country, or be part of an official tour group. Visas are not usually granted to unaccompanied women, although exceptions are sometimes made. In such cases, women entering the Kingdom on their own must be met by their sponsor and have confirmed accommodation for the duration of their stay.

Tariq (☎ 0912 235 320), a travel agent in Port Sudan, can sometimes help with negotiating a visa for Saudi Arabia.

The Red Sea

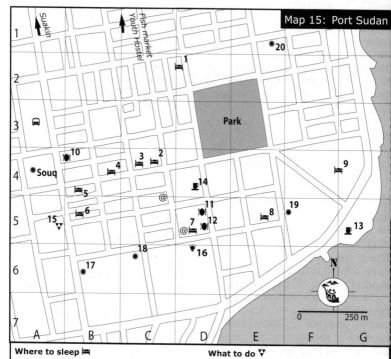

Map 15: Port Sudan

The Red Sea

PORT SUDAN

Port Sudan was established by the British in 1905 to replace Suakin as the country's main commercial port. It was felt that Suakin, lying in shallower waters, was unsuitable for the larger ships that Britain was now bringing to the country.

These days, Port Sudan has a rather faded, has-been look about it. It is still Sudan's most important sea port, and ships still linger in the docks waiting for their latest cargo to be hauled aboard, but the hustle-and-bustle of activity is nothing compared to what it was half-a-century ago.

There is a certain relaxed charm about the town centre. In the evening, **the docks** are a great place to come and drink coffee. You will see families and groups of friends sprawled on straw mats along the quayside, sipping their *jabana* or *shae bi laban*, chatting and playing cards.

You'll also see people smoking **sheesha** in this area, and there are a number of **pool tables** along the sea-front that you can make use of (an hour's pool usually costs 10-15 SDG). There are even some **fried-fish restaurants** here, although you'll get better quality nosh if you go elsewhere (see below).

Not far from this area is a **small spot where you can swim**, if the thought of sharing the waters with all those oily boats doesn't put you off.

Port Sudan is a lovely place to spend a few days and its leisurely pace of life can easily persuade you to spend longer in the town than you intended.

However, don't let the pleasant vibe in the town throw you off your guard. Port Sudan is generally less safe than Khartoum and there are a greater number of beggars. Be especially careful in the area behind the Coral Hotel, where the deserted streets, as well as the proximity to wealthy tourists, encourage some rather dubious characters to hang out.

Many people end up in Port Sudan as a stopping-off point for diving and snorkelling trips (see previous pages).

The temperature of Port Sudan is generally very hot and humid — hotter than in Khartoum, although this is tempered by the occasional breeze sweeping in from the Arabian Peninsula.

The main part of the town is not large and is quite easy to navigate.

You can either walk or take a rickshaw between areas for a few SDG.

There are two **football clubs** in the town, not far from the central bus station: Hilal El-Sahil and Hay El-Arab. Both clubs regularly host major regional and national games. A ticket costs between 10 and 40 SDG, depending on who is playing.

If you fancy doing any **sport or recreational activities** whilst here, then the best place to head for is the Coral Hotel, overlooking the water front. Here, you'll find a swimming pool, gym, table tennis court, table football and a billiard room. If you are planning on staying for awhile, you can take out a monthly or yearly membership for the hotel's fitness club. This entitles you to free use of facilities, plus a 25% discount on all food and beverage items that the hotel sells. The prices (in SDG) are as follows:

	Single	Couple	Family
1 mth	350	580	750
3 mth	580	1000	1200
6 mth	1000	1800	2100
1 yr	1800	3100	3600

Where to sleep

Many of the budget-accommodation options are located around the marketplace in the south of the town. The most down-market places charge around 20 SDG for a night in a room or 10 SDG for a bed in a dormitory.

Marhaba Hotel is a male-only *lokanda* in the centre of town. Rooms are cheap (20 SDG per night), but very basic and not particularly clean. The *lokanda* can provide fresh sheets, though, if you ask. Security is an issue in the hotel and the windows do not always lock.

A few doors down, **Sad'al** shares the same characteristics as Marhaba. Rooms are slightly cheaper — 15 SDG for a room — but other that there is not much to distinguish them.

Just next to these *lokandas* is the slightly more upmarket **Basery Plaza Hotel** (☎ 0311 121 999). Prices are somewhat higher (92 SDG per room), but the hotel is cleaner and has air-con. The hotel also has a small restaurant attached. The restaurant is often full, however, so it is wise to book in advance.

Port Sudan's **Youth Hostel** (🏠 Salabona Street; @ info@sudaneseyha. net; 🖥 www.sudaneseyha.net) is a good place to stay if you are on a budget, but want to stay somewhere that is relatively clean and comfortable. It is located a little way out of town, but in a lovely area near the fish market in Sigala, overlooking the sea. Staying in a room with two beds costs 35 SDG per person. A bed in a room that sleeps more people costs 25 SDG. You must have a YHA membership card to sleep at the hostel, which can be purchased on-the-spot for 20 SDG.

Boheine Hotel (☎ 0912 208 306) is a nice and friendly option for those that like a bit of extra luxury. The staff are extremely helpful, and the hotel has a relaxed vibe that is often missing in many higher-end hotels. Official check-out time is a thoroughly civilised 12 o'clock, and the staff are often prepared to extend this if things aren't too busy. The hotel has a fairly run-of-the-mill restaurant, with 24-hour service, which serves the usual grilled meat dishes and other Sudanese fare. A single costs 168 SDG whilst a double costs 196 SDG. The hotel has 60 rooms. Rooms come with TV, air-con, fridge and ensuite bathroom.

Okier Hotel is a large and friendly hotel not far from the university. It offers singles for 150 SDG, doubles for 200 SDG and triples for 250 SDG. All rooms are ensuite and come with a TV, air-con, and small balcony. Rooms are comfortable and clean.

Omiya is clearly in desperate need of a lick of paint and the rooms are no less tatty than the exterior. A single costs 75 SDG and comes with an air-cooling unit, very small balcony and ensuite bathroom. Not the cleanest or most comfortable place to stay, and the creaking beds are unlikely to do much good for the posture. Management can be slightly officious, too.

Rania is a cheap, yet comfortable and clean, place to stay. Staff are friendly and helpful. A single room costs 70 SDG, a double room with ensuite bathroom costs 120 SDG and a double without ensuite costs 80 SDG. All rooms come with air-con and TV.

Going more upmarket, the **Palace Basher Hotel** (☎ 0311 823 341/3 or 0912 310 373) has single rooms for 188-299 SDG and doubles for 215-312 SDG. There are even a couple of four-bed rooms, for 303 SDG. At first, it is a little hard to work out the logic behind the pricing of the rooms, since many of the more expensive rooms appear identical to the cheaper ones. Your researchers were led to believe that it was to do with the area of the hotel that the rooms were located in. The hotel has two wings: the older section, which tends to have slightly larger rooms, and the newer section, which looks more spruced up. The more expensive rooms are in the newer section, but if you don't mind a few cracks on the wall, you can often get a much nicer room in the old-er section for the same amount of money. Rooms, in any case, tend to be more luxurious than many of the other options around town. There is a small internet café on-site, and some very nice and green gardens surrounding the hotel. Rooms come with air-con, TV and ensuite bathroom.

If you really want to push the boat out, try the luxury **Coral Hotel** (☎ 0311 839 800; @ info@coral-portsudan.com; 🖥 coral-portsudan.com), perfectly located near to the docks with some fantastic views over the sea and the port. The building that the hotel is now in (originally the Red Sea Hotel) was built during the early years of the last century, and has that reclusive British-colonial charm about it. There is a Qatar airways office within the lobby. The hotel has a nice à-la-carte restaurant attached. It also organises regular buffet lunches and dinners. The hotel has a swimming pool, table football, billiard room, gym and table tennis. These are all free for guests. Non-guests can also use them for a fee. The hotel has 114 rooms, including 11 junior suites and two executive suites. A double room costs between 300 and 400 SDG per night. The hotel also has a number of business and conference rooms, the largest of which can hold up to 250 people.

Eating and drinking

The best places to eat, if you are looking for something good and reasonably-priced, are either along the docks or around the market area.

Near the docks are a couple of very **good places selling grilled meat** — just look for the crowds — as well as some more dubious ones. The style is mainly Turkish. There are also a small number of restaurants serving **fried fish**.

It is very pleasant, after eating by the docks, to go and relax on one of the nearby rugs with a **coffee** and watch the ships go by.

By the market, in front of the bus station, there are some **small stalls selling fried fish**. Their cleanliness is questionable, but they are a good option if you fancy some fresh fish. However, the choice as to how the fish is prepared is fairly limited: fried, fried or fried.

Many of the hotels also have restaurants attached. For a more luxurious meal, the **Coral** (☎ 0311 839 800) has a nice, though expensive, café and restaurant. Expect to pay around 30-45 SDG, more if you want even posher grub. The place even serves smoked salmon. Unfortunately, it does not serve fresh fish. The hotel organises buffets on most evenings. The barbecue buffet costs 85 SDG, whilst the others — such as the Chinese and Indian ones — cost 78 SDG.

There are a couple of **fast-food** places in the centre of town. **Pizza Dream** (☎ 0904 666 606) offers the standard Sudanese-style pizza. A small pizza for around 6-9 SDG (depending on the topping) is ample for a single meal, or you can go for the larger family-sized pizza, for around 22 SDG. Just next door is **Ice-Cream Dream**, where you can buy ice-cream — 4 SDG for three scoops — and fruit juice.

Not far from Pizza Dream there is a **fast-food joint** serving grilled chicken and meat, as well as burgers and fries. The name of the restaurant is written in Arabic only.

Just down the road from these fast-food restaurants, you'll come across **Al-Muhajir Cafeteria Hall**, which is a nice place to pop in for a Sudanese coffee. The café has a small outside terrace, but, alas, no cooling water jets.

The Red Sea

If you have a craving for **fresh fish** from the Red Sea, the best thing is to leave central Port Sudan and head over to the fish market at nearby Sigala.

A rickshaw to the area should cost no more than 5 SDG, although invariably the drivers will try to charge you more. You can also take a bus for 50 *piastras*, but it doesn't come quite as far as the market. You will have to walk for an additional 20 minutes or take a rickshaw for 2 SDG.

The **fish market** (Souq as-Samak) sells mouth-wateringly fresh fish, some of which are still squirming about in their baskets. Once you've paid for your fish — 10 SDG per kg, though you may be able to negotiate — you can simply take it to one of the nearby restaurants for them to grill (which will usually cost an extra 3-4 SDG).

Even if you don't fancy eating here, it is still worth taking a trip to the market for the traditional experience — all manner of unusual fish are presented in wicker baskets, and the purveyors usually don't mind you taking photos, even if you are not going to buy anything.

If you would prefer to eat at a more formal seafood restaurant, where you don't have to purchase your own fish by the kilogram, then **Al-Shara Sea Food** (☎ 0311 828 989 or 0120 910 443) just across from the market, presents one option. It's not all that cheap — 15 SDG for a grilled fish — and the service is pretty dismal, but the fish is tasty and comes with chips. The restaurant also serves grilled shrimp and shrimp sandwiches.

How to get there

Regular **buses** from Port Sudan run east to Atbara (8.5 hours, 54 SDG) or south to Kassala (8.5 hours, 45 SDG). The journey to Khartoum takes around 15 hours

The pick-up and drop-off point is in Souq as-Shabi, a 20-minute rickshaw or taxi-ride out of town. A rickshaw ride should cost you no more than 5 SDG, a taxi ride around 10 SDG.

Many of the long-distance buses leave Port Sudan very early in the morning (around 5 or 6 am). Rickshaws and taxis do run at this time, and you should be able to find one without too much difficulty, but you will probably have to position yourself on one of the main streets to catch their attention. Waiting outside one of the football clubs — Hilal El-Sahil and Hay El-Arab — is usually a good choice.

Alternatively, if you are worried about being able to catch an early-morning bus in time, there is a fairly grotty *lokanda* just a five-minute walk away from the bus station. A basic room with fan and shared bathroom will cost you 15 SDG. A night in a dorm will cost 10 SDG.

Port Sudan's New International Airport is located about 25 km out of the city. The companies that fly to and from Port Sudan are Sudan Airways and Nova Air.

The latest news on trains is that they are no longer running to and from Port Sudan, but they may resume soon. Previously, a train ran between Atbara and Port Sudan twice a month.

If you travel overland to and from Port Sudan, you need a travel permit. However, you do not need one if you fly. Permits are required for travel out of the city, going north to Red Sea Resort and south to Suakin.

If you leave Port Sudan by bus, you will need additional permission from the immigration police, even if you already have a travel permit. They have an office at the bus station and bus companies will refuse to sell you a ticket unless they have stamped a piece of paper authorising your travel. You may also be asked to pay a departure tax, which seems to vary quite arbitrarily but is usually around 30 SDG.

You are not usually asked to pay this tax if you leave Port Sudan by car or by air.

SUAKIN

Along the Red Sea coast, 50 km south of Port Sudan, lies the ancient seaport of Suakin, slowly falling into decay and ruin.

Prior to 1905, when Port Sudan was founded, Suakin was the major port in the country, full of ships carrying goods abroad and bustling with pilgrims on their way to Mecca during the Hajj.

The exact date when Suakin was established is not known for certain, although early records show that the port existed in the 12th century. The port was initially created as a way for pilgrims to get to Mecca.

In bygone days, the slave trade made Suakin a very wealthy town. People caught in Bahr al-Ghazal and White Nile State were sold by slave traders in Suakin. Every year about 3000 slaves were transported from Suakin to slave markets in Jeddah and Cairo.

This was a lucrative trade, going on for some centuries, and the money in circulation made Suakin a place of renowned beauty. Attempts to restore the buildings to their former glory were started in 1881, but now everything lies in ruins.

Suakin is fairly small and you can walk around it in a reasonably short time but, if you don't fancy this, then take a rickshaw.

THE LEGENDS OF SUAKIN

If you spend some time talking to the local Sudanese before you visit Suakin, you will be surprised by the number of people who exhibit signs of discomfort or concern for your safety.

The main cause of this fear are the cats that prowl through the streets of the town. Spending every day gorging on the discarded remains of fish, these felines have become abnormally large. Not only that, but visitors to the town come away with stories of them standing up on their hind legs to beg for food, and some have even reported hearing them speak.

The cats are believed to be possessed by the spirits of the *jinn*, which dwell within the waters of the Red Sea.

There is a small vegetable market in the centre of town and several shops on the outskirts.

The highlight of any visit to the area is a tour of Suakin Island, which is connected to the mainland by a causeway. Here, you can wander through streets full of once-beautiful buildings that are now in the final stages of crumbling away. There is an entrance fee of 10 SDG for visiting the island.

Where to sleep and eat

Sleeping options in Suakin are limited. There are a couple of run-down *lokandas* in the market area. A slightly better place to stay is a 10-minute walk from Suakin, to the outskirts of nearby Siniar. Here, you'll find **Salahin**, a clean and spacious *lokanda*, with nice enclosed courtyard. A basic but clean room costs just 10 SDG.

The Red Sea

There aren't a great deal of restaurants to choose from in Suakin. You'll find all the usual stalls selling the usual fare near the bus station and in the market.

There is also **Mistero Seafood Restaurant** just before you enter the main island. This isn't a bad place to come for fresh fish, although the quality isn't what it used to be. Dining here also gives you a great view over the sea, where fishermen in small boats bob up and down, trailing nets in the water. There is no menu for the restaurant; they just serve the catch of the day (fried), salad and bread. For this, expect to pay around 10 SDG.

How to get there

To get to the town from the centre of Port Sudan, you will need to take two buses. The first one, costing around 80 *piastras*, will take you to Hem Suakin. You can catch it from the local bus station in central Port Sudan, just next to the Hilal El-Sahil and Hay El-Arab sports clubs. The bus from Hem Suakin to Suakin costs 4-5 SDG and takes 40 minutes. There is no fixed timetable; buses just depart when they are full.

Ferries run daily between Suakin and Jeddah in Saudi Arabia (see box on p229).

RED SEA HILLS AND ARKOWIT

Whilst the coastal towns of Port Sudan and Suakin have a great deal to offer, you shouldn't overlook the magnificent hinterland of the Red Sea Hills.

It is here that you can experience something of the true tribal culture of the local Beja people. The distinctive way that the men where their *jalabia*, with a dark tunic thrown over the top. The long scimitars bourne on the hips of some of the tribesmen. The womenfolk with enormous gold rings through their nose, sometimes so big that it is a wonder they can still support their head.

Faint glimmers of this culture appear in the urban centres of Port Sudan and Suakin, but it isn't until you venture inland that you really start to appreciate this heritage: obvious tribal customs that are not put on for the tourist, but rather because they are still a traditional part of who these people are.

If you are planning a trip into the Red Sea Hills, one of the most obvious places to head for is **Arkowit** (200 km south-west of Port Sudan and 39 km from the Red Sea coast).

Located in an area popularly known as the 'clouds' tower' Arkowit is a pleasant place in which to be, both in summer and in winter, as it enjoys frequent rains and mild weather all year round.

The town was once a cool retreat for the British. It is covered with evergreen vegetation and is situated 1200 meters above sea level. The highest point is the summit of Al-Sit at 2000 metres.

Since it enjoys mild weather all year long, Arkowit is home to many different species of wildlife and vegetation, which are not so common elsewhere in Sudan. Typical examples of flora and fauna that you can find in the area include the endemic Huhuba tree and the Nubian Ibex (known by locals as the 'mountain goat').

Arkowit is known for its **ironsmiths and silversmiths**, and for the manufacture of original necklaces, armbands, silver chains and earrings. It is also a great area for **hiking**.

Whilst here, you might want to pay a visit to the **tomb of Osman Digna**, who was one of the most prominent followers of the Mahdi (p56). Digna started off as a slave-trader in Egypt, but had to give this up when the British outlawed it in 1882. In response, he joined the Mahdist cause and fought against the British colonialists, spearheading fierce campaigns around the Suakin area and, later, up to the doorsteps of Khartoum itself. He was eventually caught by the British in 1900 and spent the next eight years in an Egyptian gaol. He died in 1922, aged 90, and is still admired within Sudan for his anti-colonialist zeal.

If you want to stay in Arkowit, a new hotel — the **Jabel Alsit Resort** (☎ 0123 373 737 or 0120 794 802; @ info@jabelalsitresort.com; ⌨ www.jabelalsitresort.com) — has recently opened in the town. The building in which the hotel is housed actually used to be a hotel during British colonial rule, and was where Her Majesty's soldiers would escape the stifling heat of the lower coastal areas. The management have attempted to recapture some of that old British charm, with a certain amount of success. Rooms are comfortable and clean, and service is very efficient. All rooms come with a TV, air-con and wi-fi.

There is even a ball room, although that doesn't tend to get as much use as it should do. A twin room costs $125, a double $200 and a suite $400. All prices include tax and breakfast.

How to get there

The easiest way to reach Arkowit is with your own vehicle. Travelling there by public transport is possible, though slightly awkward.

Start by taking a bus from Port Sudan westwards, to the small market town of **Sinkat**. This should take around two-and-a-half hours and cost 8 SDG. Sinkat is in itself an interesting place to see, if only for its remoteness and traditional way of life there. That aside, there's probably not a great deal that will hold you in the town.

From Sinkat, you can either take a taxi to Arkowit (for around 100 SDG) or take a shared *boksi* (for a much more reasonable 4 SDG per person). The downside to the *boksi* is that you may have to wait awhile for it to fill up.

The Red Sea

The East
Kassala, Dinder Park

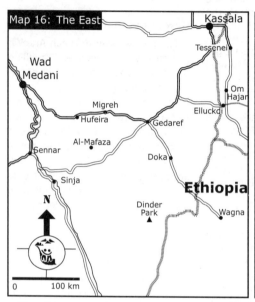

Map 16: The East

Kassala
Tessenei
Wad Medani
Om Hajar
Migreh
Elluckd
Hufeira
Gedaref
Al-Mafaza
Sennar
Doka
Sinja
Ethiopia
Dinder Park
Wagna

N

0   100 km

Highlights

- Sample Eritrean coffee on the streets of Kassala.

- Visit the spiritual heartland of the Khatmiyah sect in the Taka Mountains.

- Drink from the Totil Well and pledge to return.

- See lions in Dinder Park.

- Explore the dried river beds of the Gash.

- Experience the camel races.

The Eritrean and Ethiopian borders, in the east of North Sudan, are sprinkled with interesting places to visit. Two of the must-see destinations are Kassala and Dinder Park.

However, large scale migration of people across the border into Sudan has had a devastating effect on the area, not least on the wildlife of Dinder Park, much of which has now been hunted or poached to the brink of extinction.

Things are recovering slowly, and a concerted effort is being made to establish a sustainable tourist industry in the region, but it will be a while before things return to their former glorious days, if they ever do.

Poaching remains a constant problem in the area. Hunters ride into the forest on camels under cover of darkness and make off before morning with their valuable kills, many of which end up in the markets of Khartoum and Omdurman.

Despite their best efforts, there is little that the under-resourced park rangers have been able to do to put an end to this trade. The hope is that the fledgling tourist industry in the park will encourage the authorities to release some money in order to introduce proper policing into the area.

In Kassala, a rebel group (the Eastern Front) has been operating across the Eritrean border for a number of years (p42). This has resulted in heightened tension in the region. Things have settled down a little now and members of the rebel group have officially given up their arms. But security remains tight and your permit will be rigorously checked.

KASSALA

Overshadowed by the distinctive sugarloaf mountains of Aweitila, Totil and Taka, Kassala is one of the most picturesque places to visit in North Sudan. It is particularly popular with Sudanese newlyweds, who come to the city to celebrate their honeymoons: look out for the women adorned with golden jewellery and henna tattoos.

Men in Kassala dress in the same distinctive way as they do in the Red Sea Hills (p236), with a light brown tunic thrown over their *jalabia*. Some also wear ceremonial swords, although they are not allowed to remove them from their sheaths. The regional colours for the women's tobes are green and golden. The *tobe* is quite a bit heavier than the ones worn in other regions because of the cooler weather.

Your first impression of downtown Kassala is likely to be one of noise and chaos. There is much more hustle and bustle in the town than in other similarly-sized places elsewhere in North Sudan. Everywhere you turn you'll see traders hawking fruit and veg, often from the back of a wagon, whilst a forlorn donkey stands tethered nearby. Horse- and donkey-drawn carts careen through the town, transporting all sorts of interesting artefacts and foodstuffs. The aromas that waft up from the street are very much those of rural living, intermingled with the intriguing spices of the Eritrean-style coffee that is brewed on just about every street corner.

It is worth visiting Kassala just to experience this snapshot of life. And once the hectic pace-of-life has got too much for you, you can seek solitude by escaping to the Taka Mountains or wandering down to the banks of the Gash River.

Kassala has a very interesting range of **market stalls**, selling everything from fruit and vegetables to handicrafts. The distinctive Sudanese and Ethiopian clay pots, used to prepare coffee, are widely sold in the market and make memorable souvenirs.

Unfortunately, you have to be careful when seeking out local crafts, since much of the merchandise that appears to be locally-made is actually imported.

Also, check out **Souq an-Nissuan** (the women's market), where Sudanese ladies come to buy the material for performing their pre-matrimonial *dukhan* ceremony (p81).

A little way outside of Khartoum lie the slopes of **Jebel Totil.**

This is a lovely and picturesque area to visit, where you will find a number of cafés serving excellent Sudanese coffee, strongly-flavoured with local spices. The spot is especially popular at sunset, when you will find a number of young honeymooners enjoying the evening air. You have to pay a small fee (1 SDG) to get in.

It is here, also, that you will find the **Totil Well**. Local legend has it that, if you drink from the water of this well, then you are certain to return to Kassala.

At the base of the Taka Mountains, just below Jebel Totil, sit the ruins of the once-impressive **Khatmiyah Mosque**. Completed in 1887, the mosque was intended to provide the spiritual centre for the Khatmiyah sect. This sect, which was established in the early 19th

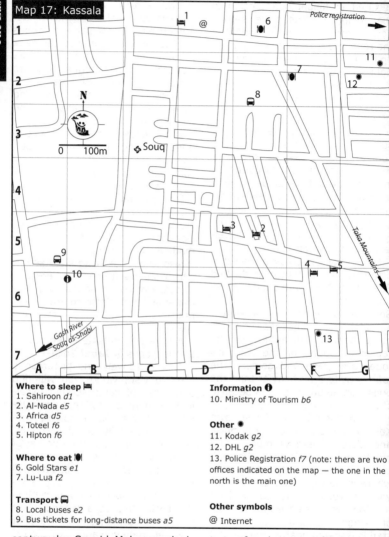

Map 17: Kassala

Where to sleep ⊨
1. Sahiroon *d1*
2. Al-Nada *e5*
3. Africa *d5*
4. Toteel *f6*
5. Hipton *f6*

Where to eat ⦿⦿⦿
6. Gold Stars *e1*
7. Lu-Lua *f2*

Transport 🚌
8. Local buses *e2*
9. Bus tickets for long-distance buses *a5*

Information ℹ️
10. Ministry of Tourism *b6*

Other ⦿
11. Kodak *g2*
12. DHL *g2*
13. Police Registration *f7* (note: there are two offices indicated on the map — the one in the north is the main one)

Other symbols
@ Internet

century by Sayyid Mohammed al-Mirghani, remains one of Sudan's most prominent religious orders.

However, only a year after its completion, the mosque was badly damaged by Mahdi forces, which at that time occupied Kassala against the Khatmiyah sect's wishes. Because of this, the mosque now has no roof and you can freely wander inside (although you should still remember to remove your shoes first).

Local legends about the mosque are popular. One suggests that, because of al-Mirghani's powers, no water falls inside the mosque when it rains, despite the lack of a roof.

Another legend foretells of the arrival of a holy man called Mohammed, who will restore the mosque to its former glory.

Regular buses run from Kassala's town centre to Jebel Totil and the Khatmiyah Mosque (direction: Khatmiyah). The bus journey should cost around 1 SDG. Alternatively, you can take a taxi to either of these places — expect to pay 15 SDG to get to the Khatmiyah Mosque and 20 SDG to get to Jebel Totil.

The **Gash River**, which runs through Kassala, is a wonderful place to explore. For much of the year, the river is a vast expanse of dry and cracked sand. This is when the local Sudanese turn out in droves to have picnics along the shore and sing traditional songs. During the rainy season, though, the river quickly fills with water and serious flooding often occurs.

Kassala is a particularly fertile part of Sudan, positively teeming with **majestic farms** that grow an abundance of local fruit, such as guava and bananas (although, in the markets, local produce is often more expensive than produce brought in from over the border). Many of these farms have splendid views of the mountains or the river, and sitting on a rug under a tree can be a great way of spending an afternoon, if you can get permission to enter the farm.

Just behind Jebel Totil lies El-Hafaya, the region's most important **camel market**. To get there, take a bus to a town called Mastura. The journey will take an hour and should cost around 2 SDG. The camel market is then a 10-minute taxi ride away (costing 10 SDG).

If you're lucky, you can even see camel races in the area. Such races have been taking place among the nomads in the region for generations, but it is only recently that the sport has become worth a lot of money. Fairly hefty bets are placed on many of the races, despite the fact that gambling is contrary to *sharia* law.

The camel market takes place every day, but there is no easy way of knowing when the races will be held. Your best bet is to ask as many locals as you can about them and see if they know when the next one will be. The staff at Sahiroon hotel (p242) seem fairly knowledgeable about the camel races, since they regularly organise tourist excursions for their guests.

Al-Bustan is a fairly new park near the town's Souq as-Shabi. It contains a small selection of fairground rides for both children and adults. There is also a restaurant. Entrance to the park costs 1 SDG and each ride costs 3 SDG. Every month a singer performs live at the park. The price for the show varies according to the fame of the singer, but is usually between 7 and 10 SDG.

Kassala is a reasonably small city and the best way to experience it is by walking. Alternatively, there is a good network of buses that take you to most places you want to go. Rickshaws are not allowed in the city and so, if you do not want to walk or take buses, your only other option is the local taxi.

When you arrive in Kassala, you should register with the local authorities. There are a couple of places to register in the town. One is in the south of the town. Another is in the north, behind Kassala's educational hospital. If you get stuck about where to register, your hotel can usually help you.

Due to a previously-high level of rebel activity in the area (p42), you will need to obtain a travel permit to visit Kassala.

Where to eat

The obvious places to go if you want to eat cheaply in Kassala are the roadside food stalls, which typically serve *fuul* or omelette.

You might also like to sample some of the regional fare. Many traditional dishes from Kassala are cooked in a large lidless pot, which is covered with black pebbles and salt. Locals say that the pebbles are essential for giving the food its unique flavour. Look out for two well-known dishes in the region: *shai'ia* (dried meat) and *gurar* (roasted meat with rice and onions). Expect to pay no more than 3 SDG for these kinds of dishes if you eat on the side of the road — more if you go to a proper restaurant.

The Eritrean-style coffee in Kassala is definitely worth sampling. It is spiced and particularly strong.

For established restaurants, try **Lu-Lua**, which opened in 2008 and is located near the main bus station in the centre of Kassala. The restaurant is clean with good service, but is slightly pricier than you might find elsewhere: a meat *sha'urma* costs 2 SDG, a burger 4 SDG, and a whole chicken 20 SDG. The restaurant also serves pizzas. You can get a medium chicken pizza for 13 SDG.

Not far from Lu-Lua is a Sudanese pizzeria called **Gold Stars**. A small pizza costs 8 SDG, a medium 15 SDG and a large 20 SDG. The restaurant also serves *sha'urma* for 3 SDG.

There are a few good places in the market selling fruit juice. Try **Laziz** or **Arrau'abi,** where a fresh orange or guava juice costs as little as 1 SDG.

Where to sleep

Most of the hotels and *lokandas* are located in the market area. The *lokandas* are typically more expensive than those in other cities and usually only accept men.

Toteel is a one of the better options for a cheap night's rest. Service is friendly and rooms are a lot cleaner than many of the other *lokandas* in the market place. For a twin room, which comes with en-suite shower and toilet, expect to pay 30 SDG. The drawback to the hotel is that, during the day, the room can become like an oven. This is probably due to the security measures in place, which are good for protecting your belongings but not for letting air in: solid bars on the window and a sturdy metal door. The solitary fan on the ceiling does little to limit your discomfort.

Africa Hotel is a small and basic *lokanda* not far from the market. A rough-and-ready room, containing one or two beds, costs 30 SDG.

El-Tayef Hotel is another cheap *lokanda*, with rooms costing 25 SDG. It is located to the east of the town centre. There is a nice courtyard just outside the building, where tea ladies work.

Hipton (☎ 0411 822 357/8) is head-and-shoulders above other hotels in Kassala in terms of service provided. It is located east of the market, in an area called al-Mantega Sinaia. The prices are a little higher than you might pay elsewhere, though: 83 SDG for a relatively small room, containing either two or three beds. All rooms come with an ensuite bathroom, fridge, television and air-conditioning. The hotel has a restaurant on the roof, where you can enjoy some fantastic views of Kassala and the Taka mountains. Breakfast is not included in the price, however.

Sahiroon (☎ 0411 827 707) is to the south of the market, behind Kassala and Faid Technology Institute. Rooms start at 65 SDG, excluding breakfast. The hotel has a garden for entertainment at night. This hotel is a popular choice for honeymooners in the town, and the staff at the hotel are very good at providing tourist advice and arranging tours. The hotel can also arrange taxis. Some of the staff speak a little English.

Al-Nada Hotel, in the centre of the market behind Souq Haikota (which sells sugar and oil), charges 70 SDG for a room with two beds. Service is terribly unfriendly and rooms are far from being the cleanest. Cockroaches are a problem in many of the rooms.

Al-Mek Nimir is a men-only *lokanda* situated north of the market, in an area called 'Botek Of Giadda', where you will find many stalls selling imported clothes from Saudi Arabia. Beds cost 15 SDG for a night.

There is even a **Youth Hostel** in the town (⌨ www.sudaneseyha.net; @ info@sudaneseyha.net), close to Osman Digna Street. Staying in a room with two beds costs 35 SDG per person. A night's sleep in a room with more than two beds costs 25 SDG. You must have a YHA card to sleep at the hostel, which can be purchased on-the-spot for 20 SDG.

Getting there

Kassala has two bus stations. The local station, Al-Mougaf al-Ham, is just next to Souq al-Kabier. Souq as-Shabi, which serves national destinations, is a 20-minute car journey west of the town centre.

This inconvenient location can make it tricky to find transportation early in the morning, which is when many of the long-distance buses depart. Fortunately, long-distance buses coming late at night stop in the town centre, which makes life a little easier.

The cheapest way to travel between downtown Kassala and Souq as-Shabi is to take a local bus for 70 *piastras*. A taxi should cost no more than 7 SDG, although you may have to pay more if you take a taxi at night or in the early hours of the morning, when no other transportation is running. Even so, resist paying much more than 10 SDG — taxi drivers who do the night-runs are remorseless in what they ask for.

Tickets for the long-distance buses can be purchased in the centre of town (see map), so you should only need to travel to Souq as-Shabi when you are ready to take the bus.

The coach journey from Khartoum to Kassala costs 58 SDG and takes between eight and nine hours. Travelling as far as Wad Medani costs 44 SDG and takes around six hours.

DINDER PARK

Dinder National Park is the biggest nature reserve in North Sudan, covering 10,000 km². In the past, its rich variety of fauna put it right up there with other famous parks in Africa, but now, sadly, a great deal of the wildlife has been killed by poachers or refugees trying to escape the war in neighbouring countries.

Elephants and other big game are extinct in the park. The animals you are most likely to see include baboons, deer, ostriches, warthogs and a startlingly-large number of bird species. There are a few lions in the park, too, so with luck you may see one of those.

The park has three areas that are open for safari, including four water holes where you have a better chance of spotting lions. Three safaris should be enough to cover all the areas in the park that are accessible to the public.

You can usually arrange with the safari lodge when you wish to go on a safari, but it is strongly advisable to start very early in the morning (before 7 am) or early in the evening (just after 5 pm). This is when the day is cooler, and you are more likely to see the animals coming down to the waterside to drink. Other times may be suggested — either by the safari lodge or by the Wildlife Police — but you should be prepared to use your own initiative and arrange to go out when you feel conditions are best for seeing the wildlife.

To visit the park, you will need to have your own vehicle. If you want to fully enjoy the safari, go in a pick-up truck. This might be a little more uncomfortable, but it will allow you to stand up outside during the safari.

A travel permit is required for the park. You can obtain one for free from the Ministry of Tourism on Mashtal Street in Khartoum.

When to go

The park is open for visitors from December until the beginning of June, depending on the start and end of the rainy season (the park is extremely difficult to get to when it rains). The best time to visit the park is at the start of the season, since this is when vegetation is at its greenest.

Where to eat and sleep

There is only one place to stay in the park: the **Dinder Tourist Camp** (☎ 0183 244 574 or +0183 246 504 or 0912 374 057 or 0916 744 276; @ nadus_tourism@yahoo.com). In Khartoum, the Ministry of Tourism, on Mashtal Street in Riyad, can give

you additional information about the camp, including how to book.

The camp has a dozen or so round huts made of cement, each containing two rooms with a fan. The rooms are fairly basic: just a few beds in each, although there is an ensuite bathroom. This accommodation costs 130 SDG per person per night, which includes three meals and two safaris (with your own car, but with a guide from the Wildlife Police).

Electricity for the camp is provided through a combination of eco-friendly solar panels and generators. Electricity stops at around midnight and starts again at 10 am.

How to get there

Dinder Park is located 600 km from Khartoum, and takes between 10 and 12 hours to reach by car. It is fairly straightforward to get to Dinder Village by car from Khartoum. Take the road as far as Wad Medani. From there, head for Sennar, then Sinja and, finally, Dinder Village.

Dinder Village lies on the outskirts of the reserve, but, even from here, it takes a minimum of four hours before you get within sight of the park. A four-wheel-drive, or off-road vehicle, is essential for this leg of the journey.

There are no signs between Dinder Village and Dinder Park. Once you arrive in Dinder Village, you must report to the headquarters of the Wildlife Police. They will check your documents and escort you to the park.

The road from Dinder Village to Dinder Park is particularly interesting. You will pass several small villages, where you can buy basic items. The Dinder River crosses some of these villages, creating some spectacular scenery.

The Centre
Wad Medani, Sennar, Kosti, Aba Island,

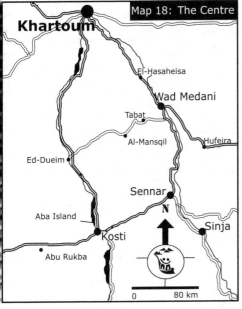

Map 18: The Centre

Khartoum

El-Hasaheisa

Wad Medani

Tabat

Al-Mansqil

Hufeira

Ed-Dueim

Sennar

N

Aba Island

Sinja

Kosti

Abu Rukba

0   80 km

Highlights

- Take a trip to Aba Island, spiritual homeland of the Mahdi movement.

- Visit the Kenana sugar factory.

- Wander down to Kosti's docks and watch shipworkers load and unload boats bound for the south.

- Relax along the banks of the Nile in Wad Medani, a popular honeymoon destination.

- Visit the historically important towns of Sennar and Sinja.

There are two roads leading south out of Khartoum. One follows the course of the Blue Nile to Wad Medani and Sennar. The other follows the White Nile down to Kosti.

Both roads cut through fairly flat and featureless terrain, which eventually opens out into North Sudan's agricultural hinterland. The main crops grown here are sorghum, wheat, millet and cotton. Watermelons and rice are also common.

Over the years, there have been many attempts to modernise agriculture in the region. In the 1920s, Wad Medani was chosen as the headquarters for Britain's ambitious Gezira scheme, which distributed water from the Blue Nile to farms in the region. During the 1970s, the area became the focal point for many of the brave — but ill-fated — attempts to bolster the country's economy through heavy investment in mechanised agriculture.

At the height of summer, the land immediately south of Khartoum becomes parched and cracked, a dreary and desolate wilderness with few points of interest along the way. But travel in the winter, after the rains have fallen, and the route tells a different story: you will discover a glistening, verdant landscape brimming with new life. And the further south you travel, the greener things become.

WAD MEDANI

Wad Medani, the capital of Gezira state, lies on the west bank of the Blue Nile, nearly 135 km south-east of Khartoum.

The town first gained prominence in 1821, when it was used by the Turkiyah army to wage war against the Funj sultanate, who had its base at nearby Sennar. In the 1920s, the British took a fresh interest in the town, when they chose it as the headquarters for their Gezira scheme.

Today, Wad Medani is a busy trading centre, with a youthful vibrancy largely thanks to the **Gezira University that is** located there. But, despite the obvious hustle-and-bustle of the town centre, there are some quiet spots that you can escape to. One of the nicest, most relaxing places to hang out in is along the **banks of the Blue Nile** where there are a number of cafés and open-air restaurants in which you can while away the afternoon.

The town's easy-going character, as well as its close proximity to Khartoum, makes it a popular destination for honeymooners.

There is not a great deal to see in the town — it is more a place where you come and just 'absorb', perhaps on your way to somewhere else.

Still, if you are bent on seeing the sights that the town has to offer, you probably should check out the University. The **Catholic Church** from 1930, which overlooks the banks of the Nile, is also interesting.

There's a **park** along the bank of the Nile, with some fairground rides, including the ubiquitous Ferris wheel. It costs 1 SDG to enter the park.

Where to sleep

If you are looking for somewhere to stay, the **Continental Hotel** (☎ 0511 843 619 or 0511 345 345 or 0912 362 180) is possibly the nicest place in town, with wonderful views over the Nile, providing you choose the right room. Being a little way away from the central market area, the hotel is a good choice for those that like their peace and quiet. The place has a nice shaded garden with an old abandoned snooker table in one corner. Rooms come with air-con, a TV and small ensuite bathroom. Prices start at 75 SDG for a single. Unfortunately, the service is a little disappointing, and the restaurant is probably not worth trying. If you do want a nice restaurant whilst staying at the Continental, try the Turkish place just next door. Here, you'll find a number of terraces overlooking the Nile, with food at very reasonable prices.

A little further down the street, you will find **Al-Neel Hotel** (☎ 0155 880 858 or 0922 356 754), which is of a similar standard to the Continental but slightly more expensive. Prices are the same for both single and double rooms — 100 SDG each — although negotiation is possible out-of-season. The rooms are very variable, so make sure you ask to have a look at them before agreeing to stay. Some have air-coolers, others have fans. Not all of them have TVs. Some come with proper toilets, others have just a hole in the ground. The staff are very friendly, but have limited English. The outdoor area is not as nice as the Continental, but the attached restaurant has a pleasant patio to sit out in. Again, the restaurant is nothing special and often seems completely deserted — but a quick burger-and-egg (5 SDG) is palatable.

In the centre of town, **Adhoua Al-Gezira** (☎ 0911 634 222) offers a much cheaper option for spending the night. A single room with two beds in it will cost 20 SDG.

The **Imperial Hotel** (☎ 0511 840 500), located between Souq as-Shabi and the centre of town, is one of the newcomers to Wad Medani's accommodation scene. Rooms are comfortable and clean, but prices are not cheap: 100 SDG for a night.

How to get there

If you take a bus to the town (two and a half hours from Khartoum, costing 17 SDG), it will drop you in Souq as-Shabi, a little way outside the main town centre. From here, you can take a bus for 70 *piastras* to get into town, or a taxi for 7 SDG.

SENNAR

A little further on from Wad Medani, heading south, is the sleepy little hamlet of Sennar. In former days, Sennar was the centre of the powerful and expansive Funj Kingdom (p54). These days there is little evidence of the town's former glory, and its epic history is all but forgotten.

There is not a great deal to do in the town. However, the pace of life in Sennar is that much slower than in nearby Wad Medani, and so it makes for a nice alternative if you want to get away from things for awhile.

Where to sleep

Sennar is not generally the first place that foreigners think of visiting in North Sudan. Nonetheless, there are a couple of reasonable hotels, along with a scattering of *lokandas* around the markets, that you'll be welcome to stay at.

Rachid (☎ 0561 822 378) is probably the nicest place in town to stay. Clean and comfortable, and prices are not unreasonable: 35 SDG to stay in a room with two beds, with shared bathroom, and 50 SDG to stay in a slightly larger room with ensuite. The place also has a rooftop restaurant.

Raeba (☎ 0912 889 004), just round the corner from Rachid, offers rooms for between 30 and 50 SDG, depending on their size and their present condition. Rooms tend to be quite variable, so ask to have a look at them before you agree to stay.

Tourism Hotel is a small *lokanda* just next to the market. A night in a dormitory costs just 5 SDG, whilst a small room with fan costs 10 SDG. The low prices are reflected in the condition of the rooms.

How to get there

Regular coaches run from Khartoum to Sennar, costing 24 SDG and taking four hours. They will drop you in Souq as-Shabi, which is a short taxi ride (7 SDG) from the main town centre.

KOSTI

Kosti is a friendly, laid-back town, conveniently situated on the banks of the White Nile. It is an important trading post between North and South Sudan, and a steady stream of boats make their way from Kosti to the Southern towns of Malakal and Juba. There is a very good tarmac road linking Kosti with Khartoum, and this provides an efficient way of getting goods to the capital.

Kosti is named after a Greek merchant who had a trading post there during the 19th century. Not much of this legacy now remains, although there is still an Orthodox church in the town.

The Centre

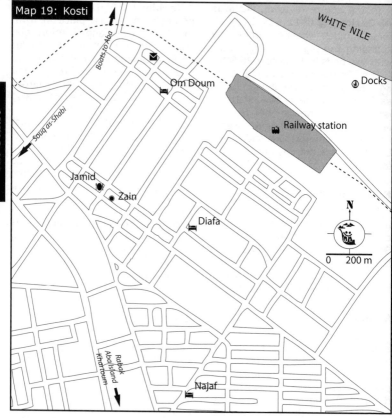

Map 19: Kosti

WHITE NILE

Boats to Aba

Om Doum

Docks

Souq as-Shabi

Railway station

Jamid

Zain

Diafa

N

0   200 m

Rabak
Aba Island
Khartoum

Najaf

Kosti has a much more agricultural feel to it than many neighbouring towns, and it sometimes feels that you can't go more than a few feet without stumbling over a sheep or donkey.

Kosti is a great place to spend a few days in, and you should consider using it as a base to explore the surrounding area. Remember, though, that Kosti is not a wealthy place so pay particular attention to your belongings whilst in the town, especially around the market areas.

The **marketplace** in the centre of town is definitely worth a visit. It is less noisy and chaotic than many others around the country. Kosti's fruit and vegetables are excellent and fairly cheap: the watermelons are particularly good.

The **docks** are the highlight of any stay in the town. Since the signing of the peace agreement between North and South in 2005, there has been a steady increase in the number of cargo ships travelling between Kosti and South Sudan. Initially, the surge in river traffic was due to a UN-backed programme to get refugees back home. Now, though, the transportation of refugees has just about stopped and been replaced instead with cargo shipping companies. Few cargo ships run northwards to

Khartoum, though; most goods to the capital are transported by road.

Many of the ship operators speak passable English, and are usually eager to practice on the few foreigners that pass by the area. You may even be able to secure passage on one of these boats, although there are still no official passenger services operating to the South. You will have to negotiate the price — 100 SDG to travel between Kosti and Juba is probably reasonable, although you will almost certainly be asked to pay more. Remember that these ship operators do have another income and you should not be coerced into over-paying.

The Nile River Transportation Company (🏠 Street 25, Amarat, Khartoum; ☎ 0183 560 037/34/36; @ info@nrtcsd.com; 🖥 nrtcsd.com) runs cargo shipping operations out of Kosti and can give you advice about making the trip down to Juba. You will need an additional permit to travel to South Sudan.

It is fascinating, and not a little saddening, to see the number of disused barges, corroded with rust and half-submerged in the water. There used to be a beautiful paddle-steamer, lying abandoned in the water, but this has now been taken away as part of an effort to smarten the area up.

Kosti has a small **football stadium**, where, if you are lucky, you can catch local games on Friday evenings for 1 to 2 SDG.

On the opposite side of the river, in Rabak, lies the famous **Kenana Sugar Factory**, a throwback to the 1970s when Jaafar Nimeiri, then President, tried to establish Sudan as the 'breadbasket' of the Middle East. Focussing on agriculture as the mainstay of the economy, he encouraged massive investment in mechanised farming. As was the

case with many similar attempts to boost the economy at that time, this one was a flop: production went down and Sudan's debt soared massively. The factory at Kenana is one of the few sites that still cling on to that era, but these days it is doing much better, and is now one of the largest producers of white sugar in the world.

Whilst in Kosti, you might also like to visit **Aba Island** in the centre of the Nile (p250), where Mohammed Ahmed famously spent fourteen years preaching in the 19th century before declaring himself to be the Mahdi (p56).

Where to eat and sleep

There are a few nice places to stay in Kosti.

Um Doum (☎ 0120 777 468) is fairly cheap and has a lovely rooftop restaurant, with scenic views of the Nile and the docks. Expect to pay significantly more for a meal there than you would in the marketplace: 10 to 15 SDG for grilled meat and salad. Um Doum is located just next to the market. The hotel has a somewhat faded look to it and could do with a new lick of paint, although rooms and bathrooms are generally clean. A room with a separate communal bathroom costs between 25 and 35 SDG, depending on the number of beds. For a room with ensuite bathroom, expect to pay between 50 and 100 SDG according to facilities. You will pay more if you want air-con and satellite TV, for example. Service in the hotel is extremely friendly and complimentary tea and biscuits in the morning are often provided.

Another popular option is **De'afa Palace** (☎ 0120 777 455), a little further away from the Nile and in the centre of town. This hotel is a very attractive and peaceful place and you will find it less noisy than staying by the market. The hotel has an attractive rustic entrance and lovely garden, with some tables and chairs where you can sit out in the evening. At last visit, the hotel was unusually run by women. A single room costs 150 SDG, and comes with air-con, a TV, cupboard, fan, fridge and ensuite bathroom. Service is friendly. The hotel is clean, but the rooms are not that big and some repairs wouldn't go amiss.

Moving a little further away from the centre of town, you find **Najaf Hotel**. With just six rooms, this is quite probably the smallest hotel in Kosti. Although rooms are not very big, they are comfortable and come with a fridge, air-cooler, fan, television and desk. The hotel has a small yard with a couple of seats. This hotel is ideal for those that like their peace and quiet. Being so far from the market and the docks, you can sit out in the yard for most of the day and not be disturbed by very much at all, apart from the occasional braying of a donkey or squawking of a chicken. A double room costs 125 SDG.

Options for gourmet eating in Kosti are extremely limited, to say the least. In the **marketplace**, you will find a number of stalls selling the usual Sudanese dishes: *fuul*, salad and grilled meat. Most of the hotels also offer similar meals, at a slightly higher cost.

On the outskirts of town, near the Zain office, **Jamid** offers very good grilled meat and Sudanese-style pizzas.

Fruit in Kosti is excellent. Try the exceedingly succulent and good-value watermelons (4-5 SDG). Bananas are good too, but mangos tend to be slightly more expensive than you might find elsewhere (3 SDG each).

How to get there

It takes four hours to drive from Khartoum to Kosti. A bus to the city costs around 29 SDG. If you're coming from Juba or Malakal in the South, then you could brave roughing it for two weeks on one of the cargo ship that travels regularly along the river. This will cost you between 100 and 200 SDG.

ABA ISLAND

Not far from Kosti, in the centre of the White Nile, lies Aba Island, the spiritual heartland of the Mahdi movement. It was here that Mohammed Ahmed came, in 1868, before he declared himself to be the prophesied redeemer of Islam in 1881. It was here, too, that Mahdi forces won a key battle against government troops in 1881, by lying in wait for them among the reeds of the Nile — a scenario that springs immediately to life the moment that you set foot on the island.

Aba Island is a welcome breath of fresh air from the parched countryside stretching between Khartoum and Kosti. Whilst there are certainly fewer trees on the island than there were during the Mahdi's time, it is still pleasantly forested.

It is worth spending some time along the banks of the Nile. The scenery there is stunning and the birdlife plentiful. Aba Island is well-known for its fishing industry and you can purchase freshly-caught fish from the fishermen there.

Iman al-Mahdi University, just next to the local *souq*, used to be the palace of the Mahdi. It became a university in 1956, shortly after the country gained independence, and now boasts 2000 students.

The architecture of the university is splendid, and you should definitely look around if you get the chance. The university is closed on

Fridays and during holiday periods, but you can usually find someone to let you in.

Look for the unique table-tennis court, which has been constructed out of an ordinary table with bricks placed across the centre for the net.

Pictures of Saddam Hussein, former President of Iraq, decorate some of the outer walls of the university; he was clearly very much of a hero here. Campus guards can be a little reluctant to let you take photos of the university, but asking nicely, with a smile, usually wins them round.

Just round the corner from the University are the headquarters of the Umma Party, the modern incarnation of the Mahdi movement. You can pop into the headquarters if you like. They are usually very welcoming, but don't count on anyone speaking English.

If you head west from the University, towards the opposite side of the island, you will eventually come across **Al-Kar Mosque**, where the Mahdi himself once used to preach. The mosque is not quite on the banks of the Nile; it is about 1 km inland.

The original mosque is now in disuse. It is set a little way back from the road and is simply a grey concrete block, derelict and dilapidated. The door is kept locked but, if you ask around, you can usually find someone to let you in. Even though the mosque is not in use anymore, you must remember to take off your shoes before you enter. Inside, amidst the dust and the grime, there are several stone tablets, reputedly with the words of the Mahdi engraved upon them.

The modern Al-Kar Mosque, which is still in regular use, is less interesting. It is a low, square building set close to the road and painted blue.

How to get there

You can get to Aba Island either by boat or by road, since a causeway now connects the island to the mainland.

Boats to Aba Island leave just north-west of Kosti's main docks; passage costs around 1 SDG.

If you want to travel to Aba by road, the turning to the island is about a 20-minute drive north of Kosti, along the road leading to Khartoum. It is poorly-signposted and easy to miss, but you will know that you are on the right track when you cross a strip of land with locals fishing off to your left.

You can get to the island by public transport, too. Simply take a minibus from the centre of Kosti to Rabak, just across the Nile. Regular minibuses leave from Rabak to the island.

It is actually better to enter the island by road, since this guarantees that you are on the right side of the island for visiting the main attractions there.

The Centre

Kordofan
El-Obeid, Dilling, Kadugli

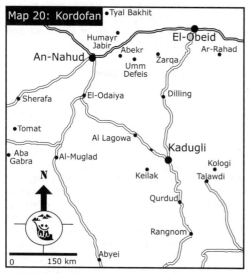

Map 20: Kordofan

Tyal Bakhit • El-Obeid
Humayr Jabir • Abekr • Ar-Rahad
An-Nahud • Zarqa
Umm Defeis
Sherafa • El-Odaiya • Dilling
Tomat
Al Lagowa • Kadugli
Aba Gabra • Al-Muglad • Kologi
Keilak • Talawdi
Qurdud
Rangnom
Abyei

N

0   150 km

Highlights

- See Mahdi memorabilia at the Sheikan Museum in El-Obeid.

- Take a trip to the famous Sheikan Battlefield.

- See traditional wrestling in the Nuba Mountains.

- Discover the importance of gum arabic in the region.

- Wander through the charming thatched villages of the Nuba people.

Whilst the terrain of North Kordofan is fairly flat and featureless, South Kordofan's terrain is broken up by the rugged outcrops of the Nuba Mountains.

The province is most famous for its production of gum arabic, a sticky resin that is secreted by the *acacia senegal* tree.

Gum arabic is used in the manufacture of many pharmaceutical drugs and fizzy drinks such as Coca-Cola.

Sudan once supplied 80% of the world's gum arabic. However, according to the World Bank, Sudan now accounts for less than 50% of total gum arabic production. Nevertheless, the industry remains extremely important to the Kordofan region. Interestingly, this is one of the few North Sudanese products exempted from American sanctions.

Kordofan used to be a single federal state but, in 1994, it was divided into three separate provinces: North Kordofan, South Kordofan and West Kordofan.

Since the signing of the Comprehensive Peace Agreement (CPA) in 2005, West Kordofan no longer exists, and the territory of this province has been divided up between North and South Kordofan, although there remains some dispute as to exactly where the borders should be drawn.

Due to its geographical position, South Kordofan has for a long time been embroiled in the country's civil war. Many people living in the Nuba Mountains feel that they have been persecuted for years at the hands of the northern Arabs, and, supported by the Sudanese People's Liberation Movement/Army

SPLM/A), have fought fiercely to protect their land.

Although the war with Khartoum has now officially ended, things remain highly volatile in the Nuba Mountains. During the research of this edition of the book, violent conflict erupted in Kadugli, the capital of South Kordofan. As with anything in Sudan, the reasons behind the conflict are complex.

The generally-accepted narrative is that an SPLM leader, Abdulaziz Al-Hilu, launched an armed rebellion in the region after losing the state election to Ahmad Haroun, a member of the ruling National Congress Party (NCP), who is now governor of the area. Khartoum, who backed Haroun, sent soldiers from the Sudan Armed Forces (SAF) to the region and began shelling the town of Kadugli, where much of the armed struggle was taking place.

This eruption of conflict has resulted in countless civilian deaths and casualties, and displaced hundreds from the town, many of whom fled northwards to El-Obeid. There were many foreign workers in the area that had to be air-lifted to safety.

Although Kadugli was the flashpoint for the conflict, the violence has also spilled over into other areas. The lovely African town of Dilling was also affected, with reports of shootings in the centre, although the locals say that things have since quietened down.

Before deciding whether or not to explore the Nuba Mountains, the best advice is to speak to people in the region and ask them how safe it is to travel there.

A permit is required for travel into the Nuba Mountains. Since the eruption of the latest conflict in Kadugli, controls have become much stricter and you will almost certainly encounter problems in the region if you do not have a valid permit.

Even with a travel permit, there are large parts of the region where you will not be able to go. With the current security problems, travelling any further south than Dilling will be difficult. You will certainly be barred from visiting Abyei, unless you have a very good reason for being there.

Due to its importance in trade, the road between El-Obeid and Khartoum is very good. The roads as far south as Kadugli have recently been improved. However, travel any further and you will find that their condition rapidly deteriorate.

EL-OBEID

El-Obeid, the capital of North Kordofan, is a major trading hub for the region, which makes it a popular stopping-off point for traders transporting their goods across Sudan. It is also a good place for travellers to stop if they are planning to visit the Nuba Mountains further south.

The soil in and around El-Obeid is very sandy, so that when it rains — which it starts to do around June or July — the water drains away quickly, unlike in Khartoum where huge puddles can stay for days.

El-Obeid is steeped in history. It is here that in 1881 the Mahdi came to raise his army of supporters in order to take on the British (p56). It was in this area, too, that the army led by General William Hicks was annihilated in 1883.

The **Sheikan battlefield**, where Hicks met his end, lies 50 km south of El Obeid. A taxi ride to the area should cost around 50 to 60 SDG. A cheaper way of getting there is to take a bus to Kasgil for 5 SDG. From there, a taxi ride to the battlefield is only another 5 SDG.

The region is still remembered as the place where Mahdi forces triumphed over the colonial invaders, but you will be disappointed if you

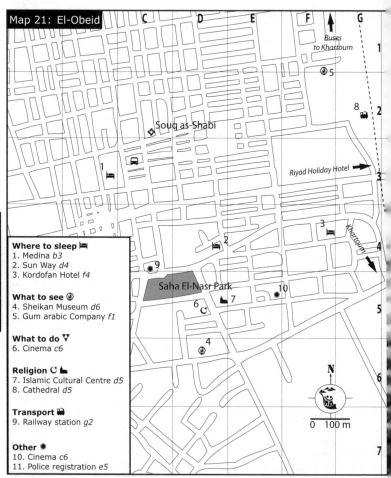

Map 21: El-Obeid

Buses to Khartoum

Souq as-Shabi

Riyad Holiday Hotel

Saha El-Nasr Park

Khartoum

Where to sleep ⛟
1. Medina *b3*
2. Sun Way *d4*
3. Kordofan Hotel *f4*

What to see ⓦ
4. Sheikan Museum *d6*
5. Gum arabic Company *f1*

What to do ⓥ
6. Cinema *c6*

Religion ☪ ⛪
7. Islamic Cultural Centre *d5*
8. Cathedral *d5*

Transport 🚉
9. Railway station *g2*

Other ◉
10. Cinema *c6*
11. Police registration *e5*

N

0   100 m

Kordofan

come to see the famous *sheikan* thorn trees that helped them win the battle. Most of the thorn trees in the region died a long time ago, largely due to desertification and deforestation.

However, you can see the famous **tabaldi tree** that Hicks reportedly climbed to try and escape Mahdi forces. The locals still know it as Hicks' Tree.

Back in town, the **Sheikan Museum** (☎ 7 am to 3 pm) not far from the Islamic Cultural Centre and the cathedral, is well-worth a visit. It is free to enter and provides

an excellent overview of some of the town's history. There are two parts to the museum. One part charts the history of the town, including the rise of the Mahdi and vanquishing of the British. The other part deals with the overall history of North Sudan, with a particular focus on the archaeological finds of the northern deserts. If you can, try and speak with the curator of the museum. At last visit, this was a young Sudanese man called Abdulla, who was a mine of fascinating facts about he country and loves to share his knowledge with visitors.

Just round the corner from the museum is the **Roman Catholic Cathedral**, one of the largest in Sudan. The cathedral was founded in 1871 by Roman Catholic missionary Daniel Comboni, who eventually became a Saint in 2003.

The church is often locked, but there is usually someone around that is happy to open it for you. Inside, you will find some fabulous stained glass windows and fresco paintings. A particularly noticeable one lies above the alter at the front, depicting Comboni and the famous Sudanese slave Josephine Bakhita (see box). Although Comboni and Bakhita would probably not have crossed paths in any meaningful way (Comboni died when Bakhita was just 12), the painting in the cathedral represents Comboni's ardent fight against slavery, and the triumph of Bakhita to transcend the unhappy life that she was born into.

It is interesting to note the close proximity of the cathedral to the Islamic Cultural Centre, on the other side of the street: an indication, perhaps, of the importance of El-Obeid as a crossover point between Christian and Muslim worlds.

It's really worth trying to attend a Sunday service at the cathedral. The building will be almost overflowing with African Christians, and the colours and vibrancy of African services are breathtaking to behold.

Not far from the cathedral, there is a **park** with a few rides in, including a Ferris wheel.

The **Gum arabic Company**, which produces most of Sudan's gum arabic, is located in Souq as-Shabi, El-Obeid's sprawling market area. Whilst this is not a usual tourist destination, you might be able to get permission to look around if you ask the right people.

JOSEPHINE BAKHITA

Josephine Bakhita was a former Sudanese slave who eventually became a saint

Little is known about her early life. She was born in a small village just outside Nyala in Darfur, probably around 1869. When she was still fairly young — perhaps no more than nine — she was kidnapped by Arab slave traders and brought to El-Obeid, where she became a slave. The name she is known by — Bakhita — means 'lucky' in Arabic and was given to her by one of her slave masters.

In 1883, with El-Obeid under control of Mahdi revolutionaries, Bakhita was sold to the Italian vice-consul Callisto Legnani. She was taken to Italy, where she fell under the employ of one of Legnani's close friends, Augusto Michieli.

When the Michieli family returned for a time to Sudan, Bakhita was entrusted to a group of Canossian Sisters in Venice. It was there that she came to know God and, after several months in the catechumenate, she received the sacraments of Christian initiation and was given a new name: Josephine. When the Michieli family came to take her back, Bakhita said she preferred to remain with the Sisters. Although the Michieli family wanted her to return to Sudan with them, a ruling in the Italian courts said that, since slavery was forbidden according to Italian law, they had no power over her.

Bakhita remained with the sisters until she died in 1947. She was canonized in 2000.

Remember that you should register in El-Obeid when you get there. You can do this in the offices just to the east of the cathedral.

How to get there

It takes around eight hours to drive from Khartoum to El-Obeid. Regular **coaches** depart early in the morning from Souq as-Shabi in Khartoum, costing 57 SDG one way. Coaches from El-Obeid to Khartoum also leave in the early hours of the morning. The bus station in El-Obeid is located about 15 minutes' walk north of the town centre. You have to pay 1 SDG to enter the bus station, irrespective of whether you are catching a bus or not.

El-Obeid is situated on the main **railway** line between Khartoum and Nyala. However, train services to and from the city are highly erratic and it is likely to take you a long time to get to your destination if you use the train. If you are planning to pick up a train from El-Obeid, you will just have to wait until you see one passing through; local rail staff are unable to provide any more reliable information.

Sudan Airways operates regular **flights** between Khartoum and El-Obeid. They take just over one hour and cost 373 SDG.

Where to sleep

Sun Way is one of the pricier hotels in town. A single costs between 180-200 SDG, whilst a double costs 250-280 SDG. Prices depend on the size of the room. Rooms come with air-con, TV, cupboard facilities, fridge and small ensuite bathroom. Rooms are comfortable and clean, and the English-speaking staff are very friendly. However, many of the rooms do have an odd, though not particularly unpleasant, musty smell about them. The hotel's restaurant offers food at reasonable prices. Just outside the hotel, there is a small play area for children, which includes slides and climbing frames.

Hotel Medina (☎ 0611 823 605) must surely be the friendliest hotel in town, and the staff are generally willing to help with any problem that you have, including accompanying you to the local authorities so that you can register. The rooms are nice, clean and comfortable. A standard single costs 60 SDG. The showers and toilets (hole in the ground) are shared, usually one between two rooms. The bathroom is kept locked and can only be opened by the occupant of the relevant room. This limited sharing of bathrooms has the result that they are spotlessly clean. The rooms have no air-conditioning, but the very efficient and high-powered fan in the ceiling makes up for this. The hotel also has a few more deluxe rooms, which include air-con and ensuite bathroom. But, with these costing 200 SDG each, you might be better off sticking with the perfectly comfortable and clean cheaper option. The place is a little tricky to find, since there is no name written on the outside of the building. It is down a small cul-de-sac, with *sheesha* stores on either side.

Marakech (☎ 0122 610 134) is a small and not terribly clean *lokanda* in the market area. Expect to pay 7 SDG for a bed or 15 SDG for a small room.

If you are not on a budget, **Riyad Holiday Hotel** (☎ 0122 425 189 or 0912 303 808) is probably the nicest place to stay in town. This hotel is where the majority of oil workers stay whilst in the city, and is, accordingly, fancy. The furnishings are more lavish than you will find elsewhere. There is a restaurant on the top floor, which offers some decent international food at reasonable prices, as well as the more usual *sha'urma* and burgers (4-5 SDG). You can also get fresh fish here (most commonly Nile perch) for around 20 SDG. Rooms start at 200 SDG for a single and 250 SDG for a double. The hotel offers *sheesha* for 5 SDG.. The hotel is a little way from the town centre, in the direction of Kordofan University.

Close to the cathedral, **Kordofan Hotel** (☎ 0611 823 020 or 0121 195 726) offers comfortable rooms with satellite TV. The staff are friendly and prices are reasonable. A single room with outside toilet costs 69 SDG. A double room costs 92 SDG (with outside toilet and shower) or 139 SDG (for an ensuite). A three-bed ensuite costs 172 SDG. The hotel has a total of 21 rooms. There is a small restaurant in the grounds of the hotel that serves grilled chicken and meat. It isn't always open, though.

Eating and drinking

Inexpensive eating in El-Obeid is not a problem, but don't expect much in the way of variety. Grilled meat, bread, *fuul* and salad are the most popular dishes. El-Obeid is a long way from the Nile, or indeed any water source and, therefore, fish is difficult to find.

The best place to look for cheap eateries is in the marketplace, where *fuul* is ladled out by the bucketload. There are also one or two burger joints in town.

Some of the fancier hotels — such as Riyad Holiday Hotel and Sun Way — offer a more international-style of menu, although prices tend to be high and the quality isn't always great.

DILLING

Dilling pronounced 'Dillenj' — is a wonderful little town on the outskirts of the Nuba Mountains, midway between El-Obeid and Kadugli.

There is a fantastic **African-style souq** in the centre of the town, which is quite distinct from the Islamic *souqs* that you find if you travel further north. Here, you will find oddities such as fried crickets (a particular delicacy

of the Nuba people), dried gourds, the *gongleze* fruit of the *tabaldi* (baobab) tree, sun-dried tomatoes, and hand-woven straw dish coverers. You can spend a really interesting few hours just marvelling at these goods. There is also a **small university** in the town.

Where to sleep and eat

The best way of finding accommodation in the town is to ask about *lokandas* in the market area. One that you might like to try calls itself the **Dilling Arous El-Gibal Hotel** (☎ 0912 230 925). Single rooms, with ensuite, start at 30 SDG, although the price is usually negotiable. A bed in the courtyard outside will cost around 10 SDG. Electricity in Dilling is pretty up-and-down and many places, including the aforementioned *lokanda*, have electricity for only a few hours a day.

There are a few places where you can eat *fuul* and grilled meat, mainly on the edge of the market or around the bus station.

Getting there

Buses for Dilling leave regularly from Salahin bus station on the southern outskirts of El-Obeid. To get to this station, you can either take a mini-bus from the centre of town (costing 1 SDG) or a taxi for between 4 and 5 SDG.

There is no fixed timetable for the buses from Salahin; they simply leave when they are full. To catch one, you must add your name to a list. Once enough people have put their names down, the driver will announce that the bus is ready to depart. Depending on when you are travelling, you may have to wait a few hours for the bus to fill up. A one-way ticket to Dilling costs 15 SDG.

If you don't want to spend time waiting for the bus to fill up, an alternative is to take a taxi, which should cost around 60 SDG. If you can find three other people willing to share the taxi with you, the cost will be the same as the bus, whilst the comfort is significantly greater.

Either way, it takes around two hours to get from El-Obeid to Dilling.

The road leading south from El-Obeid is unexpectedly flat, with the only real distraction being the occasional village of low-lying thatched huts, with their unique conical shape. About an hour before Dilling, however, the road rises slightly and jagged peaks start to break through the uniform terrain. By the time the bus pulls into the town, you will find yourself surrounded by the Nuba Mountains.

KADUGLI

Information on Kadugli is optimistically included here in the hope that the situation in the town improves during the lifetime of this book. At the time of publication, travel to the town was not recommended — skirmishes from an armed rebellion that started in June 2011 continue in the town, and the region is awash with light arms. Before this latest conflict began, Kadugli was a lovely mid-sized town in the Nuba Mountains that was just starting to open up to tourism. The hope is that, once the violence in the area ends, visitors will again be able to appreciate the town's beauty — and see something of its tragic, war-scarred past.

The opening of a new tarmac road between Dilling and Kadugli has halved the time that it takes to travel between the two towns. The journey now takes just two hours instead of four to five.

The eruption of conflict in the town put an end to regular bus services between Dilling and Kadugli. Such services are only just starting to resume.

A bus between the two towns costs 15 SDG and leaves when it is full. You can also take a taxi for around 60 SDG. Again, consider sharing — this will significantly reduce the price.

Direct buses used to run between El-Obeid and Kadugli and may resume in the future. They would generally depart early in the morning. There was even a bus leaving early in the morning from Kadugli all the way back to Khartoum, which operated only on some days of the week. This service has been suspended for the time-being, though.

The scenery between Dilling and Kadugli is enchanting: much greener and more mountainous than the lands further north, and you will quickly see the twisted scrubland start to give way to actual forest.

Kadugli is the capital of South Kordofan and a nice place for appreciating some of the great scenery of the Nuba Mountains proper. There is a lively *souq* to walk around and some of the paths leading up into the mountains afford great views of the town.

Even before the latest fighting, Kadugli was much more affected by the civil war than Dilling, and the signs of war were obvious in the town: many people their missing limbs, eyes or sometimes sanity. When the dust settles on the latest uprising, the tragic scars of war will be just as stark.

Kadugli was also a base for many aid agencies working in the region, many of which had to be air-lifted to safety when the latest troubles began. Gas-guzzling four-wheel drive vehicles were a hallmark of what the town had become. If you want to stay in the town, the best thing to do is ask people in the *souq* for the nearest *lokanda*. For eating purposes, there are a number of cheap places serving *fuul* and grilled meat, particularly around the bus station and edge of the market.

Sudan

Camel ride in the northern deserts - VP

Building new roads in South Sudan - LP

Local Bedouin herder stops for morning *chai* - LA

Fortifications of Omdurman - VP

Elephant sculpture - VP

Strumming the Arabic lute - IS

A fisherman casts his net into the
Red Sea - AO

Sufi child - IS

Left: Moving by
boat in North
Sudan - LA

Serving up *fuul* on the streets of Khartoum - VP

Harsh desert conditions claim the skeleton of a camel - AL

Contemplating life half-way up a pyramid in Karima - VP

Pumping water in a rural village in South Sudan - JW

Sharing dinner with villagers just outside Sennar - VP

The demonic cats of Suakin - VP

Sudanese *mulah* - VP

Typical food at a
Sudanese wedding -VP

Sudanese drinks: *chai*, *chai
bel leban* and *jabana* -VP

Stewing tea - VP

Sudanese food presented
on a *sinaia* - VP

Syrian food - VP

Hanging fish out to dry
in the midday sun on the
shores of Lake Nubia - LA

Sunset over Omdurman - VP

Sunrise over Dinder Park - VP

Traditional village in South Sudan - JW

Sudanese vegetable stall - VP

A Sudanese village near Gedaref - VP

The Third Cataract - AL

Traditional horse and cart transportation - VP

Air-conditioned buses - TS

Amjad - TS

Rickshaws - TS

Boda-bodas - VP

Sufi practitioner - VP

South Sudanese woman - LA

Cooking *khudra*, a spinach-
like stew - JW

North Sudanese wedding - VP

Man in *jalabia* - VP

Tombs in El-Kurru - VP

Kids in
Khartoum - VP

South Sudan
border - BEP

The pyramids at Nuri (p999) - VP

Camels bound for life? - VP

Bird's-eye view of temples in Karima - VP

Ferry to Dongola - VP

Relaxing on the banks of the Nile, Kalagla - VP

Eating camel meat at Souq al-Naaga - VP

Darfur
El-Fasher, El-Geneina, Nyala

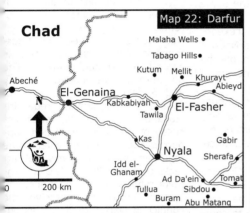

Map 22: Darfur

Chad

Malaha Wells •
Tabago Hills •
Kutum Mellit
Khurayt
Abieyd
Abeché
El-Genaina
Kabkabiyah
El-Fasher
Tawila
Kas Gabir
Nyala Sherafa
Idd el-Ghanam
Ad Da'ein Tomat
Tullua Sibdou
Buram Abu Matang

200 km

Highlights

- Discover a land rarely frequented by tourists.

- Learn about the Fur sultanate at the Ali Dinar Museum in El-Fasher.

- Behold the beauty of Jebel Marra, North Sudan's highest peak.

Given Darfur's multitude of problems, the region is unlikely to feature on the itineraries of most casual visitors to Sudan. In fact, for many, obtaining a visa to the region is notoriously difficult. These days, controls are rigorous throughout Darfur and you are certain to have problems if you try to visit the area without permission. Even United Nations personnel and aid workers have difficulty moving about.

Rules and regulations keep changing as far as obtaining permission goes, so it is best to ask at the Ministry of Humanitarian Affairs (Khartoum 2, south of Qurashi Park) for the latest information. Without a good reason for going to Darfur, your application for permission is likely to be refused — which means that many tourists never get the chance to go there.

The easiest way to secure permission is to be invited to the region by someone already living or working there. Teachers may be able to find a school in Darfur willing to sponsor their applications.

Following the indictment of President Omar al-Bashir for war crimes by the International Criminal Court (ICC) — see page 68 — the government expelled many aid workers and expats from the region in protest.

Many have now been allowed to return. Therefore, coming to Sudan for work purposes may bring you into contact with Darfur, in which case this section will come in useful.

Others who visit Sudan may decide that the trouble of getting to Darfur, coupled with the lack of tourist facilities, means that it is best to give the area a miss.

In terms of security, Darfur is not as safe as many other areas of North Sudan. The low-level conflict still going on there is very real, and civilians continue to get caught up in it. Banditry is rife on the roads, particularly near the Chadian border and between Kordofan and

El-Fasher, and so you are strongly advised against taking the overland route, unless you go as part of an armoured convoy.

Although the United Nations Mission in Sudan (UNMIS) left the country on 9 July 2011, the same day that South Sudan officially gained independence, peacekeeping troops from the United Nations and African Union remain on the ground in Darfur, in a joint operation known as UNAMID.

However, the mission continues to be under-resourced and simply cannot monitor every part of the land area, which is as big as France. If you stick to the three major cities — Nyala (to the south), El-Geneina (to the west) and El-Fasher (to the north) — you should be okay. However, reports continue to come in of lawlessness within the town centres, including armed raids on banks and petrol stations. In the past, rebel groups have also deliberately targeted foreigners, in the belief that forcing them out of Sudan will cut off a valuable source of income for the regime in Khartoum.

Despite efforts by the international community to secure peace in Darfur, many rebels have still not laid down their weapons and fresh outbreaks of violence are common. Check the latest situation with your national embassy to make sure that you do not become an innocent victim of such violence.

UNAMID publishes a very informative monthly magazine about Darfur, including how the problems in the region are being tackled and any cultural events that are taking place. You can find the latest issues of the magazine at: 🖵 unamid.unmissions.org.

UNDERSTANDING DARFUR

There are many misapprehensions about the reasons behind the fighting in Darfur and Western news reports often add to the confusion.

The latest conflict in the region erupted in 2003, when a group of rebels, claiming that the region was being neglected by Khartoum, launched a series of attacks against government targets. The government responded quickly and ferociously with a series of counter-attacks against rebel installations. It has also been accused of providing arms and support to the *janjaweed*, a fearsome mounted militia, to carry out attacks on local villages. The government refutes these allegations.

Many incorrectly perceive the conflict in Darfur to be an extension of the country's 21-year-long north-south civil war, which officially came to an end in 2005. In reality, the conflicts are quite separate, although the rebel forces in the two regions inevitably have connections.

Moreover, the conflict in Darfur is often portrayed as a battle between Arabs in Khartoum and black Africans. Again, this is an incorrect way of viewing things, since many of the rebels in Darfur are themselves of Arabic origin.

There are many different rebel groups operating in the region, each with a slightly different agenda. The spectrum of rebel groups changes all the time. New rebel factions frequently splinter away from larger groups, as upcoming rebel leaders seek to carve out powerbases of their own. Occasionally, rebel groups with similar agendas forge alliances together, in the belief that they stand a better chance of realising their aims if they are united. The shifting composition of rebel groups represents a large-scale power struggle within the region, and is one of the factors that prevents the emergence of a single formidable force that is capable of taking on the government in Khartoum.

The UN, and others, have been pressing for a reduction in the number of rebel groups, since it is easier to negotiate with people who share the same demands. The reality is, though, that many of the rebels have inherently different backgrounds and, therefore, agendas. The UN says that there are still five distinct rebel groups in Darfur, all wielding considerable power: the Sudanese Liberation Army Unity (SLA-Unity), the United Resistance Front, two Sudanese Liberation Movement (SLM) factions — one led by Abdul Wahid and the other by Abdul Shafie — and the Justice and Equality Movement (JEM).

In practice, there are more groups than these five, but they are not generally considered significant.

It is worth mentioning the origins of two of the rebel groups here.

The SLA was established at the end of the 1980s, in response to what was seen as a concerted attempt by the government to 'Islamicise' the area. The make-up of this rebel group is primarily black-African. Since its formation, the group has splintered into several different factions, the most influential of which is probably the one led by Abdul Wahid.

Wahid spent five years living in Paris, where he endured widespread criticism for preferring the Champs Elisées to the wild bush of Darfur. Recently, Wahid has returned to Sudan, where he continues to campaign for the toppling of the National Congress Party (NCP).

Choosing to stay in Paris for so long was not the only controversial decision that Wahid made. In 2008, he opened an office in Israel. This provoked widespread condemnation from people within his own movement, and appeared to validate Khartoum's claims that the rebellion in Darfur was orchestrated by the Jewish state.

JEM has quite different roots. In the 1990s, Hassan al-Turabi, erstwhile ally of President Omar al-Bashir (p65), sought to extend his influence within Darfur by bringing a number of Muslims from the region into the government. When Turabi fell out of favour with Bashir in 1999, his Darfuri cohorts were also expelled from office and went on to form JEM. Most senior JEM members are Arabic, with a strongly Islamic agenda, although some non-Arabs have joined the movement in the belief that it provides the best opportunity for waging war against Khartoum.

Like the SLA, JEM has also splintered into different factions. The most prominent of these is the one led by Khalil Ibrahim, a former lawyer. JEM has been particularly active in targeting oil installations and kidnapping foreign oil workers, to force them out of the region. In May 2008, JEM launched an attack on the capital of Khartoum (p66).

JEM is widely believed to receive backing, including money and arms, from Chad — a claim that the Chadian government refutes.

The Darfur conflict is further complicated by tribal divisions, and many of the units fighting each other have a long history of ethnic rivalry. Some in the international community accuse the government of using this rivalry to spark clashes between different tribes, thereby detracting the rebels from threatening Khartoum.

Many rebel groups have been split along tribal lines. One of the reasons that JEM may have secured backing from Chad is that many of the group's members come from the Zaghawa tribe, which is also the tribe that dominates the Chadian government.

One other dimension of this multifacetted conflict is the way in which competition for increasingly scarce resources has brought rival groups into closer contact with one another. Rapid desertification of the region has had a hand in this.

An unenthusiastic attempt at a peace agreement was attempted in 2005, when Mini Minawi, who leads a faction of the SLM, was much-applauded by the international community for attempting to make peace with the government. But other rebel groups refused to sign and, at the end of 2010, Minawi tore up the agreement and fled to South Sudan, where he continues to oppose Khartoum. Recently, Minawi has aligned himself with Wahid in a bid to bring down the government.

EL-FASHER

The large market town of El-Fasher is the capital of North Darfur. In former times, it was an important trading post for camel caravans crossing the deserts between the east and the west.

Sultan Abdul Rahman al-Rashed founded the town in the 18th century as the capital of the Fur sultanate, and it remained as such until 1916, when the province was integrated into the rest of Sudan by the British (p54). The name 'El-Fasher' is actually derived from the Arabic for royal courtyard.

El-Fasher's former importance has now faded and, surrounded by bleak desert, the region has become fairly poor. These days, the town is best known as the headquarters of UNAMID.

Such increased interest from the United Nations and the African Union, as well as a scattering of other humanitarian organisations, may actually save the city from terminal decline. Already, the town is showing signs of revival, with one or two restaurants gaining prominence in the area.

Nonetheless, those who work in El-Fasher still complain that there remains precious little to do in the evenings, advising those who come to live here to bring an ample supply of DVDs.

For sightseeing opportunities, the best thing to do is to make for the **Ali Dinar Museum**, which is housed in the old palace of the Fur sultanate. The museum is quite small (you probably don't need much more than half-an-hour to walk round it), but it contains a fascinating collection of memorabilia from the era of the Fur Sultanate. Look out for the two large drums made of copper as you enter — they would be used to declare war or to announce a death sentence.

In the centre of El-Fasher, not far from El-Naga arena, the **Council for Development Through Cultural Reality** holds regular evenings of poetry, art exhibitions, theatre shows and musical concerts.

For eating, the best places to try are **Marsland** (well-known for its pizzas and also does a decent burger and chips) and **Roast House**, which arguably serves the best fried chicken you will find in the whole of Darfur. Both restaurants are located in the centre of town.

Decent accommodation options in the town are still fairly limited, but the World Food Programme (WFP) office is sometimes able to offer a bed for the night. Alternatively, you could try one of the grubby *lokandas* in the market.

How to get there

There are regular flights to El-Fasher from Khartoum (p95). Alternatively, if you work for an NGO, you may be able to secure a flight on one of the flights to the region that are organised by the WFP.

NYALA AND JEBEL MARRA

Overshadowed by the magnificent volcanic ridge of Jebel Marra, Nyala is set in truly wonderful surroundings. Once a popular destination for trekkers intent on clambering up the slopes of the nearby mountains, the town now has that same discoloured look that other parts of Darfur now have: scarred by years of fighting in the region.

Like other major towns in western Sudan, Nyala has a large population of foreign aid workers, and consequently there have been gradual improvements in the town.

In more peaceful days, Nyala was a popular base from which to explore the lower slopes of the nearby Jebel Marra. These days, obtaining permission to do anything in the way of trekking is likely to prove impossible. The area surrounding Nyala remains highly volatile and it is not recommended that you travel very far outside the main town. Nyala may yet be restored as a popular tourist destination, but first a lasting peace must return to the region — something that does not look as though it is about to happen in the near future.

The **Marra Plateau** is vast, covering more than 12,000 km, reaching all the way from the Tabago Hills north of El-Fasher to the Tebella Plateau south of Zallingei, near the Chadian border. Jebel Marra itself, the second-highest peak in Sudan,

lies between Nyala and Zallingei. It is an old volcano, widely thought to be extinct, although some experts have recently suggested that it may just be dormant. The wildlife of the region has sadly been depleted by war and poaching, but some animals still remain — including baboons, gazelles and a variety of birds. The scenery of the region is stunning and, hopefully, when the fighting dies down, visitors to Darfur will be able to properly appreciate it again.

Good and cheap sleeping options are extremely limited in Nyala, and the hotels that have recently opened there are very expensive. **Coral Hotel** (🖳 www.coral-international.com), which has branches in both Khartoum and Port Sudan, will shortly open in Nyala.

How to get there

The easiest way of getting to Nyala from Khartoum is to fly (p95), but you can also take the train that runs once a month between the two places. The train journey takes between four and five days. Departure times change frequently, and you should consult the local train station for the latest details.

EL-GENEINA

El-Geneina is a small and dusty town some 50 km from Sudan's border with Chad. Whilst other major towns in the region have prospered from the presence of UN and humanitarian workers, with new buildings being thrown up and new restaurants opening, El-Geneina remains a rather despondent place in which to be. This is despite the large presence of relief workers in the town.

Its most notable characteristic is the large number of refugee camps that engulf it, providing shelter for

Darfur

those who have fled the fighting in Darfur and across the border, in Chad.

Nonetheless, El-Geneina does display some of the hallmarks of a destination for expat workers. There is a swimming pool within the complex of the World Food Programme. Use of the pool is at the discretion of the head of the WFP office in the town. Expat workers can usually use the pool for free, but local Sudanese are not permitted access to the pool

Good restaurants in El-Geneina are still a distant vision. If you want to eat out, your best bet is to try one of the grubby stalls in the market area, which serve the usual selection of *fuul*, *asida* and *agashay*.

South Sudan
Juba, Malakal and Wau

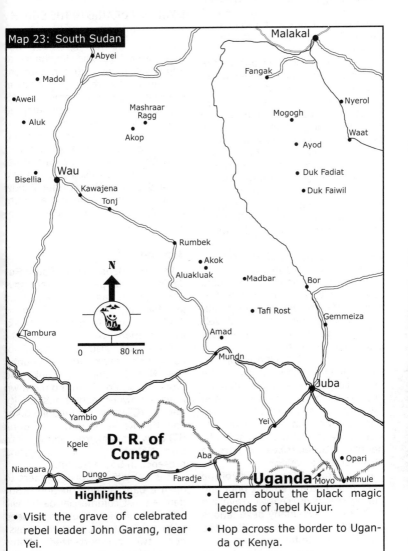

Map 23: South Sudan

Malakal
Abyei
Fangak
Madol
Nyerol
Aweil
Mashraar Ragg
Mogogh
Waat
Aluk
Akop
Ayod
Wau
Duk Fadiat
Bisellia
Kawajena
Duk Faiwil
Tonj
Rumbek
Akok
Aluakluak
Madbar
Bor
N
Tafi Rost
Gemmeiza
Tambura
Amad
0   80 km
Mundn
Juba
Yambio
Yei
D. R. of Congo
Kpele
Opari
Niangara
Aba
Dungo
Faradje
Uganda
Moyo
Nimule

Highlights

- Visit the grave of celebrated rebel leader John Garang, near Yei.

- Experience the vibrant nightlife of Juba.

- Learn about the black magic legends of Jebel Kujur.

- Hop across the border to Uganda or Kenya.

- Meet the native tribes of South Sudan.

On July 9, 2011, after decades of conflict with Khartoum, South Sudan finally gained its independence. Celebrations to mark the occasion were held in both the North and the South. But, amidst all the rejoicing, there lay the tacit acceptance that some of the biggest challenges for the world's newest country still lie ahead.

South Sudan is now one of the weakest and most undeveloped countries in the world. Outside of Juba, the country lacks basic infrastructure. Roads are in a terrible condition, and in rural areas access to basic amenities (such as health care and education) is difficult.

Many of the essential conditions for a functioning state are still not in place. Security forces lack training and equipment. Countless laws and procedures are still not in place, creating ambiguity for those that want to conduct business in the country. The media industry continues to look rather threadbare.

NGOs and humanitarian workers have been pouring into South Sudan in order to help the country get on to its feet, and things are developing at lightening speed, but there is still a long way to go.

Travel in South Sudan is far less safe than in the North. Many people in the country have known nothing but war for most of their lives, and the region is still awash with guns. Banditry is rife on many roads outside of the main cities and sporadic fighting between tribes can flare up at a moment's notice.

Road infrastructure outside of the main urban areas remains poor and during the rainy season travelling by bus or car to many destinations is simply not possible. Often the only option is to fly.

South Sudan is classified by the United Nations as a non-family destination, which to an extent defines the profile of foreigners that come to work in the country. Expats will generally be young and unattached, and you will see few children accompanying them.

LIVING & WORKING IN THE SOUTH

South Sudan is very much a country-in-the-making. It has therefore not yet had the chance to implement many of the investment and labour laws that are in place in the North (p186). In some instances, legislation has been adopted from the laws of the North. In other cases, the regulatory environment represents an amalgamation of British Common Law and tribal customary practices. There is still a great deal of ambiguity about how things should be done in the South, but this should become clearer going forwards.

Banking

Prior to independence, South Sudan's banking operations were governed by the Bank of Sudan based in Khartoum. Now, the Bank of South Sudan is in charge of banking operations.

There are also a number of commercial banks in the county. The Nile Commercial Bank and Ivory Bank are both homegrown privately-owned institutions. Equity Bank (💻 www.equitybank.co.ke) and the Kenya Commercial Bank (💻 www.kcbbankgroup.com), both from Nairobi, also have a strong presence in South Sudan.

It is not difficult for foreigners to open a bank account in South Sudan — most commercial banks will offer this service. You simply need to turn up with a copy of your passport, two passport-sized photos and a letter of introduction from the company or organisation that you are working for.

Communication

TELEPHONES

Your choice of phone package depends on whether you plan to just use it within South Sudan, or might need to use it outside the country.

Viva Cell offers cheaper rates than other mobile phone providers. However, it only works within South Sudan and is useless if you take it anywhere else, including to the North.

MTN (⌨ www.mtn.com) offers very good coverage in most of the main towns in South Sudan, and works outside the country.

Zain (⌨ www.zain.com) is also available, although its coverage in the country is not as good.

Sudani, the North Sudan provider, no longer operates in the South.

Gemtel is a private company in South Sudan that was given permission by Uganda to use its dialing code +256. However, there was some dispute about the legality of this and so, following independence, the company decided to make the switchover to the South Sudan dialing code. This switchover was happening as we were going to press and will be completed by December 15, 2011. Gemtel phones do not work outside the country.

You can pick up a SIM card for your phone from street vendors or from official offices of the phone company that you want to go with. On the street, the SIM card will cost between 10 and 15 SSP, whilst it will cost around 5 SSP if you buy it directly from the telecoms provider.

Top-up cards are widely available from shops and street vendors, in denominations of 2, 5, 10 and 20 SSP.

SUDAN COUNTRY CODE

On October 1, 2011 South Sudan got its very own country code. To dial the country from abroad, you should no longer use the prefix for North Sudan telephone numbers (+249) but the newer country code +211.

INTERNET

Internet in South Sudan is still very under-developed and it is not widely available outside of the main urban centres. Even within cities, it can be incredibly slow and not really suitable for heavy-duty streaming. Because of this, voice communication software such as Skype does not always work

ADSL connections are not available in the South and those that want to get an Internet connection usually rely on dongles from the main mobile phone providers (Zain or MTN), which plug into your USB port.

Internet cafés are available throughout the main cities in South Sudan, but surprisingly expensive. Expect to pay at least 10 SSP per hour.

Many of the larger hotels also have wireless internet, although they are now always willing to let non-residents make use of it.

POSTAL SERVICE

There is presently no door-to-door delivery service in South Sudan and it is not yet possible to open an individual PO Box with the local Post Office. In fact, in many areas Post Offices still do not exist.

If you want to send a package to Sudan, your best option is to use DHL (⌨ www.dhl.com) and TNT (⌨ www.tnt.com). This assumes that the delivery end point is Juba. If you want to send anything elsewhere in South Sudan, then you are better off using the delivery channels of a large company or organisation that has operations in the South.

Visas and permits

South Sudan has opened a number of representations around the world, which are responsible for issuing visas for entry into the country. Where there is no representation in your home country, it may be possible to get the visa through an embassy of a neighbouring country instead, such as that of Uganda. The Interior Ministry has also said that arrangements are being made to allow the issuance of the visa at certain border points, although how this will work remains to be seen.

The standard visa is valid for a period of 30 days and is for a single entry. If you want to stay longer, or you want to apply to work in the country, you should speak to your local South Sudan representative office about the latest requirements.

If you find an organisation that is prepared to employ you in South Sudan, it is usually not difficult to get permission to stay in the country on a work visa. However, the work visa is generally tied to a particular employer and, if you change employer, you will need to apply for another one.

Opening a business

There are countless opportunities for business investment in South Sudan, and the government is actively encouraging foreign private-sector money to help develop the region.

As with the North, the government is prepared to give a better deal for those that are committed to long-term investment and are actually prepared to introduce some lasting benefit to the country. Those that are simply planning to import goods to the country may face high levels of tax and other costs.

South Sudan's Chamber of Commerce (☎ 0955 122 462; @ info@ s s c h a m b e r - c o m m e r c e . o r g ; 🖥 www.sschamber-commerce.org) in Juba can give you more details about latest requirements.

If you need any printing services, then there are a couple of options:

Artzone (☎ 0977 120 454 or 0977 251 148) is a small Kenyan-owned printing house in Juba. It can supply stickers, logos, T-shirts and business cards.

Afri Star has been running for longer and is the only offset printing press in Juba. It offers printing for manuals, books, posters and business cards. The place is owned by Nadi Kudsi (☎ 0957 104 640). The printer himself is an Indian chap called Babu (☎ 0957 189 231).

Schools and family

The UN has designated Juba a non-family destination. You will not find any schools of international-standard here, and few workers choose to bring their family here.

If you do have a family and plan to work here, then you could consider basing your family in nearby Kampala or Nairobi — where there are a number of international schools — whilst you work in South Sudan.

Media

If you are in Juba, you can listen to the BBC World Service by tuning into 88.2 FM.

The most popular newspapers in the South are the Citizen and the Juba Post. The Khartoum Monitor has recently relocated to the South from the North and is now circulated here.

You can also find Kenyan papers, the Nation being the most popular.

Newspapers are usually sold by street vendors at bus stations or in the markets.

How to find a job

At the moment, it is not all that difficult for a foreigner to find a job in South Sudan. Vast quantities of development and investment money is now flowing into the country, and this is creating all sorts of different opportunities.

Inevitably, the most common jobs are with NGOs, who are looking for people pretty much all the time. To find this kind of job, consider approaching NGOs directly. The UN also has a large operation in the country.

The need for language teachers — especially English — is also growing.

Following independence, South Sudan announced that English will become the official language of the country. Pressure is mounting to discourage the use of Arabic, which is widely spoken in Juba but carries with it the unwelcome reminder of domination by the North. Since being unable to speak English is likely to block many Sudanese from certain jobs, the desire to learn English is only going to grow. The difficulty, though, is how to earn a decent salary from this profession, since many of those that want to learn English do not have the means to pay. The trick is to find a charity or NGO willing to offer courses.

French teachers can always call in at the French Cultural Centre in Juba, which is located on the University campus.

Accommodation

Decent rental accommodation is expensive in South Sudan. There are currently no estate agents to help you find a place to live, although some of the larger organisations based in the South offer this service for their staff.

When flat-hunting, the best thing to do is speak to others living in the region or to consult the Jubalicious Google Group (⌨ groups.google.com/group/jubalicious).

JUBA

Juba was founded around 1830, close to Gondokoro (the southernmost outpost of the Ottoman Empire). Many explorers, such as Samuel Baker, set off from Gondokoro in search of the source of the river Nile.

As Khartoum has been galloping forwards in an orgy of development since the signing of the peace agreement in 2005, Juba has been mimicking this progress in the South. The result is an African city that feels modern, fresh and exciting — but one that is still stranded in a wilderness of shoddy infrastructure, tribal rivalry and deep-rooted poverty.

Whilst humanitarian and UN workers have been leaving North Sudan, they retain a strong presence in the South. It is this, plus Juba's relative remoteness (it is surrounded by poor roads in an area that is still economically weak), that has pushed prices in the city up so dramatically. Both food and accommodation can be expensive.

Prices are starting to fall slowly, though. This is partially due to increased competition and partially because of better transport connections to the neighbouring countries of Uganda and Kenya.

South Sudan

South Sudan

Map 24: West Juba

HAI AMARAT

← Bor

HAI KUWAIT

HAI SORA

Acacia Village

Old Customs

49
Ⅲ 70
69 Ⅲ
51
76
61

71 Ⅲ

52

1 Ⅱ
2 Ⅱ

2

3

4

New Customs

Yei →

South Sudan

0 250 m

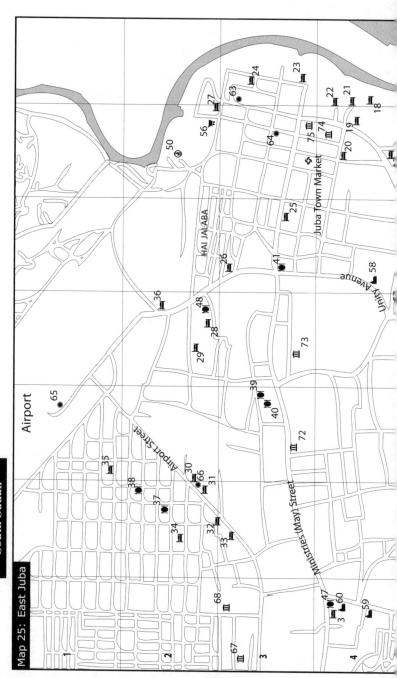

Map 25: East Juba

South Sudan

Airport

Airport Street

Ministries (May) Street

Unity Avenue

Juba Town Market

HAI JALABA

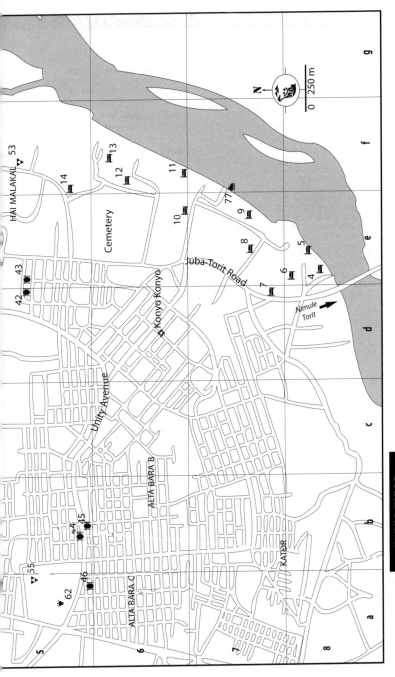

Juba

Where to sleep 🛏
1. Jebel Lodge *b3 [p270]*
2. Rock City *b3 [p270]*
3. South Sudan Hotel *a4 [p272]*
4. Da Vinci's Lodge *e8 [p273]*
5. Juba Bridge Hotel *e8 [p273]*
6. Heron Camp *e8 [p273]*
7. Saalam *d7 [p273]*
8. Bros Camp *e7 [p273]*
9. Intra Africa *e7 [p273]*
10. Civicon *e6 [p273]*
11. Sunflower Camp *f6 [p273]*
12. Mango Camp *f6 [p273]*
13. Afex Camp *f6 [p273]*
14. Bedouin Lodge *f5 [p273]*
15. Quality *f4 [p272]*
16. Star *g5 [p273]*
17. New York Hotel *f4 [p272]*
18. Akok Camp *g4 [p272]*
19. Juba Grand *f4 [p272]*
20. South Sudan II *f4 [p272]*
21. Raymok Hotel *g4 [p272]*
22. River Nile Residence *g4 [p272]*
23. Hamza *g3 [p272]*
24. Summer Palace *g3 [p272]*
25. Paradise *e3 [p272]*
26. New Sudan Hotel *e3 [p272]*
27. Juba Raha *f2 [p272]*
28. Logali House *d2 [p272]*
29. Shalom *d2 [p272]*
30. Olympic Hotel *c2 [p272]*
31. Glory Hotel *b2 [p272]*
32. Panache *b2 [p272]*
33. Paradiso *b3 [p272]*
34. Dolce Vita *b2 [p272]*
35. Asmara *c1 [p272]*
36. Sahara Hotel *d2 [p272]*

Where to eat 🍴
37. Arkel *b2 [p272]*
38. Airport View Motel *b2 [p272]*
39. Mai Thai *c3 [p272]*
40. Home and Away *c3 [p272]*
41. Central Pub *e3 [p272]*
42. Spice 'n' herbs *d5 [p273]*
43. Queen of Sheeba *e5 [p273]*
44. Wonderful Chinese *b5 [p273]*
45. International *b5 [p273]*
46. Shanghai *a5 [p273]*
47. Millennium *a4 [p272]*
48. Havana *d2 [p272]*
49. Kololo Bar *g3 [p270]*

What to see 👁
50. Central Equatoria Nursery *f2 [p272]*
51. John Garang's Memorial *g4 [p270]*

52. Jebel Kujur *a3 [p270]*

What to do ⛹
53. Football stadium *f5 [p273]*
54. Nyakuron Cultural Centre *g5 [p271]*
55. French Cultural Centre *a5 [p273]*

Where to shop 🛒
56. JIT Supermarket *f2 [p272]*

Religion ⛪
57. All Saints Cathedral *d4 [p272]*
58. St Joseph's *e4 [p272]*
59. SIL Compound (Juba International Fellowship) *a4 [p272]*
60. Juba Christian Centre *a4 [p272]*
61. Seventh Day Adventist Church *f3 [p270]*

Education and courses 🎓
62. Juba University *a5 [p273]*

Tour operators ●
63. Muthaiga Travel *g3 [p272]*
64. Charleston Travel *f3 [p272]*

Car hire ●
65. Juba Interlink Services *c1 [p272]*
66. MCAC Car Hire *b2 [p272]*

Embassies 🏛
67. EU Compound (EU, Dutch, French and British Embassies) *a3 [p272]*

NGOs and official buildings 🏛
68. USAID *a3 [p272]*
69. Main Ministries *g3 [p270]*
70. National Assembly *g3 [p270]*
71. World Food Programme *a2 [p270]*
72. UNDP *c3 [p272]*
73. UNICEF *d3 [p272]*
74. Police headquarters *f4 [p272]*
75. Prison *f3 [p272]*

Transport 🚌 ⛴
76. Local and long-distance buses *g4 [p270]*
77. Port (ferries to Malakal and Kosti) *f7 [p273]*

Other ●
78. South Sudan TV *g5 [p271]*

South Sudan

In stark contrast to Khartoum, Juba's nightlife is positively buzzing, and this is one of the reasons why many people living in the North like to escape to the city for periodic breaks. Alcohol is completely legal in the South and a number of nightclubs and restaurants stay open well beyond 11 pm.

Remember that Juba is not as safe as many cities in North Sudan. There have been reports of raids on foreign-owned camps, which has led to periodic camp closures and occasional curfews being put in place. There have also been some incidents of *boda-boda* drivers being shot at night, which is why many of them prefer not to work much after 7 pm or so.

Visiting the town on foot during the day is usually fine, but it is not recommended to walk at night. After dark, you really need to have your own vehicle or to find someone who can give you a lift — there is a big lack of taxis in the city, and *boda-boda* drivers usually only work during the day.

As for any large city, the usual precautions apply when visiting Juba. Do not display signs of excessive wealth, lock cars and houses when not in use, and take care when walking in urban areas, especially at night.

Lying on the banks of the Nile, in close proximity to the Ugandan and Kenyan borders, Juba has developed into an important trading centre. Since the arrival of peace, trade has picked up along the Nile and cargo ships regularly travel down from Kosti in the North. Merchants from Uganda and Kenya are also starting to return to the city.

Tour companies

Charleston Travel (☎ 0957 236 676; @ info@charleston.co.ke; 🖳 www.charleston.co.ke), a Kenyan travel agency, has a branch in Juba's town centre, in the old KCB building not far from the Sun Air offices. The agency can help arrange hotel bookings, car hire and flight reservations.

Muthaiga Travel, a Nairobi-based tour operator, has offices in Juba (☎ +882 164 333 2622/5350 or 0122 204 515 or 0126 761 775 or 0955 117 903 or 0927 314 195; @ mtljuba@yahoo.co.uk; 🖳 www.muthaigatravel.com) and can help organise safari tours in South Sudan, as well as in Uganda, Kenya and Tanzania. Unusually for a company in Juba, you don't have to pay cash — you can simply give your credit card details and payment will go through Nairobi.

Andrew Belcher (☎ 0955 213 730 or +254 722 515 498 or 0977 114 824; @ andrewbelcher@hotmail.com or andrew@ssasltd.com), the manager of Bedouin Lodge, can help organise rafting trips, overland safaris and aerial excursions.

Shopping

Juba has a number of open-air markets that are worth visiting whilst in the city. **Old Customs**, not far from the central bus station, used to be the main market of Juba, but it has recently been downsized to make way for an expansion of Juba University.

The market sells non-perishable items (including clothes, plasticware, buckets, cleaning products and some toiletries) as well as a good selection of fruit and vegetables (onions, tomatoes, cabbages, bananas, pineapples, guavas and mangoes). Many products from Uganda and Kenya are sold here; these are becoming easier to find and cheaper as trade routes to the south improve.

Many of the traders that had to move as a result of the downsizing of the market have now relocated to **New Customs**, otherwise known as 'Jebel Market', which is on the outskirts of town, not far from the slopes of Jebel Kujur. This market is now bigger than Old Customs, but it is also better structured and laid out.

Closer to the river, **Konyo Konyo** is particularly noted for its fish, meat, fruit and vegetables. Most hardware items can be found in Konyo Konyo, along with clothing and toiletry stalls.

Juba Town market, in the centre of the city, is smaller and easier to navigate than the other markets. However, it also has a smaller range of products than can be found elsewhere.

One of the best **supermarkets** for expats is JIT, which sells everything from household appliance to imported foodstuffs.

If you want to take back with you some **traditional artefacts** from South Sudan, look out for the Roots Project. This is a charity that has been set up to help women earn a living through traditional arts and crafts. Products include jewellery, pottery, and embroidery. Some of the things that these women produce are truly beautiful and not at expensive — plus, by buying through them, you will be supporting a local culture that over the past decades has struggled so hard to survive. Anyieth (☎ 0955 235 806) is the woman that co-ordinates the Roots Project in Juba. Their showroom is located in the Nimra Talata area of the city, behind the basketball court. Look out for the orange structure with a thatched roof.

Another women's self-help group is Lulu Works, which is not far from the JIT supermarket, opposite a mosque. The women produce a range of **natural products** known as Lulu Life, which are sold in stores and supermarkets throughout the city. It is also possible to visit their workshop and buy the products there. They are happy to receive visitors. Eunice (☎ 0913 551 962) is the manager.

There are currently no **bookshops** in Juba. The best thing to do, if you need some fresh reading material, is to find a fellow expat to swap with. Alternatively, **Juba University** has a huge library, which is partially stocked by the Books For Sudan project (🖵 booksforsudan. soasunion.org). This is organised through the School of Oriental and African Studies (SOAS), part of the University of London.

Jebel Lodge has a book corner where books can be exchanged, but it is pretty small.

What to do

Social gatherings

As with Khartoum, social life in Juba very much revolves around the expat community, which regularly organises events and activities. If you want to get involved in such events, the best thing to do is to hook up with your fellow expats once in the city.

There is a **Google Group** called Jubalicious (🖵 groups.google.com/group/jubalicious), which often lists events that have been organised by other expats and provides a forum for foreigners in the city to meet one another. You need to be accepted as a member of the group, though.

Cultural events

Nyakuron Cultural Centre (☎ 0922 214 447 or 0122 747 960 or 0977 239 051 or 0977 185 943;

South Sudan

@ nyakuronculturalcenter@yahoo.com), just across from South Sudan TV, regularly hosts music events and cultural shows, such as the **Miss South Sudan beauty** contest that takes place in November or December every year. The centre's conference centre can hold up to 250 people, whilst the outside grounds can hold more than 15,000. The centre also has a large **cinema**, which occasionally screens films in English. The seats are comfortable, but unfortunately there is no air-conditioning. It also occasionally hosts **film festivals**. There are some **pool tables** that you can use at the centre.

The **French Cultural Centre**, within the campus of Juba University, also occasionally hosts cultural events and film screenings.

Regular **concerts and shows** are put on once a month by Words and Artists Pictures (WAPI), which supports local artists. Performers have to come from either North or South Sudan. The group has a dedicated Facebook page, where you can find more information about upcoming shows. The South Sudan Artist Association (SSAA) — southsudanartists.org — is also trying to promote local artists and details of events that they organise are usually available on their website.

POOL

Pool tables are available at the **Nyakuron Cultural Centre**, **Da Vinci Lodge** (p289) **Panache** (p284) and **International Restaurant** (p293).

SPORT

A number of the larger hotels offer sports facilities. The UN's offices in Juba also have sports facilities that expats who are working in the city can use. To make use of these facilities, you simply need to provide an ID card from your organisation or your private ID. You also need your own gear for doing these sports.

Tennis can be played at Acacia Village (p282) or the UN compound.

You can **swim** at Acacia Village (p282) and Jebel Lodge (p282). Swimming in the Nile can be dangerous. If you do so, you risk contracting a water-bourne infection, being carried away by the strong current or becoming a crocodile's dinner.

There is a large, fully air-conditioned **gym** at the UN compound. **Aerobics with barbell stretching** takes place there every Monday and Friday, between 6.30 and 7.30 pm.

Many of the larger hotels also have gyms. These are largely reserved for guests, but some may be prepared to let non-residents use them for a small fee. Try Jebel Lodge (p282) or Civicon Oasis Camp (p291).

The UN offices in Juba have **basketball courts**, **volleyball courts** and a new two-kilometre **running track**.

Touch rugby and **ultimate frisbee** usually take place at the UN compound once a week.

The **Hash House Harriers jogging club** organises runs every Saturday evening, from around 5.30 pm. The runs usually end with drinks at someone's house. Details of where the runs take place are posted on the Jubalicious Google Group.

NILE CRUISES

A popular activity is to take a **cruise on the Nile**. The government restricts how far up and down the river you can go, so if you do take a boat out yourself, without knowing exactly where the limits lie, you could have problems. There is a boat available for rent at Da Vinci Lodge (p289). You can arrange for lunch and drinks to be taken on board.

LIVE MUSIC AND DANCE

Ethiopian dancing and singing takes place every evening at Juba Bridge Hotel (p289), and nightly at Star Hotel (p285).

There is **live music** every Wednesday and Thursday at Mango Camp (p290). African bands play at Rock City (p282) in the evenings between Wednesday and Saturday.

DANCE CLASSES

If you want to dance **salsa**, then both De'Havana (p292) and Natos Lounge Bar & Grill (p293) hold regular sessions.

MASSAGE, BEAUTY AND SPA

If you want a **massage**, there is a Kenyan woman in the city that comes highly recommended by expats. Her name is Esther (☎ 0977 127 825 or 0977 127 824). She is available for house-calls and an hour's massage will cost 90 SSP. She also does other beauty treatments, like haircuts, waxing, nails, and makeup. She is always very busy and you often have to make a booking quite a bit in advance.

Courses

Regular **Arabic** courses, catering for all levels, are run at Juba University.

For **French** courses, there is a branch of the French Cultural Centre located on university campus, which runs courses from beginner through to advanced. Thirty hours of teaching, spread over 10 weeks, costs 150 SSP. University students

pay a reduced rate of just 90 SSP. Each 10-week courses constitutes one unit. There are four units for the beginner stage, four for the intermediate and two for the advanced. At the end of each stage, a certificate is provided. Once all stages have been successfully completed, a diploma from France is awarded.

Where to worship

Juba has a healthy mix of religions and faiths. As one might expect for the capital of South Sudan, there is a large **Christians** community in the city. The major denominations are **Catholic** and **Anglican**, but recently many others have started appearing in the city. There are many **Muslims** in the city, too.

The churches in the city usually hold services in three different languages — one in English, one in Arabic and one in a tribal dialect — so you should check the appropriate time before turning up.

One of the hippest churches to go to is the **Juba Christian Centre (JCC)**, which is located in Bulluk, on the road that joins Ministries Street with Juba University, just behind South Sudan Hotel. This church has a large, youthful congregation. Sermons are often accompanied by a lively choir, a great band and much dancing and clapping. Sunday services take place at 8.30 am (for English) and 11 am (for Arabic). You should go early if you want a good seat — most people just sit outside on plastic chairs, since the interior becomes so packed.

The Seventh-Day Adventist Church (SDA) is located just north of Old Customs market. Services are mostly in English and Arabic. The church also runs bible study sessions on Saturdays from 9.30 to 11.30 am.

St Josephs is a small church close to the centre of town, which is particularly popular with expats. It is on the main road, in the compound of the Arch Dioceses of Juba. On Sunday, there are three services — the tribal language of Bari at 8 am, English at 10 am and Arabic at 11.30 am.

All Saints Cathedral, an Anglican church, is located at the roundabout in Hai Cinema, next to the Petronas petrol station on the road to Malakia. It is a relatively big building on a very big compound. On Sunday, Arabic services take place at 9 am, English at 11 am and Zande at 1 pm.

St Teresa Cathedral, a Catholic church, is on a hill in the middle of Kator, a residential district. Services are in Bari, Arabic and English.

Juba International Fellowship meets every Sunday evening at 5.15 pm at the SIL Compound near Juba University, for worship, prayer and Bible study.

Jehova Witnesses can worship in the Kingdom Hall that is just next to the Nyakuron Cultural Centre.

For **Mormons**, there is a Church of Jesus Christ of Latter day Saints near Rock City.

For Muslims, there are **mosques** all over town. A particularly high number are concentrated in the town centre.

What to see

In the centre of town, not far from Old Customs Market, is the grave of the celebrated rebel leader **John Garang** (p64). For a man who was so influential in Sudanese politics, the burial site is rather disappointing: a fairly flimsy structure, nothing like the proper mausoleums you might find commemorating the lives of other such men. However, if you spend a moment talking to the men that stand guard over the grave, you will quickly discover just how revered the man still is in the South.

Heading out of Juba, on the road that leads towards Yei, is **Rock City**. This town is worth visiting for the local mountain, **Jebel Kujur**, that overshadows it. If you climb a little way up this mountain, you get some fantastic panoramic views of the area. According to tribal tradition, Jebel Kujur is an ancient site steeped in black magic

Here you find a number of stone quarries, where local villagers are digging for stones in order to lay on the road.

Along the banks of the Nile, not far from Juba Town, you will find the Central Equatoria Nursery. It is a very nice place to come and relax, and you can also buy seedlings and shrubs there.

Internet spots

Many of the larger hotels have wireless internet for their guests, although they are not always keen for non-residents to use the service.

There are numerous internet cafés scattered throughout the city, especially in Juba Town, but the price is not cheap: 10-15 SSP usually buys you an hour.

Nyakuron Cultural Centre has a fast internet café, as well as photocopiers and printers.

Central Pub has a small internet café attached, which costs 10 SSP per hour.

How to get there

There are regular **flights** to Juba from Khartoum in North Sudan and from Nairobi (Kenya) and Entebbe (Uganda). There are no direct flights from Europe or America to Juba — you usually have to change in one of these other places.

South Sudan

The most popular airlines for flights to Juba are:

- **Feeder Airlines** (🏠 Behind Nile Commercial Bank, Juba Town; ☎ 0912 865 397 or 0918 266 955; @ feederpride@yahoo.com; 🖥 feederairlines.com).

- **Sudan Airways** (☎ 0187 011 000; 🖥 www.sudanair.com).

- **Sun Air** (🏠 Amin Mohamed Building, opposite KCB Bank, Juba Town; ☎ 0126 189 918 or 0121 127 856; 🖥 www.sunairgroup.com).

- **Fly 540** (☎ +254 722 540 540 or +254 733 540 540; @ info@fly540.com; 🖥 www.fly540.com).

- **Marsland Aviation** (☎ 0183 289 618/19; 🖥 www.marsland-avi.com).

- **Air Uganda** (☎ 0977 153 912; @ info@air-uganda.com; 🖥 www.air-uganda.com).

- **748 Air Services** (☎ 0955 079 662 or 0977 102 833; @ sales@748airservices.com; 🖥 www.748airservices.com).

- **Jet Link** (☎ +254 208 275 31/4; @ admin@jetlink.co.ke; 🖥 www.jetlink.co.ke).

- **Kenya Airways** (🖥 www.kenya-airways.com).

- **Eagle Air** (☎ 0977 102 991/2; @ reservations@eagleair-ug.com; 🖥 www.eagleair-ug.com).

Regular **buses** also travel between Juba and Kampala in Uganda. Some buses even go as far as Nairobi in Kenya, but via Kampala — it is not yet safe to travel across the Kenyan border. A bus to Kampala takes 12 hours and costs around 100 SSP. The journey to Nairobi takes 30 hours and costs 150 SSP. Juba's long-distance bus station is in Customs Market. You can simply turn up at the market and buy a ticket. Buses for Kenya and Uganda usually leave early in the morning.

There are growing number of companies that serve these destinations. Two of the more comfortable and reliable ones for travelling to Uganda and Kenya are Kampala Coach and Nation Dit.

Coach companies are starting to expand their operations in the South, and it is now possible to travel from Juba to Nimule, Yei, Rumbek and Wau.

Due to persistent insecurity on the roads, it is not recommended to travel overland to North Sudan, and no commercial coach currently runs there. Besides safety concerns, the poor condition of roads running north make travel in this direction exceedingly difficult.

It is, however, possible to travel by **riverboat** between Juba and Kosti. Simply turn up at the docks and try to negotiate passage with one of the cargo ships there — expect to pay between 100-200 SSP for the trip, which takes around two weeks.

How to get around

Juba is not an easy place to get around in without your own transport. Not only is the city fairly spread out, but the United Nations advises against doing much in the way of walking, for safety reasons.

The most convenient way to get around the city is to take a motorbike taxi (***boda-boda***). This will take you to most places in the city for around 5 SSP. Travelling from downtown Juba to Rock City will cost around 15 SSP.

In terms of safety, *boda-boda* drivers can be quite variable. If you are a little bit uneasy about tearing through the streets of Juba on the back of a motobike, without wearing a helmet, ask the driver to take things easy. They are usually quite obliging.

If you're going to be in the city for any length of time, the best thing to do is find a *boda-boda* driver that you trust and store his number on your phone, so that you can call him up whenever you need a lift.

Boda-boda drivers, though, do not generally like to work after nightfall. If you are going to be coming back late, you should either take your own car or to arrange a lift with someone else.

A **minibus** network also runs throughout the town. However, minibuses are not able to go everywhere in the city. For example, they can't go up to the airport or along Ministries Street.

It is not possible to hail a **taxi** in the city, although there are a few taxi companies that now operate in Juba. Simply call them to arrange a time that you would like to be picked up, although prices are high, especially at night (a charge of 80 SSP for a short trip in town is not unusual).

Juba Transporters Ltd. (☎ 0955 305 254 or 0772 335 942; @ kaka.dennis6@gmail.com), run by a Ugandan, is fairly reliable.

Other drivers that are recommended by expats living in Juba include **Patrick** (☎ 0977 188 266), **Barakat** (☎ 0926 253 451) and **Colins** (☎ 0977 225 915).

If you want to have your own vehicle whilst in the city, and your organisation doesn't provide one, there are a few decent **car rental companies** available.

Juba Interlink Services (☎ 0923 647 445) is an upmarket car hire company with offices just next to the airport. It supplies executive vehicles for government ministers and special functions such as weddings. All prices include driver plus fuel. The smaller vehicles — such as the Prado GX — cost $300 a day, whilst the executive land cruisers — such as the V8 — cost $500. The higher-class vehicles — the Range Rover and Mercedes — are popular for weddings or official functions, and cost $650 a day. It is not usually necessary to book — simply turn up at the offices — but if you want to be certain that a particular vehicle is available then it is worth phoning ahead.

For less high-end cars, try **MCAC** (☎ 0955 155 560 or 0955 284 700; @ mcac_car@yahoo.com or mcac.car@gmail.com), which is just next door to Olympic Hotel and run by a friendly Sudanese-Australian. A car with driver will cost around 200 SSP a day, although fuel is extra.

Another option is to **buy your own car**, although this is likely to be very expensive because of high import costs. To save some money, many expats buy a used car in Kenya or Uganda and then drive it up. In fact, if you look closely at the cars in Juba, you will notice that many have the steering wheel on the right rather than the left, because this is the correct side for Kenya.

Some people also buy vehicles — usually the more high-end models, such as Humbers — from Dubai and ship them over.

Golden Arrow (☎ 0915 611 340) has a Toyota show room near Rock City.

Muthaiga Travel (☎ 0955 117 903 or 0927 314 195; @ mtljuba@yahoo.co.uk; 🖵 www.muthaigatravel.com) can also provide help with car hire.

Where to sleep

If you are looking for cheap and affordable places to stay, you are going to be out of luck in Juba. The unremitting needs of the UN and NGO workers in the city have pushed accommodation prices up considerably.

Nevertheless, more and more hotels are opening up in the city, and competition is beginning to bring prices down.

Much of the accommodation in Juba looks fairly temporary: often in tents, prefabricated buildings or container cabins that could be quickly loaded on to the back of a lorry should war return.

However, now that a lasting peace for South Sudan seems to be taking hold, these temporary measures are slowly being replaced with more permanent structures. At the moment, a number of hotels in the city have both temporary buildings and more permanent ones.

Most hotels offer different prices depending on how many meals you want to take there — whether you want full board, half board, breakfast only or no meal at all. The price ranges we use in the listings below usually depend on the numbers of meals taken

WESTERN OUTSKIRTS

Rock City (☗ Jebel Kujur; ☎ 0977 255 634; @ katwalo@hotmail.com) is set in the mountains, a little way outside of Juba. It is a lovely location for the hotel, but disappointingly the rooms are not as luxurious as one might expect for the price. There are only three permanent rooms (doubles), costing 250 SSP each. The rest of the accommodation is in tents: 100 SSP for a double. Prices do not include meals. You also have to pay extra for the internet — $20 for a connection that lasts for the duration of your stay. There is a rather mediocre restaurant next door (a main costs 20-30 SSP), which has live music Wed-Sat, from 8 pm until late. The bands tend to have Congolese, Ugandan and South African influences. The rooms don't have air-con or TV, and there is often no hot water. They come with a fan, self-contained toilet and a shower. There are plans to build a swimming pool in the hotel.

Jebel Lodge (☗ Jebel Kujur; ☎ 0955 035 586; @ thejebellodge@gmail.com), just next door, is a much more comfortable option. Singles cost $150-187, doubles $180-217 and executive suites $220-257. Guests have free access to wireless internet, a small gym and the pool. A laundry service is also provided. There are 55 rooms available. Secure parking spaces are available for residents and visitors. The hotel serves decent pizzas for 25 SSP.

Acacia Village (☗ Not far from Jebel Kujur, on the road leading west out of Juba; ☎ 0977 254 216; @ info@acaciavillage.com; ☐ www.acaciavillage.com) is a good option if you want to get away from the hustle-and-bustle of city life. The hotel has earnt a reputation as being one of the poshest places to stay, in a beautiful location with wonderfully-kept lawns and gardens. The rooms are constructed from roughly-hewn stone. There is a friendly bar on the premises, with an incredible selection of drinks and an excellent restaurant that serves everything from burgers to traditional pizzas cooked in a wood-fired over. Many expats consider these to be the best pizzas in town. The hotel has a swimming pool and tennis court. The high location of the hotel makes it cooler than other places down in town. The hotel has 10 cottages and 15 tents. The hotel is smaller than Jebel Lodge and has a less commercial feel to it.

NEAR OLD CUSTOMS

South Sudan Hotel (🏠 Ministries Street; ☎ 0126 663 440 or 0129 396 723 or 0955 136 454 or 0977 126 361 or 0959 000 074 or 0959 000 073; @ southsudanhotel@yahoo.com or frontofficereservations@gmail.com) has more of a European feel to it, with some lovely Italian-style courtyards and meandering passageways, which one can imagine are quite easy to get lost in. The interior could do with a lick of paint, though. People visiting on official government business often stay in this hotel. There are 69 rooms. All come with a TV, air-con, a big bed and ensuite bathroom. Some rooms also have a fridge. Singles cost $100-120 (standard) or $140-170 (VIP). Doubles cost $150-180. The hotel has free wi-fi and a laundry service (3 SSP for a shirt plus trousers). The hotel's restaurant offers European-style cooking, both *à-la-carte* (30 SSP for a dish) and a buffet (40 SSP). Conference facilities are also available at the hotel: $50 per day for a room that seats up to 15 people, $200 for up to 75 people and $300 for up to 100 people.

NEAR AIRPORT

Asmara (🏠 Off Airport Street; ☎ 0955 057 011, 0927 121 889 or 0955 131 388; @ asmara_juba@yahoo.com) is a lovely little place with a friendly vibe. It is rather more secluded than some of the others, which seems to add to its laid-back charm. It is also one of the few hotels where the staff are relaxed about non-residents coming to use the wireless internet, although out of courtesy you should probably buy a drink. The downside to the

hotel is that, because it is set some way off the main road, when it rains the approach becomes exceedingly flooded and you need a *boda-boda* or a good pair of wellies to get there. The hotel offers single rooms ($90-130) and doubles ($100-140). The hotel has 20 rooms, each generously proportioned, with ensuite shower, satellite TV and air-con. A free laundry service is provided for guests. The restaurant serves decent Ethiopian food (15-25 SSP) for a main. There's also an Indian menu (20-26 SSP for a curry), but only when there is enough demand (which is rarely).

Red Sea Hotel (🏠 Off Airport Street; ☎ 0926 660 931 or 0955 028 674 or 0955 014 590; @ redseahoteljuba@yahoo.com) — a curious choice of name, given that South Sudan is a landlocked country and the Red Sea is thousands of kilometres away — is rather tucked away and not on a main road. This makes it a little hard to get to when it rains, but the place is friendly enough. Single rooms go for $100 a night, and doubles for $140. Prices include breakfast, but not lunch and dinner, which you can get for 18-25 SSP. Food includes a range of grilled meat, chicken and fish dishes — as well as a limited selection of vegetarian meals. The hotel has 22 rooms. A free laundry service is available for guests, plus wi-fi. The rooms are rather on the small side, although the big bed makes up for this. All come with TV, air-con and ensuite bathroom.

Panache (🏠 Airport Street) is an Indian-owned hotel with friendly, professional service. There are actually two hotels owned by the same people, both near each other. The newer one, which opened in 2010, is both nicer and cheaper to stay in. Rooms here cost $100-130. In the other hotel they cost $120-150. All

South Sudan

rooms are equipped with satellite TV, air-con unit and ensuite shower and toilet. Rooms are big with a generous bed. There are 17 rooms in the newer hotel and 20 rooms in the older one. Wi-fi is available for guests. There is also an internet café that non-guests can use at the rate of 5 SSP for half an hour. A small, sparsely-equipped gym is located in the second hotel, which guests can use. The food served in the restaurant is Indian-themed. A main meal will cost 25-35 SSP, and you really shouldn't forget the *lassi* for 8 SSP. There is a pool table in the restaurant.

Chaay Hotel (🏠 Off Airport Street; ☎ 0955 042 347) is a nice option for those on a budget, who want somewhere cheap and clean to stay, relatively close to the airport. Of course, you get what you pay for: rooms don't have air-con (although they do come with a fan) and internet is not available. Moreover, many of the staff have only a fairly shaky grasp of English. A single costs 120 SSP and a double 150 SSP. Don't expect to get breakfast for this, but the restaurant serves delicious Ethiopian breakfasts for only a few SSP. This hotel has a much more local, African feel to it than some of the others — which can be a plus.

Glory Hotel (🏠 Airport Street; ☎ 0926 660 851 or 0955 595 550 or +256 785 489 448 or +971 509 495 213; @ glorycompanies@ gmail.com or amanhailom@yahoo. com) is a friendly and relaxed hotel, although the rooms are a little tatty. A plus of this hotel is that it has a big screen with projector, which is often used to show big sporting events such as football matches. All rooms come with air-con, a fairly large bed, a rather nice TV set and an ensuite shower. Free access to wi-fi is provided, although

this tends to be quite slow. A laundry service is included in the price. There are 19 rooms in total. Singles cost $110-140, whilst doubles cost $130-160. The style of food served in the hotel restaurant is Ethiopian, although a more continental breakfast is available (including omelettes and cornflakes).

Olympic Hotel (🏠 Airport Street; ☎ 0926 691 277 or 0955 040 084, 0977 256 282; @ olympic.juba@gmail.com), just next to Glory Hotel, is a similar establishment, although with marginally smarter rooms. Wireless internet is provided. All rooms come with satellite TV, air-con and ensuite shower. There is also an icecream parlour adjoined to the hotel, which can be a welcome addition when things get too hot. On the complex, you'll find a hair salon for men (10 SSP), a travel agency and MCAC car rentals (p281). A single costs $110-130, a twin $140-150 and an executive $130-180. Discounts are available for UN workers and corporate clients. Further discounts are considered for those who stay longer than a month. The restaurant serves an assortment of grilled meat and fishes (20-28 SSP for a main). Conference facilities are available at the daily rate of $200 and there is a laundry service.

Dolce Vita (🏠 Off Airport Street; ☎ 0955 035 216 or 0909 010 461) is a good option for those on a budget, who aren't too fussed about comfort but who don't want to completely rough it. There are 12 rooms in container accommodation. Each is self-contained, with satellite TV and air-con. There is even a fridge and both hot and cold water are available. However, the rooms are not all that big and the staff do not speak very good English. A single room costs $80-120. Unfortunately, there is no internet. The restaurant offers

Eritrean / Ethiopian fare, as well as some Italian / continental dishes. A main course costs 15-20 SSP.

Paradiso (🏠 Airport Street; ☎ 0955 665 050 or 0121 012 788 or 0977 12 6765; @ alemdrar@yahoo.com or paradiso.hotel@yahoo.com) is a friendly place, with reasonable prices. There are 18 rooms, although two are used for staff who live on-site. A single costs between $75-95 and a double $85-105, depending on meals taken. The hotel likes to boast that it can guarantee power 24 hours a day. Not only do they have a generator, fairly standard in most hotels, but since they are on the same power line as the ministries, the power never goes off. Food is a mixture of continental and Eritrean / Ethiopian dishes. You can get a pizza for 22-28 SSP, and an Eritrean / Ethiopian meal for 28-30 SSP.

JUBA TOWN

Juba Grand Hotel (🏠 South-east of Juba Town Market; ☎ 0955 026 142 or 0128 787 532 or 0977 260 311; @ jubagrandhotel@gmail.com) is the place to come if you want to escape the noise and chaos of the city for awhile. Although the hotel is set along the banks of the Nile, the mango trees obscure your view of it and prevent you getting there. Guests get free use of wi-fi, the gym and table-tennis. The hotel also offers a free pick-up service from the airport. Laundry is available, costing a few SSP per item. Service is very professional and on a par with a business hotel in Europe. Singles cost $160-180 and doubles $200-220. Rooms are good-sized and almost clinically clean. Each one comes with a high-tech TV, fridge, cupboard and en-suite shower. The showers look nice but tend to be very temperamental.

There are 80 rooms in the hotel and two conference halls.

Raymok Hotel (🏠 South-east of Juba Town Market; ☎ 0955 051 300) is definitely at the lower-end of Juba hotels, and consequently much more affordable than other options in the city. A single costs just 50 SSP. The hotel is fairly small, having only ten rooms, and often fills up quite quickly. The place is relaxed, laid back and friendly. The Eritrean staff do not speak very good English, but they do try to make the effort. Rooms are nothing special and there is no air-con, only fans. Internet is not available, although the management cheekily point out that occasionally you can pick up a wireless connection from neighbouring hotels. The attached restaurant is very cheap and serves excellent Eritrean fare (5 SSP for a *kitcha fit-fit*).

Star Hotel (🏠 South-east of Juba Town market; ☎ 0955 070 505 or 0955 003 903 or 0126 937 508; @ starhoteljuba@gmail.com) is in a lovely location by the banks of the Nile. Ethiopian dance takes place in the restaurant every evening, from 8 pm, apart from Tuesday. Unlike many other hotels in Juba, all rooms are solid concrete buildings rather than pre-fabricated units or another kind of temporary accommodation. A single room, with bed and breakfast, costs $130. All rooms come with air-con, satellite TV, small ensuite bathroom and fridge. Wireless and cable internet is available for guests. The buffet restaurant charges 40 SSP per person.

Hamza (🏠 East of Juba Town, near the Nile; ☎ 0922 855 057 or 0918 471 324 or 0977 106 798; @ hamzainn@gmail.com) offers fairly basic, slightly over-priced rooms. Singles cost $110-140, with doubles at $150-180. Laundry and wireless internet are included in the price. There are 60 rooms in total. Accommodation is in containers. The rough-and-ready rooms have air-con and ensuite bathroom, but no TV. The nice thing about the place is the garden outside, which is lovely and shady and contains a fountain. Meals are international.

Habesha (🏠 Juba Town; ☎ 0955 014 444 or 955 014 445; @ benyam.berhanu@gmail.com) offers singles for $150-180 and doubles for $220-250. Prices include access to free wi-fi and laundry. There are 14 rooms in total. Rooms are clean and relatively big. They come with a study table, fridge, air-con, big bed and decent shower. The weighing scales in the corner are a nice touch. The hotel offers conference facilities for rent.

Savanna (🏠 Juba Town; ☎ 0955 026 288) is extremely basic and has very small rooms, for 100 SSP each. There is no air-con or TV — just a clunky fan in the ceiling. There is no internet available. The hotel has only seven rooms. The staff are friendly but have poor English. The restaurant serves a range of Eritrean and Ethiopian dishes.

Summer Palace (🏠 Eastern end of Juba Town; ☎ 0955 109 690 or 0955 370 096; @ jubasummerhotel@gmail.com; 🖥 www.jubasummerhotel.webnode. com) is a Chinese-run hotel. There are 35 rooms, each with a fridge, ensuite shower and air-con. Rooms are in container accommodation. There is a nice Chinese restaurant attached. The hotel has a gym, free for guests. A standard single room costs $100-130 and an executive room costs $120-150. You can also rent rooms on a monthly basis, for between $1350-2000.

Juba Raha Hotel (🏠 North end of Juba Town, near JIT supermarket; ☎ 0955 114 240, or 0926 354 691; 🖥 www.jubaraha.com) has singles for $120-150 and doubles for $150-180. The restaurant mostly offers Sudanese food, although the chef can also prepare Japanese, Indian and Russian dishes on request. There is a buffet for 50 SSP every day. Rooms are a good size and come with fridge, TV and air-con. There are 75 rooms, all in containers.

South Sudan II (🏠 Next to Juba Town Market; ☎ 0977 142 344 or 0927 844 717 or 0959 000 071 or 0955 059 290; @ garangmike@ yahoo.com) used to actually be a horse stables, but was turned by a business guru into hotel accommodation. Singles cost 200-280 SSP and doubles 240-300 SSP. There are 60 rooms. Internet and laundry are both included in the price. A conference hall for 100 people is available for rent. The hotel has clearly seen better days and could do with repainting.

River Nile Residence (🏠 East of Juba Town Market; ☎ 0955 014 650 or 0977 128 345) has a small, welcoming, family-run feel to the place. Staff are mainly Indian. A single costs $120-170 and a double $160-210. The rooms are fairly basic and the wooden furniture looks as though it will fall apart the moment that you touch it. Rooms are all ensuite and come with TV. There are 20 rooms in total.

Akok Camp (🏠 South-East of Juba Town Market; ☎ 0928 312 193) is in a lovely spot on the banks of the Nile, but that is the only good thing about it. It is extremely rundown with very poor service. The tatty furniture in reception looks as though it hasn't been replaced in years and the tents are somewhat threadbare these days. There is no internet, although management promise that they were working on getting it installed (though they say they'll charge 15 SSP an hour, even for guests). This is definitely a place to avoid during the rainy season. When the rains come, the area turns into a lake and you end up having to wade to your tent. Still, if you're looking for a place to stay right on the banks of the Nile, this is more affordable than most: 100 SSP for a single and 150 SSP for a double. Prices do not include meals. There are more than 60 tents on the site.

HAI JALABA

New Sudan Hotel (🏠 Unity Avenue, near Ministries Street; ☎ 0122 325 171 or 0919 695 786 or 0914 173 597 or 0977 128 159; @ newsudanhotel@hotmail.com or akashaisam@hotmail.com) is an ugly-looking building from the outside but actually offers rather nice self-contained apartments within. There are 60 apartments all in all, consisting of a safe, fridge, TV and small kitchen area (although there is no oven). The two apartments on the top floor offer some of the best views of Juba in the whole city, really allowing you to appreciate how green the place is (at least when compared to North Sudan). Apartments cost between $200-250. The owner is particularly proud of the European-style kitchen that is used to prepare food for all the guests in the restaurant. The style of food is European — 45 SSP for dinner — but of course you can also prepared your own food in your apartment. Unusually, the owner of the hotel is from North Sudan. Wireless internet is available, but it is not free.

Sahara (🏠 Unity Avenue, near airport; ☎ 0955 171 717 or 0922 143 333 or 0129 569 755 or 0977 143 430; @ info@sahara-juba. com; 🖥 www.sahara-juba.com) is located conveniently close to the airport. The interior and rooms have nice décor, with a slightly Oriental feel to them. The place is clean and comfortable, but management can be somewhat officious and the hotel lacks the friendly atmosphere on other places in town. Prices are also a little on the high side: $180 (for a single), $220 (for a double) and $800 for a suite. They have a salon, including massage (70 SSP) and steam baths. There's also a barber — 20 SSP for a simple cut — and a laundry service. Rooms come with satellite TV, air-con, a fridge, a safe and ensuite bathroom. Accommodation is in containers but does not look too container-like. The hotel is fairly big, consisting of 88 rooms. There's a good albeit pricey restaurant attached, serving a wide range of European, Chinese and Lebanese food

Shalom (🏠 Off Unity Avenue; ☎ 0122 010 249 or 0955 035 034 or 0977 129 164; @ jubashalom@yahoo. com or booking@shalomhoteljuba. com; 🖥 www.shalomhoteljuba.com) is only worth considering if good and friendly service is not too high on your list of priorities. The sign outsides reads "a home away from home" but this claim is questionable. The staff have a terrible don't-really-care attitude, and to get them to take any interest in your stay is an uphill struggle. With such awful service, you might expect the prices to be cheaper than they are: $130 (for a single, full board) and $150 (for a double, full board). The bar serves burgers and snacks from 12 SSP and pizzas from 20 SSP. There are a total of 29 rooms in the hotel. Rooms are smallish and come with wireless internet, air-con, fridge and satellite TV.

Holiday Hotel offers rooms for $160-200. All rooms are double and can comfortably sleep one or two people. Free wi-fi is available, but you have to pay for the laundry service, which isn't cheap: 10 SSP for a pair of trousers. There are 24 rooms in total. Each is fairly basic, consisting of a fridge, satellite TV and ensuite bathroom. The English of the staff is so-so. The restaurant has a vast menu of European dishes, for 25-35 SSP. There is also a good selection of drinks and spirits.

Logali House (🏠 Off Unity Avenue; ☎ 0977 103 800 or 0957 103 800, @ laurie@logalihouse.com; 🖥 www.logalihouse.com) has a very British feel to it, with a lovely aroma of fresh toast and coffee lingering in the dining hall. Journalists and diplomats often choose to stay here when they come to town. A standard single room costs $275, a double $350 and a single container unit $185. Prices include breakfast and laundry services, but not wireless internet which is extra ($10 per hour). The hotel also rents out conference rooms. There are 19 rooms in total, including five rooms in containers.

HAI MALAKAL

New York Hotel (🏠 South of Juba Town Market; ☎ 0129 069 015 or 0977 127 193; @ newyorkhotelss@yahoo.com) offers container accommodation-style in relaxing and quiet accommodation, not far from the Nile. Singles cost $120-160. Twins cost $140-180. The restaurant offers a limited selection of food — mainly pizzas, burgers and sandwiches. The service is extremely friendly and courteous. Each room comes with a TV, fridge, basic shower and very efficient air-con. A conference room, accommodating up to 200 people, is available for rent.

Quality Hotel (🏠 South of Juba Town market; ☎ 0927 820 320 or 0977 100 044; @ hotelquality10@yahoo.com) is a clean, quiet and relaxing hotel. It has regular hot water. Rooms are a good size and come with satellite TV and ensuite bathroom, with very good shower. Customer service is excellent and very friendly, and they are good at dealing with unreasonably difficult customers. A single room costs $160-220 and a double $260-360

Paradise (🏠 Ministries Street; ☎ 0955 308 715 or 0959 000 082 or 0955 015 713 or 0977 111 409 or 0977 164 229 or 0923 325 890; 🖥 www.paradisehoteljuba.com) is very much geared towards the business customer. The Indian-run hotel offers standard singles for $120-150, deluxe singles for $150-180 and suites for $220-250. The pizza in the restaurant is particularly good. The hotel also rents out office space and conference facilities for businesses, and does outside catering. It is located not far from the Norwegian Consulate and within walking distance of Juba's central business district.

Bedouin Lodge (🏠 Just next to the cemetery; ☎ 0955 213 732 or 0977 114 824 or +254 722 515 498; @ andrew@ssasltd.com or andrewbelcher@hotmail.com; 🖥 www.accommodationjuba.com) is a very relaxing and pleasant place to stay. Accommodation used to be only in prefab units, but management is slowly changing to more permanent structures. At the time of visiting, there were six rooms in permanent buildings and 24 prefabs. The idea is that, eventually, everything will be permanent. A night in a basic prefab costs $85, whilst it costs $100 to stay in a more permanent building. Rooms come with a fridge, TV, air-con and ensuite bathroom. As you might expect, the permanent rooms are bigger and nicer. Wi-fi internet and laundry is free. The restaurant serves European-style meals for 18-35 SSP. The setting for the

South Sudan

camp is lovely and puts one in mind of a secluded jungle. There is even a little stream running through it. The camp also offers office space for rent. There is a large screen and projector for watching the main sporting events.

SOUTH-EAST JUBA

Juba Bridge Hotel (☎ By the Nile, south; ☎ 0121 609 187 or 0977 130 363 or +882 655 527 011;   @ jubabridgehotel@yahoo.com or 🖥 www.jubabridgehotel.com) is best known for its Ethiopian food and the lively Ethiopian dance shows that it puts on. Accommodation is in pre-fabricated buildings: $140-165 for a single and $180-300 for a suite. Rooms are generally quite big, and come with air-con, TV and a reasonably large bed. The decor is pleasing. However, in some of the rooms, there seems to be a strange smell emanating from the shower, which is difficult to place. Internet is not generally available in the hotel, but a cable connection can be provided if guests request it. There is also an internet café next door. A laundry service is available, costing a few SSP per item.

Heron Camp (☎ By the Nile, south; ☎ 0955 151 206 or 0128 845 114 or 0955 120 634; @ heroncampsite@yahoo.com) is one of the older camps in town, but not the nicest place you might stay at. The rooms are small and looking a little worn around the edges. The plastic garden chairs in some of the rooms just look tacky. Many of the showers are in poor conditions. And, to round everything off, the staff aren't always the most helpful. On the plus side, though, guests do get free access to the steam and sauna rooms, as well as a big and well-equipped gym. A single costs 200-350 SSP and a double

300-650 SSP There is a decent Indian restaurant within the hotel — and the service here is much better.

Da Vinci Lodge (☎ By the Nile, south; ☎ 0955 072 009 or 0977 112 648 or +882 1621 233 298 or +254 733 803 094; @ mactdavinci@yahoo.com or holgor_poehler@hotmail.com) is one of the best-loved hotels in Juba, partly because of its relaxed setting (the last of a string of hotels overlooking the Nile), partly because of its food (expensively exotic) and partly because of the service (attentive). There are two types of accommodation that you can stay in — either bungalows, of which there are four, or concrete rooms, of which there are five. Bungalows are often rented by those that are going to stay in Juba for awhile, and cost $4000 a month. Rooms, which can sleep up to two people, cost $250. Internet is not available at the hotel, although an internet dongle can be provided for guests, as long as they arrange the monthly payments. The hotel has a free laundry service and a pool table that guests can make use of. The hotel has an excellent albeit pricey restaurant, which serves ostrich and crocodile as well as a range of pizzas. The hotel can arrange boat trips.

Central Hotel (☎ North of Konyo-Konyo Market; ☎ 0955 524 609; @ sallaed22@yahoo.ie) offers two types of room: with air-con (150 SSP per person) and with fan (100 SSP per person). There is no TV in any of the rooms. The rooms are very small — it would be a struggle to fit more than one person in them. There was no internet when your researchers visited, but management promised it would be installed shortly. There are 14 rooms in total. Prices include a free laundry service. Customer service is friendly, but the hotel has a rather faded has-been look to it. The hotel is in a somewhat run-down part of Juba, not far from Konyo-Konyo market. There are probably better places to stay for the same money.

Mango Camp (⌂ By the Nile, near the cemetery; ☎ 0955 022 090) is set in lovely surroundings on the banks of the Nile. It is one of the few places in Juba where you can stay in traditional African *tukul* huts: $55-80 for a single and $65-100 for a double. The huts are clean — which is more than can be said of the communal toilets — and cosy to sleep in. However, they are fairly basic and there is no TV. There is live music every Wednesday and Thursday evening. The hotel also has a big screen for showing sporting events. Prices include free internet access and laundry. The camp has earned something of a reputation as a place frequented by ladies of the night and drunken soldiers.

Bros Camp (⌂ By the Nile, south; @ broshotel@yahoo.com) has singles for $130-160 and doubles for $160-190. There is no internet, although there is a small internet café on-site. The rooms, which are in container accommodation, come with a TV, air-con and ensuite bathroom. There are 92 rooms in total.

Afex Camp (⌂ By the Nile, south; ☎ +254 203 878 313 or +254 720 987 198 or +882 1643 334 065; @ jubabookings@afexgroup.com) is one of the oldest camps in Juba and has a well-deserved reputation for being very safe. Accommodation used to be in lovely safari-style tents, but they have just switched over to hard units. There are almost 70 rooms. Wi-fi is not available, but there is a fast internet café on-site: 7 SSP for 17 minutes. If you use your own laptop then prices are slightly less. Single accommodation costs $210-250. Prices include

breakfast. Conference facilities are also available.

Intra-Africa (⌂ By the Nile, south; ☎ 0977 128 318 or 0977 103 682; @ info.hotelintraafrca@gmail.com) has singles for $100-130 and doubles for $170-200. This includes free wi-fi connection and laundry. The hotel has a gym, salon and barber. The hotel is nicely laid out, although the rooms are fairly small. Each comes with satellite TV, air-con, shower and toilet. Accommodation is in permanent concrete units.

Royal Garden Hotel (☎ 0977 298 160 or 0955 065 235 or 0924 830 211; @ royalgarden.arden@gmail.com or karanidamary@yahoo.com) offers singles for $100-130 and doubles for $150-180. Wireless internet is available, but only accessible in the reception and restaurant. The management say that it should be extended to the rooms soon. Conference halls are available for rent. The hotel provides free bottles of water in the rooms during the day, plus one with every meal. The hotel has 40 rooms in total. Accommodation is in concrete units and includes air-con, TV and basic shower. The restaurant is principally Ethiopian and Kenyan, with a little bit of Sudanese thrown in for good measure.

Sunflower Camp (⌂ By the Nile, south; ☎ 0955 016 373; @ sunflowerinnjuba@yahoo.com) is a decent place to stay with great atmosphere. It is located close to the river in pleasant surroundings. Accommodation is mostly in containers. Single rooms are available for 240 SSP, double rooms for 320 SSP, and self-contained units for 360 SSP (single) and 440 SSP (double). Meals and 10% tax are not included. All rooms have air-con and there is a free internet service.

Free laundry is also provided twice a week.

Civicon Oasis Camp (🏠 By the Nile, south; ☎ 0122 204 798; @ civiconoasis@yahoo.com; @ www.oasiscampjuba.com)has self-contained tents and prefabricated containers. The camp is located on the banks of the Nile, just behind a squatter's camp, where refugees are living beneath corrugated iron sheets and cardboard boxes. Single rooms cost $100-140. Double occupancy in a single room is $140-175. A double room (single or double occupancy) costs $160-200. The hotel also has conference facilities for rent. There are 120 rooms in total. Rooms are fairly basic — consisting of little more than an air-con unit, TV and bed — but service is very friendly. The camp has a nice gym overlooking the river, which provides pleasant views whilst you are exercising. A laundry service is available and the camp has a boat that can be rented for trips on the Nile. There is also a very nice European-style café on the site, which has a lovely aroma of coffees and pastries emanating from it. The 'shocked gorilla' fountain that greets you as you enter the hotel is a little tacky, though.

Salaam (🏠 Juba-Torit Road; ☎ 0959 000 539; @ hotelsalaam@ yahoo.com) is a small place with rooms (single or double) for 170 SSP. It is Indian-run and very welcoming. From the outside, the lovely cottage type buildings look very inviting. The management points out that the thatched roofs keep the rooms cool at night, which is a good thing since air-con is not provided. The thin beds in the rooms look very uncomfortable. All rooms come with TV. Unfortunately, they have a perpetual damp smell about them. The hotel can also offer conference facilities. A laundry service is available for a few SSP per item. There are 16 rooms in total.

Where to eat

The variety of restaurants available in Juba continues to improve all the time, and it is not difficult to find a good selection of dishes from all over the world, to suit most tastes.

Most of the residential camps offer buffet meals for visitors for between 25 and 40 SSP, but the quality can vary considerably. Some of the better hotel restaurants are listed in this section.

Beer (most commonly Tusker, Bell and Pilsner) is served everywhere although, depending on the power supply, it may or may not be cold.

There are plenty of small shops in Juba serving traditional local food, most commonly *fuul*, chicken or mutton, served with hunks of bread. Fresh fish from the Nile is also popular. *Sha'urma* is available in many places.

There is a wide range of international cuisine available, too. Chinese and Indian restaurants are popular, and there are a large number of pizzerias (of varying quality) in the town. Eritrean and Ethiopian cuisine is also common.

Most people just turn up at restaurants — it is not necessary to call beforehand. However, some of the more popular places can get crowded fairly quickly, so it is best to turn up early. In the evening, restaurants start serving food from 7 pm, with last orders being taken around 9.30 pm.

Kololo Bar, opposite the government ministry buildings, attracts a regular lunch crowd from the ministries. It typically serves fish, goat's meat and beans. The place often plays loud music during the evenings and things can get quite rowdy.

Airport View Motel offers fairly basic meals. The usual grilled meat dishes cost between 20-25 SSP. Sandwiches and snacks are also offered (15 SSP). Despite the sign outside, don't come here looking for any rooms — there aren't any (although management says they may expand in the future). Service is fairly slow. The place is usually quite empty, though this can change when the function hall just opposite comes into use. On Sunday mornings, this hall is used as a church and on Friday/Saturday evenings it often doubles up as a nightclub.

Millennium (🏠 Ministries Street; ☎ 0912 733 904 or 0122 397 178; @ jubamillenium@yahoo.com) is a largish restaurant not far from the ministries, with an expansive garden. It's okay for a quick bite, but nothing exceptional. The usual grilled meat and kebabs are served for around 25 SSP. A daily plate of African or Oriental fare goes for 20 SSP, steaks 25 SSP and pizzas 30-35 SSP. They also have a conference hall. There is a rough edge to this restaurant.

Safari New Sudan Restaurant serves fried chicken and fish in austere surroundings. Meals cost around 10 SSP.

Mai Thai (☎ 0955 335 454 or 0955 168 950; @ barbara_04@hotmail.com or jpenka2000@yahoo.co.uk), located in the Home & Away complex, offers great Thai cooking for 20-30 SSP a meal. Service is friendly but slow. Food is very tasty and, as might be expected, rather spicy (although they are happy to tone it down for you if you ask) Food is authentic and smells terrific. The restaurant has

a lovely shady courtyard in which you can eat.

Mama Maburka's offers a cheap place to eat in a friendly and relaxed atmosphere. The food is more authentically African than many other places in Juba. The serving ladies speak reasonably good English and enjoy meeting foreigners. If you take the time to ask about the dishes on offer, they'll be happy to explain them to you. Fried meat or meat stew dishes go for 5-10 SSP. Portions are exceedingly generous and it all smells very nice.

Arkel is the place to come for a decent barbecue buffet, which can be taken in the courtyard or inside. The service is a tad on the slow side, but the quality of food is excellent, and prices are not unreasonable. The place is very popular with expats and almost always busy in the evening. There is a good salad bar, too, although there is usually a lot more salad during weekdays. For the barbecue and salad buffet, expect to pay 35 SSP.

De'Havana (☎ 0977 321 218 or 0957 321 218; @ anyaronge@yahoo.co.uk) is one of the better options for pizza in town. Prices range from 25 SSP (for a margarita) to 40 SSP (for more exotic toppings). The pizzas are not really up to European standards, but they're not bad. You can also get soup (15 SSP) and sandwiches (25 SSP). The restaurant is just next to Logali and managed by them, but owned by a businessman called Deng. The service and atmosphere are both excellent. The place is popular with Sudanese and expats alike. Salsa sessions are often put on at Havana

Central Pub (☎ 0955 065 529, 0977 163 951) is a lovely spot to eat, with a large expansive outside area that is hidden away from the main road. The food is not bad, either, with kebabs cooked outside for 30 SSP. Other grilled meat dishes cost 22-30 SSP.

Natos Lounge Bar & Grill is a popular place, with slightly unusual offerings and an exceedingly well-stocked bar. Try the octopus salad for 26 SSP and entertain yourself by wondering where they got an octopus in the middle of the jungle. Surroundings are pleasant, with more of a 'bar' than 'restaurant' feel to it, although service could be improved. Salsa sessions are often organised on week-ends.

Spice 'n' Herbs (☎ 0923 663 007 or 0977 256 969) is probably the finest Indian restaurant in Juba. The food is fresh and exceedingly tasty with a subtle blend of spices. They also have a good range of cocktails. But prices aren't cheap: 22-30 SSP and you have to pay extra for the rice and naan (12 SSP for plain boiled rice and 6 SSP for naan). The restaurant also offers Italian food — 25-30 SSP for a pizza — but you might be better off sticking with the curries. The main downside to the place is the atmosphere. Despite the Indian staff, it feels much more like a Sudanese eatery than a curry house.

Parade has decent Indian food at not unreasonable prices, but they often don't have very much on the menu.

Queen of Sheeba is one of the most distinctive Ethiopian restaurants in town, housed beneath a lovely and attractive thatched cottage. Ethiopian meals cost 21 to 30 SSP, whilst continental cost 26 to 29 SSP. The food is delicious, but the wine they offer is not so good — stick to the beer. Try the *atkilt* — an assorted vegetarian platter, served atop Ethiopian bread — and you will not be disappointed. You also probably won't be able to walk out of the restaurant on your own volition.

Solidarity (☎ 0122 34 91 52), on the road to the cultural centre, serves Sudanese food — including *asida* and fried chicken — for not very much money (5-10 SSP)

Wonderful Chinese is perhaps a little inappropriately named. The interior is grubby, which makes one wonder what state the kitchen might be in. The service is questionable and rather slow. The food is nothing special, but the portions are big. A basic meal costs 22-28 SSP. Rice and naan bread are extra. The restaurant also offers pizzas (15-25 SSP). Expats often know the place as the 'Chinese Container', since it is still in container-style accommodation.

Shanghai, just across from Juba University, is a much nicer place to come for decent Chinese food. It's tucked away and a little hard to find, but really worth persevering in your search. A basic meal costs 25-35 SSP. If you want a seafood dish, this costs 40-55 SSP. Rice is extra.

International Restaurant serves Kenyan and Ugandan food, including the well-loved *nyoma choma*, *posho* and *matoke*. Grilled meat is also available. A dish costs 30 SSP, and comes served with greens. There is a pool table in the place. There is a nice outdoor area where you can eat, too.

Kush Bar and Restaurant offers Ethiopian and Eritrean dishes for 10-15 SSP. Food is served in a traditional way, with woven dish covering. The place has a very 'pubby' feel to it, with lots of people drinking beer and talking in loud voices.

Bharel-Gebel Restaurant mainly offers Sudanese food, despite the sign outside that suggests it is an Asian restaurant. *Fuul* costs 4 SSP and grilled chicken 10 SSP

South Sudan

Home & Away Delhi, on the Home & Away complex, serves very nice cakes and pastries for 6 SSP, coffee for 10-12 SSP and sandwiches for 20-25 SSP. It smells nice and has a European feel.

Hotel Restaurants

Most hotels and camps in Juba have restaurants attached to them, but the food can often be very hit-and-miss. The following hotel-restaurants are particularly worth trying.

Bedouin Lodge (p294), east of the cemetery and not far from Afex Camp, is a comfortable, relaxing place in which to spend a few hours chilling out. Prices are a little expensive, though.

Rock City (p282), on the eastern outskirts of the city, is a great place to come for the view. Most nights of the week, the typical food is grilled chicken or fish, although they occasionally advertise special evenings when they serve Chinese food. The beer isn't always as cold as it might be and the food is only so-so, but it is a nice spot to come and relax.

Mango Camp (p290) serves decent meals for a fair price, but it is the bar that attracts most of the attention. With a good range of drinks and great music, Mango Camp is a popular drinking venue.

Da Vinci Restaurant (p289) has one of the best settings along the banks of the Nile and, if you get here in time for sunset, you will see the Nile at its best. Inside, the lighting is soft and intimate, with a welcoming ambience. The restaurant is expensive but excellent, serving such rare treats as crocodile, ostrich (70 SSP), lobster, prawns and sushi. The pizzas (30-55 SSP) are reputed to be among the best that you can get in the city, although this claim is somewhat dubious. A good selection of wines is available.

Heron Camp (p289) has one of the best Indian restaurants on-site, with very good food and friendly, attentive service.

Panache (p284) is another good choice for authentic food.

Paradise (p288) does some of the best pizzas in town.

Summer Palace (p286) has a very nice Chinese restaurant attached to it.

Jebel Lodge (p282), located on Jebel Kujur on the outskirts of Juba, serves excellent pizzas. The relaxing mountain-side setting is an added bonus.

Acacia Village (p282) goes one better, though, and serves pizzas from an authentic wood-fired oven. Definitely the best pizzas in town.

MALAKAL

Malakal lies on the White Nile, just north of the junction with the Sobat River, which flows into the country from Ethiopia, in the east.

Since colonial times, Malakal has been one of the leading cities for commerce in South Sudan. These days, it is probably second in importance only to Juba. It is particularly famous for trade in gum arabic, a sticky resin secreted by the *acacia senegal* tree and used in fizzy drinks and medicine. Cargo ships regularly stop in Malakal as they shuttle between Kosti in the North and Juba in the South.

As the true gateway to the South, Malakal served as a garrison town for northern militias during much of the civil war. There used to be a large presence of soldiers in the town. The numbers have dwindled significantly, but some still remain. Most of these soldiers come from Bahr al-Ghazal in the south-west and not from the immediate locality.

Malakal has suffered greatly during the country's civil war, and the fighting displaced thousands of people, many of whom have now returned home and are starting to rebuild their lives.

The Shilluk and Nuer are the two largest tribes in the town, although there are also significant numbers of Dinka, Murle and other ethnic groups.

Before the Egyptian incursions into South Sudan during the 19th century, Malakal lay at the heart of the expansive Shilluk kingdom, which had established itself in the region during the 15th century.

Where to sleep

There are a growing number of options for sleeping in the town.

Nile Palace (☎ 0918 771 903 or 0927 547 141), on the banks of the Nile, is one of the more up-market hotels in the town, with rooms from $120 a night. The hotel is clean and comfortable with relaxing surroundings. Rooms come with air-con and TV.

South Sudan I (☎ 0129 504 483) offers single rooms for $100-120. Rooms are fairly basic, though come with air-con, TV and fridge.

South Sudan II (☎ 0919 813 914 or 0126 067 598) is a similar place to stay, with slightly cheaper rooms: $90-120 for a single. Air-con, TV and fridge are provided.

Malakal National Hotel (☎ 0913 171 978) is a cheaper option, providing accommodation in tents for $100. There was a fire at the hotel recently and it had to shut down. How temporary this closure will be is unclear.

How to get there

During the dry season, it is possible to travel from Kosti to Malakal by road. You may also be able to negotiate passage on one of the regular cargo ships that run between the two cities. Travelling from the South is not such a good idea due to insecurity on the roads. Flying from Juba is very convenient, though: Feeder Airlines (🖥 feederairlines.com) and Ethiopian Air (🖥 www.flyethiopian.com) offer regular flights.

WAU

Wau, the capital of West Bahr al-Ghazal State, lies in the heart of the war-torn south. The fighting has died away now, and the city is trying to reinvent itself as a popular place for tourists to visit, in much the same way as Juba is doing. One or two promising places to stay and eat are now emerging in the city.

The area around Wau is home to the Dinka, who graze their cattle on the surrounding plains. A great tropical forest of teak and mahogany trees starts just to the south of the town. It is difficult to explore this region unless you have your own car and a knowledgeable guide, but the area may open up to tourism in the future.

Things to see and do are still limited in the town, but if you want to cool off then Wau River Lodge has a swimming pool — 20 SSP for non-guests.

Where to sleep

The nicest place to spend the night is probably the **Wau River Lodge** (☎ 0910 600 265 or 0919 410 234 or +882 1643 333 798; @ wauriverlodge@gmail.com), located just east of the city, on the way to Rumbek. The governor's offices and Peace Hall are nearby.

Accommodation is mainly in tents with ensuite facilities. Singles are $120-140, doubles $140-160. There are also some cottages available: $170-190 (single) and $190-210 (double). All rooms and tents are now fully air-conditioned, and guests get free access to wireless internet. There is also an internet café on-site. The lodge has a restaurant and bar, as well as a swimming pool. Satellite TV is available in the main house.

Regent Hotel, just next to Wau River Lodge, offers rooms for $120-180. The hotel is clean and comfortable, although not quite in the same league as the aforementioned.

South Sudan Hotel is further away from the banks of the Nile, also offering accommodation for $120-180.

Afex (☎ 013 743 101; @ awambua@afexgroup.com) is another, slightly more downmarket option, closer to the centre of town. A night in a tent costs around $75 per person, including free wi-fi.

How to get there

It is possible to travel to Wau by road from Juba, but the roads aren't in great condition and the journey can take as long as two days. Moreover, the roads are usually only accessible during the dry season. It costs around 200 SSP to travel there by coach.

Most people, though, choose to fly instead, which is both fast and convenient.

The city marks the end of the railway line from Khartoum but, due to the long-running war, trains no longer travel to Wau.

YEI

Lying not far to the South of Juba, Yei has long been an impor-tant port-of-call for traders coming up from Uganda.

In fact, in colonial times, Yei was nicknamed 'Little London', due to its importance as a trading and communications hub.

But then war came and threw the town into chaos and devastation, along with the rest of South Sudan.

Now that peace has returned, the town is once again thriving and the town has regained some of its old energy.

The climate of Yei tends to be cooler than towns further north.

Where to sleep

There are growing number of accommodation options in the town, including some *lokanda*-type places in the centre where tradesmen from Uganda often stay.

ECS Guesthouse (☎ 0977 137 050; 🖥 yei.anglican.org) is owned by the Episcopal Church of Sudan, and is located within the church compound. It has rooms for 30 SSP, with shared bathroom. Rooms with ensuite cost 60 SSP.

Referendum Hotel (☎ 0977 121 973) has rooms for 30 SSP a night.

Executive Guest House (☎ 0977 101 469) is a little further outside the town centre. Rooms are around 50 SSP a night.

Twin Hotel (☎ 0977 238 111) provides accommodation in containers.

How to get there

The road from Juba to Yei is still not brilliant and so buses can take as long as 12 hours to reach here. The journey costs around 35 SSP). Many buses from Uganda, heading northwards, also pass by Yei.

TORIT

A hundred and forty kilometres east of Juba, on the road that runs towards Kenya, lies the capital of Eastern Equatoria State.

There is not a great deal to see and do in the town. It has been one of the centre-points to the war between North and South Sudan, and is now struggling to rebuild.

Torit is often credited with sowing the first seeds of discontent with British rule, and providing the first soldiers that championed the South's bid for independence. Subsequently, Torit also produced some noticeable rebel soldiers that fought for the South Sudanese People's Liberation Army (SPLA) against Khartoum's domination of the country. In fact, for many years Torit was the political headquarters of the SPLM/A.

NGO workers regularly come to the town.

Where to sleep

If you're planning on staying in Torit, you could try **Kinati Lodge** (☎ 0977 173 050) or **Safari Link Guesthouse** (☎ 0977 153 965). Both places charge around 60 SSP a night.

How to get there

It is not generally safe to travel by land to the town, either from the east or the west. Land mines, left over from the cruel civil war, still litter the surrounding countryside and periodically claim lives. Moreover, highway robberies occur not infrequently along this stretch of road.

For this reason, most people prefer to fly to the town. There is a small airport very close to the centre and regular flights there operate out of Juba.

South Sudan

Ethnographers estimate that there are more than a 100 different languages spoken in North and South Sudan combined. However, Arabic is by far the most widely-spoken language. It remains the official language of the North and a variation of it — known as 'Juba Arabic' — is also spoken in the main urban centres of the South (although, with independence, more and more Southerners are preferring to rely on English rather than Arabic as the common language).

Whilst there are similarities between Sudanese Arabic and the Arabic spoken in other countries, you should be aware that there are also many differences. Even once you have mastered the basics of Sudanese Arabic, you may have difficulties making yourself understood in other regions of the Arabic world.

'Juba Arabic' has been heavily influenced by regional tribal dialects and is therefore quite different from the Arabic that is spoken in the North.

This chapter gives you a foundation in spoken Sudanese Arabic, using phrases and scenarios that might be immediately useful to you when you arrive in the country.

For reasons of clarity, this chapter focuses on the Arabic that is spoken in North Sudan. This is likely to be the strand of Arabic that is most useful to visitors to the country, particularly as the popularity of Juba Arabic appears to be dwindling.

There is no official written form of Sudanese Arabic. If you encounter Arabic writing whilst in Sudan, you will see that it is closer to classical Arabic than to the local dialects spoken on the street.

PRONUNCIATION

For those who are unfamiliar with Arabic, trying to master some of the distinctive sounds in the language can be a little daunting, to say the least.

Learning the Sudanese way of speaking is not helped by the fact that the locals indiscriminately 'eat' their words, and often pronounce the same word in different ways according to the sentence in which it appears.

Not only this, but many of the sounds that you will find in the language have no equivalent in English or in many other languages.

The best way to learn the different sounds is to listen to as many conversations as possible and to try to repeat the phrases in this chapter slowly to yourself. You can download a series of Arabic audio clips from *The City Trail* website (⌨ www.thecitytrail.com), which should also help you with the pronunciation. These audio files have been specially produced by native Sudanese speakers, to give you a good idea of how spoken Arabic sounds in the country. You will need to enter the ISBN number of this book, as well as the 'Audio Download Code' that you will find on the very first page of this book.

Arabic has two sounds that are particularly tricky for non-Arabs to produce. One is the *ein* sound, which is made at the back of the throat and sounds a little like someone being strangled. The other sound is the glottal stop, which is similar to the *ein*, but a little less guttural and made without tensing the muscles at the back of the throat so forcefully.

In the transliterations that follow, both the *ein* sound and the glottal stop are represented with a single apostrophe ('). They are both similar sounds, and you will be understood if you say them in the same way. However, in order to really appreciate the differences, you should download and listen to the audio files that are available on the website to support this book.

Arabic has both long and short vowels. In the following pages, two of the same vowels together signify a long vowel. An alternative way of transliterating vowels, which you may find in some renditions of Arabic, is to draw a short dash above them, as in ā.

Another peculiarity you should be aware of in Sudanese Arabic is that the word for 'and' ('*wa*') is often pronounced as 'u'. However, for consistency and ease of understanding, we have represented this word as '*wa*' throughout the text. In general, if 'and' precedes a vowel sound, it should be pronounced as '*wa*', otherwise it should be pronounced as 'u'.

We use a few common vowel combinations (diphthongs) in the text.

ay	signifies an 'a' sound as in 'lane'.
ai	signifies an 'i' sound as in 'why'.

GRAMMAR

Pronouns

I	*ana*
you (m)	*inta*
you (f)	*inti*
he	*hu*
she	*hı*
we	*nihna*
you (pl)	*intu*
they	*hum*

Possessive

To indicate possession in Arabic, simply add a short sound to the end of the noun:

my book	kitab-i
your book (m)	kitab-ak
your book (f)	kitab-ik
his book	kitab-oo
her book	kitab-a
our book	kitab-na
your book (pl)	kitab-kum
their book	kitab-hum

In Arabic, there is no direct equivalent of the English verb 'to have'. Instead, if you wish to express possession, you can use the word '*ind*', followed by the relevant sound as indicated in the table above.

I have money   *Indi guroosh*

To be

CONJUNCTION OF 'TO BE'			
Pronouns	**Past**	**Subjunctive**	**Future**
ana	kunta	akuun	hakuun
nihna	kunna	nakuun	hankuun
inta	kunta	takuun	hatkuun
inti	kunti	takuuni	hatkuuni
intu	kuntu	takuunu	hatkuunu
hu	kaan	yakuun	haykuun
hi	kaanat	takuun	hatkuun
hum	kaanu	yakuunu	haykuunu

In the simple present tense, the verb 'to be' ('*kaan*') is usually omitted.

I am happy   *Ana saiyeed*

However, it is commonly found in other tenses.

Yesterday I was happy (past)	*Umbarich ana kunta saiyeed*
I want to be happy (subjunctive)	*Ana a'ayeez akuun saiyeed*
I'm happy when I see you (conditional)	*Ana hakuun saiyeed laman ashufak*
Tomorrow, I will be happy (future)	*Bookra, ana hakuun saiyeed*

Tenses

Whilst the tenses used in Arabic are broadly similar to those in English, there are some peculiarities that you should be aware of.

The past tense is fairly similar to English.

I went to Amarat   *Ana mashayt Amarat*

The present tense in Arabic is usually used for actions that are repeated regularly.

I go to work every day   *Ana bamshi al-shoghul kuliyoum*

The present conjugation is also often used to express the future.

I will go to work tomorrow   *Ana bamshi al-shoghul bookra*

However, verbs also have their own future tense which can be used instead (adding 'h' or 'ha' to the start of the verb, rather than 'b' or 'ba').

I will go to work tomorrow   *Ana hamshi al-shoghul bookra*

Verbs in Arabic have their own subjunctive form.

I want to go to work tomorrow   *Ana a'ayeez amshi al-shoghul bookra*

Like English, the imperative form in Arabic either relates to the second person plural or the second person singular. In general, there are three variations of the imperative for each verb. However, when the masculine form of the verb finishes with a feminine ending, then there are just two forms.

Go away (to a man or a woman)   *Amshi*
Go away (to a group of people)   *Amshu*

The active participle is similar to the English present continuous. It is used to describe an action that is happening at the moment, or is about to happen.

I am cooking   *Ana taabikh*

Masculine and feminine

Feminine adjectives and nouns generally end with an 'a'. You can usually change a masculine adjective or a noun relating to humans to its feminine form simply by adding an 'a':

teacher   *ustaz (m)*   *ustaza (f)*

The plural

The plural of a noun is formed by adding '*iin*' to the masculine form and '*aat*' to the feminine form.

	Singular	Plural
Sudanese	sudani (m)	sudaaniin (m pl)
thing	haja (f)	hajaat (f pl)

Unfortunately, though, this is only a general rule and there are plenty of exceptions, all of which need to be learned by heart.

	Singular	Plural
bag	shanta	shinat
man, husband	rajil	rujaal
light	noor	anwar
day	youm	aiyyam

Arabic also has something called the 'dual form', which can be used to express things in twos. If a noun ends in a vowel, the dual is formed by adding 'tayn'. Otherwise, it is formed by adding 'ayn'.

once	marra	twice	marratayn
1000	alf	2000	alfayn
one year	sana	two years	sanatayn

The plural in Arabic is only used for quantities between two and 10. If you want to refer to items in quantities of 11 or more, you must revert to the singular again.

one pen	galam (wahid)
two pens	galamayn / itneen agleam
three pens	talaata agleam
11 pens	hiddashar galam

Demonstratives

this (m)	da
this (f)	di
that (m)	daak
that (f)	diik
these (m/f)	del
those (m/f)	dek / delaak

Colours

It is worth mentioning colours here, simply because of the dramatic way in which most of them change between the feminine and masculine forms.

black	assuad (m)	sauda (f)
blue	azrag (m)	zarga (f)
brown	bunni (m)	bunneeya (f)

green	akhdar (m)	khadra (f)
orange	bortugali (m)	bortugaleeya (f)
red	ahmar (m)	hamra (f)
white	abyad (m)	bayda (f)

Comparative and superlative

Unlike English, Arabic uses the same word for both the comparative and the superlative.

better	the best	ahsaan
fast	the fastest	asra'aa'
fatter	the fattest	asmaan
further	the furthest	aba'aad
happier	the happiest	asa'aad
more beautiful	the most beautiful	ajmaal
nearer	the nearest	agraab
taller / longer	the tallest / longest	atwaal
thinner	the thinnest	ada'aaf
worse	the worst	aka'aab

VOCABULARY

Greetings and pleasantries

How are you?[1]	Kayfak / kayfik / kayfkum? Izzayak / izzayik / izzaykum?
(I am) fine	Tamam
(I am) good	Kwayees
(I am) very well (literally: 100%)	Meeya meeya
Hi (literally: welcome)	Marhab
Good morning	Sabah al-khaiir
Good morning (reply)	Sabah al-nur
Good evening	Masah al-khaiir
Good evening (reply)	Masah al-nur
Hello (literally: peace be upon you)	As-salam alaykum
Hello (literally: and upon you be peace)	Wa alaykum as-salam
Congratulations	Mabruuk
Sorry[2]	Malesh
I am sorry[3]	Ana asif (m) / ana asfa (f)
Excuse me[4]	Lao sematha (m) / lao semathi (f)

Sudanese Arabic

[1] The different ways in which you can say 'How are you?' are very similar and there is essentially no difference between them. Some people consider '*izzayak*' to be slightly more formal — you might not want to say it to your boss, for example — but in Sudan the two expressions are used more-or-less interchangeably.

[2] '*Malesh*' is a word that you will hear a lot whilst in Sudan. It is routinely used to apologise for something — for example, if you arrive late for an appointment — but does not usually convey deep regrets.

[3] '*Ana asif*', on the other hand, is used to express sincere regret when you have done something wrong. For example, you might use the phrase if you shut someone's hand in the door.

[4] '*Lao sematha*' is often used if you are trying to attract someone's attention — perhaps when stopping someone on the street to ask for directions.

Numbers

Once you have learnt the numbers between zero and 10, it is not too difficult to master the other numbers.

Between 11 and 19, numbers are formed by adding '*shar*' to (a variation of) the single-digit numbers.

The numbers divisible by 10 are constructed by adding '*iin*' to (a variation of) the single-digit numbers.

Numbers in the hundreds can be formed by prefixing the number that you want to the word for a hundred ('*meeya*').

Combinations of numbers are put together in a different order from the English way of thinking. For example, instead of saying 'twenty-five', you would say '*khamsa wa ishriin*' ('five and twenty').

1	*wahid*	20	*ishriin*
2	*itneen*	25	*khamsa wa ishriin*
3	*talaata*	30	*talaatiin*
4	*arbaa*	40	*arbaa'iin*
5	*khamsa*	50	*khamsiin*
6	*sita*	60	*sittiin*
7	*sabaa*	70	*sabaa'iin*
8	*tamaniya*	80	*tamaniin*
9	*tisaa*	90	*tisaa'iin*
10	*ashara*	100	*meeya*
11	*hiddashar*	150	*meeya wa khamsiin*
12	*itnashar*	200	*mittayn*
13	*talaatashar*	500	*khomsomeeya*
14	*arbaatashar*	1000	*alf*
15	*khamistashar*	2000	*alfayn*

Expressing time

a month ago	*gabli shahar*
day	*youm*
in a month	*ba'ad shahar*
month	*shahar*
the day after tomorrow	*ba'ad bookra*
time	*zamen*
today	*al-layla*
tomorrow	*bookra*
What is the time?	*Sa'aha kam?* *Zamen kam?*
year	*sana*
yesterday	*umbaarih*

Days of the week

Monday	*youm al-itneen*
Tuesday	*youm al-talaata*
Wednesday	*youm al-arbaa*
Thursday	*youm al-khamis*
Friday	*youm al-juma*
Saturday	*youm al-sabit*
Sunday	*youm al-ahad*

Months

In Sudan, there are two common ways of expressing the Gregorian months. One way is simply to express the month as a number between one and 12. The other way uses a similar pronunciation to English.

In some Arabic countries, there is also another name for the months of the Gregorian calendar. However, these names are not generally used in Sudan, apart from in academic circles, and so they are not included here.

January	*shahar wahid*	*yanaiyar*
February	*shahar itneen*	*febraiyar*
March	*shahar talaata*	*maris*
April	*shahar arbaa*	*abril*
May	*shahar khamsa*	*maiyoo*
June	*shahar sita*	*yoonio*
July	*shahar sabaa*	*yoolio*
August	*shahar tamaniya*	*augostos*
September	*shahar tisaa*	*sebtember*
October	*shahar ashara*	*oktober*
November	*shahar hiddashar*	*november*

| December | *shahar itnashar* | *december* |

Questions

Where?	*Wayn?*
To where?	*Le wayn?*
From where?	*Min wayn?*
Who?	*Minu?*
How?	*Kayf?*
How much/many?	*Kam?*
How much does it cost?	*Be kam?*
Why?	*Lay?*
When?	*Mitayn?*
Is there any water?	*Fi moiya?*
Yes, there is.	*Aiwa, fi.*
No, there isn't.	*La, ma fi.*
What is that?	*Da shinoo?*
How do I get to Amarat?	*Kayf amshi Amarat?*

Prepositions

about	*'an*
above	*foqh*
after	*ba'ad*
before	*gabli*
between	*bayn*
from	*min*
in	*fi*
in front of	*giddaam*
near	*jamb*
on	*'ala*
outside	*barra*
to / for	*lei*
under	*tihit*
with (cheese)	*bel (jipna)*
with (him)	*maa (hu)*

USEFUL EXPRESSIONS

Introductions

| My name is Johnny. | *Ismi Johnny.* |

I am from England.	*Ana min Ingelterra.*
I am a teacher. I work in the American School.	*Ana ustaz. Ana shaghal fi al-Madrasa al-Amerikia.*
I live in Amarat, Street 15	*Ana sakin (m) / sakna (f) fi Amarat, Sharia Khamistashar.*
I arrived five months ago.	*Ana jiit gabli khamsa shuhur.*
I will stay here for one year.	*Ha ago'ud hina lei mudat sana.*
What's your name?	*Ismak (m) / ismik (f) minu?*
Where do you work?	*Inta (m) / inti (f) shaghal(a) wayn?*
What company do you work for?	*Inta (m) / inti (f) shaghal(a) fi yaato sharika?*

Professions

director / manager	*mudir(a)*
doctor	*diktor(a)* *tabiib(a)*
engineer	*muhandis(a)*
journalist	*sahafi(ya)*
teacher	*ustaz(a)*
translator	*mutarjim(a)*
volunteer	*muttowa' (m)* *muttowiya (f)*

Places

ambulance	*isaaf*
café	*café*
company	*sharika*
embassy	*safara*
hospital	*mustashfa*
hotel	*fundoq*
office	*maktab*
organisation	*moonazama*
police station	*gisim bolis*
post office	*bariid*
restaurant	*mat'aam*
shop	*dookkan* *baqalla*

Permits

exit and re-entry visa	*tashirat khuruj wa dukhuul*
exit visa	*tashirat khuruj*

Sudanese Arabic

photography permit	*isin tasweirr*
registration office	*maktab tasjil al ajanip*
residence permit	*irama*
travel permit	*isin safar / tasrieh safar*
work permit	*isin amel*

Feelings

I am hungry	*Ana ja'an(a)*
I am angry with you[1]	*Ana za'alan(a) minak (to m)*
	Ana za'alan(a) minik (to f)
I am full	*Ana shaba'an(a)*
I am happy	*Ana farhaan(a)*
	Ana sa'eed(a)
I am sad	*Ana za'alan(a)*
I am thirsty	*Ana a'atshan(a)*
I am tired	*Ana ta'aban(a)*

[1] Note that 'I am sad' is the same as 'I am angry'. I general, the Sudanese do not make a distinction between the two. Therefore, if your father dies, you might express your emotions as: *'ana za'alan'*. Equally, if your little brother breaks your CD player, you might say *'ana za'alan minak'*.

SITUATION DIALOGUES

In the shop	**Fi ad-dukkan**
Good morning.	*Sabah al-khair.*
Good morning. I would like some bread, three eggs and some matches.	*Sabah al-nur. Ana a'ayeez ash-terri a'aish wa talaata beedaat wa kibrita.*
Do you need anything else?	*Tani daiyir haja?*
Yes, I would like some green tea. How much does it cost?	*Ai, daiyir shai akhdar. Da be kam?*
The big one is 12 and the small one is four.	*Al-kabira bay itnashar wa al-saghiira bay arbaa.*
Give me the small one.	*Addiini as-saghiira.*
Is that everything?	*Da kullu?*
I would like some soap powder (for clothes).	*Ana a'ayeez sabuun boodra.*
This one costs two and this one costs 12.	*Da be itneen wa da be itnashar.*
I would like the big one.	*Ana daiyir al-kabiira.*
How much is the total?	*Da kullu be kam?*

That will be 20 SDG.	*Da kullu be ishriin jenayh.*
Thank you.	*Shukraan.*
Here is your change.	*Itfaddaal al-baghi.*
Thank you.	*Shukraan.*

In the restaurant	**Fi al-mat'aam**
Good evening.	*Masah al-khair.*
Good evening. Welcome.	*Masah al-noor. Marhab itfaddaal.*
Could you give me the menu please?	*Mumkin taddini al-menu lao sematha?*
Here it is.	*Itfaddaal.*
It is all in Arabic. Could you tell me what you have, please?	*Di kullu bel arabi. Mumkin taorini inda-kum shinoo, lao sematha?*
We have tomato soup, barbe-cued chicken or meat, and falafel.	*Indana shorbat tomatem, ferakh mashu-ee wa laham wa tameeya.*
Do you have any fish?	*Indakum samak?*
No, sorry, it is finished.	*La, malesh, kimil.*
Okay. I would like soup and some chicken.	*Taiyib, Ana daiyir shorba wa ferakh.*
I'll have the same.	*Ana bardu nafs ash-shee.*
For a drink, I would like fresh guava juice and a big bottle of water.	*Mashrubaat ana daiyir a'asiir jawafa fresh wa moiya kabira.*
Here it is.	*Itfaddaal.*
Thanks.	*Shukraan.*

After the meal...

The bill, please?	*Al-hisaab, lao samatha.*
It is 34 jenayh.	*Arbaa wa talaatiin jenayh.*
Goodbye.	*Ma'a salaama.*

Receiving guests	**Istiqbal al-diyoof**
What would you like to drink? Coffee, tea or fruit juice?	*Daiyir tashrab shinoo? Gahawa, shai walla a'asiir?*
Tea with milk.	*Shai leban.*
How much sugar?	*Sooar kayf?*
One spoon.	*Ma'alaga wahida.*
Thank you.	*Shukraan.*

When the tea arrives...

It is very good.	*Samih.*

Are you hungry? Can I give you something to eat?

No, really, thank you. I have eaten already.[1]

Inta ja'an? Mumkin a'amil layk haja takoola?

La, walahee, shukraan. Akalta.

[1] The Sudanese are extremely hospitable people and will insist, often quite forcefully, that you accept their hospitality. If you really do not wish to eat or drink what they are offering, 'walahee' is a good way of firmly, but politely, declining.

Taking a taxi

Hello.

I need to go to the British Embassy in Al-Baladeyah Street, next to the German Embassy.

Okay, please get in (literally: ride).

How much does it cost?

Don't worry.

No, really, how much?[1]

20 jenayh.

That is a lot. I always pay 10.

Okay, 10, come in.

Please turn left.

At the next street, turn right.

Please stop here.

Here it is.

Thank you. Goodbye.

Yakhood taxi

Salam alaykum.

Ana mashee as-safara al-britaa-neeya, fi Sharia al-Baladeyah, jamb as-safara al-Almaaneeya.

Tayib, arkab.

Be kam?

Ma mushkela.

La, la be kam.

Isriin jenayh.

La, katiira. Ana tawalee bedfa'a ashara.

Taiyib, ashara, arkab.

Lao sematha, lif shimaal.

Ash sharia al-jai, lif yamiin.

Lao sematha agiif hina.

Itfaddaal.

Shukraan. Ma'a salama.

[1] You will find that many taxi drivers prefer to negotiate the price after they have delivered you the service. Sometimes you have to negotiate quite hard to insist that they tell you what the price will be beforehand.

At the hospital

Good morning. I need a doctor.

Why? What do you feel?

I haven't been feeling well since yesterday. I have a fever, I have diarrhoea and I have been vomiting.

Okay, please have a seat. When the doctor is free we will call you.

Thank you.

Fil-mustashfa

Sabab al-khiir. Ana daiyir diktor.

Lay? Hassi be shinoo?

Min umbarih, bil-leyl ana ma hassi inni tamam. Indi humma wa is-hal wa toorash

Taiyib, faddaal. Laman yakoon ad-diktor faadi nihna hankalimak

Shukraan.

After some minutes...

Could you enter the second room on the left? A doctor is waiting for you.

Did you say the second on the right?

No, sir, the second on the left.

Okay thanks.

Good morning. I was told that you have problems with your stomach and your head.

Yes, I have.

What did you eat yesterday?

Yesterday, I went to the camel market and I ate lunch there. In the evening, I ate pizza.

When did you start to feel sick?

During the night, I woke up because I had cramps and I had to go to the toilet.

Okay, let's do a blood test.

Mumkin takhoosh fi al-qorfa at-tania be shamaalak. Ad-diktor moontazrak.

Gulta at-tania be yamini?

La, ya sayeed, at-tania be shamaalak.

Taiyeeb, shukraan.

Sabab al-khiir. Galu lei indak mashaakil fi ma'adatak wa raasak.

Aiwa indi.

Umbarih akalta shinu?

Umbarih ana masheet souq al-naga wa akalta al-ghada hinak. Wa fil-mughrib ana akalta bitza.

Wa mitayn bigheet a'ayan?

Fi asna al-leyl ana saheed a'ashan kaan indi maqus wa kaan lazim amshi al-hammam.

Taiyib. Yalla a'amil fahas ad-dam.

After the blood test...

There is no malaria in the results. It is possible that it was something you ate. Take these pills twice a day, before eating and drink a lot of water.

Thank you doctor.

May God give you health.

Ma fi malaria fil-natiija. Mum-kin a'ashan haja akaltaha. Khud al-haboob di marratayn fil-youm, gabli ma takul wa tashrab moiya katiira.

Shukraan diktor.

Allah yiddik al-a'ahfia.

SOME VOCABULARY

Kitchen	*Matbakh*	**Bathroom**	*Hammam*
bowl	*koreeya*	brush	*forsha*
cooker	*halla*	comb	*moshot*
fork	*shoka*	deodorant	*muziil*
freezer	*frezer*	electric razor	*makanet haylaya*
fridge	*talaaja*	perfume	*riha*
glass / cup	*kobaiya*	shampoo	*shamboo*
knife	*sakkeen*	soap	*sabuuna*
plate	*siineeya*	toothbrush	*forshet asnaan*

spoon	ma'alaga	toothpaste	ma'ajuun
Food	Ta'aam	**Furniture**	Athath
aubergine	asuad	bed	sariir
banana	mohz	chair	koorsee
butter	zibda	desk	maktab
courgette	koza	door	baab
grape	'ainap	mirror	miraiya
grapefruit	grayn	pillow	makhada
juice	a'asiir	pillowcase	kiis makhada
mango	manga	sheet (for a bed)	milaiya
oil (for cooking)	zayt	sofa	kanaba
onion	bassal	table	tarabayza
orange	bortuqan	television	television
pepper	fil fil	wardrobe	doolab
potato	bataatis		
salt	mileh		
tomato	tomaatem		
water	moiya		

VERB CONJUGATION

Verbs in Arabic are conjugated by taking the three consonant sounds that form the root (or stem) and inserting the appropriate vowel sounds. When talking about verbs in Arabic, one tends to refer to them in the third-person past, rather than in the infinitive.

To help you understand these concepts, consider the verb *tabakh* (to cook). *Tabakh* means 'he cooks', but it is also used to indicate the infinitive of the verb.

Tabakh is a regular verb. It is formed with the three hard consonants ('T'-'B'-'K'). The following tables show how vowels can be integrated into these three consonants in order to create all of the tenses you might need.

There are three other types of verbs, which include a softer vowel-sound somewhere within the three-consonant construction. For example, *haba* (to like) is formed from the root ('H'-'B'-'A').

The following verb conjugations include examples from all of the four main class of verbs. The stem of the root is given according to the format CVC, where 'C' indicates a hard consonant and 'V' indicates a softer vowel sound.

Tabakh (to cook)

Pronouns	Past	Subjunctive	Present
ana	tabakhta	atbokh	batbokh
nihna	tabakhna	natbokh	binatbokh
inta	tabakhta	tatbokh	bitatbokh
inti	tabakhti	tatbokhi	bitatbokhi
intu	tabakhtu	tatbukhu	bitatbukhu
hu	tabakh	yatbokh	bitbokh
hi	tabakhat	tatbokh	bitatbokh
hum	tabakhoo	yatbukhoo	bitbukhoo

Imperative
atbokh (m)
atbokhi (f)
atbukhu (pl)

Active participle
taabikh (m)
taabkha (f)
taabkhiin (pl)

'Arif (to know)

Pronouns	Past	Subjunctive	Present
ana	'arifta	'arif	ba'rif
nihna	'arifna	n'arif	bin'arif
inta	'arifta	t'arif	bit'arif
inti	'arifti	t'arifi	bit'arifi
intu	'ariftu	t'arifu	bit'arifu
hu	'arif	y'arif	bi'arif
hi	'arifat	t'arif	bit'arif
hum	'arifu	y'arifu	b'arifu

Imperative
'arif (m)
'arifi (f)
'arifu (pl)

Active participle
'arif (m)
'arifa (f)
'arifiin (pl)

Other verbs that fall into this pattern: *safar* (to travel), *'amal* (to do or make), *fakara* (to think), *fatah* (to open), *gafal* (to close), *daf'a* (to pay).

Sudanese Arabic

Wasal (to arrive)

Pronouns	Past	Subjunctive	Present
ana	wasalta	asal	basal
nihna	waslna	nasal	binasal
inta	wasalta	tasal	bitasal
inti	wasalti	tasali	bitasli
intu	wasaltu	tasalu	bitasalo
hu	wasal	yasal	biyasal
hi	wasalat	tasal	bitasal
hum	wasaloo	yasaloo	biyasaloo

Imperative	Active participle
asal (m)	tasal (m)
asali (f)	tasala (f)
asaloo (pl)	tasaliin (pl)

Akal (to eat)

Pronouns	Past	Subjunctive	Present
ana	akul	akul	bakul
nihna	akalna	nakul	binakul
inta	akalta	takul	bitakul
inti	akalti	takli	bitakli
intu	akaltu	takulu	bitakloo
hu	akal	yakul	biyakul
hi	akalat	takul	bitakul
hum	akaloo	yakloo	biyakloo

Imperative	Active participle
ukul (m)	makil (m)
ukli (f)	makla (f)
ukloo (pl)	makiliin (pl)

Other verbs that fall into this pattern: *wagaf* (to stop), *wazan* (to weigh), *akhad* (to take), *assas* (to establish / to set up).

Laaga (to meet someone)

Pronouns	Past	Subjunctive	Present
ana	laagayt	alaagi	balaagi
nihna	laagayna	nalaagi	binlaagi
inta	laagayt	talaaga	bitlaaga
inti	laagayti	talaagi	bitlaagi
intu	laagaytu	talaagu	bitlaagu
hu	laaga	yilaagi	bilaagi
hi	laagat	talaagi	bitlaagi
hum	laagoo	yilaagoo	bilaagoo

Imperative
lagi (m)
lagi (f)
lagu (pl)

Active participle
mulagi (m)
mulagia (f)
mulagiin (pl)

Gaal (to say)

Pronouns	Past	Subjunctive	Present
ana	guulta	aguul	baguul
nihna	guulna	naguul	binaguul
inta	guulta	taguul	bitaguul
inti	guulti	taguuli	bitaguuli
intu	guultu	taguulu	bitaguulu
hu	gaal	yaguul	biguul
hi	gaalat	taguul	bitaguul
hum	gaaloo	yaguuloo	biguuloo

Imperative
guul (m)
guuli (f)
guuloo (pl)

Active participle
guyl (m)
guyla (f)
guyliin (pl)

Sudanese Arabic

Saal (to ask)

Pronouns	Past	Subjunctive	Present
ana	sa'alta	asa'al	basa'al
nihna	sa'alna	nasa'al	binsa'al
inta	sa'alta	tasa'al	bitasa'al
inti	sa'alti	tasa'ali	bitasa'ali
intu	sa'altu	tasa'alu	bitasa'alu
hu	sa'al	yasa'al	bisa'al
hi	sa'alat	tasa'al	bitsa'al
hum	sa'aloo	yasa'aloo	bisa'aloo

Imperative
asal (m)
asali (f)
asaloo (pl)

Active participle
sa'il (m)
sa'il a (f)
sa'iliin (pl)

Other verbs that fall into this pattern: *zaar* (to visit), *ghaar* (to be jealous), *taar* (to fly).

Masha (to go)

Pronouns	Past	Subjunctive	Present
ana	mashayt	amshee	bamshee
nihna	mashayna	namshee	binamshee
inta	mashayt	tamshee	bitamshee
inti	mashayti	tamshee	bitamshee
intu	mashaytu	tamshoo	bitamshoo
hu	masha	yamshee	biyamshee
hi	mashaat	tamshee	bitamshee
hum	mashoo	yamshoo	bimshoo

Imperative
imshi (m)
imshi (f)
amshu (pl)

Active participle
mashi (m)
masha (f)
mashin (pl)

Liga (to find)

Pronouns	Past	Subjunctive	Present
ana	ligeet	alga	balga
nihna	ligeena	nalga	binalga
inta	ligeet	talga	bitalga
inti	ligeeti	talgi	bitalgi
intu	ligeetu	talgu	bitalgu
hu	liga	yelga	bilga
hi	ligat	talga	bitalga
hum	ligoo	yelgoo	bilgoo

Imperative
alga (m)
algee (f)
algu (pl)

Active participle
lagee (m)
lageea (f)
lageen (pl)

Haba (to like / to love)

Pronouns	Past	Subjunctive	Present
ana	habayt	ahib	bahib
nihna	habayna	nahib	binhib
inta	habayt	tahib	bit'hib
inti	habayti	tahibi	bit'hibi
intu	habaytu	tahibu	bit'hibu
hu	haba	yahib	bihib
hi	habat	tahib	bit'hib
hum	haboo	yahiboo	bihiboo

Imperative
hib (m)
hibi (f)
hiboo (pl)

Active participle
habi (m)
haba (f)
habiin (pl)

Sudanese Arabic

Gara (to read / to study)

Pronouns	Past	Subjunctive	Present
ana	gareet	agra	bagra
nihna	gareena	nagra	binagra
inta	gareet	tagra	bitagra
inti	gareeti	tagri	bitagri
intu	gareetu	tagru	bitagru
hu	gara	yagra	bigra
hi	garat	tagra	bitagra
hum	garoo	yagroo	bigru

Imperative
agra (m)
agri (f)
agru (pl)

Active participle
gari (m)
garia (f)
gariin (pl)

Ishtara (to buy)

Pronouns	Past	Subjunctive	Present
ana	ishtarayt	ishteri	bashteri
nihna	ishtarayna	nishteri	binishteri
inta	ishtarayt	tashteri	bitishteri
inti	ishtarayti	tishteri	bitishteri
intu	ishtaraytu	tishtaru	bitishtaru
hu	ishtara	yishteri	bishteri
hi	ishtarat	tishteri	bitishteri
hum	ishtaroo	yishtaru	bishtaru

Imperative
ishteri (m)
ishteri (f)
ishtaru (pl)

Active participle
mushteri (m)
mushteria (f)
mushterin (pl)

Fihim (to understand)

Pronouns	Past	Subjunctive	Present
ana	fihimta	bafham	afham
nihna	fihimna	binafham	nafham
inta	fihimta	bitafham	tafham
inti	fihimti	bitafhmi	tafahmi
intu	fihimtu	bitafhamu	tafhamu
hu	fihim	bifham	ifham
hi	fihimat	bitafham	tafham
hum	fihmu	bifhamu	ifhamu

Imperative
afham (m)
afhami (f)
afhamu (pl)

Active participle
faahim (m)
faahma (f)
faahmin (pl)

Further Reading

GENERAL HISTORY

A History of the Sudan by PM Holt and MW Daly, Longman, 2000

Probably the most comprehensive account of contemporary Sudanese history that you are likely to come across. Lecturers at the University of Khartoum swear by it.

Sudan: Race, Religion and Violence by Jok Madot Jok

An ambitious book by a Sudanese social scientist, which aims to show how Sudan's many different conflicts have helped to shape the country.

Darfur and the Failure of an African State by Richard Cockett

The former African Editor of the Economist takes an intelligent and introspective view of what has gone wrong with Sudan since independence — and how things can be fixed.

COLONIAL HISTORY

Khartoum: The Ultimate Imperial Adventure by Michael Asher

A colourful account of British and Egyptian military campaigns in Sudan between 1883 and 1998. The book deals with the Mahdi's triumph over the colonial imperialists, and subsequent efforts by the British to reclaim the country.

The River War by Winston Churchill, 1899

A gripping first-hand account of Britain's attempt to recapture Sudan from the Mahdi, under the command of General Herbert Kitchener.

With Kitchener to Khartoum by G.W.Steevens

Another first-hand account of the 1898 Sudan campaign, written by a journalist for the *Daily Mail*.

The Mahdi of Sudan and the Death of General Gordon by Fergus Nicoll, The History Press, 2005

An excellent historical account of the Mahdi uprising and the assassination of General Charles Gordon.

Jihad: The Mahdi Rebellion in the Sudan by Murray S. Fradin, Author's Choice Press, 2003

Another well-researched book about the Mahdi in the 19th century.

ARCHAEOLOGY

The Kingdom of Kush by Derek Welsby, Marcus Wiener, 1996

An excellent and very accessible overview of the evolution of the Kushite kingdoms of northern Sudan, providing an insight into the lives of the Black Pharaohs more than 2000 years ago.

The Medieval Kingdoms of Nubia by Derek Welsby, British Museum Press, 2002

Written in a similar vein to *The Kingdom of Kush*, Welsby now takes the opportunity to explore the rise and fall of Nubia.

DARFUR

Saving Darfur by Rob Crilly

A highly compelling account of why Darfur is in the mess that it is in, combining great political analysis with the personal experiences of a journalist in the field.

Darfur: The Ambiguous Genocide by Gérard Prunier, Cornell University Press, 2005

Told by a master historian of contemporary Africa, this book sets out to explain how the ethnological makeup of Sudan has contributed to the current crisis in Darfur, and why it poses such a significant threat to the government in Khartoum.

Darfur: A Short History of a Long War by Julie Flint and Alex de Waal, Zed Books, 2006

This book examines the complex history of Darfur and looks at how the governments of Sudan and Libya have manipulated the conflict for their own ends.

The Devil Came on Horseback: Bearing Witness to the Genocide in Darfur by Brian Steidle and Gretchen Steidle Wallace, Public Affairs, 2007

The impassioned memoir of a US marine, who was stationed in Sudan between 2004 and 2006. Good if you are interested in a first-hand account of life on the ground.

TRAVEL WRITING

The Weekenders by Alex Garland, W.F. Deedes, Tony Hawks, and Irvine Welsh, Ebury Press, 2001

A collection of short stories and travel writing from the Sudan, from some well-known contemporary writers. The stories are very mixed — some tragically naïve and others darkly disturbing.

The Life of My Choice by Wilfred Thesiger, W. W. Norton & Company, 1987

The autography of one of Sudan's most notable explorers, written towards the end of his life. It takes a look at life in Sudan in the 1930s, when Britain was in control of the country.

The Translator: A Tribesman's Memoir of Darfur by Daoud Hari, Thorndike Press, 2008

A wonderful, heart-stopping read about a native Darfuri translator who fled the fighting in his home town, only to return to work with reporters and UN investigators in crisis situations.

SOUTH SUDAN

Emma's War by Deborah Scroggins, Vintage, 2004

This book tells the story of a 27-year-old aid worker who marries a local rebel leader, and the struggle she faced in having to sacrifice some of her own ideals for the love of her husband.

What is the What by David Eggers, Penguin, 2008

A beautiful story of a former child soldier that is forced to serve with the Southern rebels after being taken from his family. Eggers ingeniously weaves fact and fiction together for an epic tale of adventure, tragedy, loss and survival.

The Lost Boys of Sudan: An American Story of the Refugee Experience by Mark Bixler, University of Georgia Press, 2005

The inspiring tale of four young men who fled Sudan's civil war to eventually settle in America. An often touching tale of a struggle through tragic circumstances.

FICTION

The Season of the Migration to the North by Tayeb Salih, Penguin Classics, 1969

Regarded as a classic in contemporary Sudanese writing, Salih explores cross-cultural experiences by telling the story of a villager returning to his native village in North Sudan, having spent several years studying in England.

ETHNOGRAPHY

The Nuer: A Description of the Modes of Livelihood and Political Institutions of a Nilotic People by E. E. Evans-Pritchard, Oxford University Press, 1969

A look at societal structures through the eyes of one of south Sudan's ethnic groups.

Witchcraft, Oracles and Magic among the Azande (abridged) by E. E. Evans-Pritchard and Eva Gillies, 1976, Oxford University Press

Academic but accessible, this work looks at life among the Azande tribe, a tribe found in the south-west corner of South Sudan as well as some other African nations.

Divinity and Experience: the Religion of the Dinka by Godfrey Lienhardt, Clarenden Press, 1961

An insightful look at one of Sudan's most prominent tribes, who continue to shape Sudanese politics through their involvement in government.

Kwanim Pa: the Making of the Uduk People, Oxford University Press, 1980

A well-regarded study into a tribal people that live along the Ethiopian border and became very much caught up in the North-South civil war.

ISLAM

Seeking Sanctuary by Hilda Reilly, Eye Books, 2005

A fascinating insight into what draws Western Muslim converts to North Sudan. The book works so effectively because it lets the converts themselves describe their own spiritual journeys. Anyone that has been to North Sudan will find it difficult not to relate to the book in some way.

A Brief Guide to Islam: Faith, Religion, Politics by Paul Grieve, Running Press, 2006

An excellent introductory text to Islam, written by a non-Muslim who makes a brave attempt to dispel some of the myths that pervade in the West.

VIDEOS AND FILMS

Lost Boys of Sudan, Megan Mylan and Jon Shenk, 2003

A classic feature-length documentary film that follows the journey of two Sudanese refugees as they make their way from Africa to America. Nominated for the prestigious Emmy television award, this is definitely one film about Sudan that is worth seeing.

World Without Sun (*Le Monde Sans Soleil*), Jacques Cousteau, 1964

A celebrated documentary by pioneering underwater explorer Jacques Cousteau, chronicling an early attempt to create an underwater environment suitable for humans to live and work in. Filmed in the Red Sea, just off Port Sudan.

The Message, Moustapha Akkad, 1976

A sensitively-directed film chronicling the life and times of Prophet Mohammed. Funded with Libyan money, and well-regarded by Sudanese, definitely worth checking out.

Listings

NORTH SUDAN (+249)

Airports and airlines

Airport (Khartoum)
🕿 0183 774 405 or 0183 788 194 or 0183 780 129

Air France
🏠 Qasar Street, Central Khartoum; 🕿 0183-776606

British Airways
🏠 International Airport, Amarat; 🕿 0183 797 277

BMI
🏠 Jamhouriya Street, Central Khartoum; 🕿 0183 774 764

Egypt Air
🏠 Qasar Street; 🕿 0183 771 259 or 0183 780 064

Emirates
🏠 Jamhouriya Street, Central Khartoum; 🕿 0183 799 899

Ethiopian Airlines
🏠 Jamhouriya Street, Central Khartoum; 🕿 0183-781884 or 0183 762 088

Gulf Air
🏠 Jamhouriya Street, Central Khartoum; 🕿 0183 776 525 or 0183 778 503

Kenya Airways and KLM
Ali Abdul Latif Street, Central Khartoum; 🕿 0183 781 080

Lufthansa
🏠 Tayar Murad Street, Central Khartoum; 🕿 0183 771 322

Marsland Aviation
🕿 0183 483 311

Mid Airlines
🕿 0183 576 641 or 0183 792 167

Qatar Airways
🏠 Jamhouriya Street, Central Khartoum; 🕿 0183 761 304

Royal Jordanian
🏠 Central Khartoum; 🕿 0183 762 743

Saudi Airlines
🏠 Ali Abdul Latif Street, Central Khartoum; 🕿 0183 771 633 or 0183 780 425

Sudan Airways
🕿 0183 764 034 or 0183 481 579

Sun Air
🏠 International Airport, Amarat; 🕿 0183 763 636

Syrian Air
🕿 0183 761 351

Yemen Airlines
🕿 0183 797 979

Banks

Animal Resources Bank
🏠 Afriqia Street, off Street 3, Amarat; 🕿 0183 472 025

Bank of Khartoum
🏠 Jamhouriya Street, Central Khartoum; 🕿 0183 770 170

Bank of Sudan;
🏠 Mogran; 🕿 0183 778 064

Byblos Bank Africa
🏠 Street 21, Amarat; 🕿 0183 566 444; 🖥 www.byblosbank.com

Faisal Islamic Bank
🏠 El-Fayhaa Commercial Centre, Ali Abdul Latif Street, Central Khartoum; 🕿 0183 741 326; @ fibsudan@fibsudan.com; 🖥 www.fibsudan.com

Islamic Co-operative Development Bank
🏠 Tenmia Tower, Kolyat Eltib Street, Central Khartoum; 🕿 0183 774 124; 🖥 www.iscob.com

Sudanese French Bank
🏠 Qasar Street, Central Khartoum; 🕿 0183 784 902

Bookshops

Khartoum Modern Bookshop
🏠 Zubeir Pasha Street, Central Khartoum; 🕿 0103 774 425

Marawi Bookshop
🏠 Barlaman Street; Central Khartoum; 🕿 0183 773 435

Nile Bookshop
🏠 Street 41, Amarat; 🕿 0183 463 749; @ info@thenilebookshop.com; 🖥 www.thenilebookshop.com

New Bookshop
🏠 Zubeir Pasha Street, Central Khartoum; 🕿 0183 774 425

Sudan Bookshop
🏠 Tayar Murad Street; ☎ 0183 772 089

Sudanese House for Books
🏠 Baladeyah Street, Central Khartoum; ☎ 0183 780 031

Car Rental

5M
🏠 Cathrina Street, Khartoum 2; ☎ 0183 460 438 or 0183 462 962 or 0913 118 464 or 0912 010 385; @ mickey5m1@gmail.com; 💻 www.5mrentacar.com

Nice Limousine
☎ 0912 331 852; @ mano@nicelimousine.com

Europcar
☎ 0183 74661 or 0915 000 692; 💻 www.europcar.com

Abu Harba Limousine
🏠 East of the Sudanese French Bank, Khartoum 2; ☎ 0912 345 227; @ nwaisa@abuharba.com; 💻 www.abuharba.com

Seven for Car Rent
🏠 On the corner of Beu-Yokwan Street and Jazeera Street, Khartoum 3; ☎ 0914 450 024; @ malibs@hotmail.com or mohamed.alibs@seven.elnefeigroup.com

Abu Tarha Car Rental
🏠 Grand Holiday Villa Hotel, Nile Avenue; ☎ 0183 762 698 or 0912 359 743; @ contact@abutarha.com; 💻 www.abutarha.com

Car Retail

Nefeidi Motors
🏠 Barlaman Street, Central Khartoum; ☎ 0183 762 021; @ nefgroup@hotmail.com; 💻 www.elnefeindigroup.com

Golden Arrow
🏠 Al-Ghada Street, New Industrial Area; ☎ 0183 579 481/87/97; @ nefgroup@hotmail.com; 💻 www.elnefeindigroup.com

Dal Motors
🏠 Afriqia Street, Soba; ☎ 0183 232 777

Al-Safwa Motors
🏠 Kafouri, Bahri; ☎ 0185 343 878

Clubs

German Club
🏠 Street 1, Amarat; ☎ 0183 462 438

Greek Club
🏠 Khartoum 2, near Assaha Village; ☎ 0183 467 577

Doctors

CARDIOLOGISTS

Dr Siham Ahmed Hassab El Rasoul
☎ 0183 489 977 or 0911 144 611

DENTISTS

Dr Ahmed Bakri
☎ 0183 473 244

Dr Maher Saad
☎ 0183 22 20 86 or 0183 22 30 61

Dr Salwa Makram
☎ 0912 347 373 or 0183 468 975

GENERAL

Dr Girgis Kilada
☎ 0912 303 959

Dr Mohammed Ibrahim
☎ 0912 351 276

Dr Mohammed Sirag
☎ 0912 300 370

OBSTETRICIANS

Dr Audrey T. Samaan
☎ 0183 771 578 or 0183 771 852

OPTICIANS

Nour Optic
🏠 Sahara Hotel Block, off Al-Jamhouriya Street, Central Khartoum

Mekka Eye Hospital
🏠 Al-Noos Street, Riyad

PAEDIATRICIANS

Dr Amanda Tadros
☎ 0183 771 578 or 0183 771 852 or 0912 206 846

Dr El Tahir Medani Elshibly
☎ 0183 273 997 or 0183 777 446

Dr Sara Yahia
☎ 0912 288 109 or 0183 225 332

PHYSIOTHERAPISTS

Dr Ragie
☎ 09 123 03727

Dr Ernie
☎ 09 129 09326

TROPICAL DISEASE SPECIALISTS

Dr Hala Abuzeid Ahmed
☎ 0912 870 425

Dr Musa Mohammed Khair
☎ 0912 306 833

Embassies and consular representations

Australia (HC)
🏠 Baladeyah Street, Central Khartoum; ☎ 0183 780 034

Bangladesh (HC)
🏠 Street 15, Amarat; ☎ 0183 472 315

Belgium (HC)
🏠 Street 33, Amarat; ☎ 0183 489232

Bulgaria (HC)
🏠 Street 31, Amarat; ☎ 0183 787 642

Canada
🏠 North end of Afriqia Street; ☎ 0156 550 500; @ khrtm@international.gc.ca

China
🏠 Manshea; ☎ 0183 272 730 or 0183 272 603

Congo
🏠 Street 13, Amarat; ☎ 0183 471 125

Czech Republic (HC)
🏠 Mustafa Elamin Building, Bahri; ☎ 0183 778 044 or 0183 778 045

Egypt
🏠 Jama'a Street, Central Khartoum; ☎ 0183 777 646 or 0183 778 741

Eritrea
🏠 Street 39, Khartoum 2; ☎ 0183 483 834/43

Ethiopia
🏠 Near Turab Faroub cemetery, Khartoum South; ☎ 0183 471 379 or 0183 471 156

European Union
🏠 Osman Digna Street, Central Khartoum; ☎ 0183 775 054 or 0183 775 148

Finland (HC)
🏠 Barlaman Street, Central Khartoum; ☎ 0183 774 304

France
🏠 Street 13, Amarat; ☎ 0183 471 082 or 474 893

Germany
🏠 Baladeyah Street, Central Khartoum; ☎ 0183 777 975 or 0183 777 990

Greece
🏠 Jamhouriya Street, Central Khartoum; ☎ 0183 765 901

India
🏠 Afriqia Street, Khartoum South; ☎ 0183 471 202

Indonesia
🏠 Street 60, Riyad; ☎ 0183 225 106 or 0183 229 106

Italy
🏠 Street 39, Khartoum 2; ☎ 0183 471 614 or 0183 471 616

Japan
🏠 Street 43, Khartoum 2; ☎ 0183 775 875 or 0183 471 600

Jordan
🏠 Street 33, Amarat; ☎ 0183 471 164 or 0183 475 090

Kenya
🏠 Street 3, Amarat; ☎ 0183 463 758 or 0183 475 090

Korea
🏠 Street 1, Amarat; ☎ 0183 471 136

Lebanon
🏠 Street 5, Amarat; ☎ 0183 461 320 or 0183 461 295

Libya
🏠 Riyad; ☎ 0183 222 457 or 0183 222 085

Malaysia
🏠 Street 3; ☎ 0183 482 763 or 0183 482 764

Morocco
🏠 Street 7, Amarat; ☎ 0183 471 603

Netherlands
🏠 Street 47, Khartoum 2; ☎ 0183 471 200 or 0183 471 198

Nigeria
🏠 Mek Nimir Street, Central Khartoum; ☎ 0183 779 121 or 0183 779 120

Oman
🏠 Street 1, Amarat; ☎ 0183 471 605 or 0183 471 606

Poland (HC)
🏠 Mohammed Najeeb Street, off Street 41, Amarat, ☎ 0183 471 830

Somalia
🏠 Street 23, Amarat; ☎ 0183 471 151

Spain
🏠 In front of Khartoum International Fair, Burri; ☎ 0183 763 639 or 0183 269 891

Norway
🏠 Street 63, next to UNICEF, Khartoum 2; ☎ 0183 578 336 or 0183 578 343

Listings

Pakistan
🏠 Riyad; ☎ 0183 225 503 or 0183 223 445

Qatar
🏠 Street 11, Amarat; ☎ 0183 471 622 or 0183 471 621

Romania
🏠 Kafouri, Bahri; 0185 330 113

Russia
🏠 Street 5, Amarat; ☎ 0183 471 043

Saudi Arabia
🏠 Street 29, Amarat; ☎ 0183 472 583 or 0183 472 584

Sweden (HC)
🏠 Barlaman Street, Central Khartoum; ☎ 0183 780 500 or 0183 785 036

Malta
🏠 Ibrahim El Mufti Street, Khartoum 2

Switzerland
🏠 Street 7, Amarat; ☎ 0183 471 010 or 0183 471 115

Syria
🏠 Street 3, Amarat; ☎ 0183 471 152 or 0183 471 153

Tunisia
🏠 Street 15, Amarat; ☎ 0183 487 947

Turkey
🏠 Baladeyah Street, Central Khartoum; ☎ 0183 794 215

Uganda
🏠 Abujana street, Khartoum East; ☎ 0183 797 867

United Arab Emirates
☎ 0183 471 094

United Kingdom
🏠 Baladeyah Street, Central Khartoum; ☎ 0183 777 105 or 0183 770 769

United States of America
🏠 Kilo 10, Soba; ☎ 0183 022 000

Yemen
🏠 Street 11, Amarat; ☎ 0183 471 623 or 0183 471 625

Emergency services

Ambulance
☎ 911

Ambulance (Khartoum)
☎ 0912 306 224 or 0183 786 500

Ambulance (Omdurman)
☎ 0187 553 100

Fire station (Khartoum)
☎ 0183 774 444

Fire station (Omdurman)
☎ 187 554 439

Police (emergency only)
☎ 999

Police station (Khartoum)
☎ 0183 773 333

Police station (Omdurman)
☎ 0187 553 333

Traffic police
☎ 0183 780 043 or 0183 777 777

Water (Khartoum)
☎ 0183 778 640

Water (Omdurman)
☎ 0187 551 190

Exchange bureaux

UAE exchange
🏠 Afra Mall (also a branch in Khartoum 2 market area); ☎ 0183 791 142 or 0183 250 294

Government ministries

Agriculture and Forestry
☎ 0183 781 387 or 0183 771 919

Animal Resources
☎ 0183 476 129 or 0183 476 131

Cabinet Affairs
☎ 0183 775 300 or 0183 770 966

Civil Aviation
☎ 0183 778 896 or 0183 795 037

Education and Guidance
☎ 0183 778 955 or 0183 778 906

Electricity
☎ 0183 770 686 or 0183 776 321

Energy & Mining
☎ 0183 773 315 or 0183 775 595

Environment and Physical Development
☎ 0183 773 832 or 0183 472 665

External Relations
☎ 0183 777 301 or 0183 780 542

Federal Government
☎ 0183 775 000 or 0183 775 003

Finance and National Economy;
☎ 0183 776 794 or 0183 771 368

Foreign Trade
☎ 0183 772 973 or 0183 770 940

Health
☎ 0183 772 067 or 0183 773 001

Higher Education and Scientific Research
☎ 0183 773 064 or 0183 773 073

Industry
☎ 0183 778 940 or 0183 789 641

Information and Communications
☎ 0183 789 609

Internal Affairs
☎ 0183 772 754 or 0183 777 380

International Co-operation
  ☎ 0183 772 169
Investment
  ☎ 0183 787 199 or 0183 760 848
Irrigation
  ☎ 0183 777 082 or 0183 772 409
Justice
  ☎ 0183 779 173 or 0183 774 525
Labour and Administrative Reform
  ☎ 0183 775 551 or 0183 773 770
National Defence
  ☎ 0183 707 309 or 0183 707 710
Roads and Bridges
  ☎ 0183 772 361 or 0183 775 935
Science and Technology
  ☎ 0183 761 154 or 0183 799 217
Tourism and National Heritage
  ☎ 0183 482 627 or 0183 472 604
Transport
  ☎ 0183 775 290 or 0183 773 001
Welfare and Social Development
  ☎ 0183 775 832 or 0183 779 753

Hospitals

Academy Diagnostic Centre
  🏠 Riyad, near Tutti Frutti; ☎ 0183 229 956 or 0183 229 959 or 0183 228 614
Doctor Clinic
  🏠 Afriqia Street, off Street 37, Amarat; ☎ 0183 475 374 or 0183 464 419
El-Faisal Specialized Hospital
  🏠 Hosbitalia Street, Central Khartoum
Fedail Medical Centre;
  🏠 Hosbitalia Street, Central Khartoum; ☎ 0183 766 661
Modem Medical Center
  🏠 Afriqia Street, across from the Kuwaiti Embassy, Amarat; ☎ 0183 471 683
Police Hospital
  🏠 Burri; ☎ 0183 265 315 or 0183 265 316
Sahiroun
  🏠 Burri; ☎ 0183 26 53 15
Shawamikh International Hospital
  🏠 Street 21, Amarat; ☎ 0155 146 666
Yastabchiroun
  🏠 Riyad; ☎ 0183 23 78 04

Non-governmental organisations (NGOs)

Action Faim
  🏠 Street 53, Amarat
Action on Disability and Development
  🏠 Street 35, Amarat
Adventist Development and Relief Agency
  🏠 Street 49, Amarat; ☎ 0183 471 608
Agency for Co-operation and Research in Development
  🏠 Nursery Street, Riyad; ☎ 0183 244 556
CARE International
  🏠 Street 55, Khartoum 2
Concern Sudan
  🏠 Riyad; ☎ 0183 256 620
Children of the World Human Rights
  🏠 Street 31, Amarat
Children Village International
  🏠 Jamhouriya Street, Central Khartoum; ☎ 0183 781 414
Emergency
  🏠 Soba
German Agro Action
  🏠 Street 33, Amarat; ☎ 0183 467 053
Help Age International Programme
  🏠 Street 33, Amarat; ☎ 0183 461 657
Hope and Home for Children
  🏠 East of Qurashi Park, Khartoum 3; ☎ 0183 482 812
Human Appeal International
  🏠 Sahafa; ☎ 0183 429 911
International Federation of the Red Cross (IFRC)
  🏠 Mek Nimir Street, Central Khartoum; ☎ 0183 771 033 or 0183 770 484
International Committee of the Red Cross
  🏠 Street 33; Amarat; ☎ 0183 476 464
International Organization for Migration
  🏠 Street 47, Amarat; ☎ 0183 570 801
International Rescue Committee
  🏠 Fardos Street, Arkowit; ☎ 0183 242 870
Médicins Sans Frontières (Holland)
  🏠 Street 33, Amarat; ☎ 0183 475 486
Médicins Sans Frontières (France)
  🏠 Khartoum 2; ☎ 0183 472 993
Oxfam
  🏠 Mogran; ☎ 0183 787 708

Listings

Save the Children (USA)
🏠 Street 21, Amarat; ☎ 0183 471 234

Save the children (Sweden)
🏠 Street 19, Amarat; ☎ 0183 471 234

Sudan Open Learning Organisation
🏠 Central Khartoum; ☎ 0183 471 059

The Leprosy Mission
🏠 Street 57, Khartoum 2; ☎ 0183 462 617

War Child (Netherlands)
🏠 Malik Street, off Street 27, Amarat

Language institutes

Catholic Language Institute in Khartoum
🏠 Street 29, Amarat; ☎ 0183 483 972

French Cultural Centre;
🏠 Ali Dinar Street, Central Khartoum; ☎ 0183 798 035; 🖥 www.ccfkhartoum.net

German Goethe-Institute
☎ 0183 777 833; 🖥 www.goethe.de/khartum

Comboni College
🏠 Khartoum and Mamoura; ☎ 0183 782 654; 🖥 www.combonikhartoum.com

Lawyers

El Tigani El Karib
🏠 Mek Nimir Street; ☎ 0183 779 998 or 0183 781 991

Ahmed Mohamed Fadl
☎ 0183 780 243 or 0183 771 220.

Wanni & Wanni
🏠 Jamhouriya Street, Khartoum Insurance Co. Building, First Floor; ☎ 0183 777 517 or 0183 778 086

Sudan Bar Association
☎ 0183 783 845

House of Legal Consultancies & Services Ltd.
🏠 Nil Street, Kuwaiti Building, 4th Tower, ☎ 0183 785 704 or 0183 790 378/9 or 0183 777 751

Sudanese Commercial Law Office
🏠 Manshea, near Chinese Embassy; ☎ 0922 530 704; @ wael.abdin@sudaneselaw.com; 🖥 www.sudaneselaw.com

House of Legal Consultancies & Services Ltd
🏠 Nil Street, Kuwaiti Building, 4th Tower; ☎ 0183 785 704 or 0183 790 378/9; @ awahab@hlcs-law.com

Omar Abdel Atti
🏠 Baraka Tower, 7th floor; ☎ 0183 776 400 or 0183 781 268; 🖥 www.omerabdelati.com

Schools

International Standard English School
🏠 Street 33, near Mohammed Najeeb, Amarat; ☎ 0155 170 446 or 0122 757 686

British Educational School
🏠 Street 1, near Mohammed Najeeb, Amarat; ☎ 0183 583 703/4/5 or 0912 148 502; @ britishinstitutes25@yahoo.co.uk

Khartoum American School
🏠 Mohammed Najeeb Street, south of the 'Kia Motors' sign; ☎ 0155 770 105/7; @ kas@krtams.org; 🖥 www.krtams.org

Khartoum International Community School (KICS)
🏠 Soba; ☎ 0183 215 000; @ principal@kics.sd; 🖥 www.kics.sd

Unity High School
🏠 Qasar Street; ☎ 0183 786 585; @ principal.uhs@hotmail.com; 🖥 www.unityhighschool.org

Ecole Française de Khartoum
🏠 Riyad; @ ecolefrancaisekhartoum@yahoo.com; 🖥 www.efk-sd.com

Sudanese Academy International School
🏠 Kafouri, near the Vatican Embassy; ☎ 0912 378 964

Holm English Medium School
🏠 Mamoura; ☎ 0183 248 614/5/8; 🖥 www.holmschool.com; @ hemsedu@yahoo.com

Khartoum Diplomatic School
🏠 Malik Street; ☎ 0183 468 003; @ info@khartoumdiplomaticschool.com; 🖥 www.khartoumdiplomaticschool-edu.com

Shipping companies

DHL
🏠 Nigomi Street, Central Khartoum; ☎ 0183 777 500

TNT
🏠 Amarat, Mohammed Najeeb, off street 55, Amarat; ☎ 0183 472 203/4/5/6

United Nations' bodies

Food and Agricultural Organisation (FAO)
🏠 Osman Digna Street, Central Khartoum; ☎ 0183 774 646
United Nations Children's Fund (UNICEF)
🏠 Street 27, Khartoum 2; ☎ 0183 471 837 or 0183 471 838
United Nations High Commissioner for Refugees (UNHCR)
🏠 Street 1, Amarat; ☎ 0183 471 101 or 0183 471 013
United Nations Humanitarian Co-ordination Unit
🏠 Jama'a Street, Central Khartoum centre
United Nations Industrial Development Organisation (UNIDO)
🏠 Jama'a Street, Central Khartoum
United Nations Population Fund (UNFPA)
🏠 Street 13, Amarat; ☎ 0183 773 547 or 0183 771 493
World Food programme (WFP)
🏠 Street 33, Amarat; ☎ 0183 471 157 or 0183 461 252 or 0183 461 594
World Health Organisation (WHO)
☎ 0183 776 471

SOUTH SUDAN (+211)

Airports and airlines

748 Air Services
☎ 0955 079 662 or 0977 102 833; @ sales@748airservices.com; 🖥 www.748airservices.com
Airport (Juba)
☎ 0811 20 800
Air Uganda
☎ 0977 153 912; @ info@air-uganda.com; 🖥 www.air-uganda.com
Eagle Air
☎ 0977 102 991/2; @ reservations@eagleair-ug.com; 🖥 www.eagleair-ug.com
Feeder Airlines
☎ 0912 865 397 or 0918 266 955; @ info@air-uganda.com; 🖥 www.air-uganda.com

Sun Air
☎ 0126 189 918 or 0121 127 856; 🖥 www.sunairgroup.com

Banks

Kenya Commercial Bank
☎ 0977 251 297 or 0955 081 493; 🖥 www.kcbbankgroup.com
Nile Commercial Bank
☎ 0977 101 931; 🖥 www.southern-sudan.com/nilebank.htm

Car Rental

Juba Interlink Services
🏠 Juba Airport; ☎ 0923 647 445
MCAC
🏠 Olympic Hotel; ☎ 0955 155 560 or 0955 284 700; @ mcac_car@yahoo.com or mcac.car@gmail.com

Car Retail

Golden Arrow
🏠 Near Rock City, Jebel Kujur; ☎ 0915 611 340

Embassies and consular representations

United Kingdom
🏠 European Union Compound, Tong Ping Road; ☎ 0955 584 193; @ ukinsouthsudan@dfid.gov.uk
Egypt
☎ 0811 823 700
France
🏠 European Union Compound, Tong Ping Road; ☎ 0957 127 549 or 0955 587 332
Germany
🏠 EU Compound, Tong Ping Road; ☎ 0956 008 021
Norway
🏠 Hai Malakal; ☎ +47 2153 6553; @ cg.juba@mfa.no
South Africa
🏠 South Tong Ping; ☎ 0912 169 992
Uganda
☎ 0811 821 555; @ consulugajuba2@yahoo.com

Government Ministries

Ministry Of Finance
☎ 0926 659 840

Ministry Of Health
☎ 0811 820 678 or 0811 820 134

Ministry Of Commerce And Industry
☎ 0811 823 473 or 0977 104 766 or 0957 104 766 or 0122 177 269

Ministry Of Water Resources & irrigation
☎ 0811 823 554 or 0811 823 580

Ministry Of Housing, Physical Planning And Environment
☎ 0955 121 646 or 0977 252 441

Ministry Of Gender, Social Welfare And Religious Affairs
☎ 0811 822 722 or 0912 843 562, or 0977 124 172

Ministry Of Energy And Mining
☎ 0811 820 824

Hospitals

Juba Medical Complex
☎ 0977 156 689; @ jcomplex@ya-hoo.com

Language institutes

🏠 On the campus of Juba University; ☎ 0955 381 983

Photographers

Jenn Warren
☎ +1 832 622 4473; @ info@jen-nwarren.net; 🖵 www.jennwarren.net

Taxis

Barakat
☎ 0926 253 451

Colins
☎ 0977 225 915

Juba Transporters Ltd.
☎ 0955 305 254 or 0772 335 942; @ kaka.dennis6@gmail.com

Patrick
☎ 0977 188 266

Index